FITZWILLIAM MUSEUM
HANDBOOKS

ENGLISH POTTERY

The books in this series provide a convenient and accessible introduction to subjects within the applied arts. Drawing examples from the world-famous collections at the Fitzwilliam Museum, they furnish the reader with a wide variety of information on many different types and forms and illustrate some of the most famous as well as the most unusual examples. A general introduction is followed by entries on sixty-four individual objects, each of which is illustrated in colour. Complete with glossaries and guides to further reading, these books will prove invaluable to all collectors and enthusiasts.

FITZWILLIAM MUSEUM HANDBOOKS

ENGLISH POTTERY

JULIA E. POOLE

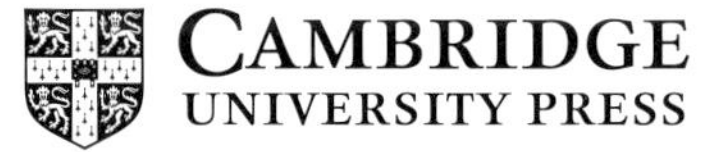

Published by the Press Syndicate of the University of Cambridge
The Pitt Building, Trumpington Street, Cambridge CB2 1RP
40 West 20th Street, New York, NY 10011-4211, USA
10 Stamford Road, Oakleigh, Melbourne 3166, Australia

First published 1995

Printed in Great Britain at the University Press, Cambridge

A catalogue record for this book is available from the British Library

Library of Congress cataloguing in publication data
Poole, Julia.
English pottery in the Fitzwilliam Museum / Julia E. Poole.
p. cm. – (Fitzwilliam Museum handbooks)
ISBN 0 521 47521 X (hardback). ISBN 0 521 47520 1 (paperback)
1. Pottery, English – Catalogs.
2. Pottery – England – Cambridge – Catalogs.
3. Fitzwilliam Museum – Catalogs.
I. Fitzwilliam Museum. II. Title. III. Series.
NK4085.P55 1995
738'.0942'07442659–dc20
94-28172 CIP

ISBN 0 521 47521 X hardback
ISBN 0 521 47520 1 paperback

TAG

To Jack Lister and Gordon Cardinal
in appreciation of their service in the
Department of Applied Art at the
Fitzwilliam Museum

CONTENTS

PREFACE

The sixty-four illustrations in this book were chosen to give an impression of the vitality and diversity of English pottery, and to outline its development between the late thirteenth and late twentieth centuries. All of them are in the Fitzwilliam Museum, but similar types are represented in many private and public collections in England, America and elsewhere.

The Museum was founded in 1816 when Richard, seventh Viscount Fitzwilliam of Merrion, bequeathed his art collection and library to the University of Cambridge, together with funds to provide suitable housing for them. The Founder's building, designed by George Basevi, was begun in 1837. Members of the University and the public were admitted in 1848, although the splendid entrance hall was not completed until 1875.

The first English pottery to enter the collection was a Wedgwood blue and white jasper portrait medallion of William Pitt, first Earl of Chatham, which was donated in 1840. Sixty years passed before the acquisition of three delftware pharmacy pots in 1901 and during the following quarter of a century only a small quantity of Wedgwood and miscellaneous pieces from other factories were received. During this period, however, the Museum acquired significant groups of Oriental and European porcelains, Islamic pottery and Italian maiolica.

Much of the pottery illustrated in this book was bequeathed to the Museum in 1928 by Dr J.W. L. Glaisher, FRS, a mathematician and fellow of Trinity College, Cambridge, or was purchased with funds which accompanied his bequest. With a few exceptions (nos. 17, 20, 49, 56 and 57), these pieces were published in Bernard Rackham's *Catalogue of the Glaisher Collection of Pottery and Porcelain in the Fitzwilliam Museum, Cambridge* (Cambridge, 1935; reprinted by the Antique Collectors' Club, Woodbridge, 1987). This has not been cited in the suggestions for further reading after each item, because the Museum's accession numbers are usually the same as the *Catalogue* numbers. Where they are not, the *Catalogue* number has been given.

Since 1928 the Museum has acquired some English pottery in most years. Some of the pieces in this book were either given by individuals (nos. 41, 43, 48, 58 and 61) or by the Friends of the Fitzwilliam (nos. 2, 54, 55, 60, 62, 63 and 64). The rest were purchased with the help of the Eastern Arts Association (no. 64) and the National Heritage Memorial Fund (no. 38) or grant-in-aid administered by the Victoria and Albert Museum (nos. 38, 50 and 59).

Permission to photograph and reproduce numbers 61, 62, 63 and 64 was kindly given by Josiah Wedgwood & Sons Limited, Janet Leach, Jane Coper, and Alan Caiger-Smith respectively. All the photographs were taken by Bridget Taylor, the Museum's Second Photographer. Josiah Wedgwood & Sons Limited also gave permission to quote from Wedgwood MS E.26-19117 under number 30. Advice on aspects of the text was gratefully received from Michael Archer, David Barker, Group Captain Frank Britton, Sharon Gater, Chris Green and Robert Stones.

Recent studies of English pottery, particularly those involving excavations, have modified some long-standing attributions by revealing new information about the industry in different parts of the country. Some of the attributions and opinions given here will doubtless need revision as new evidence is published.

INTRODUCTION

Pottery has been made in Britain since the Neolithic period (3000–2000 BC) but it was only in the second half of the eighteenth century that England took the lead as the most innovative producer in Europe. Since then the functional and aesthetic qualities of English pottery have made it as renowned as Chinese porcelain.

The most striking feature of English production as a whole is its diversity. The unglazed and lead-glazed earthenwares made during the Middle Ages were joined in the second half of the sixteenth century by tin-glazed earthenware (also known as delftware). Salt-glazed stoneware was introduced in the second half of the seventeenth, and all three continued until the end of the eighteenth century when tin-glazed earthenware gradually went out of production. In addition to these major types, English potters in the eighteenth and nineteenth centuries developed many variants of lead-glazed earthenware and stoneware. These included creamware and pearlware, jasperware and stone china.

This diversity also extended to the types of objects made. The present book deals mainly with tableware, ornaments and figures, but several other aspects of the industry were of economic importance. These included the manufacture of kitchen and dairy wares; garden pots and ornaments; pharmaceutical and industrial equipment, such as drug pots, crucibles and storage jars; architectural ceramics, ranging from colourful wall tiling to bricks and chimney pots; and, last but not least, sanitary ware such as sinks, lavatories and drainpipes.

The ability to make such an abundance of ceramic types and products depended primarily on England's geology and geography. Most parts of England have beds of clay suitable for coarse pottery; but some areas, notably North Staffordshire, have several types of clay whose properties make them appropriate for different products, such as bricks or teapots. The development of cream and white bodies in the eighteenth century was made possible by clays which are white when fired. These are found in substantial quantities only near Barnstaple and Newton Abbot in Devonshire and around Poole in Dorset. They became known as 'ball' clays because they were transported in large balls weighing about half a hundredweight. Flints, which were ground and mixed with these clays to strengthen and whiten the body, are found in the eastern and south-eastern counties, especially along the coast. England also has its own sources of tin, lead and salt for glazes, and other minerals, such as iron, for pigments. The temperate climate ensured that there was plentiful timber for firing kilns and when timber began to be scarce in the seventeenth century, coal was available in North Staffordshire and elsewhere. Good harbours and navigable rivers, such as the Severn, Weaver and Trent, aided the transportation of raw materials, which otherwise had to be carried laboriously overland by packhorses or carts. The construction of canals in the eighteenth century and railways in the nineteenth made transport easier and faster.

The availability of raw materials, fuel and nearby markets determined the areas which were to emerge as major centres of production during the late seventeenth and eighteenth centuries. These included London and Bristol; the cluster of North Staffordshire villages which eventually became known as the Potteries, now Stoke-on-Trent; Liverpool; Nottingham and Derbyshire; Leeds and other towns in Yorkshire; and Sunderland and Newcastle-upon-Tyne in the north-east. Significantly, several of these were also ports from which pottery could be exported to the colonies or Europe.

The gradual concentration of large-scale production in a few areas did not lessen the variety of English pottery. Numerous small rural and urban potteries continued to carry on a thriving local trade in slipware and other earthenwares. Among the most flourishing between the seventeenth to nineteenth centuries were potteries at Tickenhall in Derbyshire, the Harlow area in Essex (no. 6 below); Wrotham in Kent (no. 7), Barnstaple, Bideford (no. 52) and Fremington in North Devon; Donyatt in Somerset; Rye, Chailey and several other villages in Sussex; and the Halifax area of Yorkshire. During the nineteenth century many of these small potteries, especially those in towns, were driven out of business by decline in demand for their rustic products, and by the vast output of cheap wares from the industrialized potteries. This decline was partly offset by the Art Pottery Movement of the late nineteenth and early twentieth centuries (nos. 54, 56 and 58). This created a demand for hand-crafted decorative ware, and encouraged some country potters to devote themselves wholly or partly to these instead of traditional earthenware (no. 57). Even so, by 1920 few of these small potteries survived and the depression of the 1930s reduced the number even further.

Fortunately, the Studio Pottery Movement of the 1920s and 1930s introduced a different kind of hand-crafted pottery, with an emphasis on form and glazes rather than superficial decoration. Potteries set up at St Ives in Cornwall by Bernard Leach in 1920 (no. 62), and at Winchcombe in Gloucestershire by

Michael Cardew in 1926, played an important role in bringing about a revival of small-scale potting. After the Second World War, studio pottery became increasingly fashionable, and numerous kilns were set up during the next half century. Unlike earlier small potteries, these have not been restricted to areas where raw materials and fuel are available. Most now have gas or electric kilns, and can, if necessary, obtain ready-prepared clay from industrial suppliers. Their output includes earthenware and stoneware for the home or garden, and highly individualistic ornamental ceramics which have won international acclaim (nos. 63 and 64).

During the same period the number of industrial potteries has declined dramatically through closure or amalgamation. Stricter health regulations and adverse economic conditions have obliged manufacturers to modernize their production methods, and in some factories hand work has been reduced to a minimum. These changes have not stemmed the inventiveness of the industry, and the period from about 1940 to 1990 has been described aptly as one of 'Dynamic Design'.

Socio-economic factors also played an important role in encouraging diversity in English pottery. The production of a broad range of high-quality domestic ware and ornaments was promoted by demand from a substantial urban and rural middle class, whose prosperity increased between the seventeenth and twentieth centuries. The larger class of working people provided a market for country pottery and the cheaper, less fashionable wares from the major centres. English pottery was not used a great deal by the wealthiest members of society before the 1760s, when its greatly improved quality made it acceptable. However, before this they purchased large amounts of pottery for use by their households, and made occasional purchases for themselves: for example, in 1755 the Duchess of Bedford bought a service of dishes and plates from Thomas Whieldon, perhaps for her personal use. The importance of gaining aristocratic and royal custom was fully appreciated by Wedgwood, who was delighted when he received a commission from Queen Charlotte in 1765.

The increasing popularity of tea and coffee during the late seventeenth and eighteenth centuries, and the adoption of more elaborate ways of serving meals with numerous dishes on the table at once, created a demand for a greater variety of tableware with specialized functions. The enormous range of items available by the late eighteenth century is shown by the pattern books issued by Wedgwood (1774), the Leeds Pottery (1783, 1794) and the Castleford Pottery (1796).

During the early eighteenth century tableware in the wealthiest households was usually of silver, glass and Oriental porcelain, although a little Continental porcelain was also imported, mainly from Meissen and Sèvres. The absence of porcelain manufacture in England before the 1740s was very advantageous to the pottery industry. It encouraged the production of attractively decorated delftware, and the development of refined earthenwares and stonewares to cater for customers who were comfortably off but could not afford porcelain. Pewter, the most common alternative, continued to be used by some middle-class people, such as the actor, David Garrick (1717–79), but by the late eighteenth century it was regarded as inferior to creamware or pearlware. Even after the setting up of English porcelain factories in the 1740s and 1750s, porcelain remained a luxury and its use spread only very slowly down the social scale during the late eighteenth and nineteenth centuries, mainly for tea ware and ornaments. The everyday dinner service in many middle-class homes has continued to be made of earthenware (no. 41), or stoneware, although a porcelain or bone china service, often received as a wedding present, may be brought out for special occasions.

The manufacture of pottery figures after the mid-eighteenth century was encouraged by the demand from the middle and lower classes for ornaments which were cheaper versions of those made in porcelain, although not all models were copied from porcelain. The subjects of early porcelain figures had appealed to aristocratic taste, but from the late eighteenth century pottery figures increasingly represented aspects of popular culture. Brightly coloured and naively realistic, they have a vitality which is absent from most porcelain figures of that period (no. 45). The typical Victorian Staffordshire figure, with its almost flat undecorated back (no. 51), was produced in large numbers for less affluent customers.

During the twentieth century pottery manufacturers have had to adapt their products to rapidly changing social conditions, especially the declining number of full-time domestic servants and the increasing number of women working outside the home. Oven-to-table ware, introduced in the 1960s, was intended to reduce washing up, and in the 1980s improved versions were developed which were both dishwasher- and freezer-proof. Everyday meals have become less formal, and as a result, demands for crockery have changed. Mugs, the ceramic equivalent of the labour-saving T-shirt, have all but ousted cups and saucers in some homes. Manufacturers have also responded inventively to a world-wide demand for resilient tableware for the burgeoning 'hospitality industry' and for large institutions such as universities.

The style of English pottery has never been completely homogeneous at any one time. Ostensibly it was influenced by contemporary styles in art and architecture. In practice, the degree of obvious kinship varied enormously. During the Middle Ages, English pottery was made in numerous regional styles, which are recognizably medieval in character, but difficult to relate to specific features of the romanesque or gothic styles. In fact, apart from floor tiles, the most overtly gothic pottery was made in the mid-nineteenth century during the heyday of revivalism. The 'Apostle' and 'York Minster' stoneware jugs whose designs were registered by Charles Meigh of Hanley in 1842 and 1846, are notable examples. During the sixteenth century the English pottery industry was underdeveloped in comparison with those on the Continent and its products did not reflect aspects of Renaissance art in the way that Italian maiolica, German stoneware or French 'Saint-Porchaire' ware did. Nevertheless it was a period of progress during which new forms and decoration were introduced.

After 1600, the finer earthenwares and stonewares made in the largest centres of production were most influenced by fashionable styles, although there was usually a time lag before one completely superseded another. The rococo style, for example, lingered on for about ten years after the introduction of neo-classicism. During the nineteenth century there was a succession of revival styles (nos. 41 and 50) and in the twentieth, some popular nineteenth-century patterns continued in production alongside contemporary designs. Pottery made in smaller urban or rural potteries was less affected by changes in fashion. Vessels such as baking dishes, flasks and harvest jugs continued to be made in traditional local styles which changed very slowly.

A stylistic gulf between the products of industrialized and small potteries continued in the twentieth century. The restrained studio pottery made in the 1920s and 1930s contrasted strongly with pottery made in the long-established factories, such as Wedgwood, Spode and Doulton (no. 60), or with the brightly coloured Art Deco wares made by newer firms such as Poole Pottery, A.E. Gray and A.J. Wilkinson. In the second half of the century a similar contrast has persisted between the work of the new wave of studio potters and pottery from factories such as Midwinter, Hornsea and Portmeirion. However, some of the more homely oven-to-table wares of the 1960s and 1970s were influenced to some extent by studio potters who worked in a country style.

In addition to the generalized influence of European art styles, the appearance of English pottery since the late sixteenth century has been influenced in two more specific ways: by immigrants, who brought in or developed new techniques (nos. 4, 14, 50); and by imported ceramics, especially from the Far East, the Low Countries, France and Germany (nos. 4, 5, 13, 18, 26 and 31). Potters also adopted the forms and decoration of objects made in non-ceramic materials, such as silver, and other metalwork (nos. 12, 21, 28 and 29).

These varied influences combined to produce pottery which is quintessentially English, despite having many features in common with pottery from other European countries. Several traits can be singled out as contributing to this Englishness, but some are more prominent in one type of ware or one period than another.

One of the most appealing qualities of much English pottery, is its robust, cheerful character. This is especially noticeable in slipwares (nos. 6, 7, 10, 15, 17 and 52) and other country pottery. It emanates from their sturdy forms, warm, earthy colouring and glossy yellowish, or treacly-brown lead glazes. Their lively decoration often incorporates inscribed good wishes or invitations to drink and be merry, which conjure up bucolic celebrations in the fire-lit parlours of farmhouses or inns. Similar qualities can be seen in some brown salt-glazed stonewares (nos. 20 and 21), in Measham ware (no. 51) and in the brightly coloured, polychrome delftwares of the seventeenth century (no. 8).

Equally characteristic is a tendency for understatement and restraint. This is frequently associated with excellent but unostentatious throwing and turning, and minute attention to details, such as applied sprigs, spouts and handles. Objects as diverse as medieval jugs and John Dwight's sophisticated marbled stonewares (no. 13) illustrate this very well, as do the neat, lead-glazed redwares and agate wares of the second and third quarter of the eighteenth century (nos. 22 and 28). Restraint was very characteristic of pottery made during the early neo-classical period. It can be seen to perfection in the plain or lightly decorated creamwares, and the elegant jasperware and black basalt made by Wedgwood and his contemporaries. It is even possible to find reticent pots among the exuberant products of the Victorian period, such as Ridgway's 'Bulrush' jug, beautifully moulded in a modest grey stoneware (no. 48).

Humour is also a prominent feature of English pottery. Slapstick comedy is represented by puzzle vessels which spilled their contents over unwitting or tipsy drinkers. These were made from at least the thirteenth century onwards, and included puzzle tygs, puzzle jugs and fuddling cups (known as Jolly Boys at Donyatt). Surprise jokes included mugs containing lifelike toads, like those made at Sunderland in the nineteenth century. Sly or moralizing humour is more common. It was often directed at a particular class, such as the clergy, or concerned relationships between the sexes. A good example of the latter is the early nineteenth-century group *The Battle for the Breeches*, which poked fun at bossy wives and their husbands. Caricature and political satire gradually became common after the introduction of transfer-printing in the mid-1750s, which enabled potters to reproduce prints and their inscriptions on ceramics. Caricatures were also made in the round, as mugs, jugs, figures and busts.

Some English pottery is funny in the sense of being amusing or quaint. Since the Middle Ages, potters and purchasers alike have delighted in vessels masquerading as something else, such as bear jugs and camel teapots (nos. 24 and 25) or the numerous versions of the Toby jug (no. 36). These fanciful or grotesque vessels were intended to be fun, but quaintness was often the unintentional result of an unsophisticated interpretation of a style, or model. One example is the peculiar but charming way that Sèvres or Meissen coloured grounds were imitated on white salt-glazed stoneware. Drawing was not always the English pot painter's strong point and human figures, such as Adam and Eve on delftware 'blue dash chargers', may now seem hilariously absurd. Yet curiously this occasional ineptitude is one of the most endearing qualities of English seventeenth- and eighteenth-century pottery.

Painting on English pottery as a whole in those centuries was rarely as sophisticated as that on Dutch delft or French *faïence*. At its best, however, English painting of floral designs, views and genre scenes is ravishingly attractive. The architectural historian Sir Nikolaus Pevsner (1902–83) in *The Englishness of English Art* (1956) noted the flair of English craftsmen and artists for the portrayal of what he termed 'Observed Life'. English potters and decorators were no exception to this. Their work abounds in illustrations of people and everyday activities, such as hunting (no. 20), farming (no. 33), drinking (nos. 17 and 36), tea-drinking (no.32), courting (no. 45) or just sitting (no. 23). These demonstrate the intimate relationship between pottery and English daily life, as do the numerous ceramics which mark the passage of life, from model cradles to memorial tiles.

Further reading Bevis Hillier, *Pottery and Porcelain 1700–1914*, 1968. Peter Brears, *The English Country Pottery, Its History and Techniques*, 1971. Lorna Weatherill, *The Pottery Trade and North Staffordshire 1660–1760*, 1971. Robert Charleston, 'The social background of English delftware', in Louis L. Lipski and Michael Archer, *Dated English Delftware*, 1984. Frances Hannah, *Ceramics, Twentieth-century Design*, 1986. Robin Emmerson, *British Teapots and Tea Drinking*, 1992.

GLOSSARY

black or bat printing Transfer-printing overglaze using a thin sheet of flexible animal glue, known as a bat. Linseed oil was applied to an engraved or etched copper plate, the surplus was removed and the glue bat was pressed to the plate. It picked up the oiled design and when applied to the ware deposited it on the surface. Powdered metallic oxide colour was dusted onto the oil and firing at 700–800°C fixed it to the glaze.

delftware Dutch and English tin-glazed earthenware, named after Delft, which became famous for it during the second half of the seventeenth century.

earthenware Opaque, porous pottery fired at temperatures between 450 and 1100°C.

ECC The English Ceramic Circle, a society which promotes the study of English pottery, porcelain and enamels by holding lectures, and publishes them in its *Transactions* (ECCT).

enamel-colours Pigments made from glass coloured with metallic oxides, ground to powder and mixed with oils, such as fat oil and turpentine. They are applied with a brush overglaze and are fired in a muffle kiln at between 700 and 800°C to fuse them with the surface.

faïence French term for tin-glazed earthenware, derived from Faenza in Italy, which was famous for whiteware in the second half of the sixteenth and seventeenth centuries.

famille rose Term coined in the nineteenth century by Albert Jacquemart to denote a palette of enamel-colours including rose pink derived from gold, used on Chinese export porcelain.

grog Ground up fired clay.

high-temperature colours Pigments derived from metallic oxides which withstand high temperatures and can therefore be applied before the glost (glaze) firing. The most commonly used oxides are cobalt for blue, copper or iron for green, antimony for yellow, manganese for brownish-purple, and cobalt and iron for black.

pearlware A very pale cream or white earthenware with lead glaze tinted pale blue by the addition of a minute quantity of cobalt. It was introduced about 1775 and was intended to resemble Oriental porcelain.

press-moulding The formation of the whole or parts of a ceramic object by pressing flattened clay into or over a mould.

Rockingham glaze A generic term for a glossy, dark-brown lead glaze named after the Rockingham pottery at Swinton, Yorkshire, but used by many other factories in the nineteenth and twentieth centuries.

salt-glaze A glaze-like surface on stoneware produced by throwing salt into the kiln when it reaches its highest temperature during firing. When the salt vaporizes, the sodium combines with the silica in the clay to create a vitreous coating which may have a pitted or freckled appearance.

sherd A fragment of pottery or porcelain.

slip Clay and water mixed to a sloppy consistency.

slip-casting The formation of the whole or parts of a ceramic object by pouring slip into a plaster of Paris mould. A wall of clay forms inside the mould as the plaster absorbs water from the slip, and when this is sufficiently thick, the excess slip is tipped out. After a period of drying, the cast shrinks and can be removed from the mould.

slip-trailing The decoration of earthenware by trailing slip onto its surface from a vessel with a narrow, usually tubular spout.

smear-glaze A slight sheen imparted to the surface of stoneware by putting a mixture of salt, potash and lead on the inside walls or at the bottom of the saggars protecting the pots during firing.

sprig A relief ornament made in a mould and, after removal, applied to the surface of an unfired pot using slip to make it adhere.

stoneware Pottery fired at temperatures between 1180 and 1400°C. It is hard, opaque and impervious to liquids.

tin-glaze A glaze made of sand, potash and lead oxide, opacified and whitened by tin oxide. Tin-glaze was applied to once-fired or biscuit vessels. After it had dried for a short time, but was still damp and absorbent, they were painted and fired again.

tyg A drinking vessel with more than two handles or two set close together. It is said to have been used in Staffordshire as another word for a porringer, but its use to denote taller drinking vessels with several handles has not been traced further back than the nineteenth century.

underglaze transfer-printing Decoration using transfers of damp tissue paper printed with ceramic colour from a heated engraved copper plate. The transfers are placed face down on the once-fired (biscuit) ware, and are rubbed until the design is transferred. The tissue is then removed with water, and the colour is hardened on by firing at about 700°C before glazing and firing again at a higher temperature. This method is now described as flat-press printing. Paper transfers may also be used for onglaze printing.

waster A vessel or fragment which has been damaged during firing or later in the process of manufacture, and has been abandoned as waste.

1

JUG

SCARBOROUGH, YORKSHIRE,

c. 1250–1300

Pale buff earthenware, decorated with applied points of clay under iron-streaked, copper-green lead glaze. Height 32.3 cm. Glaisher Catalogue 11–1928.

Throughout the Middle Ages pottery making was widespread in England and there were many local and regional styles. The pots from most kilns were sold or bartered locally, but the ware from some, such as those in Stamford and Scarborough, had a much wider distribution.

A pottery industry developed at Scarborough after the founding of the castle in the reign of King Stephen (1135–54) and flourished until the mid-fourteenth century, when the town declined in importance. The pots were made of a reddish, pinkish-buff or off-white fabric, depending on date, and copper-green or yellow lead glazes are typical. As well as food containers, such as pipkins and bowls, the potters made aquamaniles in the shape of animals, and large jugs exuberantly decorated with modelled knights on horseback, or with bearded masks and arms below the spouts. Others were less extravagantly decorated with applied scales, strips and pellets of clay.

Excavated and chance finds have shown that Scarborough ware was exported to many places in north- and south-eastern England and as far away as Aberdeen, Bergen and Bruges. This jug was found in a passage under a house in St Paul's Street, Stamford, Lincolnshire. Part of its handle has been restored, but the rest is remarkably well preserved. A jug of this kind was probably used for serving drinks or for hand washing at meals. Plainer examples were used for many different purposes such as fetching water from wells and taking drinks to labourers in the fields. When full, they were fairly heavy and in illuminated manuscripts are shown being carried on the head or shoulder.

Further reading P.G. Farmer, *An Introduction to Scarborough Ware and a Reassessment of Knight Jugs*, 1979. P.G. Farmer and N.C. Farmer, 'The dating of the Scarborough ware pottery industry', *Medieval Ceramics*, 6 (1982), pp. 66–86. Michael R. McCarthy and Catherine M. Brooks, *Medieval Pottery in Britain* AD 900–1600, 1988.

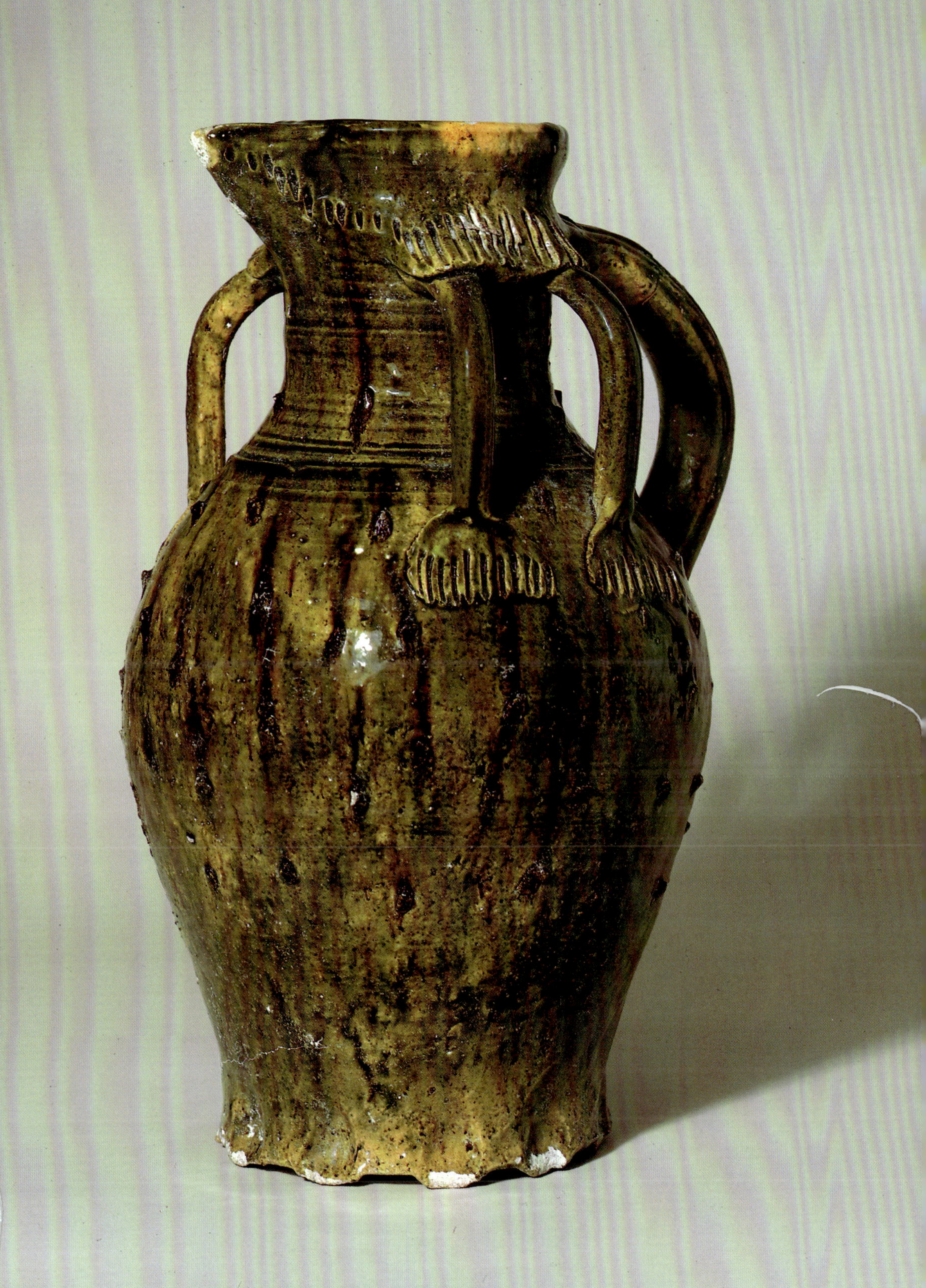

2

DRINKING POT

PROBABLY MADE IN ENGLAND, *c.* 1545–60.

Red earthenware with treacly-brown lead glaze, mounted in silver-gilt with engraved decoration. Mark: an incised cross with W and N beside it. Silver unmarked. Height 14.9 cm. M.5–1954.

Between about 1530 and 1590 there was a fashion for pottery drinking vessels with silver-gilt or silver mounts and covers. It began in Court circles and spread gradually to the country gentry, prosperous yeomen and merchants. In 1558 Etienne Perlin noted in his *Description of England* that the English drank great quantities of beer, not 'out of glasses, but from earthern pots with silver handles and covers, and this even in houses of persons of middling fortune'.

Most of these pots are of brown salt-glazed stoneware from the Rhineland or coloured tin-glazed earthenware from the Low Countries. Their silver covers and mounts, which protected the edges and gave them a more luxurious appearance, were made in London or a few other towns, such as Exeter and Norwich. Brightly coloured Isnik pottery jugs imported from Turkey were also treated in this way. Mounted lead-glazed earthenware pots, which were probably made in England, are less common. This example shows the squat, short-necked form popular during the mid-sixteenth century. A taller pot in the Victoria and Albert Museum has mounts with London hallmarks for 1546–7.

Further reading Philippa Glanville, *Silver in Tudor and Early Stuart England*, *Victoria and Albert Museum*, 1990, pp. 330–9 and p. 419, no. 35.

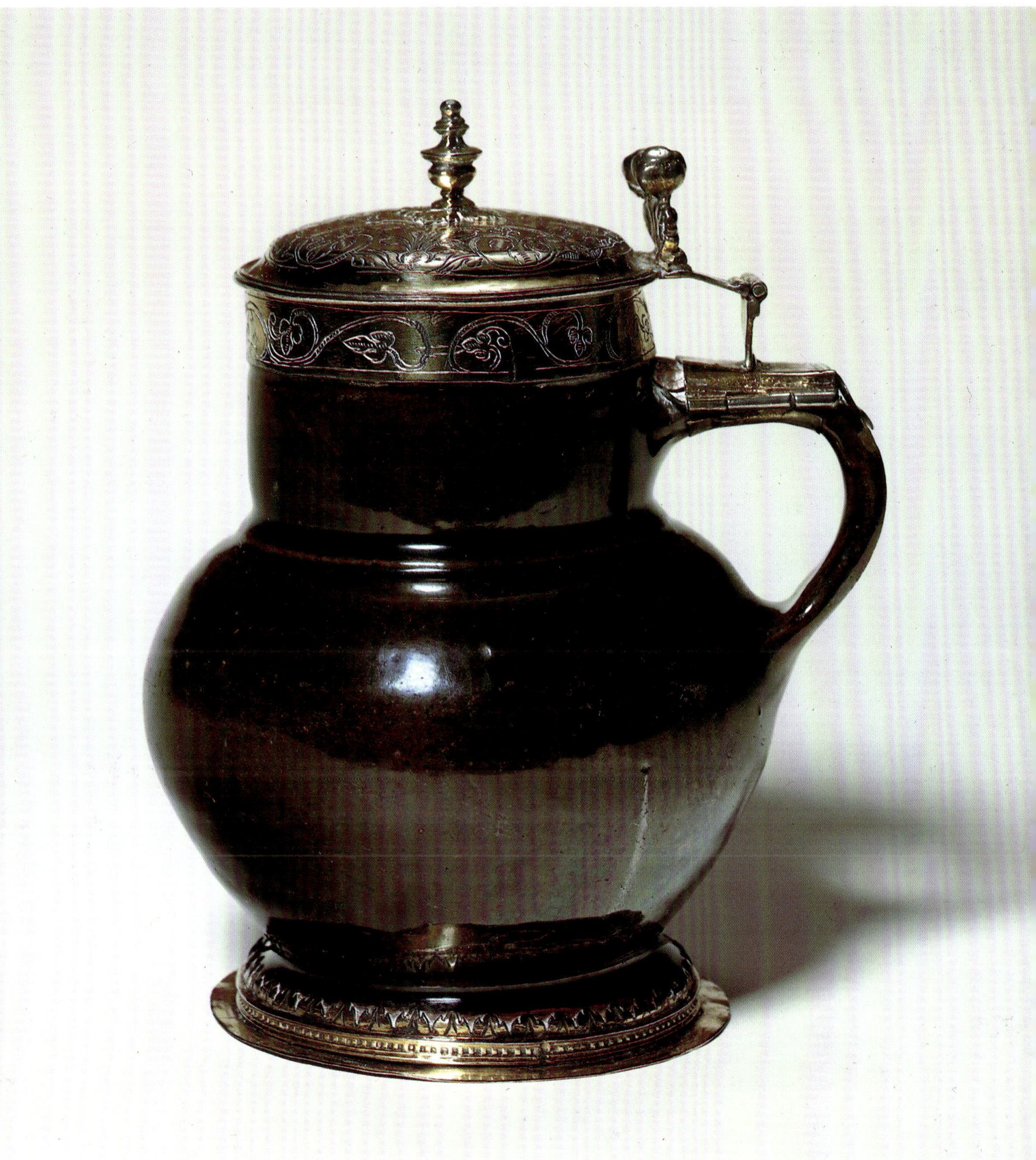

3

FLAGON

PROBABLY DERBYSHIRE
OR STAFFORDSHIRE,
1630–60.

Dark red earthenware covered with glossy black, iron-stained lead glaze. Height 29.4 cm. Glaisher Catalogue 23–1928.

During the seventeenth century two types of homely pottery known as Midlands yellow-ware and Midlands blackware were widespread in northern and central England, and extended south of London into Surrey and Kent. Yellow-ware, has a pale buff body with a warm yellow lead glaze, and survives mainly in the form of cups, candlesticks, cooking vessels and chamber pots. Blackware had a red body with black or very dark brown iron-stained lead glaze. It had developed from black-glazed Cistercian ware, made in the late Middle Ages, and first recorded in the late nineteenth century at the sites of Cistercian abbeys in Yorkshire.

This flagon, found at Youlgreave in Derbyshire on 1 May 1861, is a handsome example. Most seventeenth-century blackwares were drinking or serving vessels, such as mugs, beakers, flagons and jugs. Horizontal rilling or corrugations like those on this flagon were characteristic. In the eighteenth century blackware became more refined, and by the 1750s and 1760s Staffordshire potters were making attractive tea and coffee utensils.

Further reading Peter C.D. Brears, *The English Country Pottery*, 1971, pp. 37–9. David Barker and Pat Halfpenny, *Unearthing Staffordshire*, 1990, pp. 34–5.

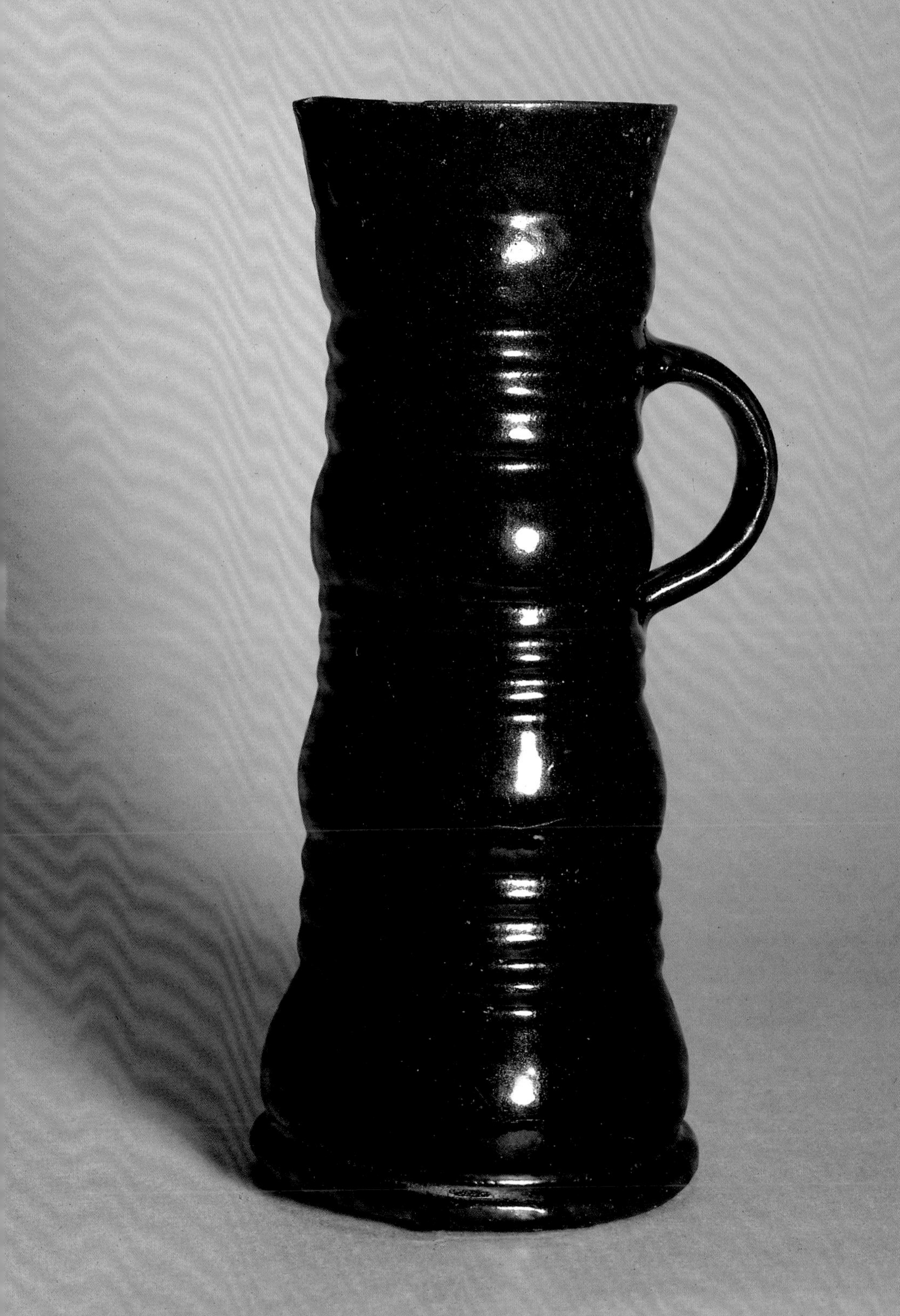

4

BOTTLE

CHRISTIAN WILHELM'S POTTERY,
SOUTHWARK, DATED 1628.

Tin-glazed earthenware painted in cobalt-blue.
Height 19.4 cm. C.5–1931 *(Glaisher Catalogue 1293).*

Tin-glazed earthenware was probably introduced into England by Jasper Andries and Jacob Jansen, who came over from Antwerp and settled in Norwich in 1567. By 1571 Jansen had moved to London, where he was recorded as a 'Pott-maker' in Duke's Place, Aldgate, along with six other Flemish potters. After Jansen's death in 1593 the pottery continued in existence until at least 1603 and probably as late as 1615. Very little intact pottery can be attributed to Aldgate and it is only from the 1620s that substantial quantities of tin-glazed ware survives which can be attributed firmly to potteries in the London area.

By then Chinese blue and white porcelain of the late Ming Dynasty (1368–1644), imported by the Dutch and English East India Companies, was creating a demand which European potters attempted to satisfy by imitating its decoration on the white surface of tin-glazed earthenware. This bottle, decorated with a late Ming design traditionally known as 'bird on rock', is one of the earliest examples of the influence of Chinese blue and white porcelain on English ceramics. Its date of 1628 is significant, for in that year a patent for the manufacture of galliware, the contemporary term for tin-glazed earthenware, was granted to Christian Wilhelm, the proprietor of a pottery at Pickleherring in Southwark, on the south bank of the Thames. Local records indicate that his pottery was probably in Vine Yard, a short distance south of Pickleherring Street. It was operating by 1618 and continued until the early eighteenth century. The 'bird on rock' pattern can be associated with Wilhelm because it occurs on kiln wasters found nearby at Potter's Fields, Southwark. After Wilhelm's death in 1630, his son-in-law Thomas Townsend inherited the pottery and appears to have continued making this pattern until the early 1640s.

Further reading Ivor Noël Hume, *Early English Delftware from London and Virginia*, 1977. Frank Britton, *London Delftware*, 1987, pp. 18–29 and 34–6.

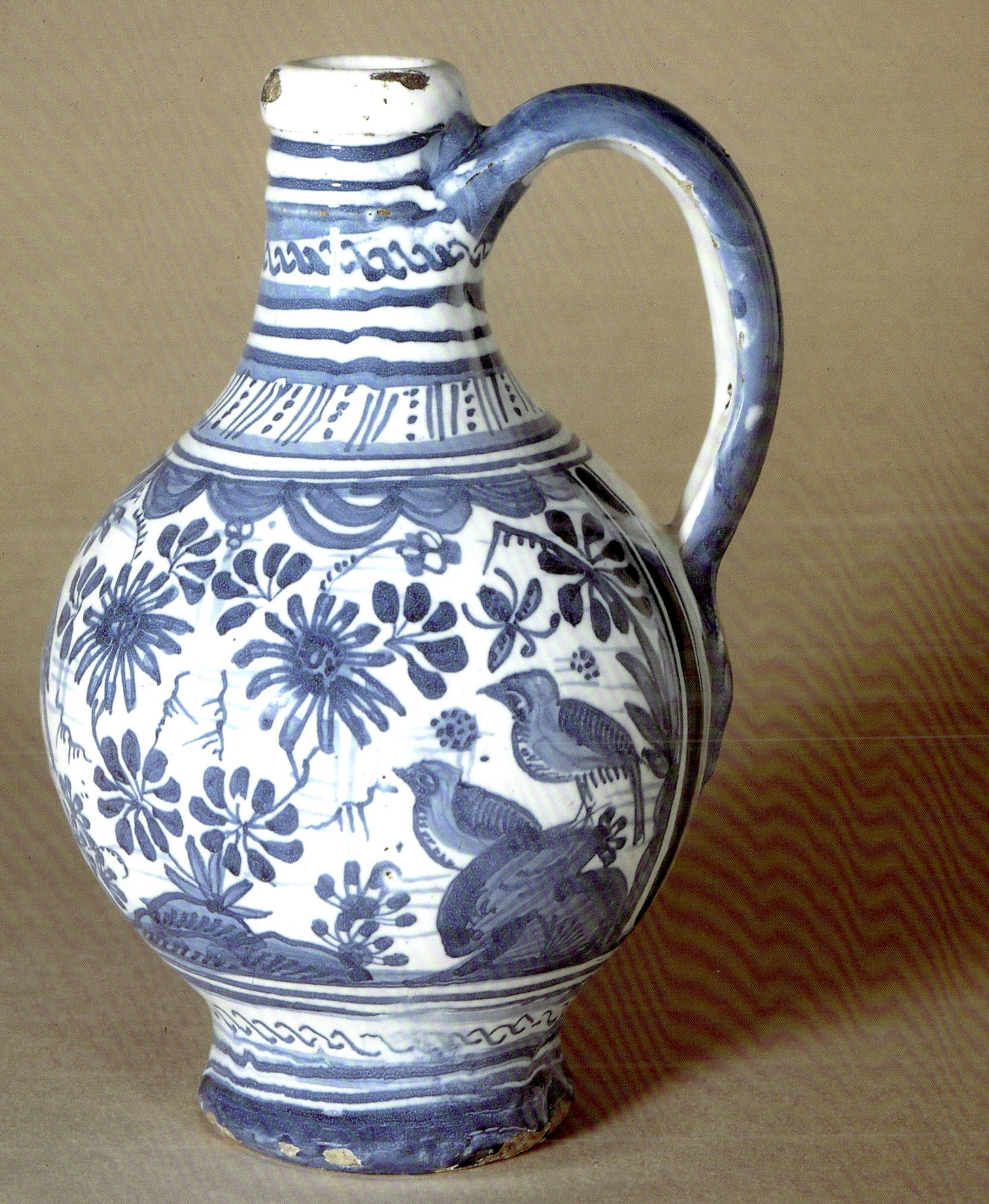

5

DISH

SOUTHWARK, 1651.

Earthenware, moulded, tin-glazed and painted in high-temperature colours; initialled and dated on the back 'C^{D}M/1651'. Length 48.8 cm, width 40.5 cm. C.1422–1928.

This dish reproduces a French lead-glazed earthenware dish of a pattern once attributed to the great French potter, Bernard Palissy (*c.* 1510–90), but probably made by Claude Berthélémy at Fontainebleau, south of Paris, in the early seventeenth century. Claude Beaulat, a potter who had worked there around 1600, had become a merchant in London by 1621, and it seems probable that such dishes were imported by him or other members of the French merchant community. The shape and central scene, known as *La Fécondité* (fertility), were copied faithfully, but the addition of polychrome decoration painted on white tin-glaze, produced an entirely different effect from the richly coloured translucent lead glazes on the French models.

These tin-glazed dishes must have looked very handsome when displayed on dressers and they remained popular for many years. The earliest known tin-glazed *La Fécondité* dish, dated 1633 and inscribed with the names of its owners 'STEPHEN FORTVNE & ELIZABETH', is in an American private collection. Several others, including the one Fitzwilliam's example, bear a date and the initials of a man and wife. The latest surviving examples, in the City Museum and Art Gallery, Birmingham and the Victoria and Albert Museum, London, both painted in blue instead of polychrome, were made in 1697, long after Palissy ware had gone out of fashion.

Further reading Bernard Rackham, 'Bernard Palissy and Lambeth Delft', ECCT, 4, Part 5 (1959), pp. 61–4. Louis L. Lipski and Michael Archer, *Dated English Delftware*, 1984. Frank Britton, 'Bernard Palissy and London Delftware', ECCT, 14, Part 2 (1991), pp. 169–76.

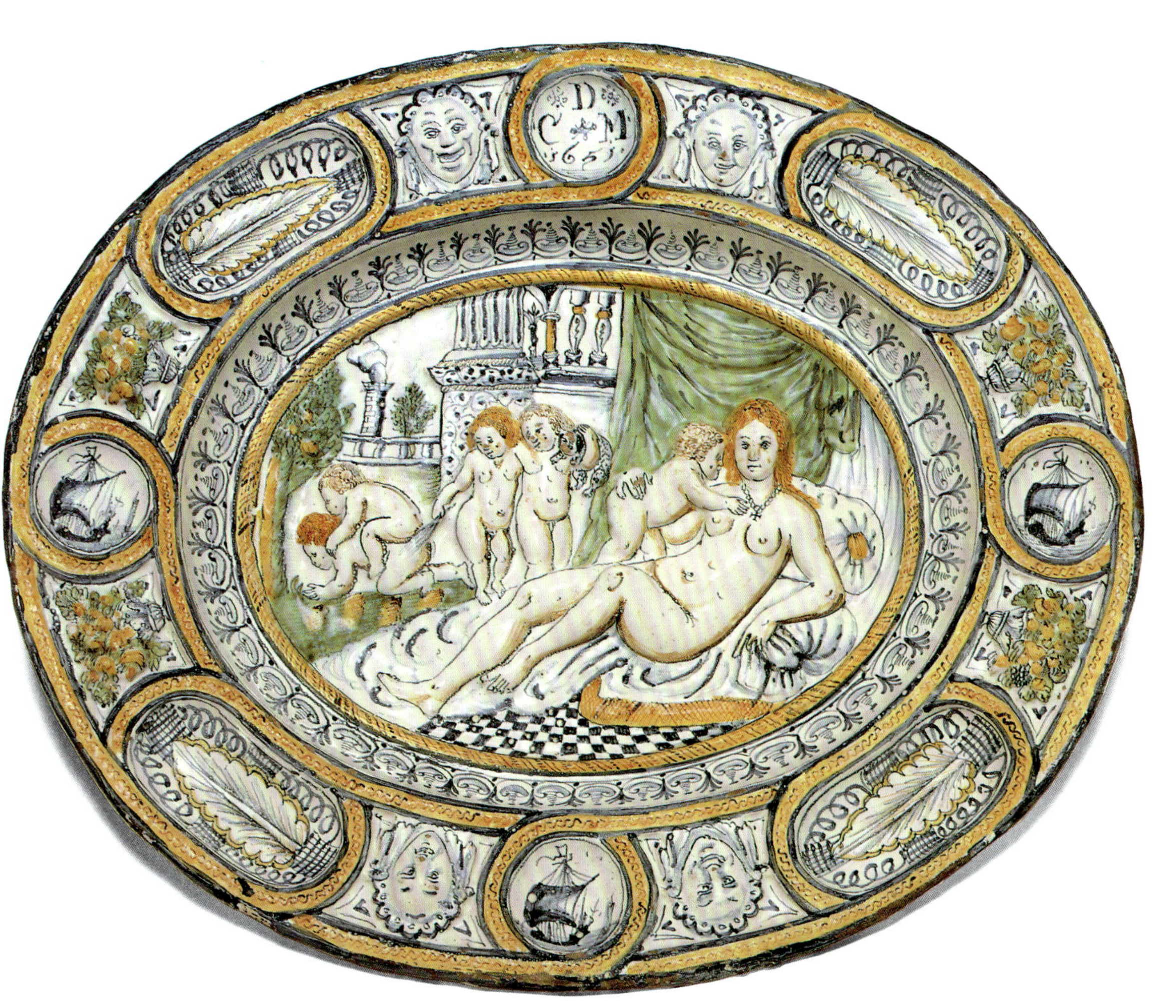

6

JUG

PROBABLY HARLOW,
ESSEX, c. 1630–60.

Red earthenware with white slip-trailed decoration under yellowish lead glaze. Height 28.4 cm. Glaisher Catalogue 40–1928.

The development of the New Town at Harlow in Essex during the 1950s led to the discovery of kiln sites and great quantities of sherds at Latton Street and Potter Street in the parish of Latton. Some sherds matched mid-seventeenth-century pottery known as Metropolitan Slipware because much of it had been found in the City of London. Its place of manufacture had previously been uncertain, but can now be identified as the Harlow area, which was conveniently situated on the road from Newmarket to London.

The slip-trailed motifs on this jug correspond to sherds from Potter Street, but it differs from many complete vessels of this type in lacking a pious inscription round its body or neck. A smaller jug and a bowl in the Museum's collection bear the exhortations 'REMEMBER GOD' and 'FAST AND PRAY'. Such inscriptions are an indication of the fervent religious sentiments prevalent in England during the mid-seventeenth century, and a reminder of the ever-present threat of death from plague and other causes in that period.

Further reading E. F. Newton and E. Bibbings, 'Seventeenth century pottery sites at Harlow, Essex', *Essex Archaeological Society Transactions*, 25 (N.S.), Part III (1960), pp. 358–77. Ronald Cooper, *English Slipware Dishes 1650–1850*, 1968, pp. 22–30.

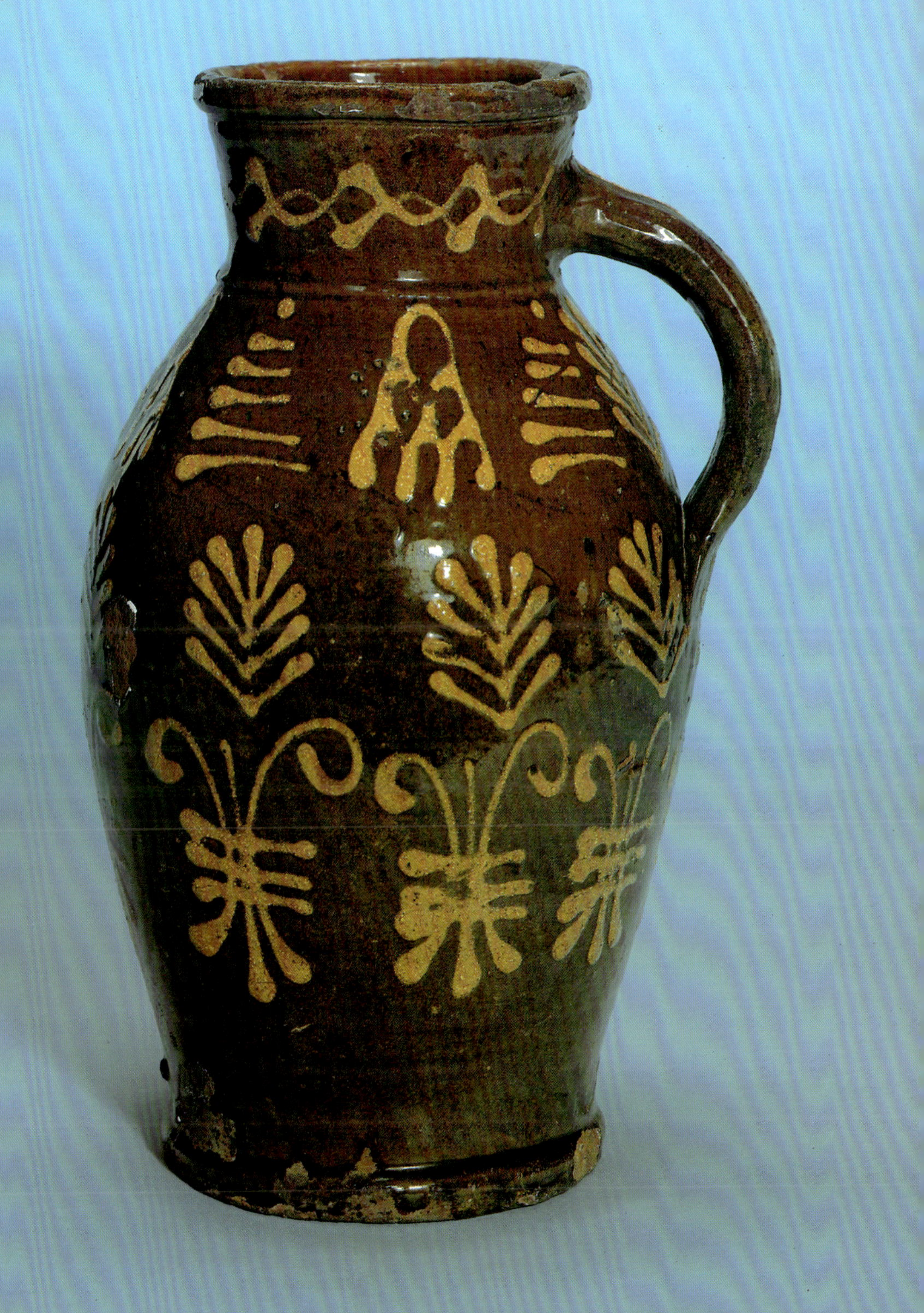

7

TWO-HANDLED TYG

WROTHAM, KENT; INITIALLED 'HI',
PROBABLY FOR THE POTTER HENRY IFIELD,
AND DATED 1668.

Reddish-brown earthenware decorated with white clay under yellowish lead glaze. Height 14.5 cm. C.120–1928.

Drinking cups with more than one handle were the great speciality of Wrotham potters in the seventeenth century and have been described as tygs by collectors since the nineteenth century. They were made of red or brown clay decorated in white with slip-trailing, prunts and heraldic motifs on applied pads of clay, which appear yellow under the lead glaze. Many of them bear dates and the potter's initials, sometimes accompanied by one or two other sets of initials, presumably those of their owners. Twisted two-colour edges and white bun-shaped finials were features of the double-loop handles, usually three or four, but on this example only two.

Searches of the Wrotham parish registers, made between 1906 and 1912 for Dr J.W.L. Glaisher, revealed the names of several persons whose initials coincide with those found repeatedly on Wrotham slipware, and who were therefore probably potters. HI is known from dated tygs and jugs bearing his initials to have been working between about 1652 and 1669. He was probably the Henry Ifield baptised in 1633, listed in the Hearth Tax Rolls of 1663–4 and buried on 18 October 1673.

Further reading A.J.B.Kiddell, 'Wrotham slipware and the Wrotham brickyard', ECCT, 3, Part 2 (1954), pp. 105–18.

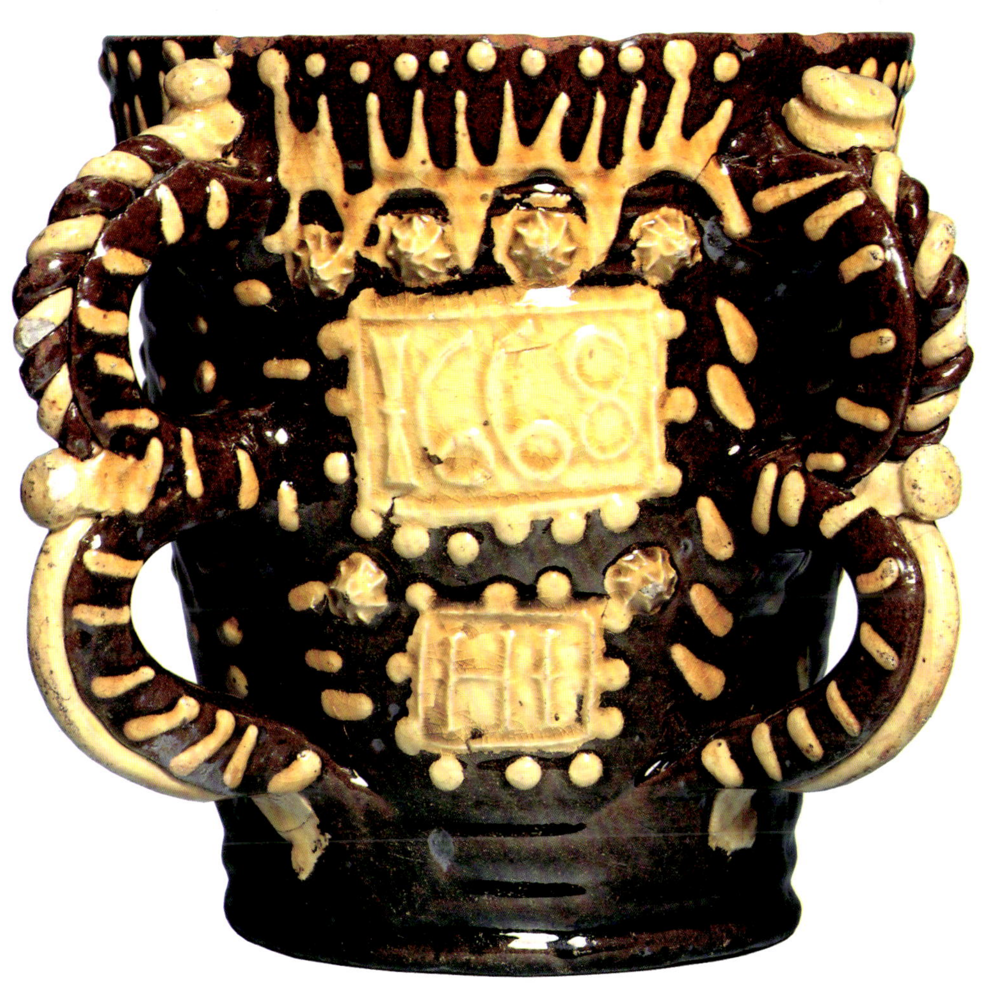
1668

8

TULIP CHARGER

LONDON, 1661.

Tin-glazed earthenware painted in high-temperature colours; initialled and dated 'W/WS 16:61'. Height 7.7 cm, diameter 48.5 cm. C.1426–1928.

Large delftware dishes, known today as chargers, were made between about 1600 and 1740. Most of them are decorated with variants of a few simple themes: geometrical patterns, fruit and foliage, tulips and other flowers arranged in a vase or growing from a mound, Adam and Eve with the Tree of Knowledge, and portraits of monarchs or other persons. Less common subjects include biblical scenes, the royal yacht, windmills, and unicorns. The rims are usually encircled by slanting blue dashes, hence the term 'blue dash chargers' coined by the Rev. E.A. Downman, who published a book with that title in 1919.

Tulip mania developed in Holland during the 1620s and 1630s and spread from there to England and other Western European countries. After the Restoration in 1660, Dutch influence on the arts in England was very strong and for about thirty years floral decoration of all kinds, including cut flowers in vases, was extremely fashionable. Tulip chargers were an expression of this love of flowers. This is the earliest dated example with a blue dash edge but they were probably made from the late 1650s. Unlike most chargers which have curved sides, it has a shallow well and a broad rim decorated with pomegranates and parti-coloured leaves. These originated on the Continent but their arrangement in panels alternating with panels of trellis pattern suggests that the decorator was influenced by the borders of Chinese blue and white porcelain dishes of the Wanli period (1573–1619).

Further reading Michael Archer, 'The dating of Delftware chargers', *ECCT*, 11, Part 2 (1982), pp. 112–21. Louis L. Lipski and Michael Archer, *Dated English Delftware*, 1984, pp. 16–36.

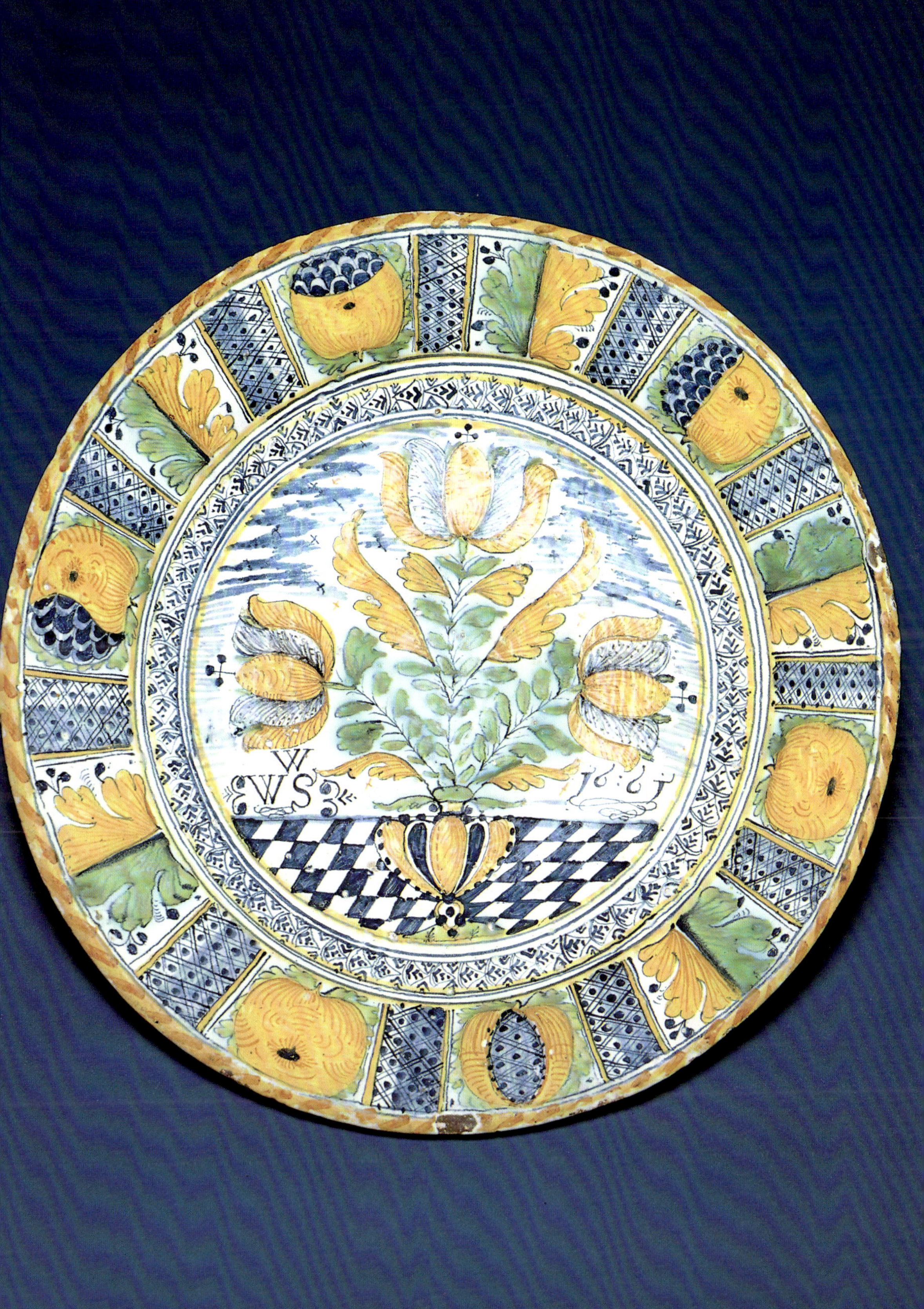
W
WS

9

NOBODY

LONDON, 1675.

Tin-glazed earthenware painted in high-temperature colours and inscribed 'M/RM/1675' on the base. Height 23.3 cm. C.1433–1928.

Free-standing ceramic models of humans or animals were rarely made in England before the second half of the seventeenth century. This quaint little man is one of the earliest made in delftware. He represents Nobody, that conveniently invisible person who for centuries has been blamed for careless breakages and other petty misdemeanours. By the late sixteenth century he was envisaged as a bodiless man whose head and arms projected from voluminous breeches. Just such a figure was illustrated on the title page of *Nobody and Somebody*, a play published in London in 1606. Although fashions changed, this image of Nobody persisted, and the delftware figure of 1675 is very like the earlier illustration, except that he holds a pipe. This reflects the fact that by the mid-seventeenth century the English had become a nation of pipe smokers.

Two more delftware Nobodies have survived: one, dated 1682, at Colonial Williamsburg, Virginia, the other in the Victoria and Albert Museum, where there is also a Chinese porcelain version. The last two have hat-shaped covers and presumably the others had them when new. The figures are hollow, and it has been suggested that they were tobacco jars. This seems unlikely because it would have been difficult to extract tobacco through the narrow opening in their head.

Further reading Gerta Calmann, 'The picture of Nobody', *Journal of the Warburg and Courtauld Institutes*, 23, (1960), pp. 60–104. Louis L. Lipski and Michael Archer, *Dated English Delftware*, 1984, p. 416.

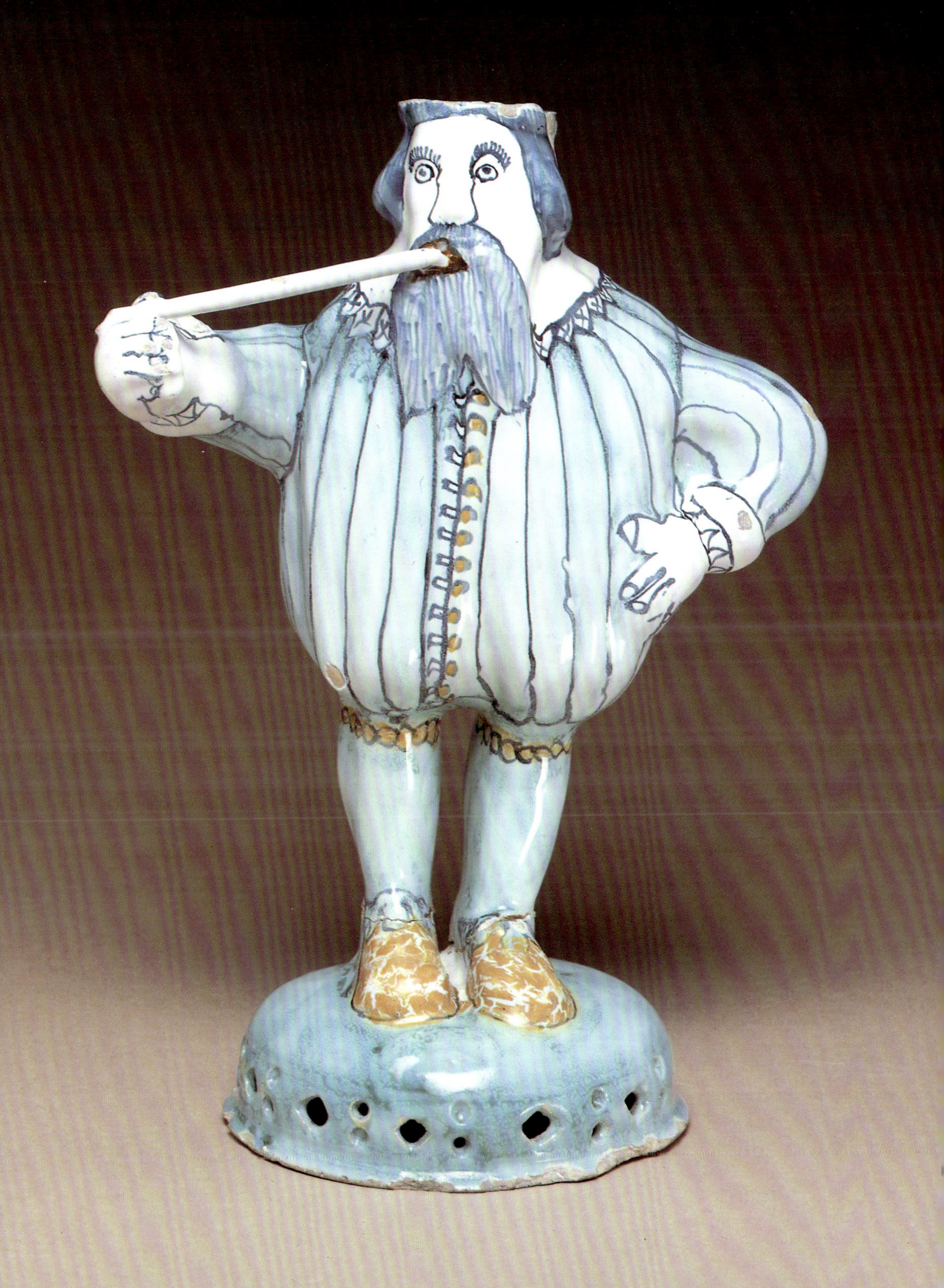

10

DISH

THOMAS TOFT,
STAFFORDSHIRE,
c. 1662–85.

Earthenware decorated with slip-trailing under lead glaze. Diameter 42.5 cm.
C.207–1928.

Staffordshire slipware dishes owe their distinctive character to virtuoso slip-trailing and highly stylized images. The fronts were usually coated with white slip onto which the design was trailed in light and dark red, and sometimes dotted in white. Then powdered lead ore was sprinkled over the surface to produce a yellowish glaze. During firing the decoration sometimes blurred, but on this example the trailing has remained wonderfully crisp. The couple probably represent Charles II and Catherine of Braganza, who were married in 1662. The trellis border is typical of Staffordshire dishes, but occasionally radiating heads or tulips were trailed round the rims.

Thomas Toft is the best known of the seventeenth-century Staffordshire slipware potters, but very little is known about his life. He was probably the Thomas Toft who married in 1663, paid Hearth Tax at the village of Stanley in 1663 and 1666 and was buried at Stoke on 3 December 1689. Over thirty signed dishes have been recorded but a few of them may have been made by his son, also Thomas Toft. What Toft senior made other than dishes is largely conjectural. Only four pieces of hollow ware bearing his name are known, among them a small jug in the Fitzwilliam Museum (C.1–1937).

Further reading Ronald G. Cooper, *English Slipware Dishes 1650–1850*, 1968, pp. 48–70.

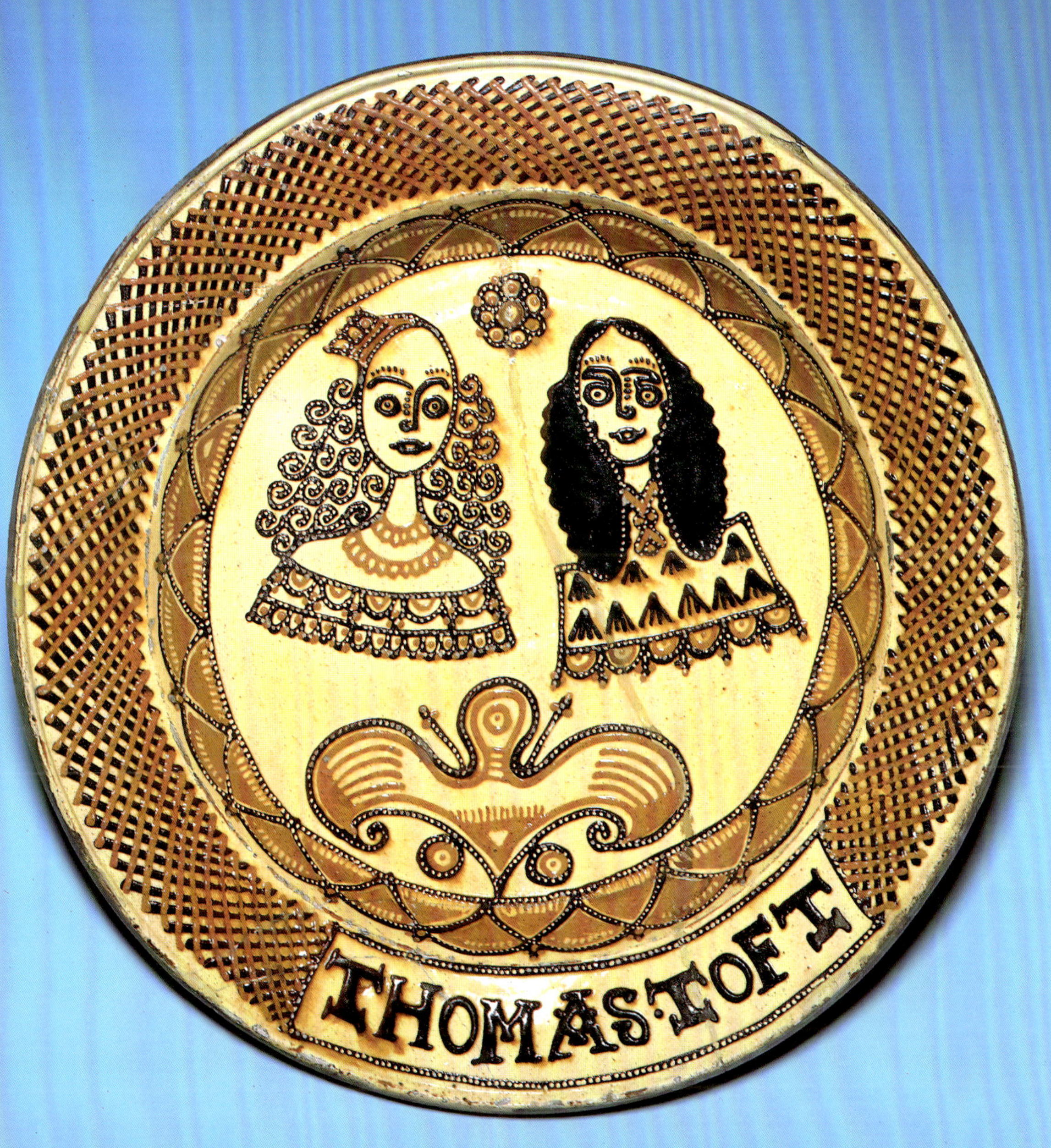
THOMAS·TOFT

11

POSSET POT AND SALVER

LONDON OR BRISTOL,
1685 AND 1686.

Tin-glazed earthenware painted in cobalt-blue; the bases inscribed 'T/C.A/1685' and 'T/C.A/1686'. Pot height 31.1 cm. Salver diameter 23.8 cm.
C.1504–1928.

In the seventeenth and early eighteenth centuries posset was both a drink and a comforting remedy for minor ailments. It was made from warm milk curdled with ale or wine and flavoured with sugar and spices. Posset pots could be made of pewter, silver, earthenware or, from the last quarter of the seventeenth century, glass. They usually had two handles and a cover, and some had a spout through which the posset was sucked or poured. The earliest recorded delftware pot, dated 1631 (Fitzwilliam Museum, C.1294–1928), has straight sides and an almost flat cover. Pots with curved sides had been introduced by the 1650s and, judging by dated examples, predominated by the 1680s.

The importance of posset at social gatherings is indicated by the elaborate forms of the largest pots of the 1680s and 1690s. Their handles and covers were decorated with curlicues and serpents and the covers often had a finial in the shape of a bird perching on a globe. To complement this, some pots had bird-shaped feet. A little later, about 1699–1705, covers shaped like crowns were fashionable. These large pots are usually decorated with flowers, European scenes or Chinese figures in landscapes derived from late Ming porcelain. Smaller pots may be similarly decorated, but they and the larger types are often plain except for a coat of arms or a cartouche containing the owner's initials.

Salvers, which were necessary to catch drips from the spout, are now much rarer than pots. The European decoration on this one does not match the pot and as it was made a year later, it may have been a replacement or may have accompanied another pot belonging to the same owner. Its edge has been restored.

Further reading *Frank Britton, English Delftware in the Bristol Collection*, 1982, pp. 68–75. Louis L. Lipski and Michael Archer, *Dated English Delftware*, 1984, pp. 200–18.

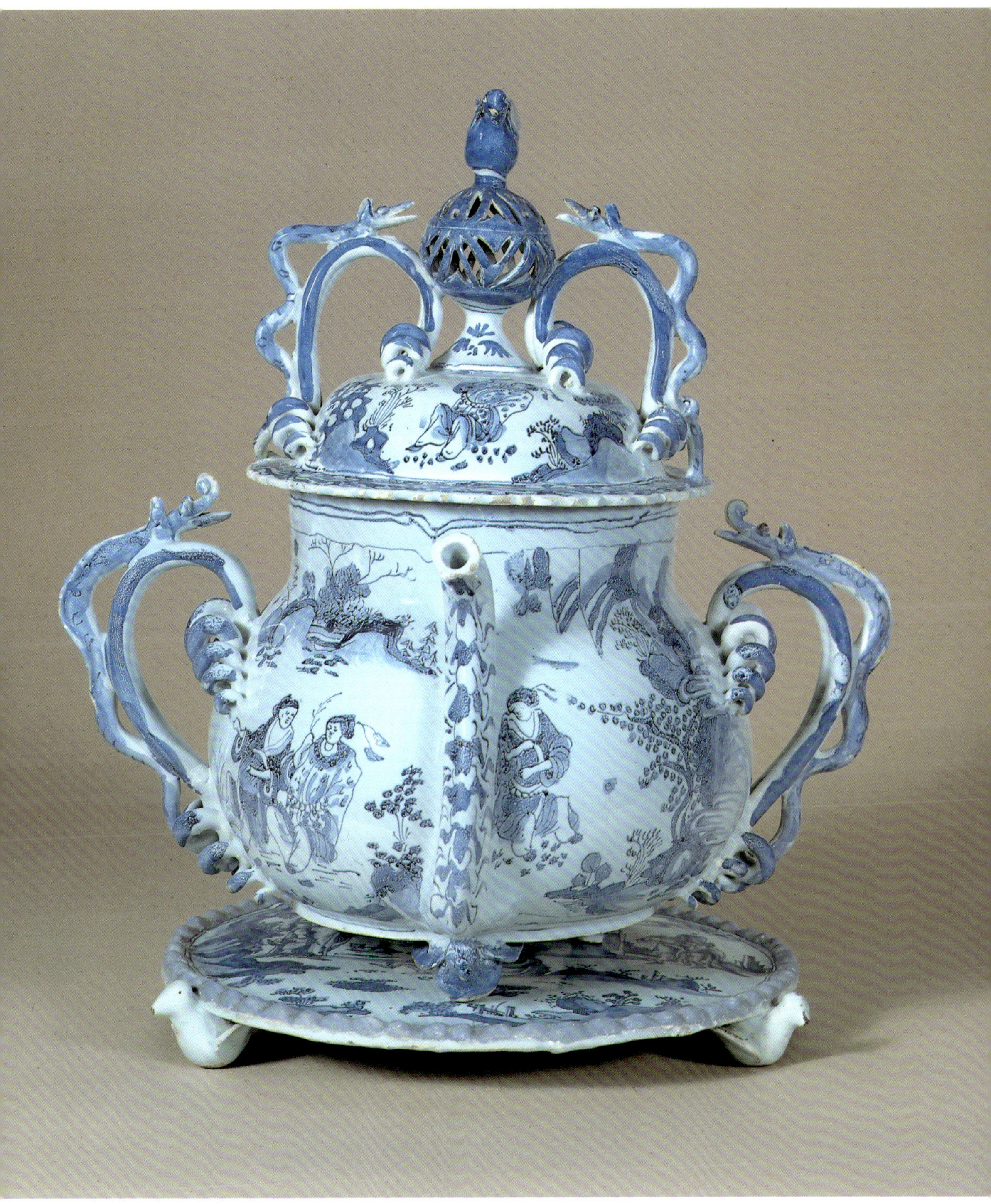

12

CISTERN

LONDON, PERHAPS NORFOLK HOUSE, LAMBETH, c. 1680–1700.

Earthenware with dark blue tin-glaze painted in white enamel. Height 14 cm, length 25.5 cm. C.1386–1928

Dark blue *faïence* decorated with white or coloured enamels was made at Nevers in France from the mid-seventeenth to early eighteenth centuries. London potters probably acquired the technique from Nevers, although they may also have been influenced by Japanese porcelain with blue glaze which was imported by the Dutch from the 1660s. Sherds of blue delftware have been found on the site of the Norfolk House pottery in Lambeth, but it may have been made elsewhere in London and at Brislington, near Bristol. The decoration, always in white, comprises floral patterns, random splodges and Oriental landscapes with figures. These Oriental designs, featuring brush-like trees and shrubs, were probably derived from Japanese blue and white porcelain in Chinese Transitional style.

This water cistern or wine cooler is a notable example of a ceramic vessel whose shape derives from metalwork (see also nos. 28 and 29). Its swelling oval form, with lion's mask and ring handles at each end, imitates the massive silver cisterns which were in fashion in the 1670s and 1680s. The few surviving blue delft cisterns are much smaller and can only just accommodate one of the bulbous glass bottles made in the late seventeenth century. Analogous Oriental decoration occurs on a monteith in the City Museum and Art Gallery, Stoke-on-Trent (421P 1935). Monteiths were circular or oval bowls with notched rims, from which wine glasses were suspended by their feet to cool in cold water or ice.

Further reading Michael Archer, *English Delftware*, 1973, p. 28, nos. 53–5. Michael Archer and Brian Morgan, *Fair as China Dishes*, English Delftware, 1987, pp. 40–1. Frank Britton, *London Delftware*, 1987, pp. 52–3 and pp. 135–6, nos. 98–101.

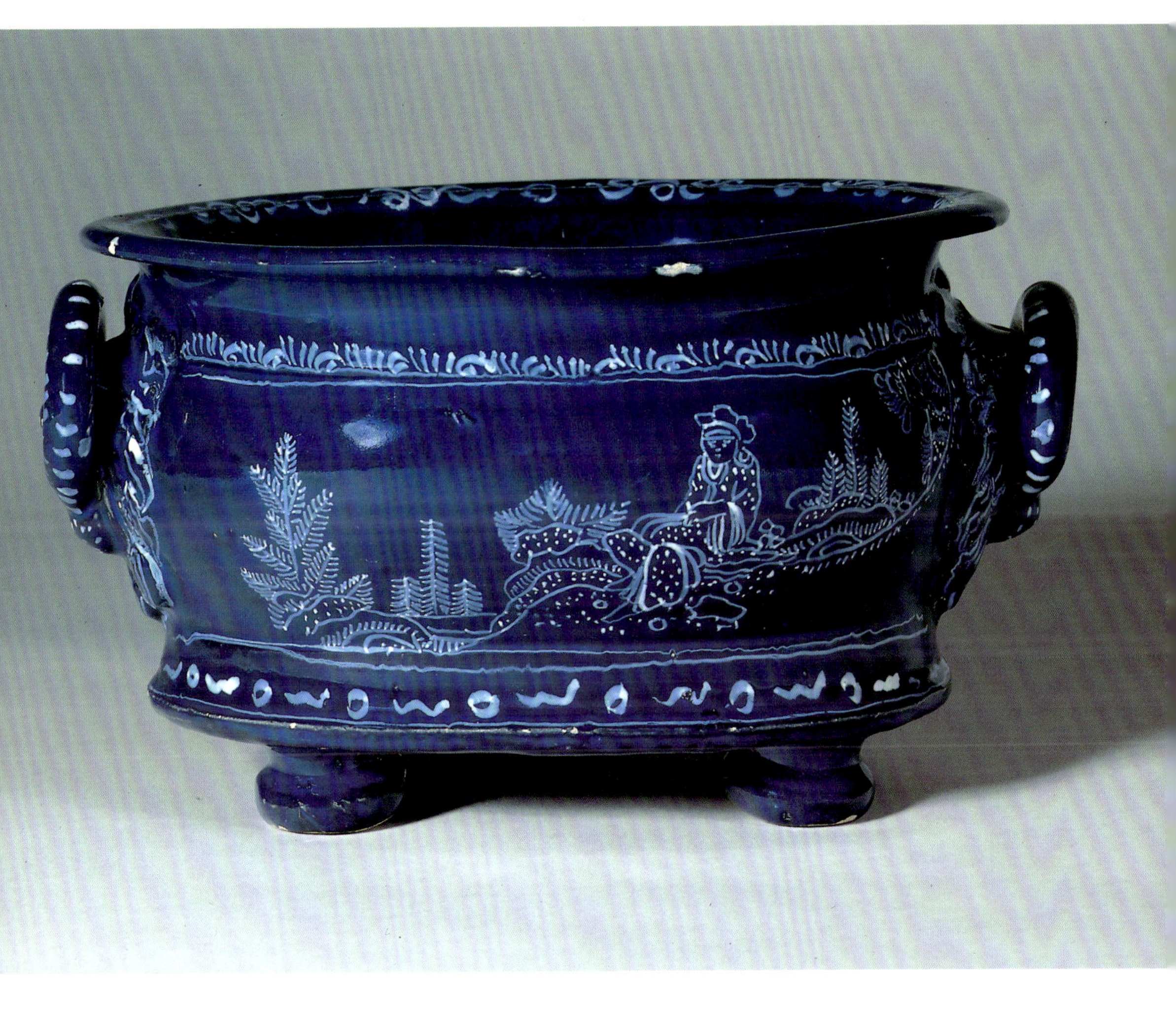

13

BOTTLE

JOHN DWIGHT'S POTTERY, FULHAM, c. 1689–94.

Salt-glazed stoneware with marbled bands, thrown, turned and decorated with applied reliefs: overlapping busts of William III and Mary II, a flying bird, two Merry Andrews (clowns), a winged cherub's head, a crane and a medallion with initial C amongst foliage.
Height 17 cm. C.1194–1928.

Glass bottles made in England before about 1650 were not very strong and during the sixteenth and seventeenth centuries hundreds of thousands of sturdy salt-glazed stoneware bottles were imported from the Rhineland to serve as containers for wine and other liquids, such as perfumed waters. Several attempts were made to produce them here, for example, at Woolwich about 1660, but these ventures were short lived. The first person to master the technique of salt-glazing and to continue successfully for a long period was John Dwight (c. 1633/6–1703). During the late 1660s Dwight, a lawyer by profession, was Registrar of the diocese of Chester and conducted experiments to produce stoneware at Wigan. In 1671/2 he moved to Fulham and in April 1672 was granted a patent for making 'China and Persian ware' and also 'the Stone Ware vulgarly called Collogne Ware'. In 1684 a renewal of the patent included various other types, among them 'marbled Porcellane Vessels' but there is no evidence that the experimental porcelain made by Dwight in the 1670s was produced commercially.

The 'sprigs' on this bottle were made with brass stamps, some of which were found at the Fulham pottery in the 1860s and were later acquired by British Museum. The initials AR on one of them probably stand for the medallist Reinier or Regnier Arondeux (c.1655–1727). The bottle remained in the possession of Dwight's descendants until 1861–2 and in 1871 was sold at auction with other heirlooms which included two similar bottles now in the British Museum and the Victoria and Albert Museum.

Further reading D. Haselgrove and J. Murray, 'John Dwight's Fulham Pottery 1672–1978, a collection of documentary sources', *Journal of Ceramic History*, 11 (1979). A. Oswald, R.J.C. Hildyard and R.G. Hughes, *English Brown Stoneware 1670–1900*, 1982, pp. 25-32. Jonathan Horne, *John Dwight 'The Master Potter of Fulham' 1672–1703*, 1992.

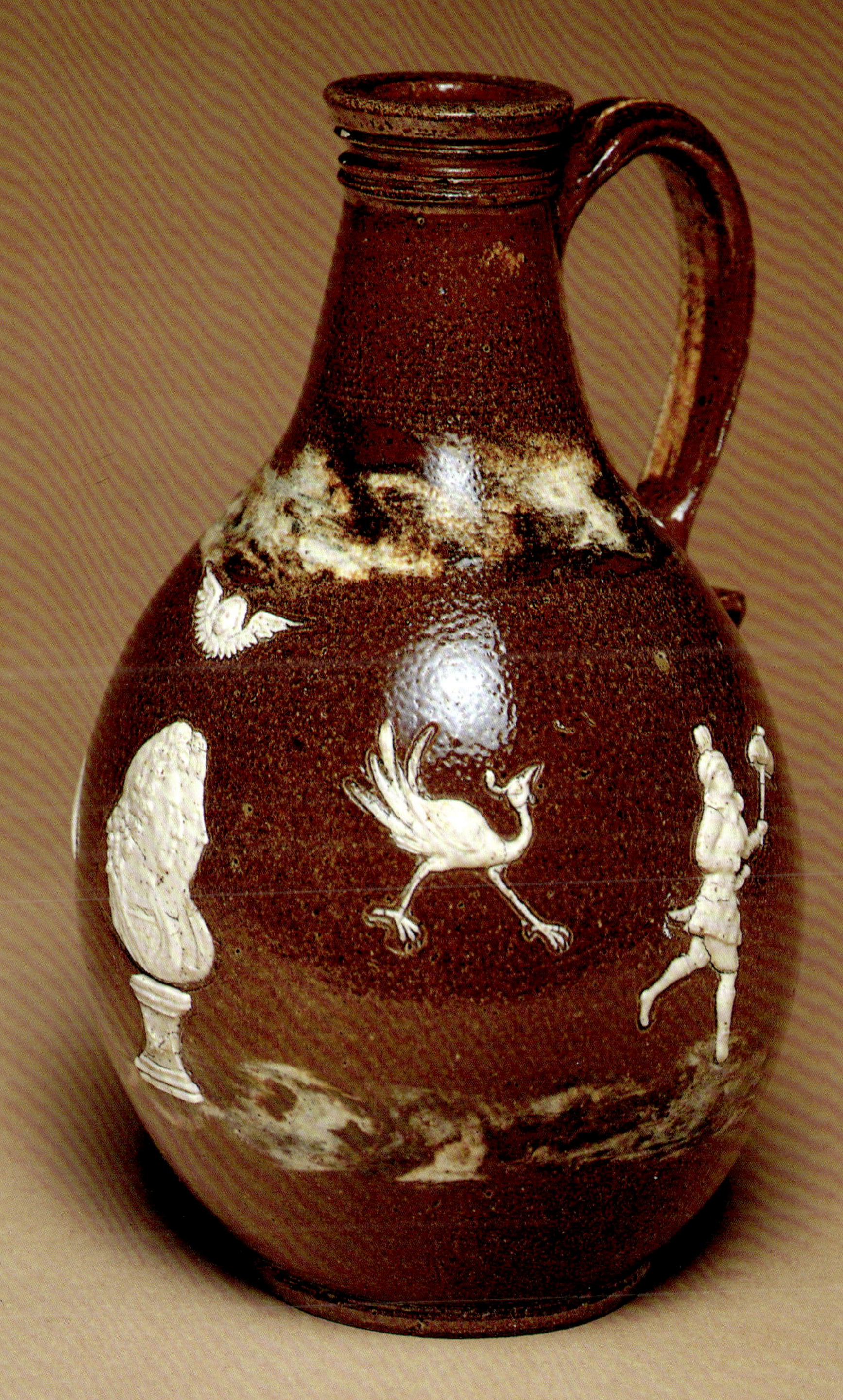

14

MUG

DAVID AND JOHN PHILLIP ELERS,
PROBABLY BRADWELL WOOD, STAFFORDSHIRE, *c.* 1691–8.

Red dry-bodied stoneware, with turned bands and mould-applied decoration of chrysanthemum sprays, three snails and a Merry Andrew. Height 10.1 cm. C.454–1928.

Red stoneware originated in China and by about 1670 it was being imported from Yixing by the Dutch. Teapots were especially prized because of their heat-retaining properties, and were imitated at Delft from the early 1670s. The first person to make red stoneware in England was probably John Dwight, whose patent of 1684 included 'opacous redd and darke coloured Porcellane or China'. Some fragments of redware were found during excavations at the Fulham pottery, but it is not certain that Dwight produced it on a commercial scale. Late seventeenth-century redware is generally attributed to David and John Phillip Elers, immigrants of German origin who had settled in London before 1686, when David was recorded as a shop owner near St Clement's church. They were silversmiths, but David claimed to have learned the art of stoneware manufacture at Cologne.

David Elers was probably making pottery in Staffordshire by 1691, and in 1693 the brothers were recorded as making red teapots there and at Vauxhall. This resulted in them being sued by John Dwight for infringement of his patent. After reaching an agreement with him, the Elers continued their business at Bradwell Wood, near Newcastle-under-Lyme, until 1698 when they moved back to Vauxhall. By 1700 they were bankrupt and both turned to china dealing, John Phillip in Dublin and David in London.

Apart from teapots, the Elers are credited with beakers, globular and straight-sided mugs, and tankards. Some of these were slip-cast and turned on a lathe to smooth their contours or to create raised bands on the exterior. Relief decoration was applied from metal moulds which left faint outlines on the surface. The chrysanthemum sprays on this mug were derived from Chinese stoneware. The dancing man is a buffoon or clown, often called a Merry Andrew in the seventeenth century.

Further reading W.B. Honey, 'Elers Ware', *ECCT*, 1, no. 2 (1934), pp. 7–16. Rhoda Edwards, 'London potters circa 1570–1710', *Journal of Ceramic History*, 6 (1974), pp. 60–2. Margaret Macfarlane, 'A red stoneware tea-pot', *National Art Collections Fund Review*, 1990, pp. 109–13.

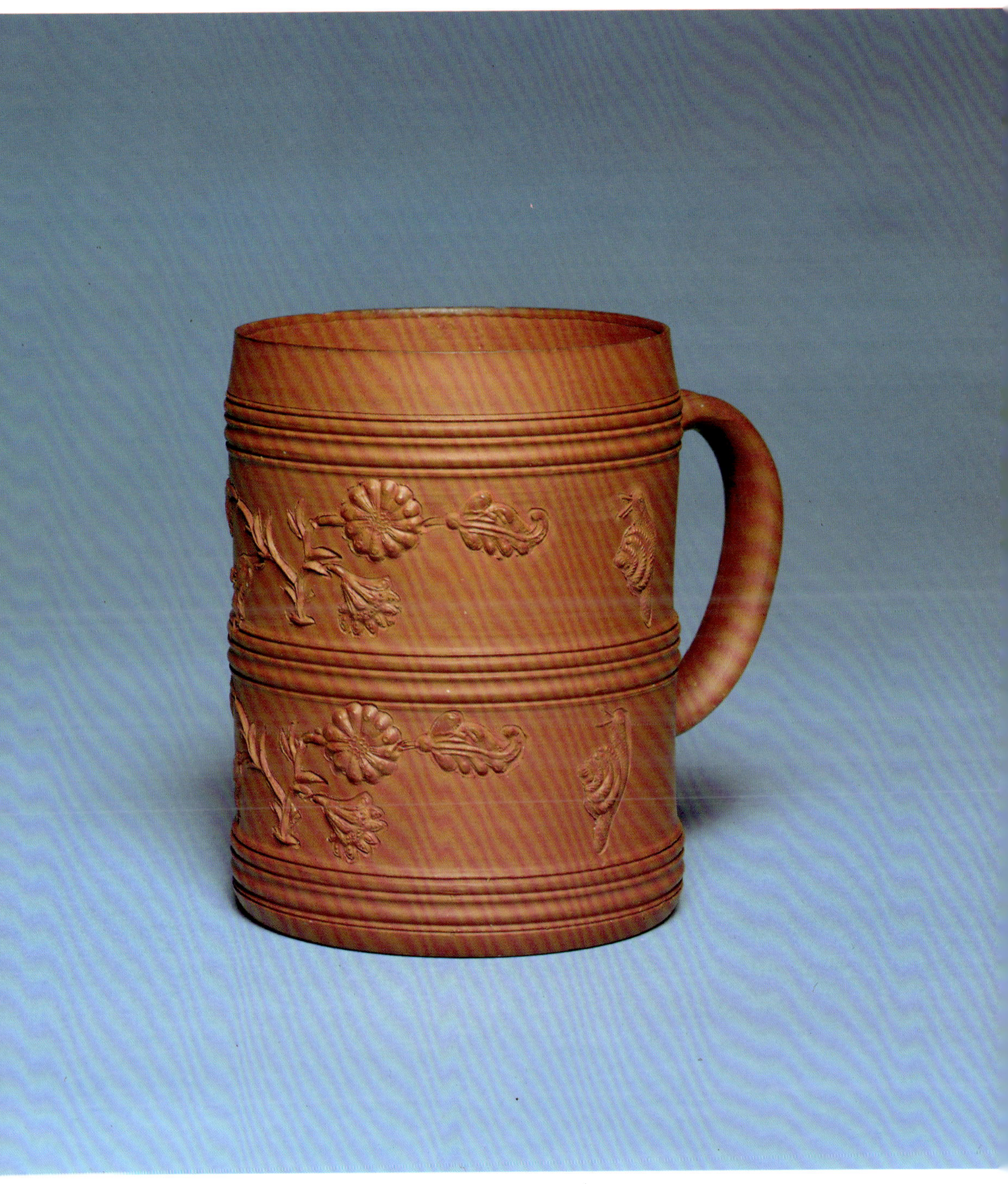

15

JUG

STAFFORDSHIRE,

c. 1680–1710.

Buff earthenware, decorated outside with marbled and feathered slips under lead glaze. Height 26.5 cm. C.311–1928.

An outstanding quality of Staffordshire slipware is that it is both handsome and functional. This sturdy jug holds exactly five pints when full to the brim and could have been used for serving or storage. At first glance the handle seems rather small for the overall size and weight. Nevertheless the vessel is easy to lift or tip forward and, although it has no lip, pours well without dripping, providing it is not too full.

The fascinating decoration on the exterior was produced by a combination of marbling and feathering techniques. The flagon was coated with orange slip (visible inside and on the handle). Then a series of lines of white and dark red-brown slips were trailed over the outside and were made to run together to create a variegated effect. According to Dr Plot in his *Natural History of Staffordshire*, 1686, this was done with a wire brush, but shaking or joggling can produce similar results. After that a pointed tool or quill was drawn through and across the slip to drag it into a feathered pattern reminiscent of the end papers of old books.

Further reading Bernard Rackham, *Early Staffordshire Pottery*, 1951, pp. 5–14. Mary Wondrausch, *Slipware*, 1986, pp. 26–8.

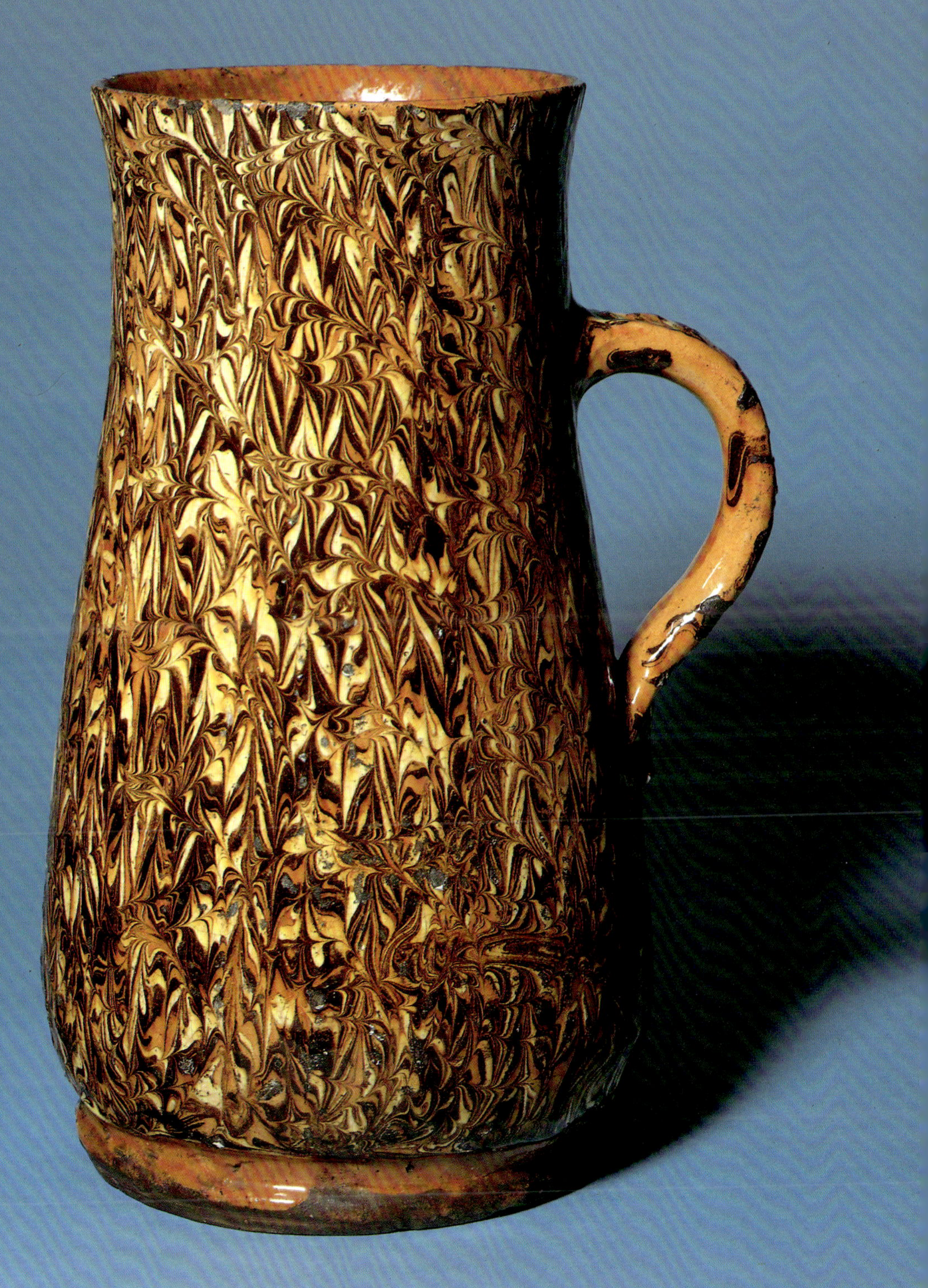

16

COVERED CUP WITH FOUR HANDLES AND A WHISTLE

PROBABLY SOUTH WILTSHIRE, DATED 1718.

Pale red earthenware with incised decoration under dark brown mottled lead glaze. Inscribed round the rim 'COM GOOD WEMAИ DRINK OF ThE BEST IOИE [JOAN] MY LADY AИD ALL ThE REST 1718'. *Height 29 cm.* C.368–1928.

In country districts fashions in pottery changed slowly and homely vessels in late seventeenth-century styles persisted well into the eighteenth, despite the trend for more refined drinking and tablewares. The Fitzwilliam has cups similar to this dated 1692 and 1737, the latter inscribed with the toast 'DRINK ABOVT AND SEE HOW MERY WE SHALL BE'. It was still common then for a group of drinkers to share a large cup and the provision of several handles made it easy to pass such 'loving' cups from one person to another. The whistles which fit into a loop on the side of some cups are said to have been used to call for more liquor, but they often stuck to the vessel during firing and can never have been used.

It is not certain where this class of brown-glazed ware originated. A considerable number of examples were in the possession of families in the Salisbury area in the late nineteenth century and others further south at places such as Ringwood and Southampton. It therefore seems likely that they were made in South Wiltshire or Dorset. Several villages in the district of Alderholt and Verwood in Dorset had potteries which operated from the fourteenth to the early twentieth century, but excavations have so far yielded very little brown-glazed ware.

Further reading Peter Brears, *The English Country Pottery*, 1971, pp. 47–8. David Algar, Anthony Light and Penny Copland-Griffiths, *The Verwood and District Potteries*, 1987.

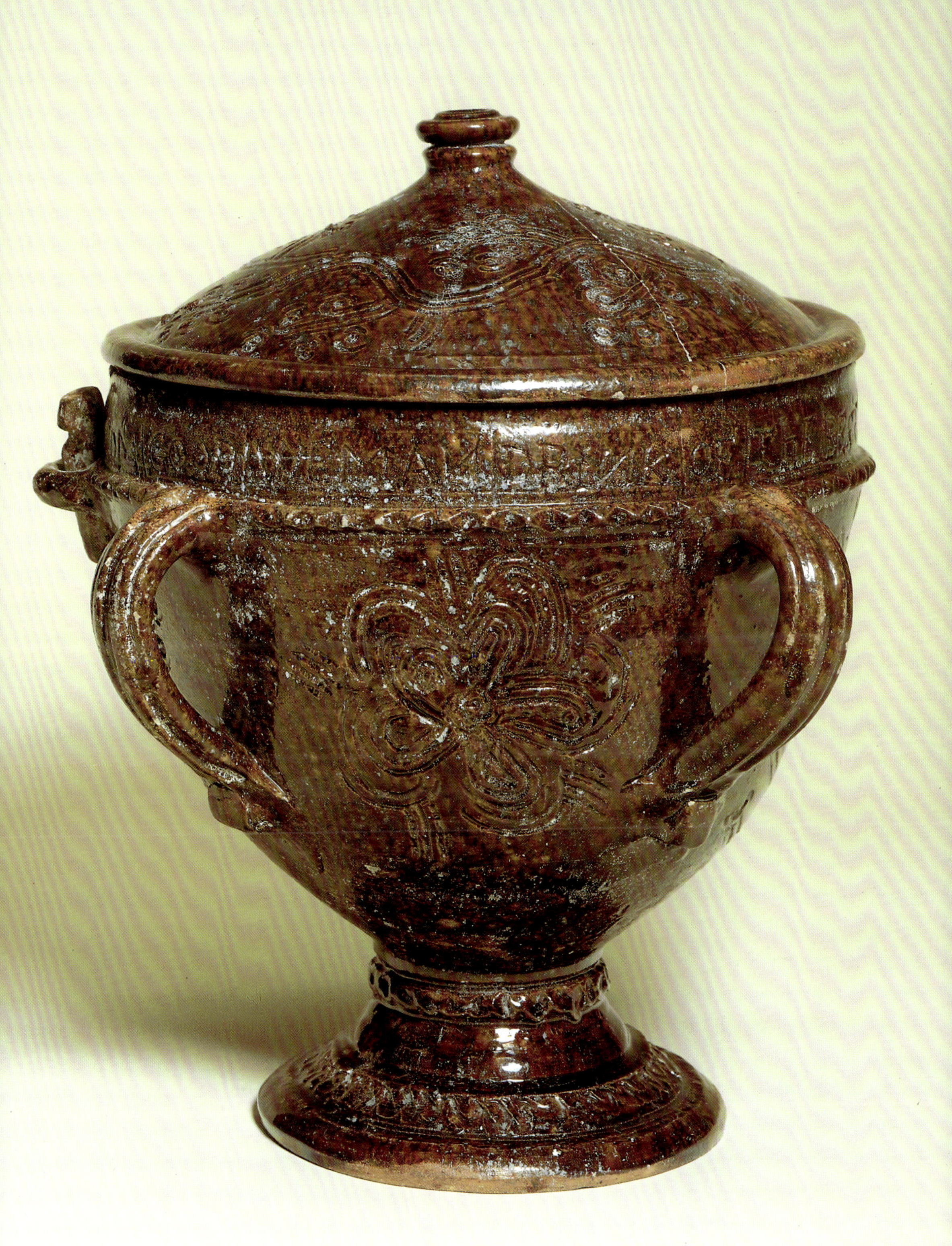

17

DISH

SAMUEL MALKIN,

BURSLEM, C. 1720–30.

Earthenware, moulded and decorated with slip under lead glaze; inscribed 'Wee three Logerheads' and initialled 'S M'. Diameter 35.5 cm. EC.3–1942.

The title of this dish is a sly joke, for the viewer is the third loggerhead or fool. The convivial scene suggests that it may have been made for an inn, perhaps a forerunner of the present 'Loggerheads', on the road between Newcastle-under-Lyme and Market Drayton. Unlike seventeenth-century slip-trailed dishes (no. 10), which were thrown, this was made on a convex earthenware 'hump mould', the back of which had been incised with the design before firing. A flat 'bat' of clay was pressed over the mould and, when it had dried sufficiently, was removed with the design in relief on the interior. Then decoration in coloured slips and lead glaze was applied and the dish was fired.

Samuel Malkin usually signed with initials only but his identity is known from a dish with his name in full, now in the British Museum. The front is decorated with a clock face inscribed 'Samuel Malkin/The Maker/in burslam 17' which, as the clock hand points to 12, suggests that it was made in 1712 or 1729. The latest date on a dish initialled 'S M' is 1734 and he probably died in 1741. The parish register records the burial of a Samuel Malkin, described as the 'old parish clerk of Burslem', a vocation which seems appropriate for a potter who inscribed some of his dishes with proverbial or biblical inscriptions such as the ominous 'Remember Lot's Wife Luke 17:32' on a dish of 1726 also in the Fitzwilliam (C.201–1928).

Further reading Hugh Tait, 'Samuel Malkin and the 'SM' slipware dishes', I and II, *Apollo*, 65 (January and February 1957), pp. 3–6 and 48–51. Ronald Cooper, *English Slipware Dishes 1650–1850*, 1968, pp. 100–7.

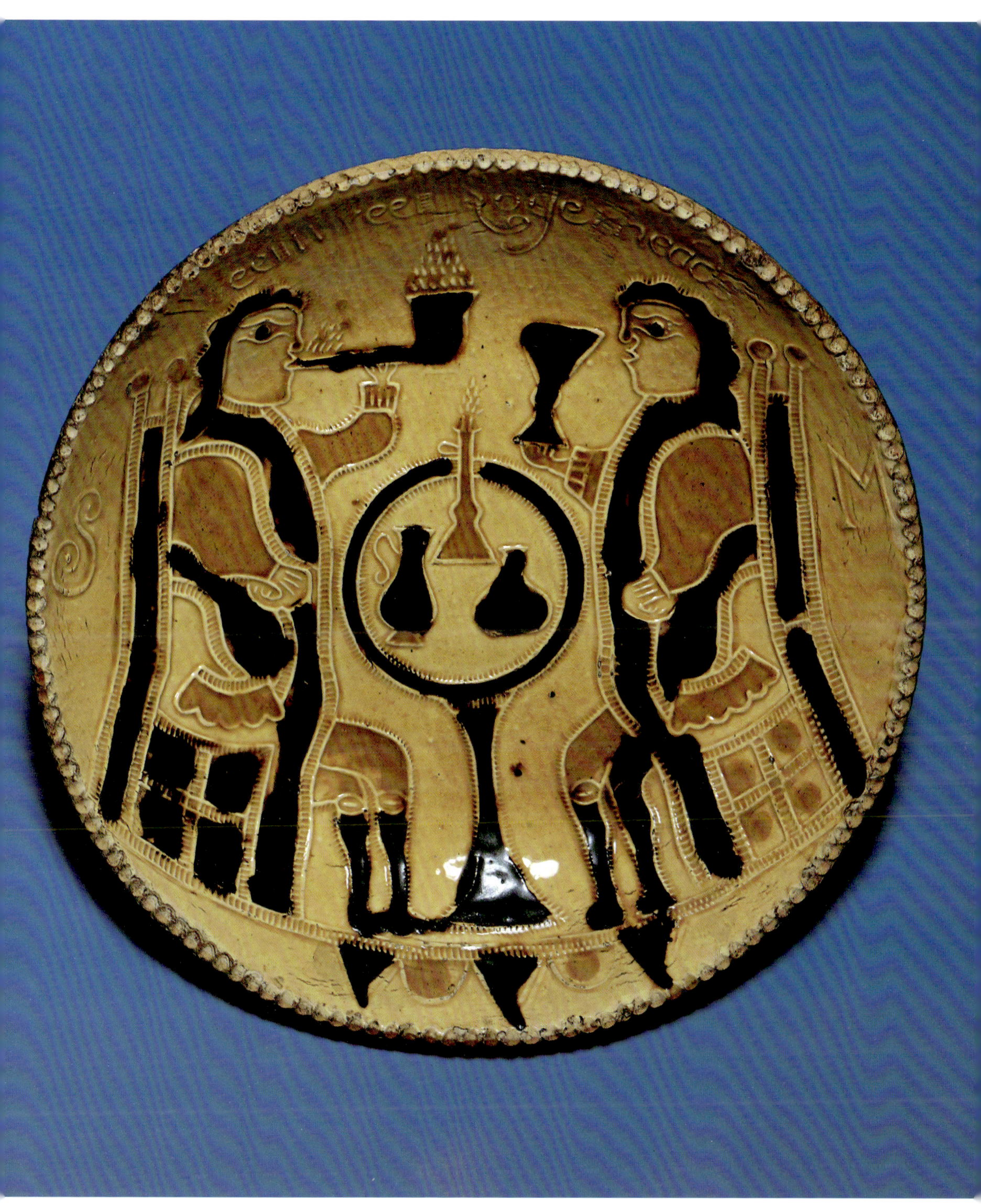

18

SIX CHINOISERIE TILES

BRISTOL OR LONDON, *c.* 1720–50.

Tin-glazed earthenware painted in high-temperature colours. 12.8 or 12.9 cm square. C.1705–1928.

Tiled fire-surrounds were being constructed in England during the 1630s, but the fashion was not widespread until the 1660s. At first demand was met by imported Dutch tiles but from at least 1676 they were made in England. In that year Jan Ariens van Hamme, an immigrant potter from Delft, was granted a patent for the manufacture of tiles and is thought to have set up a pottery at Lambeth. After his death in 1680 the patent lapsed and other potters there and at Vauxhall took up tile-making. At first they were not very successful and Dutch tiles continued to be imported, despite restrictions imposed in 1672 and 1677 to protect the English delftware industry. By the 1720s, however, the techniques of tile-making had been mastered and large quantities were being produced in the London area, and in Liverpool and Bristol.

Apart from fire-surrounds, tiles were used for decorative wall panels, pictures and shop signs. Completely tiled reception rooms, like those which survive on the Continent, did not become fashionable in England, but extensive wall tiling was used in bath houses, dairies, kitchens and other household offices.

The majority of late seventeenth- and eighteenth-century English tiles were painted in blue or manganese, or both. Polychrome tiles were much less common until the mid-eighteenth century, when large quantities were made at Liverpool. The brightly coloured scenes on these tiles were influenced by Chinese porcelain of the reign of Kangxi (1662–1722). Comparable decoration occurs on tableware attributed to Bristol made during the 1720s and 1730s, but it is not certain that these tiles were made there rather than in London.

Further reading Anthony Ray, *English Delftware Tiles*, 1973. Jonathan Horne, *English Tin-glazed Tiles*, 1989.

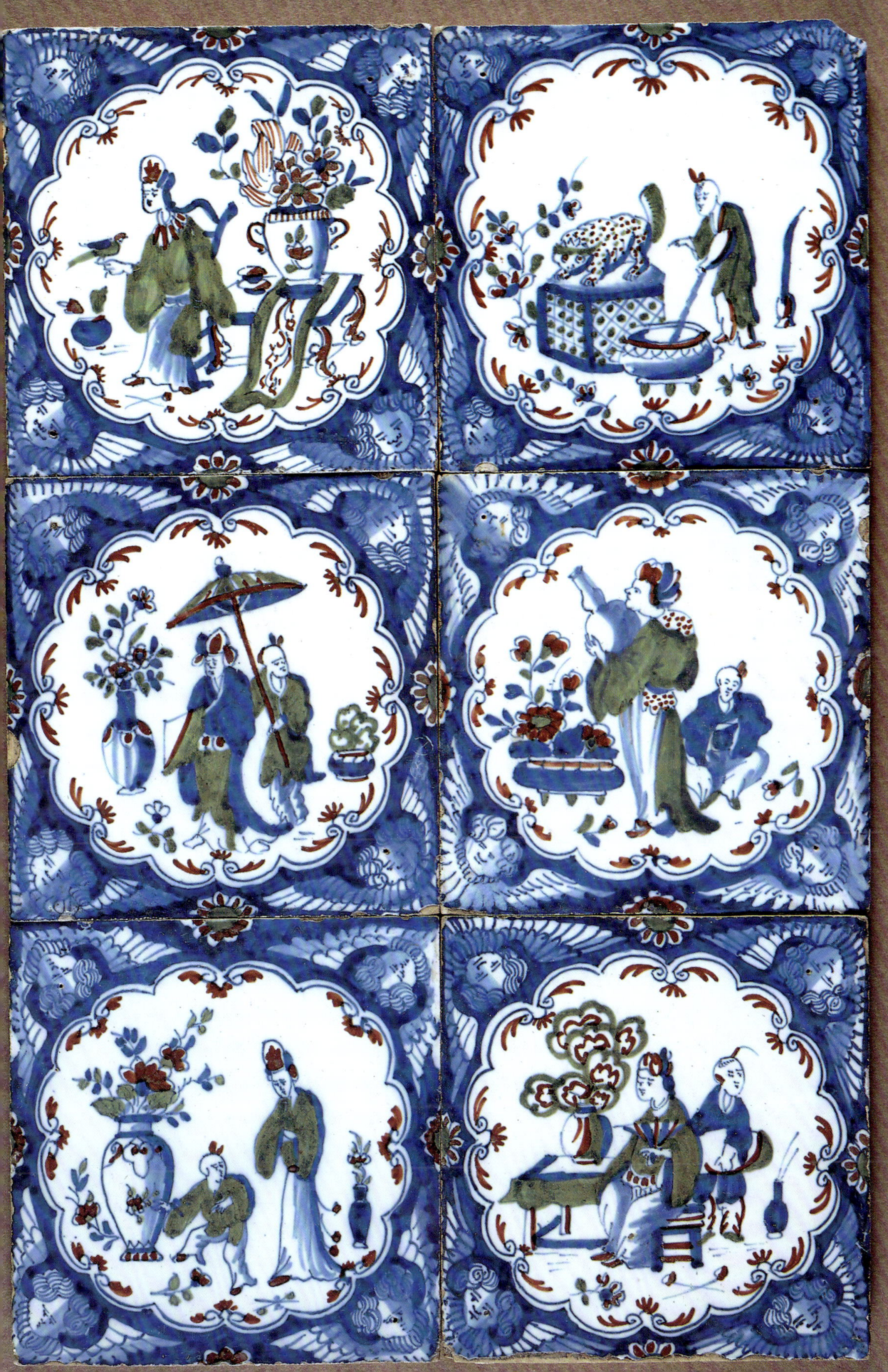

19

PUNCH BOWL AND COVER

LIVERPOOL, 1724.

Tin-glazed earthenware painted in blue.
The inside of the bowl bears the arms of Liverpool, and the inside of the lid is inscribed 'THOMAS BOOTLE/ESQUIRE MEMBER/OF PARLIAMENT/FOR LIVERPOOLE/1724'.
Height 59 cm. C.1716–1928.

English merchants in the east were drinking punch by the 1630s, but it was not widely known in England until the reign of Charles II (1660–85). Much favoured by seamen, it soon became popular with all classes of society and remained so until the nineteenth century. Delftware punch bowls exist with dates from 1681 to 1779. Their decoration is extremely varied, including drinking parties, landscapes and hunting scenes, portraits, flowers and ships. Many of them bear names and dates, or short phrases such as 'Prosperity to the flock'.

This imposing example, decorated with Chinese landscapes, was probably made at Liverpool, where the first of several delftware factories had been established in 1710. It comprises a large bowl and a three-part lid containing two smaller bowls, perhaps for spices and lemons. The bowl was made for Thomas Bootle (1685–1754), a prominent lawyer, who was returned unopposed to parliament for Liverpool in 1724 after two unsuccessful attempts. It would be interesting to know whether he bought it for himself, or if it was given to him by his supporters, who included several local landowners in opposition to the city council. In 1726 Bootle became Mayor of Liverpool, but he resigned in 1727 so that he could stand for parliament again. He was re-elected, and held the seat until 1734.

Further reading Romney Sedgwick, *The History of the House of Commons 1714–1754*, vol. 1, 1970, pp. 270–1 and 473–4. Louis L. Lipski and Michael Archer, *Dated English Delftware*, 1984, pp. 235–94.

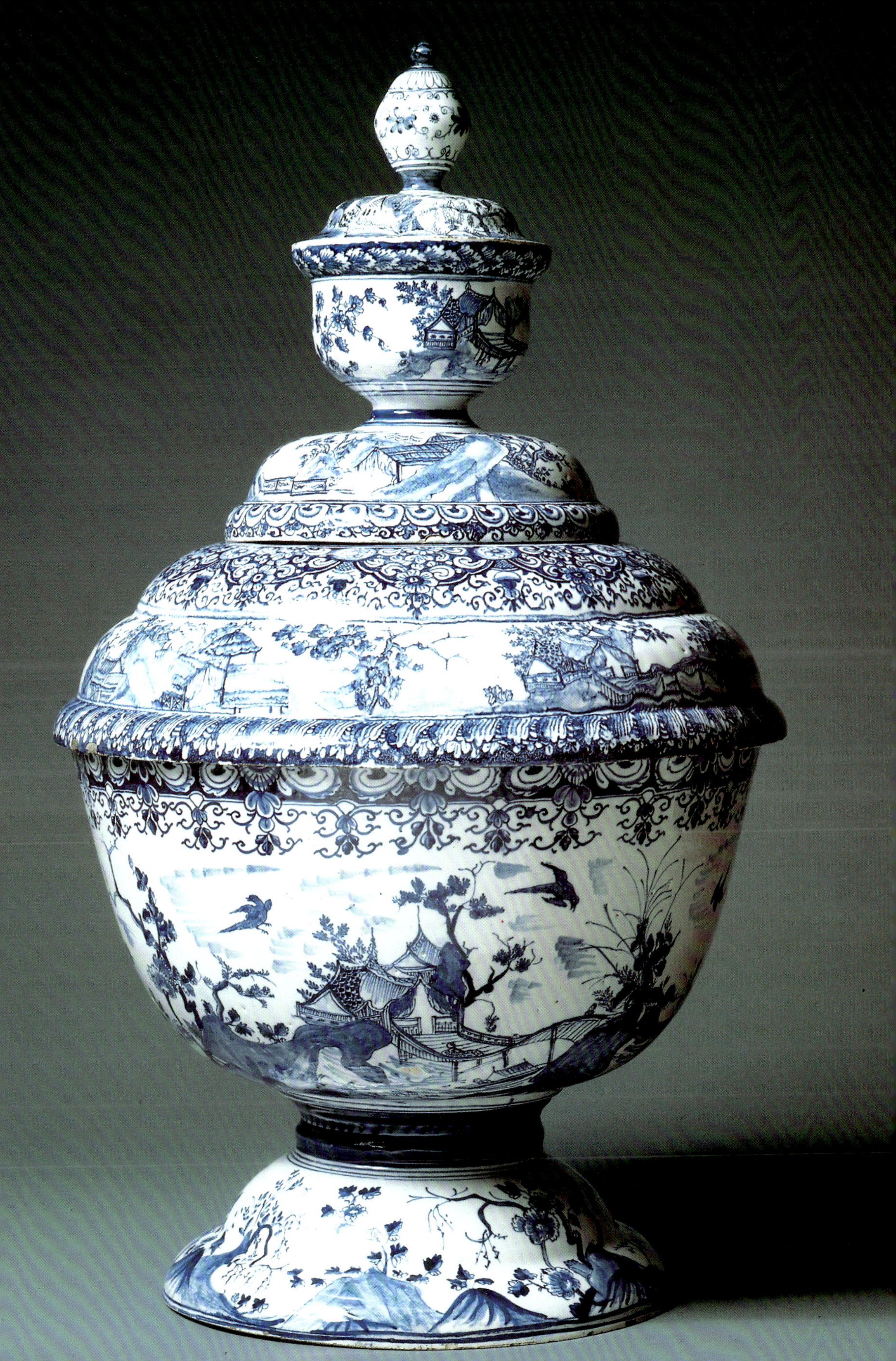

20

HUNTING MUG

PROBABLY VAUXHALL POTTERY, 1730.

Salt-glazed stoneware with incised and applied decoration and the inscription 'Drink about Boys to the Pious Memory of Queen Ann/Mary Bayley/1730'. Height 21.5 cm. C.2–1937.

Hunting was a ubiquitous sport in the eighteenth century, whether for hares, the commonest form, or for foxes and stags. Its popularity is reflected in the frequent occurrence of hunting scenes on English ceramics, such as the brown salt-glazed stoneware 'hunting mugs' made in London and Bristol. These are decorated on the exterior with an applied hare, stag or fox hunt, usually with several other motifs above, such as busts of monarchs, inn signs, the arms of City Companies, punch-drinking scenes and cottages. In addition, some bear their owner's initials or name and a date, occasionally accompanied by a place name or the owner's occupation.

This mug belongs to a group which all have the hunt proceeding in a clockwise direction. They were probably made at the Vauxhall Pottery between about 1713 and 1744, the dates on the earliest and latest recorded specimens. Some are inscribed round the rim with a toast to the memory of Queen Anne or two lines from the second verse of a popular hunting ballad, 'On Banstead Downs a hare we found / Which led us all a smoaking round.' On this mug the toast is accompanied by a bust of Queen Anne flanked by beefeaters, an incised church and two hand-modelled Boscobel Oaks, each harbouring a head of Charles II. The same pottery made mugs decorated with busts of George I or George II with Queen Caroline, so it seems likely that the choice of motifs reflected their owners' loyalty to the Stuart or Hanoverian lines. During the early Hanoverian period many informal political clubs met in taverns and toasting often led to brawls between rival factions.

Further reading Adrian Oswald, R.J.C. Hildyard and R.G. Hughes, *English Brown Stoneware 1670–1900*, 1982, pp. 48–50 and 244–9. Julia Poole, 'Ballads and hunting mugs', ECCT, 12, Part 2 (1985), pp. 156–60.

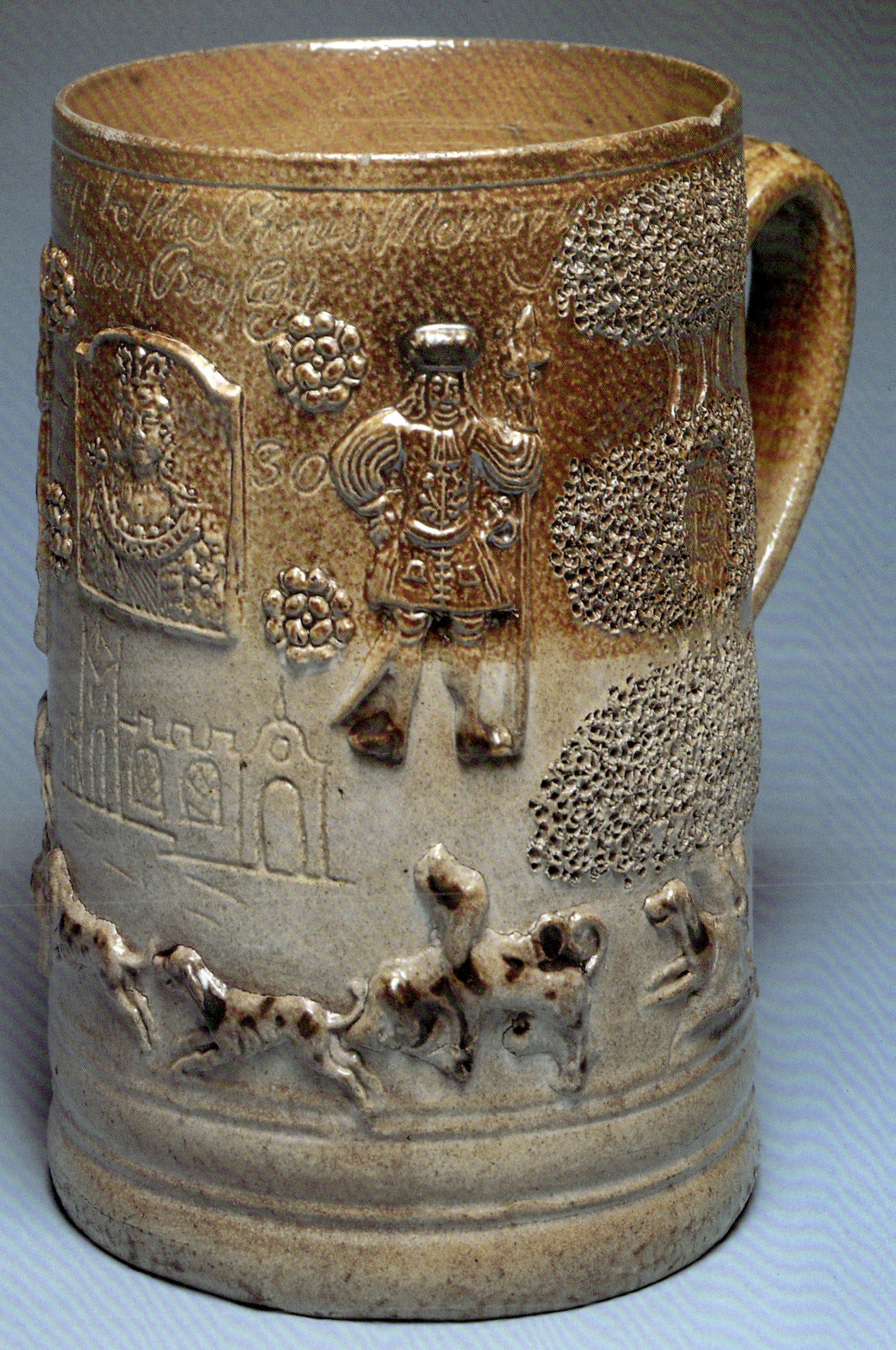
30

21

TWO-HANDLED LOVING CUP

PROBABLY NOTTINGHAM OR CRICH,

1739.

Lustrous brown salt-glazed stoneware with incised decoration; inscribed 'Thomas Smeeton &/Mary His Wife 1739'. Height 21 cm.

C.1234–1928.

James Morley of Nottingham was making brown salt-glazed stoneware by 1693, when he was sued by John Dwight of Fulham for infringement of his patent. During the early eighteenth century production increased and the industry was at its most prosperous between about 1760 and 1790. The names of over sixty Nottingham potters have been recorded but so few pieces are marked that it is rarely possible to make attributions. It is also difficult to distinguish Nottingham stonewares from those made at Crich in Derbyshire.

Nottingham was renowned for tavern mugs, and also produced a great variety of domestic pots, generally decorated with incised, cut or rouletted patterns. Two-handled cups were popular gifts, and examples inscribed with the names of a man and woman may commemorate marriages. These are modest versions of the silver two-handled cups which were the most important form of presentation plate during the eighteenth century. An overall lustrous brown colour, frequently much darker than this cup, was typical of Nottingham stoneware. It could have been achieved by dipping the pots in a thin coat of iron-bearing slip, but probably occurred naturally as a result of a high iron content in the clay and generous amounts of salt thrown into the kiln during firing.

Further reading Adrian Oswald, R.J.C. Hildyard and R.G. Hughes, *English Brown Stoneware 1670–1900*, 1982, pp. 102–38. Robin Hildyard, *Browne Muggs, English Brown Stoneware*, 1985.

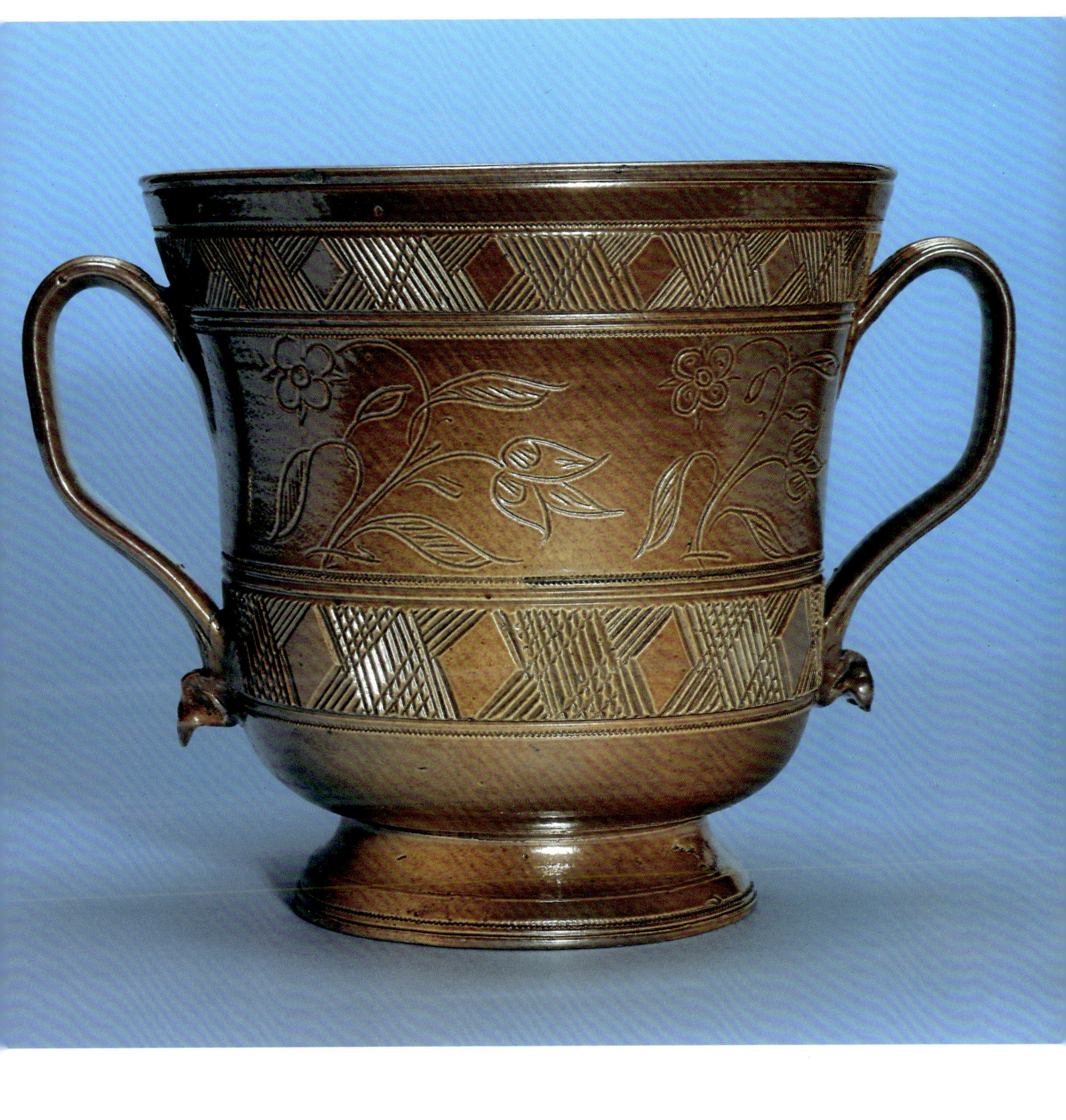

22

MILK JUG

STAFFORDSHIRE, *c.* 1725–45.

Lead-glazed agate ware with cream slip band round the rim. Height 12.3 cm. C.651–1928.

TEAPOT

STAFFORDSHIRE, *c.* 1740–50.

Red earthenware decorated with applied sprigs of the Royal Arms, with the motto DIEU ET MON DIT *(sic), squirrels and leaves, touched with cobalt under lead glaze. Height 14.9 cm, length 20 cm.* C.618–1928.

From about 1720 Staffordshire lead-glazed red earthenware became more refined in response to the demand for tea and coffee ware. Fine throwing and lathe-turning produced neat, light vessels in plain red or dark red and brown agate ware, sometimes decorated with cream slip bands round the edges. Unlike slipwares they were fired twice, once before and once after glazing. Plain redwares and those with cream clay sprigs are often referred to as Astbury ware after John Astbury (1686–1743). Some were no doubt made by him at Shelton, but similar redwares were made by many other potters, such as Samuel Bell (d. 1744) at Lower Street, Newcastle-under-Lyme between 1725 and 1744. The recovery in Broad Street, Shelton, of redwares very like Samuel Bell's shows that attributions of redware to specific potters is inadvisable unless the forms and decoration match sherds from identified sites.

A waster decorated with the Royal Arms and motto with an error which also occurs on this teapot, and a lid decorated with a squirrel were found in 1925 on the site of a pottery at Fenton Low. It is not clear who potted there in the 1740s but by 1750 it belonged to Thomas Whieldon (1719–95), who let it to William Meir in that year and in 1752 to Edward Warburton. Whieldon had occupied a factory about half a mile away at Fenton Vivian since 1747. Therefore, although this pot has traditionally been associated with Whieldon, it is not possible to confirm that attribution.

Further reading P. Bemrose, 'The Pomona Potworks, Newcastle, Staffs. Part II, Samuel Bell: his red earthenware productions 1724–44', *ECCT*, 9, Part 3 (1975), pp. 292–303. David Barker and Pat Halfpenny, *Unearthing Staffordshire*, 1990, pp. 23–33. David Barker, *William Greatbatch, a Staffordshire Potter*, 1991, pp. 81–2.

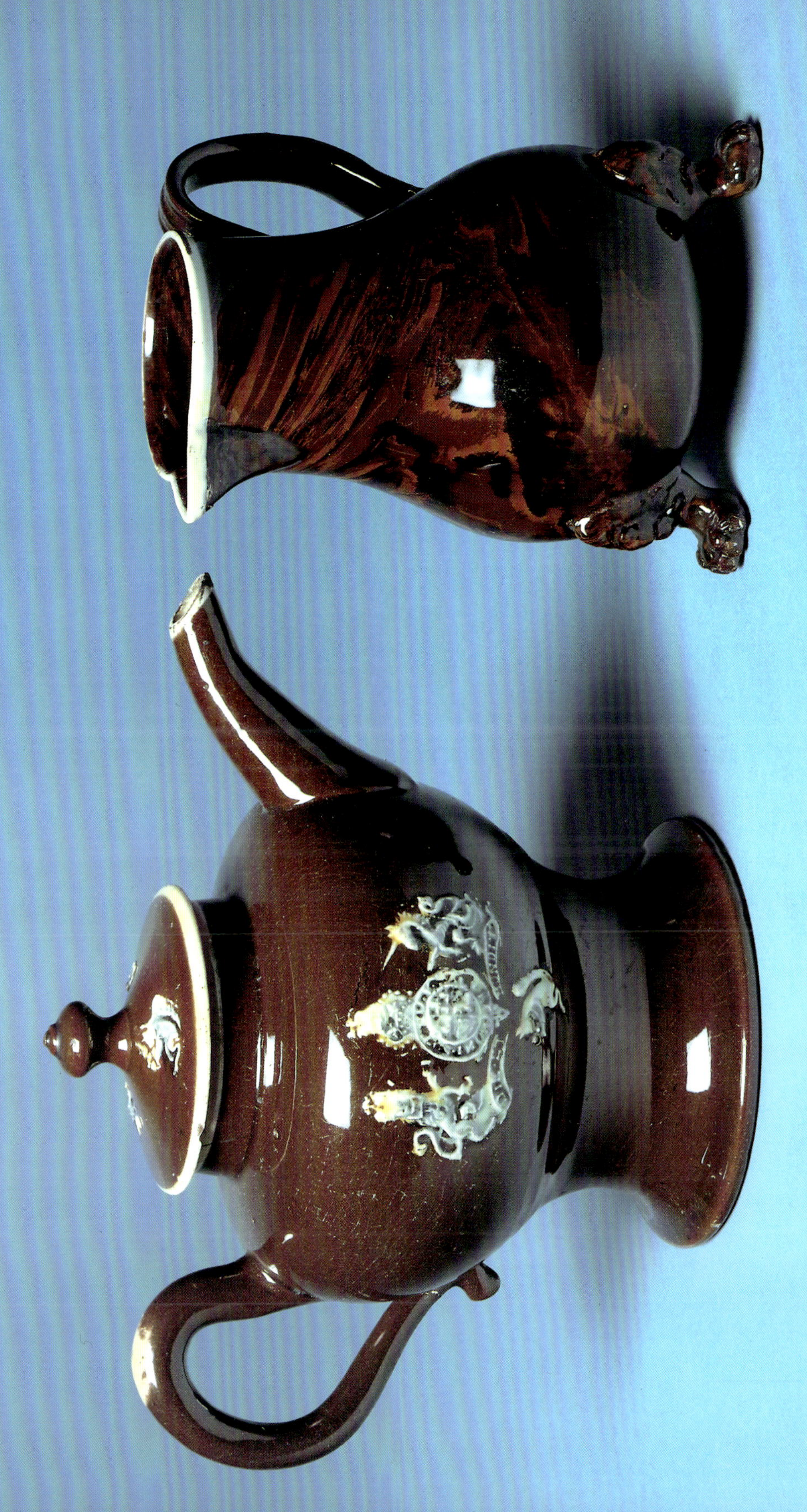

23

PEW GROUP

STAFFORDSHIRE,

C. 1740–50.

White salt-glazed stoneware
with details in brown clay and slip.
Height 16.5 cm, length 16.5 cm.
C.779–1928.

The term 'pew group' is a misnomer so entrenched in ceramic literature that it is unlikely to be changed. In fact the figures do not sit on church pews, but on high-backed settles which were common in inns and rural houses during late seventeenth and eighteenth centuries. A few of the groups have three figures, the rest two men or a couple, seated side by side in a decorous manner, suggesting shy courtship or the complacency of long years of marriage. Some of the men play bagpipes or a fiddle and lapdogs accompany several of the ladies. An exceptional group, also in the Fitzwilliam Museum, shows Adam and Eve standing beside the Tree of Knowledge (C.777–1928).

Unlike later eighteenth-century figures which were press moulded or slip-cast, pew group figures were mainly hand-modelled from strips and rolls of clay, with some press-moulded parts. Wigs, costume, musical instruments and pets are shown in a highly realistic way, and the figures' facial expressions and the slight inclination of their bodies give each an individual and sometimes humorous character.Their modellers have not been identified, but on the basis of the costume worn, the groups could have been made during the 1740s. They are so rare that it seems probable that they were made to order, or as gifts, rather than as part of the normal output of a pottery.

Further reading John E. Lerch, 'Staffordshire pew groups', *Antiques* (September 1936), pp. 104–8, reprinted in Paul Atterbury, (ed.), *English Pottery and Porcelain, an Historical Survey*, 1980, pp. 138–42. Arnold R. Mountford, *The Illustrated Guide to Staffordshire Salt-glazed Stoneware*, 1971.

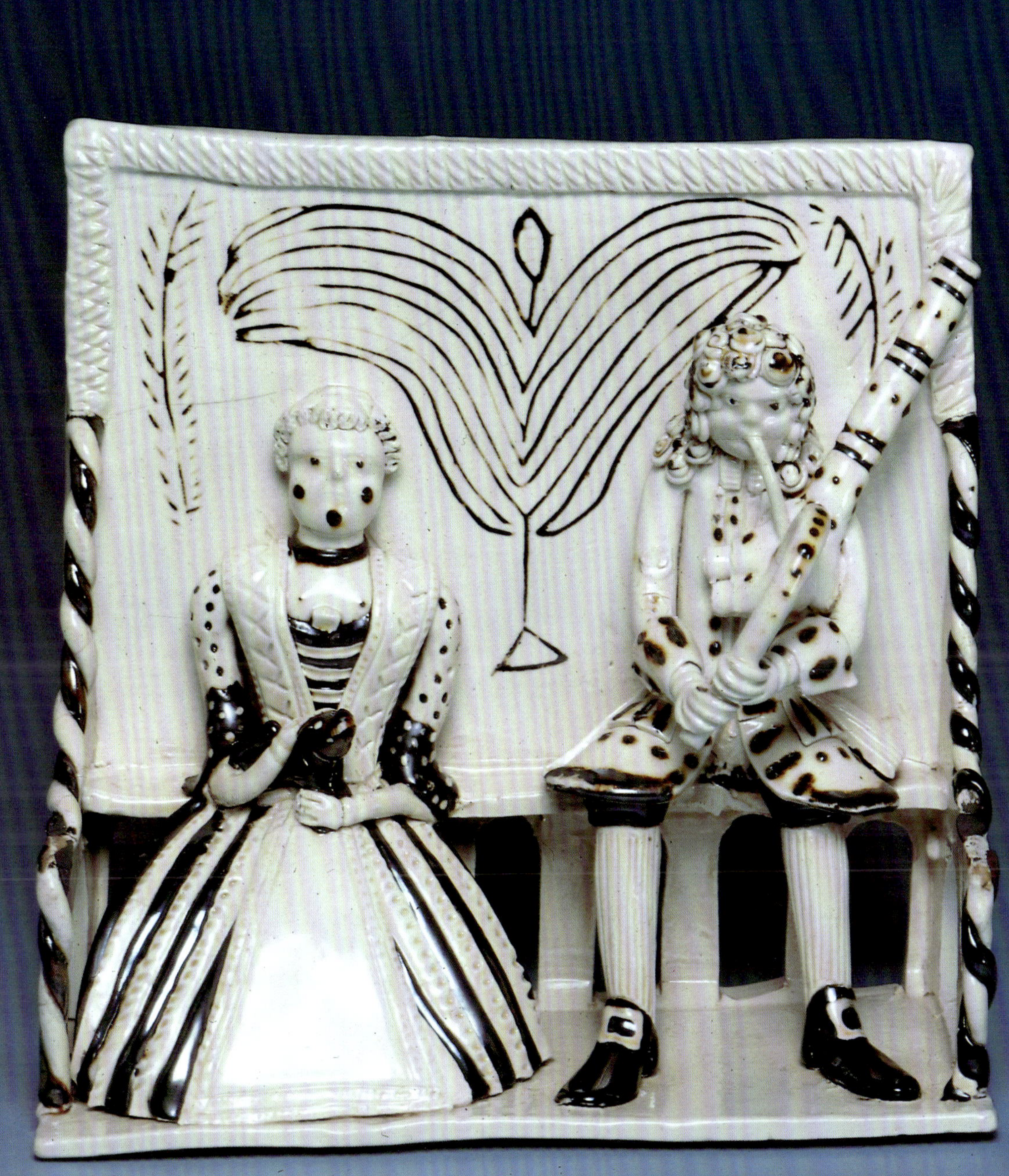

24

BEAR JUG OR JAR

STAFFORDSHIRE,

c. 1740–70.

White salt-glazed stoneware with shredded clay fur and details in brown slip. Height 24.4 cm. C.501–1928.

Bear jugs call to mind performing bears and the vicious sport of bear-baiting which were popular entertainments in the eighteenth century. White salt-glazed stoneware bears were made in Staffordshire and brown ones at Nottingham. Both types usually have a chain through their noses and some bears grasp a dog, or more rarely a musical instrument, between their front paws. Their endearingly tubby bodies have fur made of shredded clay or grog (ground up fired clay) and details such as eyes and collars are picked out in brown slip. Their heads were made separately so that they could serve as lids and cups. This allows them to be turned sideways, which gives some of the bears a very comical expression.

There are no dated brown or white bears but a rough guide to dating is the fine 'breadcrumb' fur on some examples. This also occurs in bands on white stoneware tea wares dated to the 1740s and on brown ones of about 1750–70. It is usually assumed that the bears were jugs or tobacco jars, but whatever their original function was, their high survival rate suggests that they soon became treasured ornaments.

Further reading Arnold R. Mountford, *The Illustrated Guide to Staffordshire Salt-glazed Stoneware*, 1971, pp. 65–6. Adrian Oswald, R.J.C. Hildyard and R.G. Hughes, *English Brown Stoneware 1670–1900*, 1982, pp. 126–7 and 129–30.

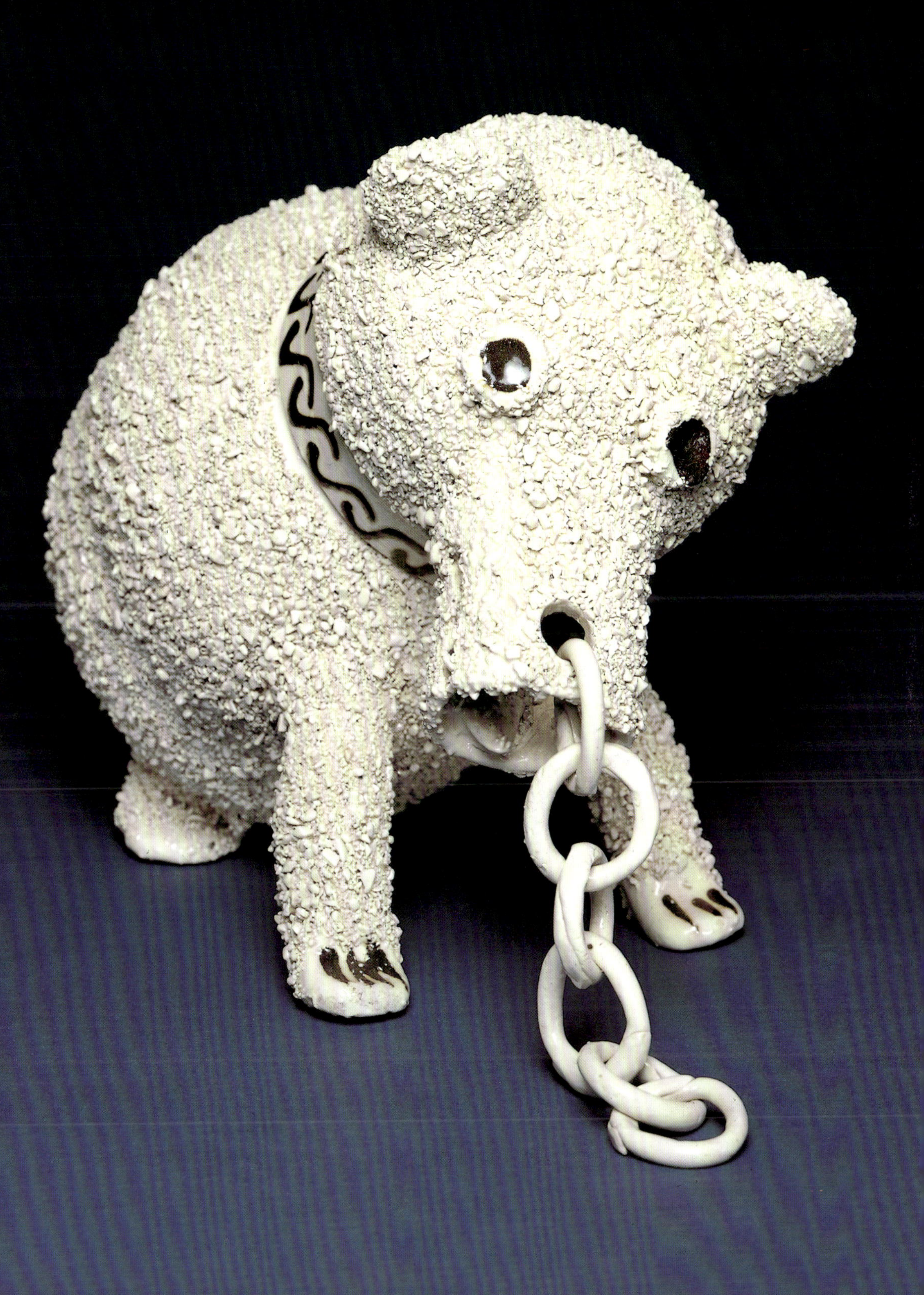

25

CAMEL AND MONKEY OR SQUIRREL TEAPOTS

STAFFORDSHIRE,

c. 1750–5.

White salt-glazed stoneware, slip-cast.
Heights 15.5 cm and 13.5 cm, lengths 18.1 cm and 12 cm. C.572 *and* C.575–1928.

White salt-glazed stoneware was produced by combining calcined flints with white ball clay imported from Devonshire and Dorset. The chronology of its early development is uncertain, but it was in use in Staffordshire shortly before 1720. By the mid-1740s potters were making extensive use of press-moulding and had begun to slip-cast in plaster of Paris moulds. These processes enabled them to make a greater range of shapes and to decorate both flat and hollow-ware with relief patterns formed at the same time as the body. They also made it possible to satisfy the demand for naturalistic and fanciful tableware which was an aspect of rococo taste.

Block cutters, who made the blocks from which the plaster of Paris moulds were taken, displayed great ingenuity in their teapot designs. Traditional globular or pear-shaped pots were decorated in relief with quaint figures, plants and geometrical patterns. Others were moulded in the shape of houses, shells, fruit and animals. This exotic camel teapot with chinoiserie decoration on the sides of the tower on its back must have had great selling appeal in an era when people were fascinated by the Ottoman Empire and the Far East. The idea for the monkey or squirrel probably came from Meissen, where in 1735 Johann Joachim Kaendler (1706–75) had modelled two amusing teapots in the shape of a squirrel and a mother monkey with two babies.

Further reading Carl Albiker, *Die Meissner Porzellantiere im 18. Jahrhundert*, 1959, pls. 223–6. Arnold R. Mountford, *The Illustrated Guide to Staffordshire Salt-Glazed Stoneware*, 1971.

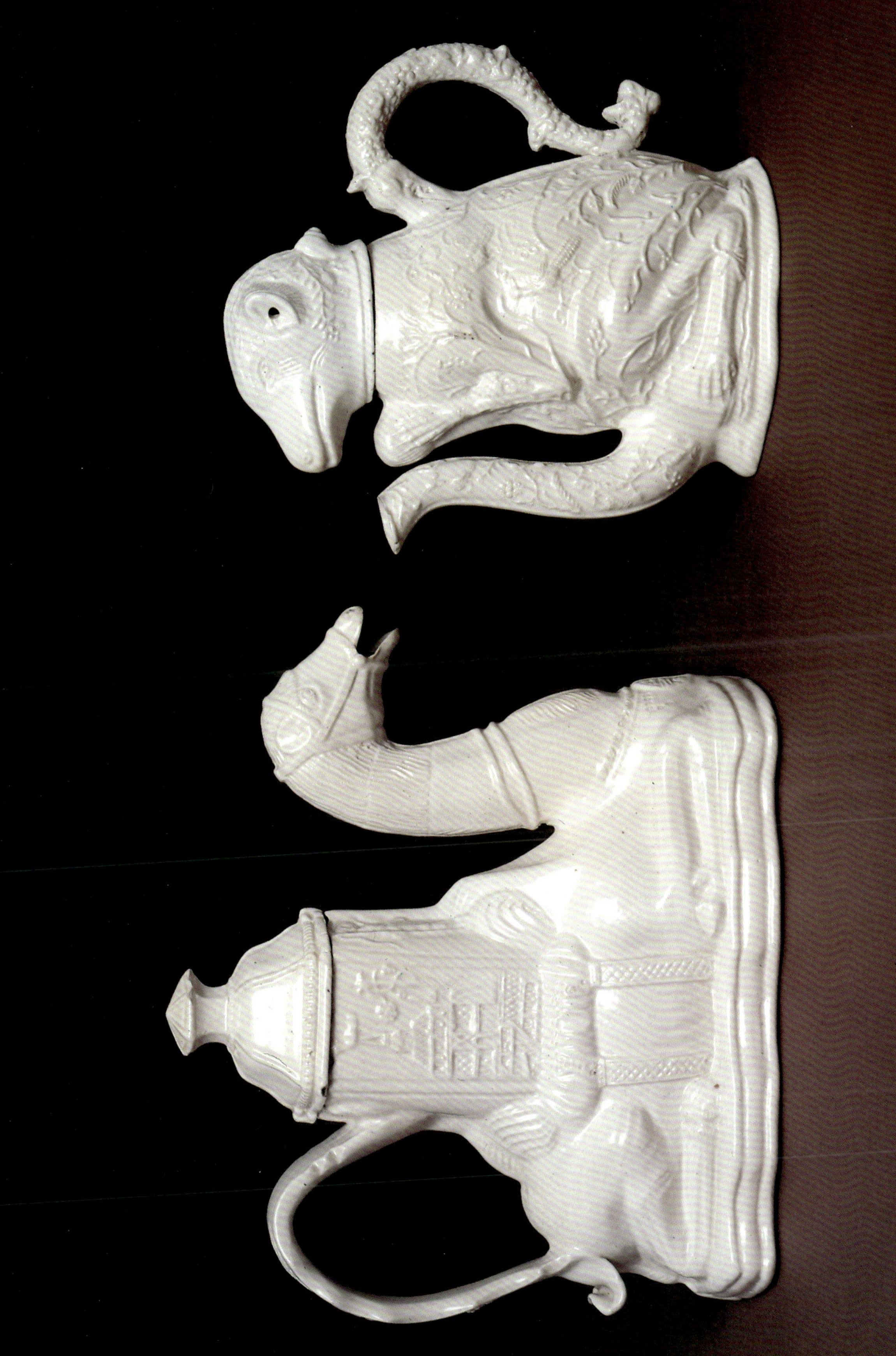

26

JUG

STAFFORDSHIRE, *c.* 1755–65.

White salt-glazed stoneware painted in polychrome enamels.
Height 18.3 cm. C.599–1928.

Overglaze decoration in coloured enamels was already in use in Staffordshire by July 1750, when it was mentioned in a letter written by Dr Richard Pococke after visiting Newcastle-under-Lyme and the pottery villages. It may have been introduced by immigrant Dutch enamellers, and for many years remained the province of specialists such as the Daniels of Cobridge and the Warburtons of Hot Lane, to whom leading potters, such as Thomas and John Wedgwood, sent their goods for decoration.

White salt-glazed stoneware with enamelled decoration was an attractive substitute for porcelain, which remained an expensive luxury, even after the setting up of English porcelain factories during the 1740s and 1750s. Chinese export porcelain provided the inspiration for many of the designs. This finely thrown and turned jug is decorated with Oriental plants and diapered borders in imitation of the *famille rose* palette. Coloured grounds and painting in reserved panels, which had been popularized in Europe by the Meissen and Sèvres porcelain factories, were imitated too, but the character of the Staffordshire salt-glazed stoneware versions was much less sophisticated and often decidedly quaint.

White salt-glazed stoneware is usually attributed to Staffordshire, but excavations or documentary evidence have shown that it was also manufactured at the Swinton and Leeds Potteries in Yorkshire, at Liverpool, Rotherham, Bovey Tracy and Chester. Its production continued into the 1770s but by about 1780 it had been superseded by creamware and pearlware.

Further reading Arnold R. Mountford, *The Illustrated Guide to Staffordshire Salt-glazed Stoneware*, 1971. City Museum and Art Gallery, Stoke-on-Trent, *Stonewares and Stone Chinas of Northern England to 1851*, the fourth exhibition from the Northern Ceramic Society, 1982, pp. 36–46.

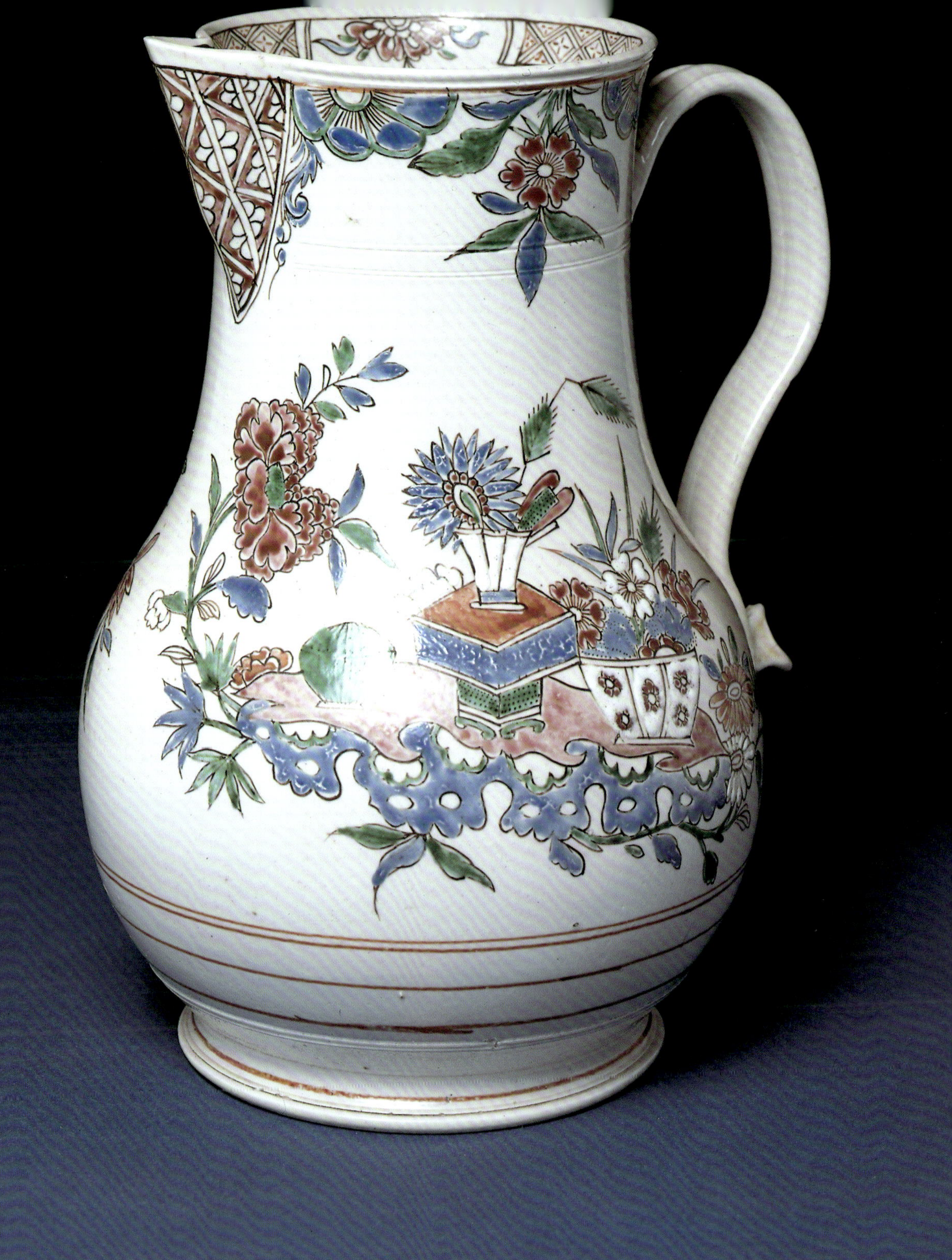

27

DISH

LIVERPOOL, c. 1755–60.

Tin-glazed earthenware painted in 'Fazackerly' colours. Diameter 45.7 cm.
C.1725–1928.

The floral design on this dish is painted in a style and colouring associated mainly with Liverpool delftware. The distinctive palette, which complements the greyish-white glaze, comprises sage–green, yellow, blue, and orange–red, pale purple and black. These colours were derived from the same metallic oxides as the traditional polychrome delftware colours. The difference lies in their tone and in the balance of the colour combinations. Blue is noticeably less prominent and green more so.

These colours have become known as 'Fazackerly colours' because they were first recorded on two mugs, initialled respectively 'TF 1757' and 'CF 1758', which were said to have been made for Thomas and Catherine Fazackerly at Samuel Shaw's pottery in Liverpool. In 1854 their son sold them to the collector, Joseph Mayer, who described them in his *History of the Art of Pottery in Liverpool*, 1855, and gave them to the Liverpool Museum. Unfortunately the mugs were destroyed during the Second World War, but water-colours showing their attractive floral decoration have survived at Liverpool City Museum.

Further reading Anthony Ray, *English Delftware Pottery in the Robert Hall Warren Collection, Ashmolean Museum*, Oxford, 1968, pp. 72–6 and 181–2. Frank Britton, *English Delftware in the Bristol Collection*, 1982, pp. 269–75.

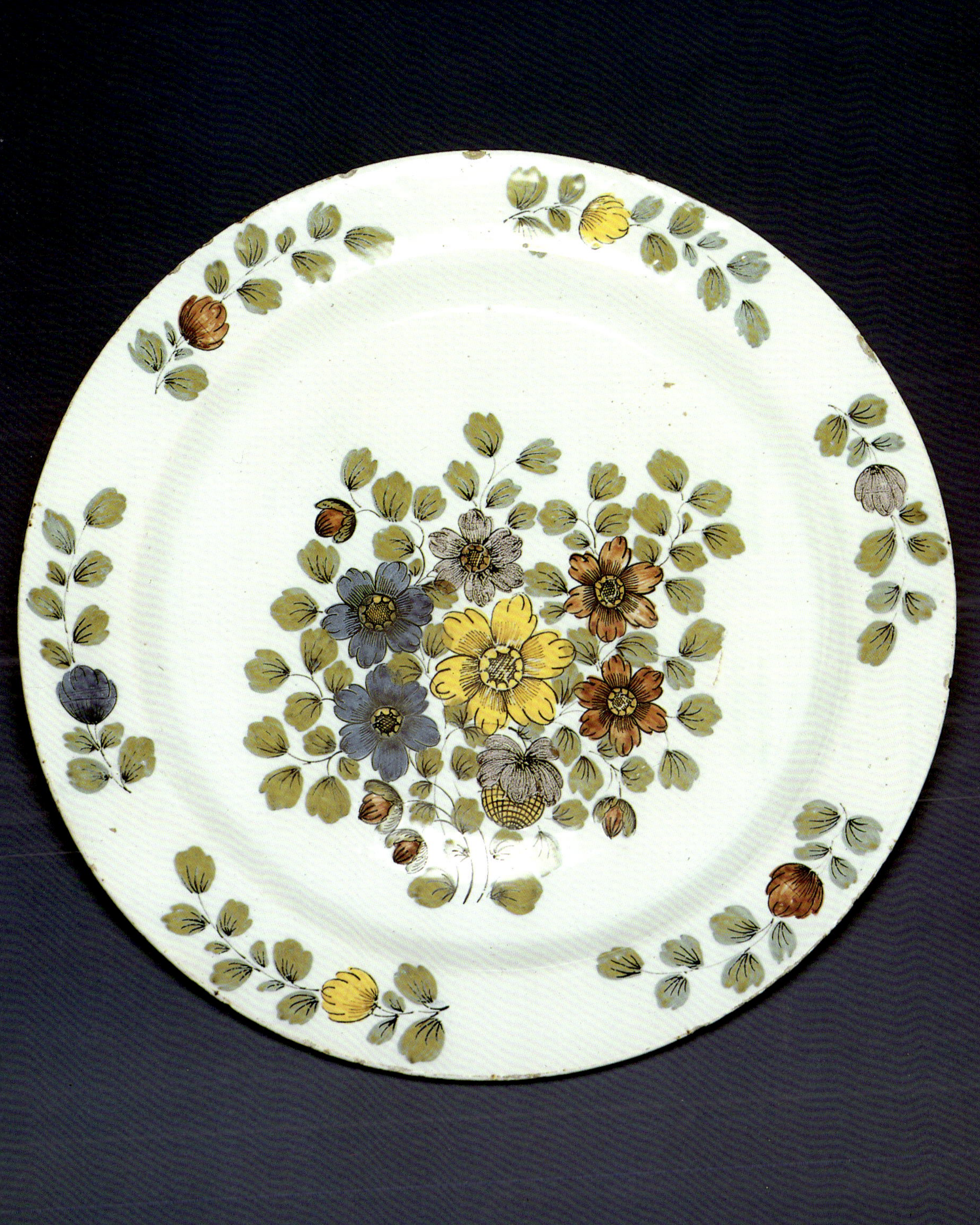

28

TEABOWL, SAUCER AND COFFEE POT

STAFFORDSHIRE,

c. 1750–65.

Reddish-brown, blue and white lead-glazed agate ware. Cup height 3.8 cm, saucer diameter 11.5 cm, pot height 25 cm.
C.654–1928 and C.35–1934.

Agate ware was made by 'wedging' together clays of different colours, which, when slabbed or thrown and turned, produced a variegated or marbled effect reminiscent of hardstones. Salt-glazed agate ware has survived mainly in the form of figures. Tablewares were usually lead-glazed, which gave them an attractive glossy surface and made them less subject to staining. In the mid-eighteenth century the dark red–brown agate of the 1720s and 1730s (see no. 22) gave way to combinations of white clay with light and dark brown, or brown and blue-stained clays. The former can produce fascinating toffee-like markings, while the latter gives a more subtle effect approaching the reflectiveness of silver. This hexagonal coffee pot with its handle at right angles to the spout is similar to silver pots of about 1720. The unassuming teabowl and saucer have walls as thin as porcelain and are pleasantly light in the hand.

Agate ware was made by numerous mid-eighteenth-century Staffordshire potters. It was still being made in the 1770s, but by then creamware had become the fashionable body for tableware.

Further reading Ross E. Taggart, *The Frank P. and Harriet C. Burnap Collection of English Pottery in the William Rockhill Nelson Gallery*, Atkins Museum, Kansas City, 1967, pp. 101–8. David Barker and Pat Halfpenny, *Unearthing Staffordshire*, 1990, pp. 31–3.

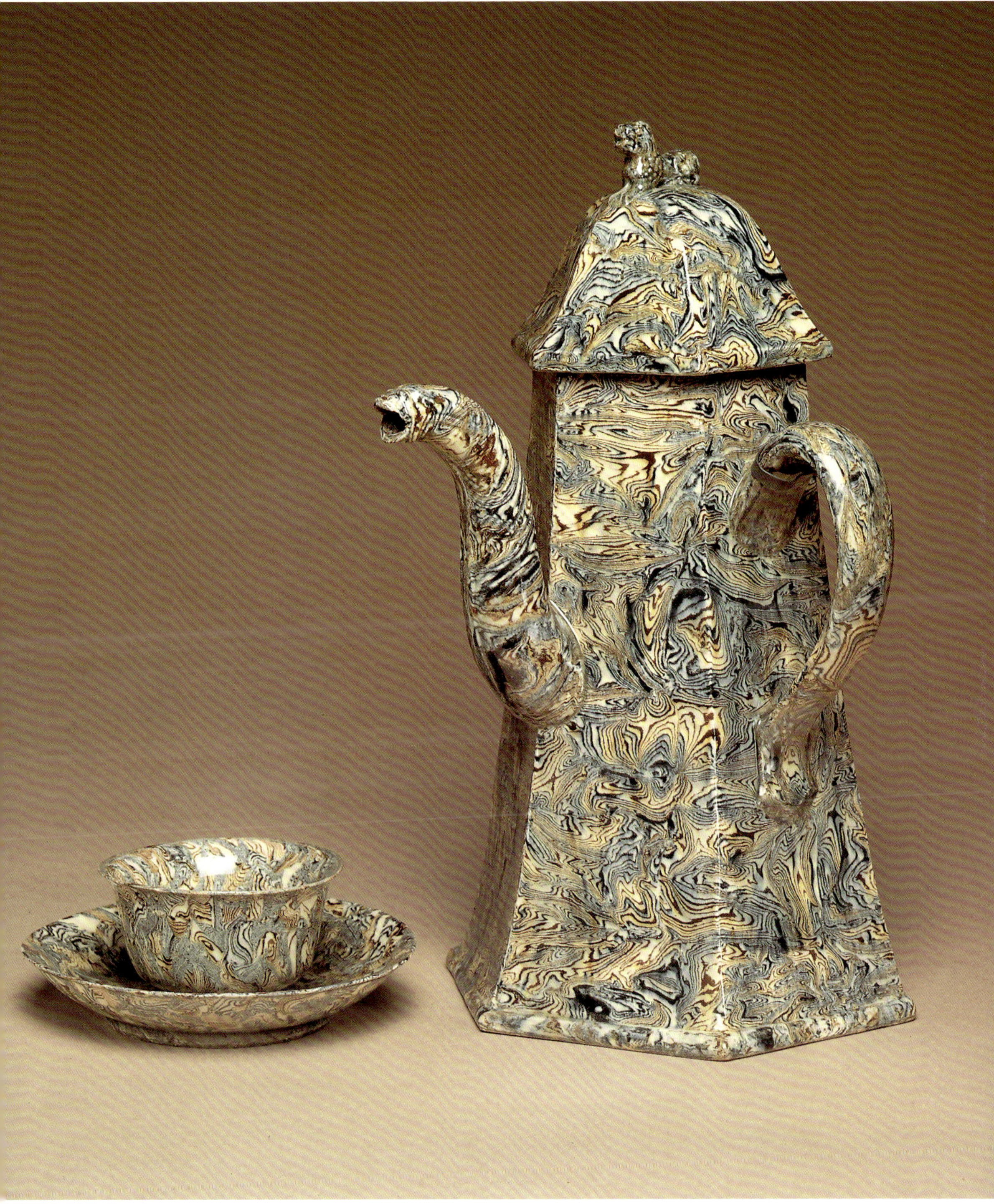

29

COFFEE POT

STAFFORDSHIRE,

1760.

Red dry-bodied stoneware with moulded handle and spout and sprigged floral ornament. The base is incised 'Joseph Edge 1760'. Height 21.3 cm. C.466–1928.

After the Elers brothers left Staffordshire red stoneware does not seem to have been made until the 1740s or 1750s, after which it remained popular for tea and coffee ware until the 1770s. In the later eighteenth and early nineteenth centuries it appeared in neo-classical guise, as *rosso antico*, the name given to it by Wedgwood in 1776.

The tapering, straight-sided body of this coffee pot is similar to silver pots of the 1720s and 1730s but it is combined with a markedly rococo handle and spout. The asymmetrically placed sprays of blossom were made in plaster of Paris moulds and after removal were applied to the surface using slip to make them adhere. Joseph Edge, whose name is incised on the base, is almost certainly the Joseph Edge, earth potter, who married Mary Newton at Stoke-on-Trent on 8 September 1759. He has not been identified as a pottery owner and was probably a workman.

Many Staffordshire potters made red stoneware between about 1745 and 1780, but only a few names can be firmly associated with it on the basis of marks or other evidence. They include Josiah Wedgwood, William Greatbatch, Richard Myatt, Thomas Barker and a member of the Astbury family. Progress in linking the widely scattered examples to these and other makers will only come about through matching their features with excavated material and the painstaking scrutiny of local records.

Further reading Robin Price, 'Some groups of English redware of the mid-eighteenth century', ECCT, 4, Part 5 (1959), pp. 1–9; 11, 5, Part 3 (1962), pp. 153–68. David Barker, 'A group of Staffordshire red stonewares of the eighteenth century', ECCT, 14, Part 2 (1991), pp. 177–98.

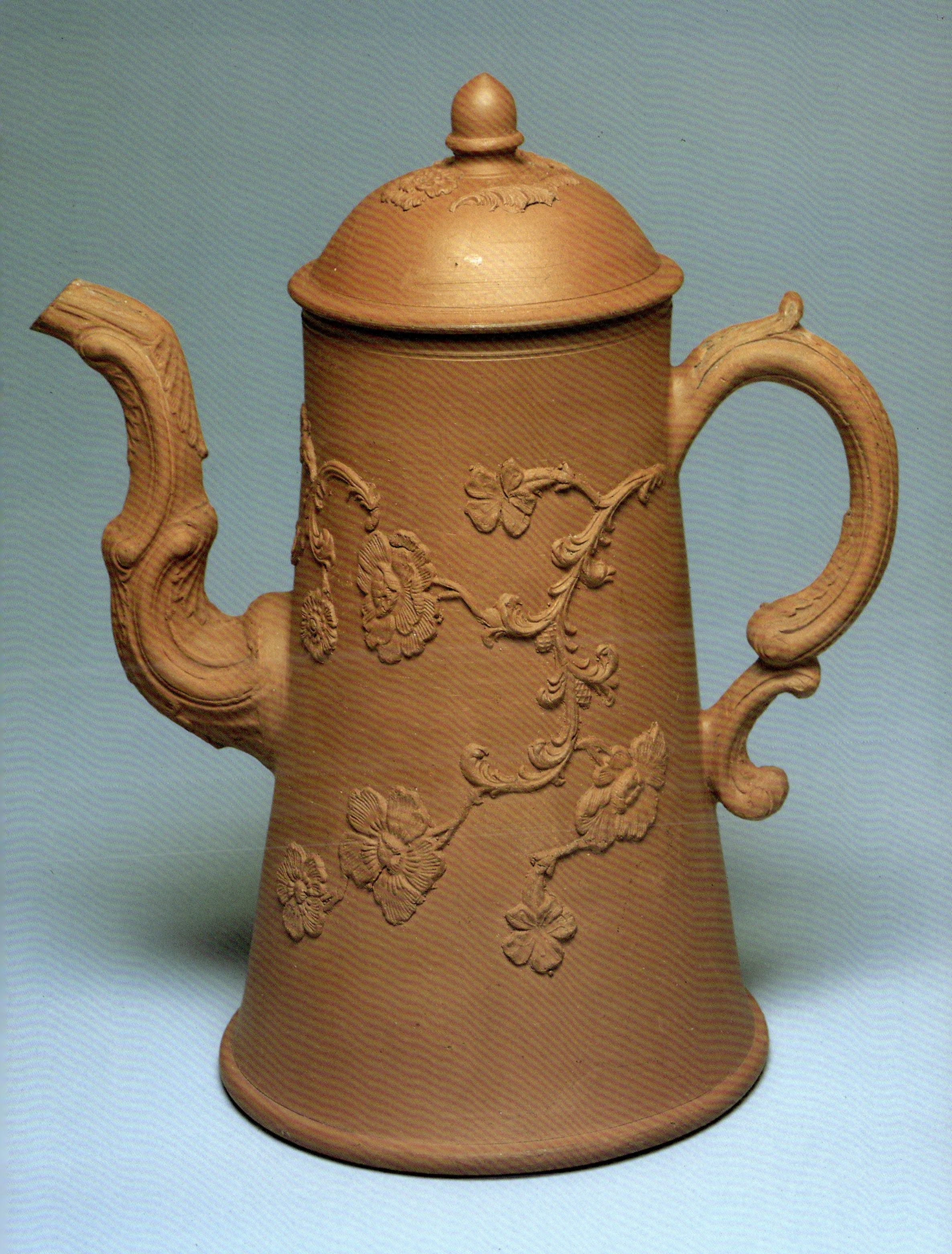

30

TEAPOT

ATTRIBUTED TO JOSIAH WEDGWOOD, BURSLEM, *c.* 1759–66.

Pale buff earthenware with applied stamped sprigs, covered with transparent green lead glaze bearing traces of oil gilding. Height 11.1 cm. C.665–1928.

Towards the end of his partnership with Thomas Whieldon of Fenton, which lasted from 1754 to 1759, Josiah Wedgwood (1730–95) developed an improved green glaze for use on earthenware. He recorded its ingredients of white lead, calcined flint and copper in his *Experiment Book* on 23 March 1759, noting later that it was 'the result of many Expts. which I made in order to introduce a new species of colored ware, to be fired along with the tortoiseshell & Agate wares in our common gloss ovens, to be of an even self color, & laid upon the ware in the form of a colored glaze'. On 1 May 1759 Wedgwood leased the Ivy House and potworks in Burslem and set up in business on his own. This teapot may have been made there or at the Brick House Works to which he moved in 1764, but the possibility that it was made at Fenton Vivian at the end of the Whieldon–Wedgwood partnership cannot be ruled out. It is unlikely to have been made long after 1 August 1766 when Wedgwood wrote to his friend and future partner, Thomas Bentley, telling him of his plans to abandon the manufacture of green glazed ware and to sell off all his existing stocks.

Many other potters adopted green glaze, notably William Greatbatch, who had also worked for Whieldon before setting up his own pottery at Lower Lane, Fenton in 1762. It went out of fashion in the late eighteenth century but returned to popularity in the nineteenth for dessert wares, many of which were moulded with leaves and basketwork.

Further reading John des Fontaines and others, *Josiah Wedgwood: 'the Arts and Sciences United'*, 1978. Robin Reilly, *Wedgwood*, vol. 1, 1989, pp. 147–80. David Barker, *William Greatbatch, a Staffordshire Potter*, 1991, pp. 251–62.

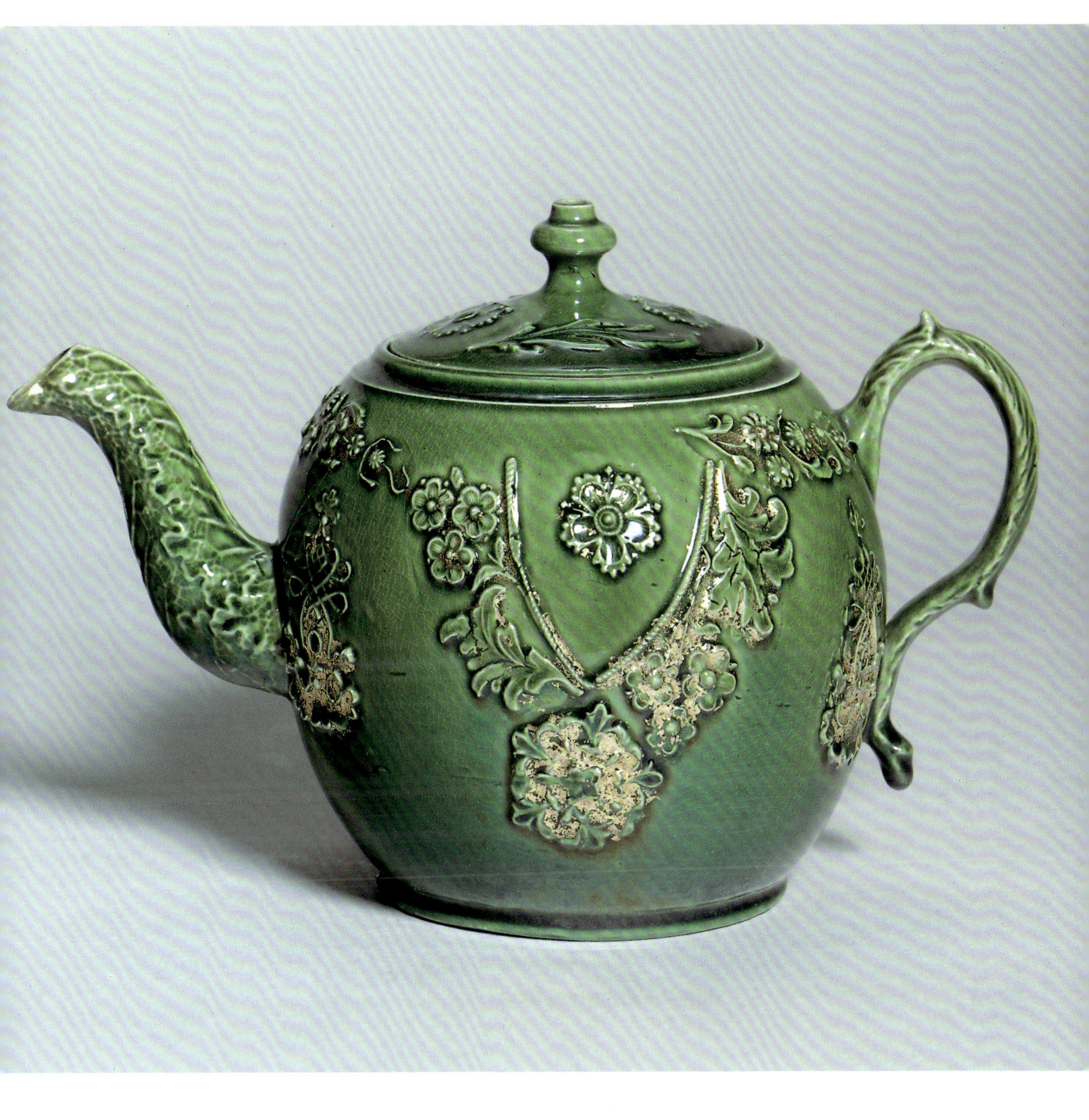

31

TUREEN

STAFFORDSHIRE,

c. 1760–5.

Cream earthenware, moulded and decorated with metallic oxides under clear lead glaze. Height 20.3 cm. C.676–1928.

Cream-coloured earthenware incorporating ground flints and white clay from Devon or Dorset, and coated with liquid lead glaze was being made in Staffordshire by the early 1740s. During the 1750s and 1760s much of it was press-moulded or slip-cast with borders or motifs in relief; applied sprigs of flowers and foliage were also popular. This lightly fluted tureen has borders of wickerwork with scrolled panels at intervals. Borders of this kind were introduced on Meissen porcelain dinner services during the 1730s and early 1740s. Other Continental and English porcelain factories imitated them, and pottery manufacturers followed, bringing this fashion to the tables of the middle classes.

Sponging or painting with metallic oxides was the most common decoration on early creamwares. The oxides were applied to the once-fired body before glazing and during the second firing melted into the glaze, producing streaked, mottled or patched coloration, described as 'Tortoiseshell'. On this tureen, cobalt, copper and manganese oxides were used, but applied sparingly, so that the yellowish-cream of the body remains visible on the exterior. Inside the colours are darker and run down the sides in streaks to a pool of green-stained glaze in the centre.

Further reading Donald Towner, *Creamware*, 1978. Stoke-on-Trent, City Museum and Art Gallery, *Creamware and Pearlware*, the fifth exhibition from the Northern Ceramic Society, 1986, pp. 14–19.

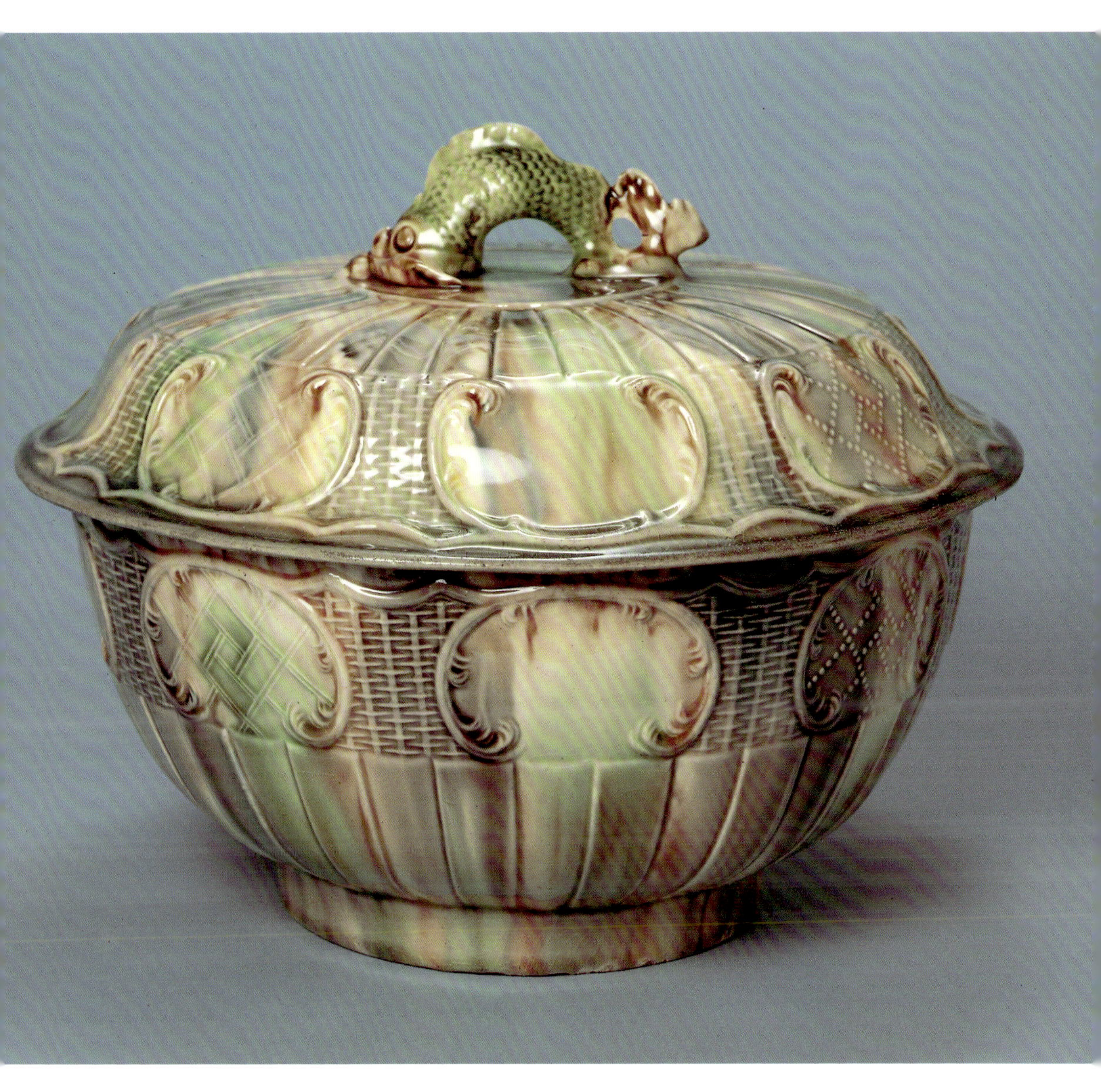

32

TEAPOT

JOSIAH WEDGWOOD, ETRURIA,
PRINTED IN LIVERPOOL BY GUY GREEN,
c. 1775–80.

Cream-coloured earthenware (Queen's Ware), printed onglaze in black. Mark: 'WEDGWOOD' impressed. Height 14 cm. C.729–1928.

During the 1760s and 1770s Josiah Wedgwood modified the body and glaze of his creamware until it was very pale in colour and not subject to crazing. This was one of his most significant achievements and contributed to the development of the durable white bodies in use today. In the autumn of 1761 Wedgwood began to send creamware to Liverpool to be printed by John Sadler and Guy Green, who had been decorating delftware tiles by that method since 1756. From 1763, he sent increasingly large amounts, and after Sadler retired in 1770, he continued to trade with Green until the early 1790s.

The pale colour and clear black printing on this teapot indicate that it was made towards the end of the 1770s. On one side it has a scene known as *The Tea Party* and on the other *The Shepherd*. Both had been used in the 1760s, but the costume of the tea-drinkers was changed to keep abreast of fashion. It used to be thought that onglaze prints like these were applied with tissue transfers, but recently convincing evidence has been put forward for the glue bat method (see glossary).

In conjunction with creamware, onglaze printed decoration was an important technical advance, allowing potters in Staffordshire, Yorkshire and elsewhere, to supply a rapidly expanding market with crockery which was elegant and cheap. Initially printing was a decorative medium in its own right, executed in black, red or lilac, but increasingly it was used to provide guidelines for hand-painting in enamels.

Further reading Donald Towner, *Creamware*, 1978, pp. 43–72. Robin Reilly, *Wedgwood*, vol. 1, 1989, pp. 181–245. David Drakard, *Printed English Pottery, History and Humour in the Reign of George III 1760–1820*, 1992.

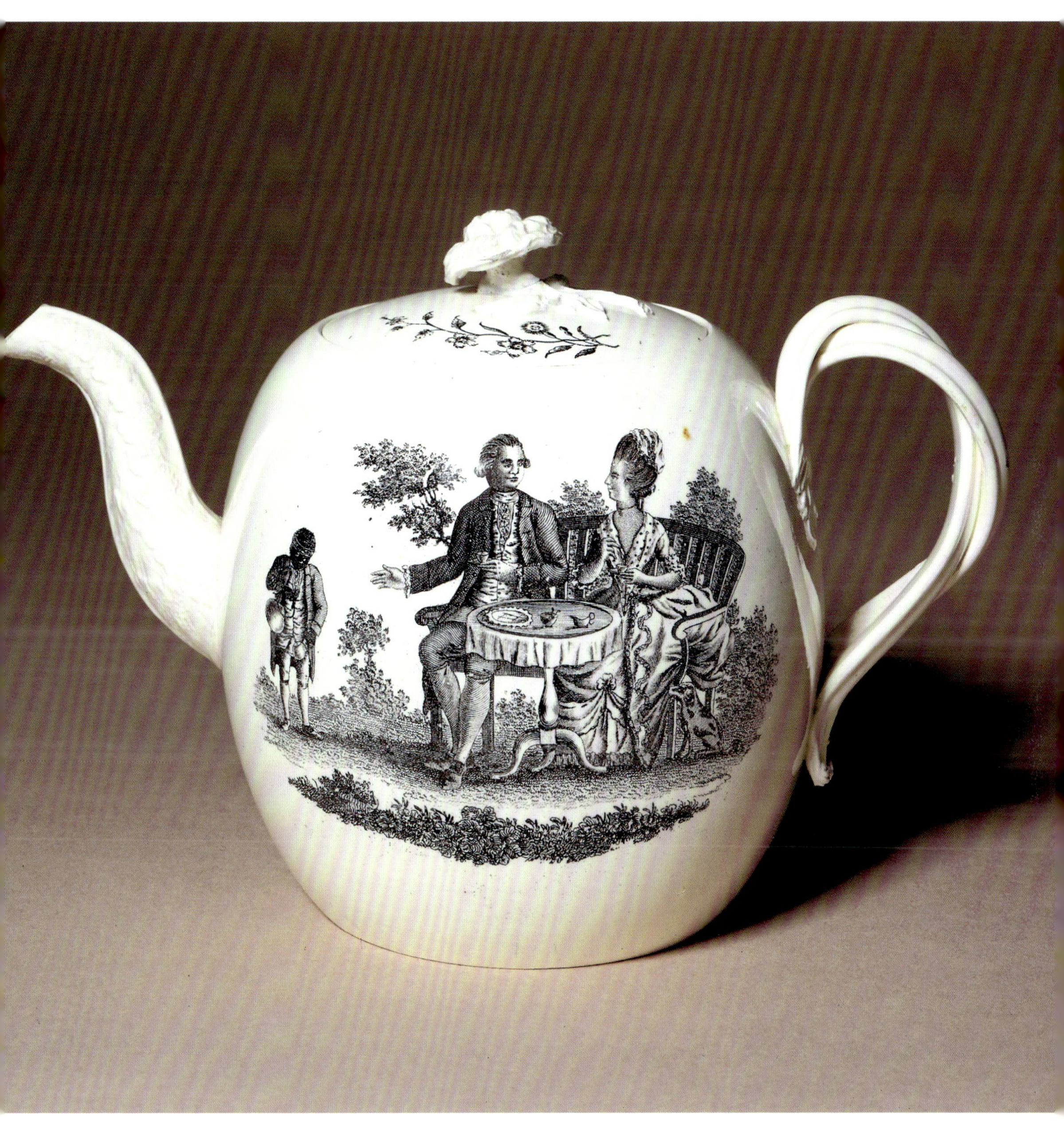

33
JUG

YORKSHIRE,
1780.

Enamelled creamware,
inscribed 'Iohn. Bridgen|1780'.
Height 24.2 *cm.* C.1055–1928.

Creamware painted overglaze with enamels was the medium for some of the most charming tablewares made in Yorkshire and Staffordshire between the 1760s and 1790s. They include many commemorative pieces, such as jugs and mugs, decorated to order with names, dates and inscriptions, sometimes accompanied by the implements of the owner's trade or scenes showing their occupation. Apart from their social interest, these documentary pieces provide an important guide to dating shapes and styles of decoration.

John Bridgen's jug is decorated with a continuous view of a farm with milking and haymaking in progress. It includes many details which are difficult to see in a reproduction, such as three chickens, a piglet and a dog sitting despondently outside his kennel; the village church, inn and windmill in the background; and on the other side, a rider allowing his horse to drink in the duck pond. The style is naive, but the painter had an excellent grasp of how to adapt his design to cover the curved surface of the jug.

Further reading David Towner, *Creamware*, 1978. Sheila Bidgood and Peter Walton, *Pots about People, Named and Dated Creamware and Pearlware* 1760–1820, catalogue of an exhibition at the Bar Convent Museum, York, 1990.

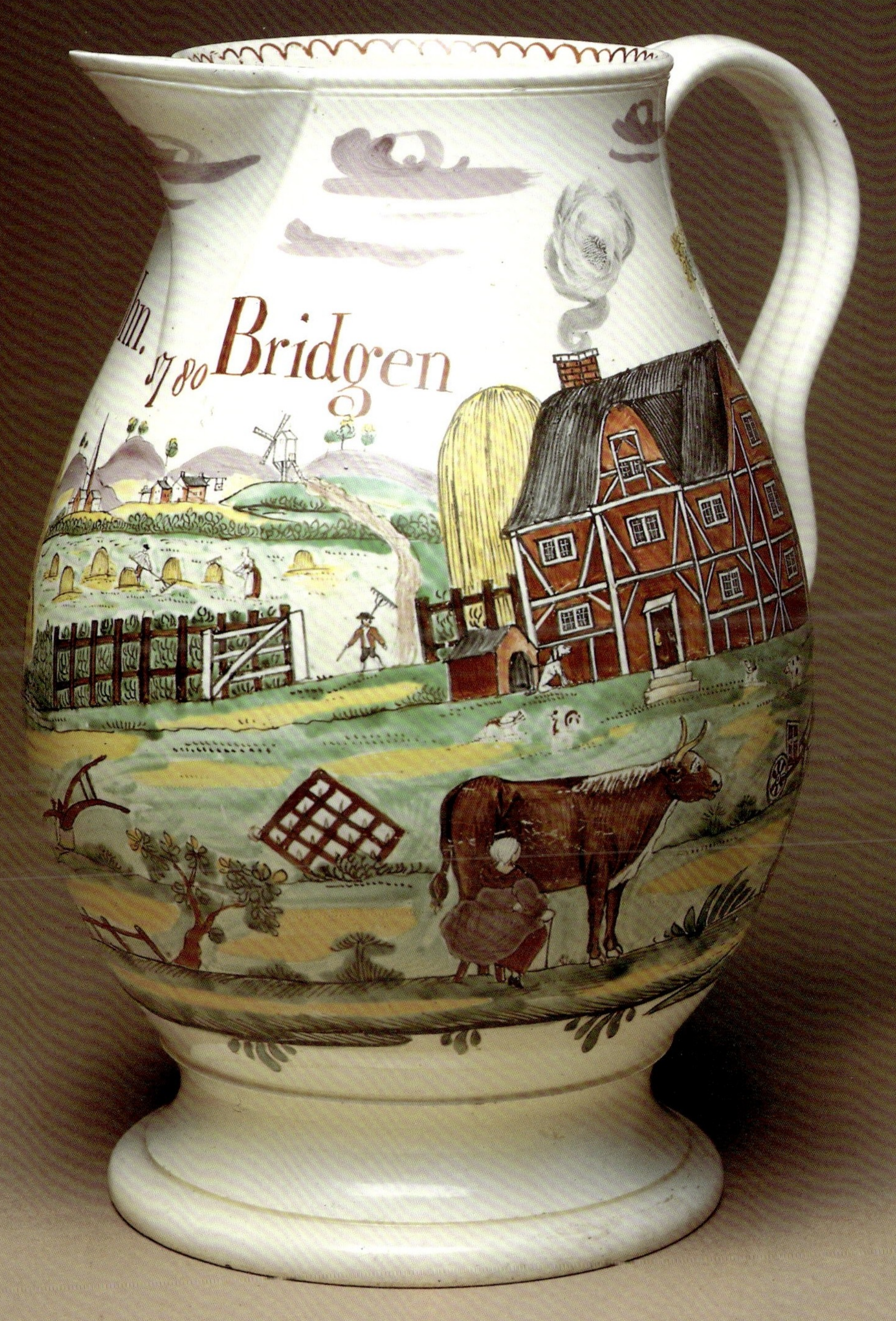
1780 Bridgen

34

CENTREPIECE

PROBABLY LEEDS POTTERY,
YORKSHIRE, c. 1780–1800.

Creamware with black enamel lettering on the bottles for oil and vinegar and the pepper caster. Height 63.5 cm. C.1063–1928.

Elaborate centrepieces were essential attributes of the well-laid dining table during the eighteenth century, particularly for the dessert. Creamware centrepieces, introduced about 1780, were a technical *tour de force*. The largest comprised a tray for condiments and a tiered arrangement of shells and branches supporting sweetmeat dishes and baskets. At the top there was an urn or classical figure, such as *Venus* or *Plenty*, which imparted a fashionably 'antique' character. The pierced cruet frames and openwork sweetmeat baskets on this example echo the pierced ornament and wirework which were features of neo-classical silver and Sheffield plate.

The Leeds Pottery, operating between 1770 and 1830, was the most important of the Yorkshire factories manufacturing creamware. The *Leeds Pattern Book* included two centrepieces, each described as a '*Grand platt menage*', and although this example does not resemble them, it seems probable that it was made there. The most likely alternative would be a Staffordshire factory such as that of James and Charles Whitehead of Hanley.

Further reading Donald Towner, *The Leeds Pottery*, 1963. Peter Walton, *Creamware and other English Pottery at Temple Newsam House, Leeds*, 1976, pp. 120–3.

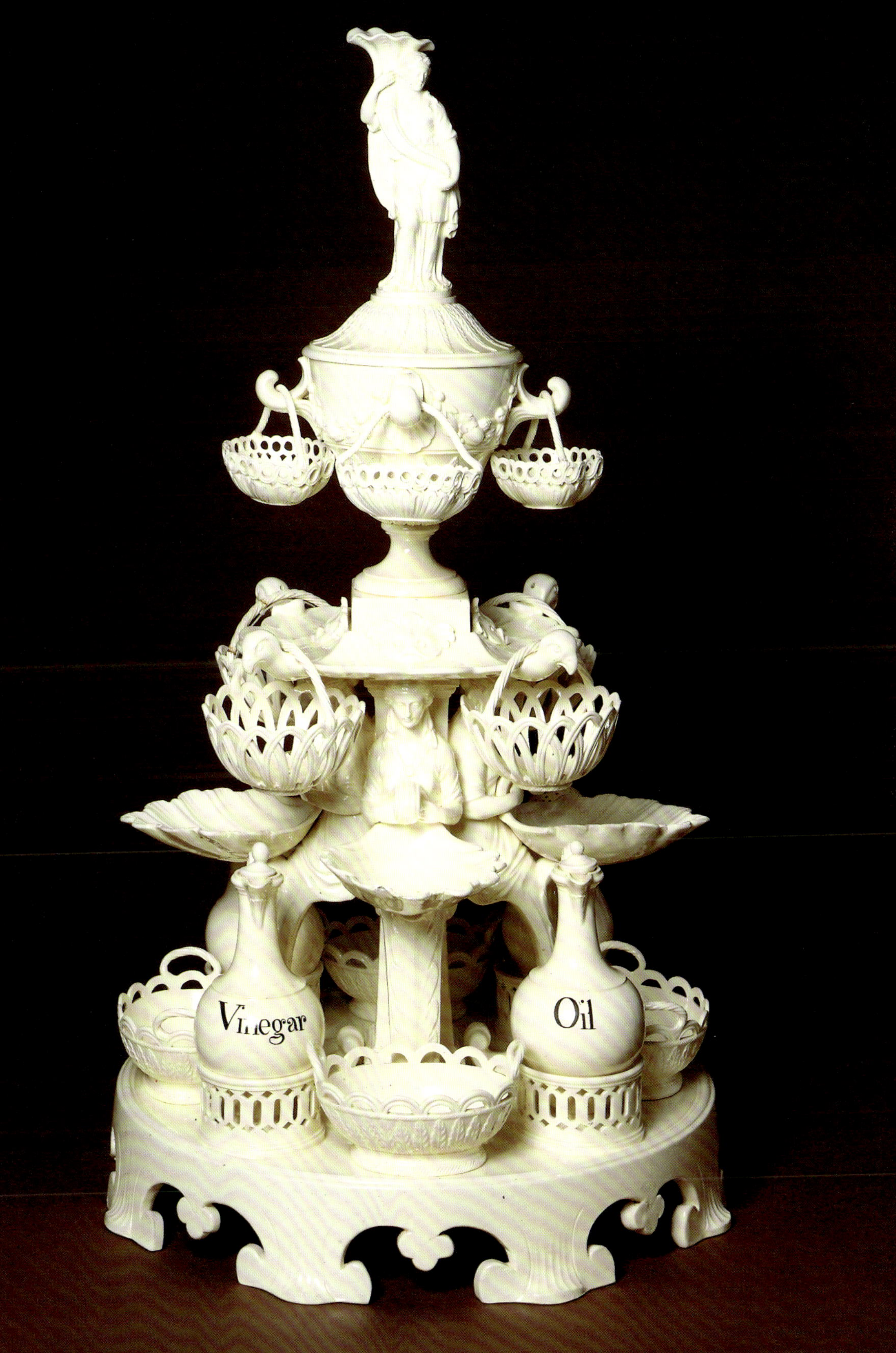
Vinegar
Oil

35

SAINT GEORGE AND THE DRAGON

STAFFORDSHIRE, c. 1780–1800.

Earthenware decorated with coloured lead glazes.
Height 25.4 cm. C.49–1930 *(Glaisher Catalogue 859).*

Coloured-glaze figures were probably introduced between 1775 and 1780. The glazes, coloured with metallic oxides to produce green, yellow, brown, blue and grey, were painted onto the once-fired model, which was then fired again. The clear glaze over the flesh areas often has a slight green or blue tinge, and the latter may be very pronounced. There are numerous models, mainly of rural, classical and biblical subjects or animals.

This class of figure was made by several potters, the best known of whom are John Wood (1746–97) and his brother Ralph Wood II (1748–95). John Wood's sales ledger for 1783–7 in the City Museum and Art Gallery, Stoke-on-Trent, mentions figures from 1783. Its entries indicate that some of the models formerly attributed to his father, Ralph Wood (1715–72), were probably made at his factory at Brownhills, Burslem. During the preceding decade Ralph II had been a glass and earthenware dealer in Bristol. He returned to Burslem in 1783 and by 1784 was in partnership with his cousin Enoch Wood. The duration of this partnership is uncertain but it had probably ended by 1790, when Enoch insured a potworks in his own name alone, and certainly before 1793, when he entered into partnership with James Caldwell (see no. 37). Models marked 'RWOOD' or 'Ra. Wood/ Burslem' were probably made after the cousins split up, and Ralph's heir, Ralph III, may have continued to use these marks until his premature death in 1801.

This model may have been derived from a bronze by Francesco Fanelli (c.1580–c.1661), who worked in England during the reign of Charles I. It was in production by November 1783, when an invoice in the Wedgwood archives records the sale by Ralph to Josiah and Thomas Wedgwood of a dozen 'George & Dragons' at 2s.0d. each. John's ledger mentions one sold for 1s.9d. in March 1784, presumably made by his factory. An example marked 'Ra.Wood/ Burslem' has been recorded, which suggests that the model continued to be made in the 1790s. It was a popular subject and also exists with underglaze painted and overglaze enamel decoration.

Further reading Frank Falkner, *The Wood Family of Burslem*, 1912. Pat Halfpenny, 'The Wood family', *Ceramics*, 3 (May–June 1986), pp. 118–26. Pat Halfpenny, *English Earthenware Figures 1740–1840*, 1991, pp. 55–99.

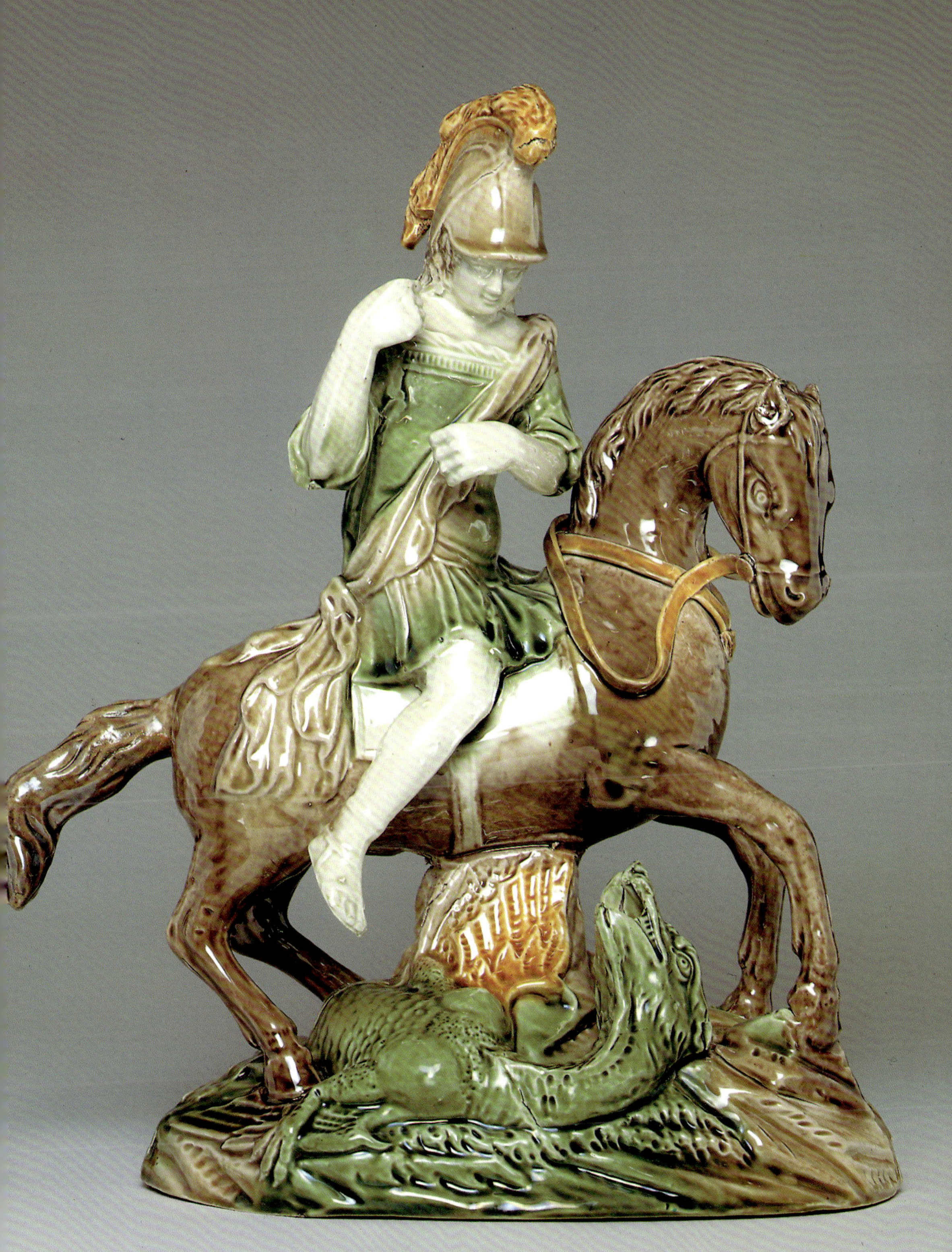

36

TOBY JUG

STAFFORDSHIRE,
c. 1790–1810.

White earthenware painted and sponged in blue, yellow, orange and grey under blue-tinted glaze. 'Pratt Ware'. Height 24.5 cm. C.752–1928.

Countless mugs, punch bowls and flasks bear witness to the importance of drinking in English social life, but none so graphically as the Toby jug, which made its debut about 1770. The origin of the name is uncertain. It may have been taken from Toby Fillpot, the subject of a song, 'The Brown Jug', published in the Rev. Francis Fawkes' *Original Poems and Translations* in 1761 and reprinted many times. It begins:

> 'Dear Tom, this brown jug that now foams with mild ale,
> (In which I will drink to sweet Nan of the Vale)
> Was once Toby Fillpot, a thirsty old soul,
> As e'er drank a bottle, or fathom'd a bowl.'

The modelling and colouring of Tobys and their accessories, such as barrels, pipes and mugs, differs from jug to jug. This classic example is decorated underglaze with the palette of metallic oxides described as 'Pratt' colours, which also included green, brown and black. Only two jugs marked 'PRATT' have been recorded and this palette was used on creamware and pearlware by many other potters in Staffordshire and elsewhere between the 1780s and 1830s. Toby jugs were also decorated with coloured glazes and with overglaze enamels.

Further reading Desmond Eyles, *Royal Doulton Character and Toby Jugs*, 1979, pp. 13–25. John and Griselda Lewis, *Pratt Ware, English and Scottish Relief Decorated and Underglaze Coloured Earthenware*, 1984.

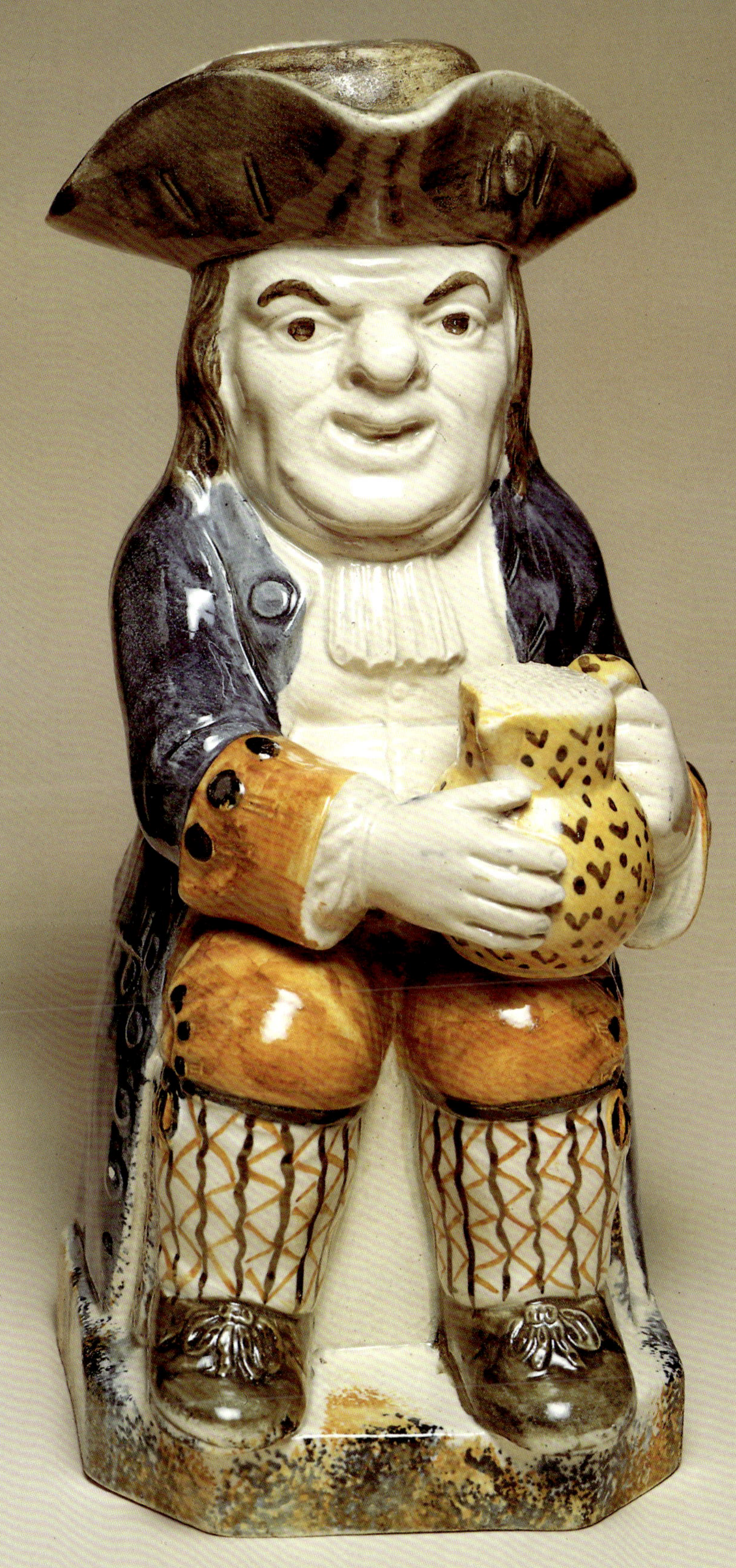

37

DEMOSTHENES

ENOCH WOOD, BURSLEM,
c. 1790–1810.

Pearlware, decorated overglaze in enamels.
Mark: 'E WOOD' impressed on the back of the base.
Height 48.2 cm. C.900–1928.

Enoch Wood (1759–1840) was one of the most prominent Staffordshire potters in the late eighteenth and early nineteenth centuries. In his youth he was a skilful modeller, and in middle age was respected as an astute businessman and an active participant in local affairs. After collaborating with his cousin Ralph Wood for an undefined period about 1784, he entered into a partnership with a lawyer, James Caldwell, which lasted from 1793 until 1818. Wood made several types of pottery during the early part of his career but is best known for his figures. Some of these were pearlware, an off-white earthenware with bluish glaze, described by contemporaries as 'china glaze'. They were decorated overglaze with enamels which included shades of pink, yellow and turquoise. This figure of the great Athenian orator, Demosthenes (384–322 BC), also known as *Eloquence*, may have been made during the 1790s or in the early nineteenth century, as Wood apparently continued to use his own mark after the commencement of his partnership with Caldwell.

Like other potters, Wood based some of his figures on earlier sculpture by making moulds from plaster casts, which were obtainable in several sizes from London sculptors. *Demosthenes* had started life in the early 1750s as a full-sized plaster statue by John Cheere (1709–87), who later sold reduced size casts of it. Wood could also have obtained this model from another London cast-maker, Charles Harris (d. 1795?), whose undated catalogue of casts of about 1790 included a *Demosthenes* and several other subjects produced as figures by Wood, such as *Fortitude*. The relief on the pedestal beside the figure shows Hermes, the messenger of the gods, who was associated with eloquence and reasoning, and therefore alludes to Demosthenes' oratorial skill.

Further reading Frank Falkner, *The Wood Family of Burslem*, 1912, pp. 38–60. J.E. Poole, *Plagiarism Personified? European Pottery and Porcelain Figures*, 1986. Pat Half-penny, *English Earthenware Figures 1740–1840*, 1991, pp. 157–69.

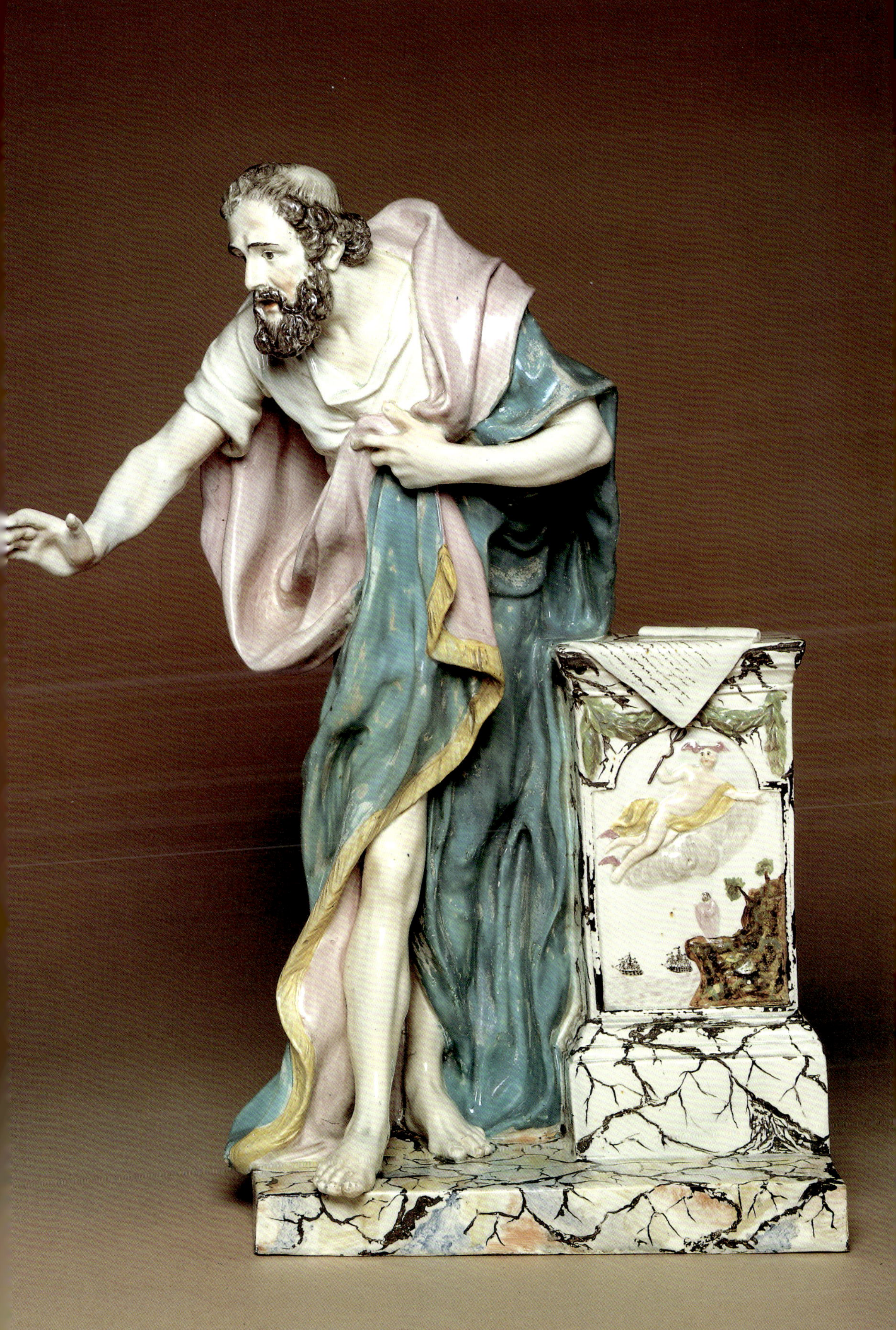

38

ERASMUS DARWIN'S PORTLAND VASE COPY

JOSIAH WEDGWOOD, ETRURIA, STAFFORDSHIRE, *c.* 1789–90.

Black jasper with applied white jasper reliefs.
Height 25.2 cm. C.20–1984.

Jasper is a fine, white, dry-bodied stoneware developed by Wedgwood between 1772 and 1775. It contains barium sulphate and can be tinted with metallic oxides to produce blue, sage-green, lilac, black and other colours. At first Wedgwood used jasper for intaglios, cameos and portrait medallions, but from the early 1780s he introduced teawares, vases and other ornamental wares in the new body.

Wedgwood's greatest technical achievement in jasper was his copy of the Roman cameo-glass *Portland Vase*. The dowager Duchess of Portland, who purchased it from Sir William Hamilton in 1784, died in 1785, and a year later Wedgwood borrowed the vase from her son, the third Duke of Portland. After studying it thoroughly, Wedgwood, his son Josiah II and his modellers Webber and Hackwood, experimented for three years before the first successful copy was achieved in the late summer of 1789. The exact number of Portland copies made in this 'first edition' before Wedgwood's death is not known. Surveys of extant vases and documents in the Wedgwood archives indicate that it was between forty and fifty, some of which were faulty.

This example is believed to be the vase sent by Wedgwood to his friend and medical adviser, Dr Erasmus Darwin of Derby in September 1789. Failing that, it must have been given to him shortly after, for there is no evidence that he purchased a Portland copy. After his death at Breadsall Priory, Derbyshire in 1802, the vase and its travelling case remained there in the possession of his unmarried daughter, Emma, who died in 1818 bequeathing it to her brother, Sir Francis Sacheverell Darwin. From him it descended in the family until it was purchased by the Fitzwilliam Museum in 1984 having been displayed on loan since 1963.

Further reading Aileen Dawson, *Masterpieces of Wedgwood in the British Museum*, 1984, pp. 112–25 and 149–50. Ian C. Freestone, William Gudenrath, Kenneth Painter and David Whitehouse, 'The Portland Vase', *Journal of Glass Studies*, 32 (1990). Elizabeth B. Adams, *The Dwight and Lucille Beeson Wedgwood Collection at the Birmingham Museum of Art, Birmingham, Alabama*, 1992, pp. 141–6.

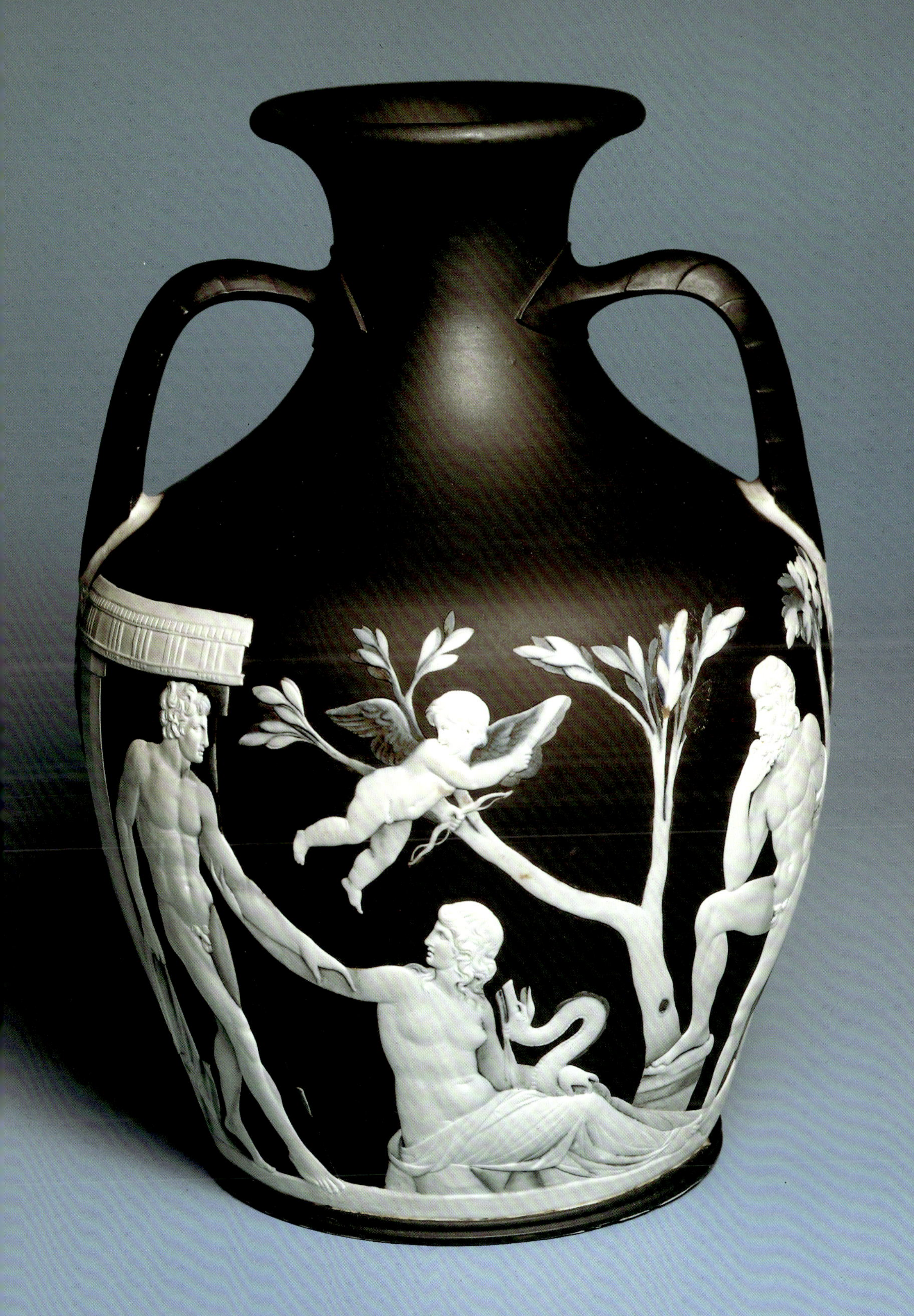

39

TEAPOT

ATTRIBUTED TO SOWTER & CO.,
MEXBOROUGH,
YORKSHIRE, c. 1800–11.

White felspathic stoneware with press-moulded body and applied reliefs, the panels outlined in blue enamel. Mark: '22' impressed. Height 16.5 cm, length 27.6 cm. C.1274–1928.

Between about 1785 and 1810 factories in Staffordshire and Yorkshire developed fine stonewares which sometimes have a slight sheen known as 'smear-glaze'. They were well suited for moulding the elegant neo-classical forms and relief ornament made fashionable by Wedgwood and other major potters such as Neale & Co. In Yorkshire, the Castleford Pottery became famous for its white felspathic stoneware, and as a result, teapots like the one illustrated became known as 'Castleford Teapots'. In fact, they were made by several factories, including one which marked its wares 'S. & C°.', perhaps for Sowter & Co. of Mexborough. This teapot has been attributed to that factory because the impressed '22' on its base is sometimes found in conjunction with 'S. & C°.', and because similar reliefs occur on teapots with that mark.

Teapots of this shaped oval form are described as silver- or commode-shaped (after the curving fronts of French chests-of-drawers). They usually have a low gallery around the lid which slides into position from the handle end instead of lifting off, a device which prevents the lid falling out when the tea is poured.

Further reading Diana Edwards Roussel, *The Castleford Pottery 1790–1821*, 1982, pp. 42–4 and pl. 92. Philip Miller and Michael Berthoud, *An Anthology of British Teapots*, 1985, p. 141. Robin Emmerson, *British Teapots and Tea Drinking*, 1992, pp. 176-82.

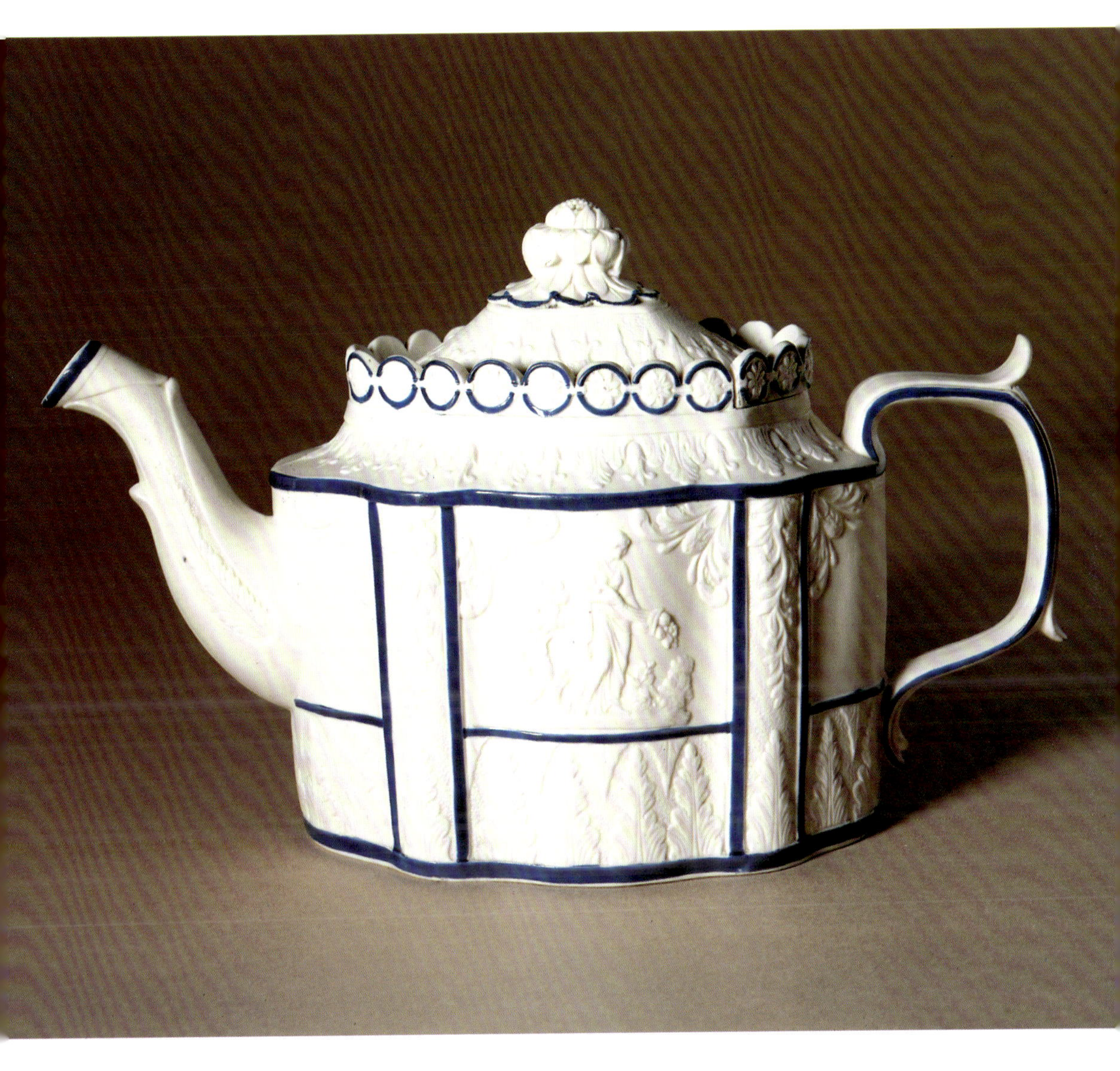

OBELISK

BRISTOL POTTERY, TEMPLE BACK,
BRISTOL, 1802.

Cream earthenware transfer-printed onglaze in brown and painted in enamel-colours with the arms of the City of Bristol and a print commemorating the Peace of Amiens. Height 74.5 cm. C.1113–1928.

The Water Lane pottery, later known as the Bristol Pottery, operated between 1682 or 1683 and 1886. It made delftware until 1777, when it was taken over by Richard Frank, who also made stoneware. His son-in-law, Joseph Ring, purchased the pottery in 1784 and in 1786 began to make creamware, which was continued after his death in 1788 by his widow and partners. Transfer-printed decoration was probably introduced after one of the latter, Henry Carter, took control in about 1797, but was little used until the 1820s.

The commemorative design on this rare model obelisk is one of the few printed patterns attributable to the pottery at the beginning of the nineteenth century. It is one of an enormous number of prints which were inspired by the Revolutionary or Napoleonic Wars, and the heart-felt relief when they were over. The design incorporates figures of Peace and Plenty on either side of an altar inscribed 'PEACE / Signed at / AMIENS/between/ENGLAND/FRANCE/ SPAIN/AND HOLLAND/March 27 1802'. In the background there is a view of the works inscribed 'Bristol Pottery'. The design also appears on mugs and was re-used with an updated inscription to celebrate the Peace of Paris in 1814.

Obelisks had been popular for funerary and other monuments in England since the sixteenth century and were associated with ancient Egypt and imperial Rome, because of the Egyptian obelisks set up there. This pottery version, painted to resemble marble, illustrates the tendency of English eighteenth- and nineteenth-century obelisks to take the form of a very pointed pyramid rather than a 'needle'.

Further reading Bristol Museum and Art Gallery, *Bristol Fine Wares 1670–1970*, 1980. Roger Price, 'Bristol potters and potteries 1600–1800', *Journal of Ceramic History*, 12 (1982), pp. 23–8. David Drakard, *Printed English Pottery, History and Humour in the Reign of George III 1760–1820*, 1992, chs. 10–14.

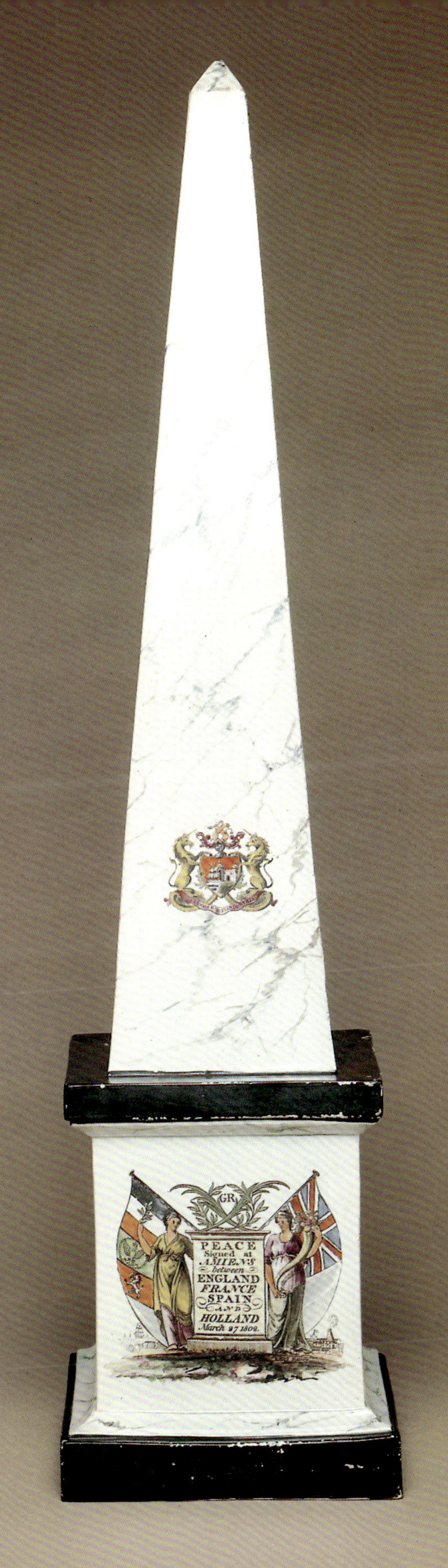
GR
PEACE
Signed at
AMIENS
between
ENGLAND
FRANCE
SPAIN
AND
HOLLAND
March 27 1802

41

DINNER PLATE

SPODE, STOKE-ON-TRENT, *c.* 1806–33.

White earthenware of 'New Indented' shape, transfer-printed underglaze in blue with 'Greek' pattern. Diameter 24.2 cm. C.89–1977.

Underglaze blue transfer-printed decoration had been introduced on English porcelain at the end of the 1750s but was not widely adopted by earthenware manufacturers until the 1780s. Josiah Spode (1733–97) is said to have introduced it at his Stoke factory in 1784 but the technique was not perfected until the early 1800s. During the proprietorship of Josiah Spode II (1755–1827) the number and variety of patterns available increased rapidly.

'Greek' pattern, introduced in 1806, catered for the demand for classical subjects created by the Greek revival. Each shape in the service was decorated with the same four vases between reserves containing different scenes derived from engravings of Greek vases in the collection of Sir William Hamilton (d. 1803). The central medallion on this plate shows Zeus in his chariot. The pattern was very popular and production continued during the Copeland and Garrett period (1833–47).

The development of underglaze blue printed earthenware was one of the outstanding successes of the British ceramic industry. Throughout the nineteenth century it was produced by hundreds of factories in Staffordshire and elsewhere, and was exported all over the world. Admittedly the quality of designs and printing was uneven, but at its best blue and white had undeniable charm and was ideal for everyday use. After about 1860 production gradually declined and there are now relatively few patterns on the market, among them Spode's 'Italian', introduced about 1816.

Further reading David Drakard and Paul Holdway, *Spode Printed Ware*, 1983, pp. 164–5. A.W. Coysh and R.K. Henrywood, *The Dictionary of Blue and White Printed Pottery 1780–1880*, vol. II, 1989, p. 95.

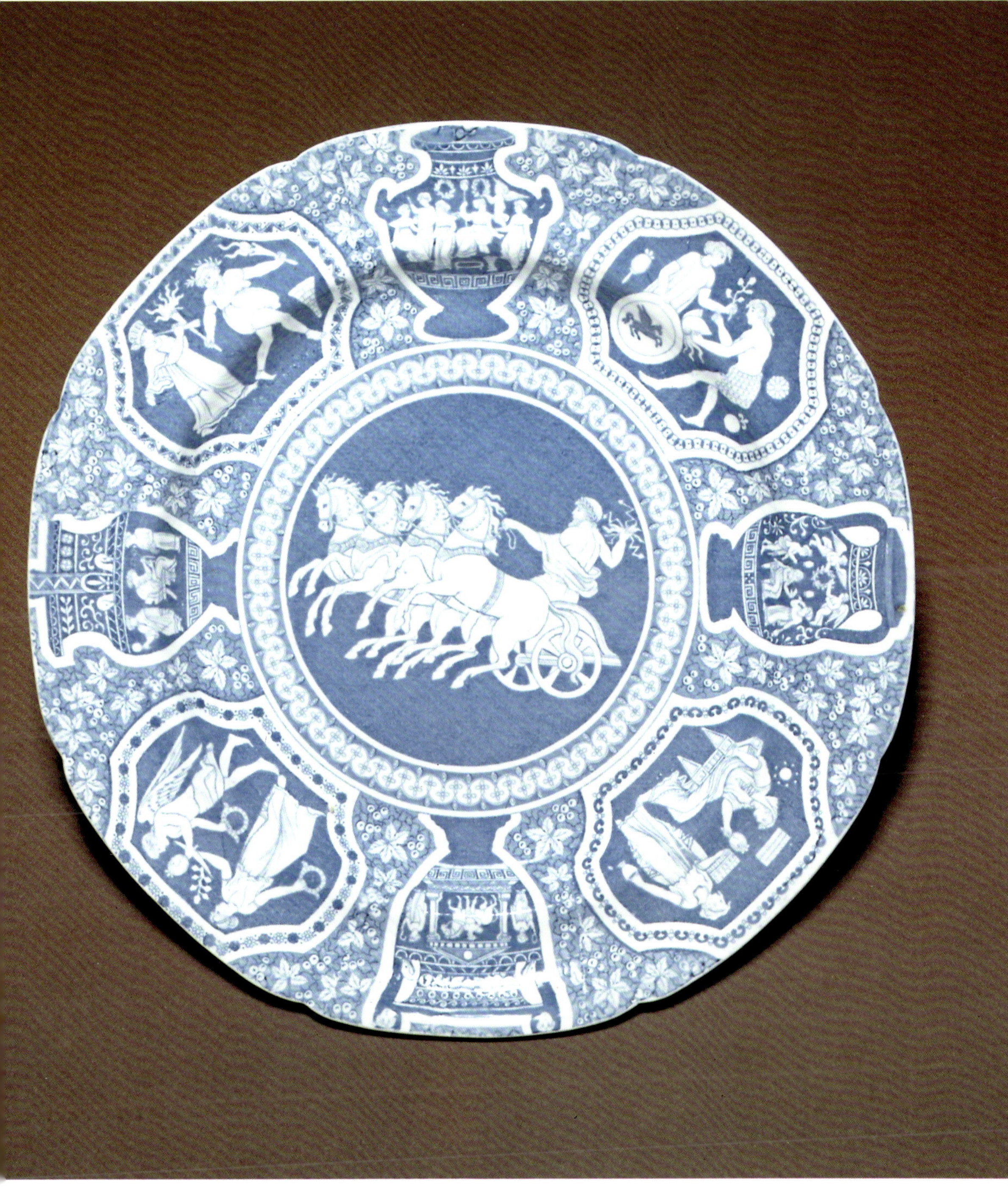

42

GARNITURE OF FIVE COVERED VASES

RICHARD WOOLLEY, LANE END, LONGTON, *c.* 1810–12.

White stoneware, decorated with applied white reliefs and partly coated in blue slip. Mark: 'WOOLLEY' impressed on each vase. Heights 38.5 cm, 21 cm and 18.5 cm. C.1266 & a-d-1928.

In the eighteenth and early nineteenth centuries vases were supplied in pairs or in chimney-piece garnitures of three, five or seven, which have rarely survived intact. These vases illustrate the jasper-like effect which could be produced by applying a coloured slip ground to fine white stoneware. The reliefs are of popular subjects which also occur on jasper and fine stonewares by other potters, such as John Turner and his sons, John and William. Until the recent discovery of another marked vase, these were the only pieces which could be firmly ascribed to Richard Woolley (1765–1825) during his occupation of the Lane End Manufactory, Longton between 1810 and 1812.

From about 1793 to 1807, Woolley had been in partnership with James Chetham at Commerce Street, Longton, and on Chetham's death he continued in partnership with his widow, Ann, until 1809. According to Simeon Shaw in *The History of the Staffordshire Potteries*, 1829, Chetham and Woolley had introduced a very fine, unglazed white body in 1795 which became known as 'Pearl', and like jasper was used 'for the finest description of ornaments'. It seems likely that Woolley would have continued to make 'Pearl' after he set up his own business, and if so, the Fitzwilliam Museum's vases are probably examples of that body.

Further reading David Hollens, 'The makers of dry bodies', ECCT, 11, Part 3 (1983), pp. 222–9. Geoffrey A. Godden, *Encylopaedia of British Porcelain Manufacturers*, 1988, p. 794.

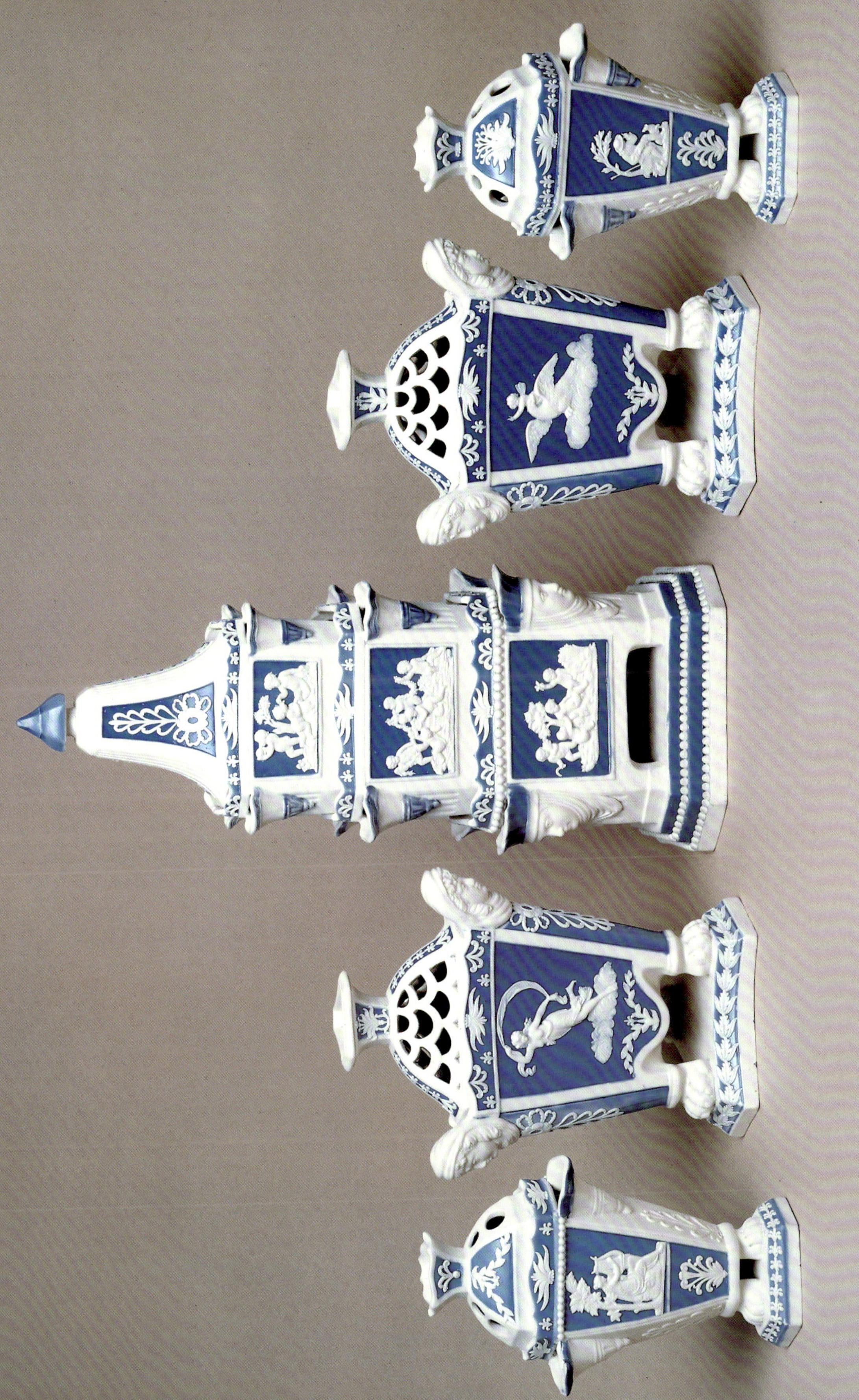

43

JUG

PROBABLY STAFFORDSHIRE OR LIVERPOOL, c. 1810–20.

Yellow-glazed earthenware decorated with black transfer-prints inscribed 'FAITH', 'HOPE' and 'CHARITY', and banded with 'silver' lustre. Height 16.4 cm. C.1–1970.

Yellow-glazed earthenware was made between about 1785 and 1835 but apparently only in small amounts, as it is one of the least common types of English pottery. Most major English collections have a few pieces, but by far the best place to see it is the National Museum of History and Technology in Washington DC, where there is a splendid collection formed by Eleanor and Jack L. Leon.

The opaque glaze, which gained its brilliant yellow from antimony, was usually applied to a cream-coloured or white body. Figures were often left plain yellow. Tablewares were usually decorated with lustre, enamels or transfer-printing in black or other colours, singly or in combinations. The enamelled decoration can be startlingly gaudy, but a greater degree of sophistication was achieved with lustre-resist patterns or black prints with lustre banding. The prints of *Faith*, *Hope* and *Charity* on this jug are among those which occur most frequently.

The few marked examples of yellow-glazed ware show that it was made in most of the important ceramic centres in England and Wales. Manufacturers included Enoch Wood, Davenport, Shorthose and Spode in Staffordshire; the Leeds and Swinton Potteries in Yorkshire; the Herculaneum Pottery at Liverpool; the Cambrian Pottery in Swansea and several firms in Sunderland and Tyneside.

Further reading Jack L. Leon, 'Yellow-glazed English earthenware', ECCT, 8, Part 1 (1971), pp. 31–41. J. Jefferson Miller II, *English Yellow-Glazed Earthenware*, 1974.

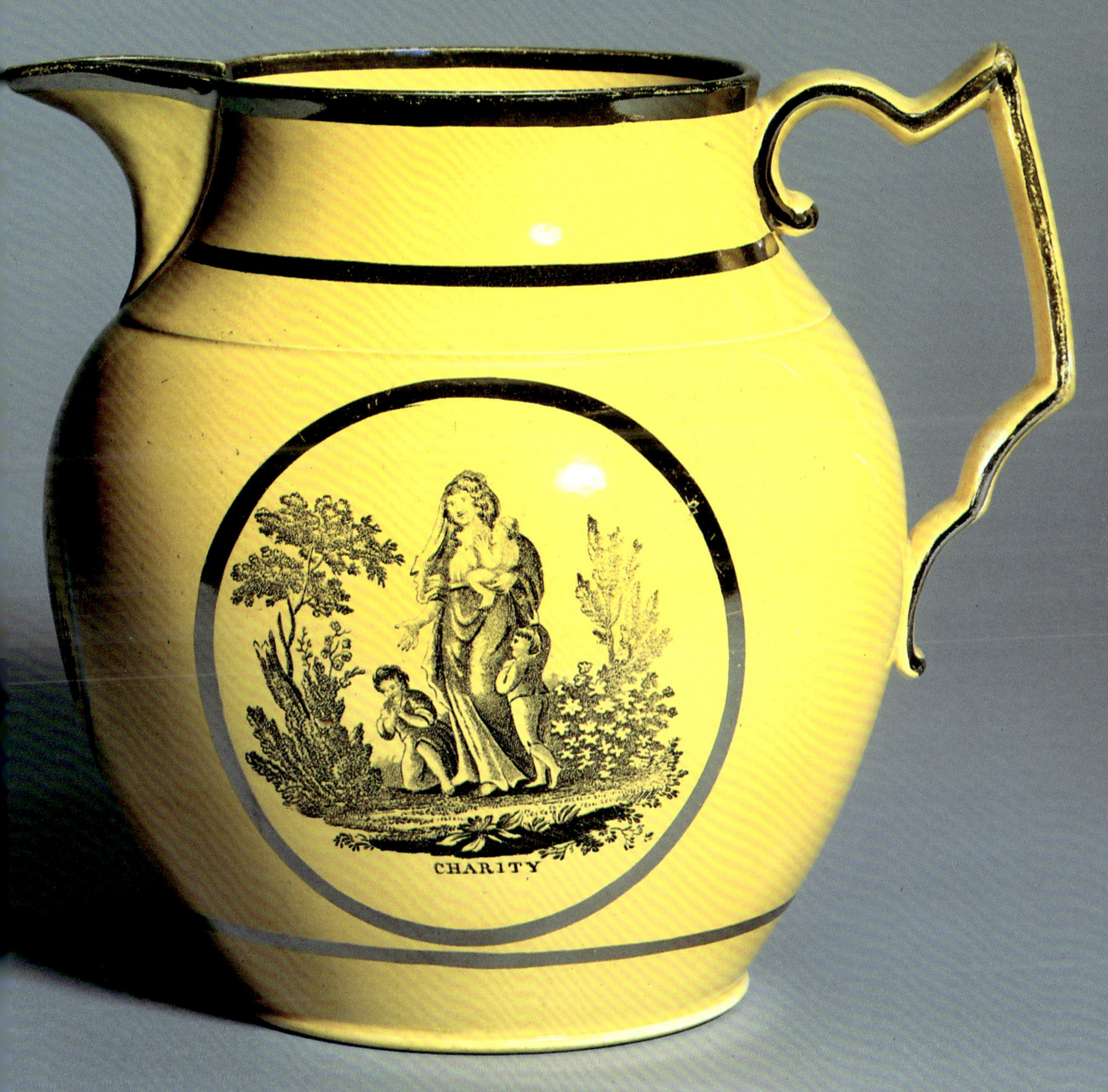
CHARITY

44

DISH

LEEDS POTTERY, YORKSHIRE, *c.* 1815–20.

*Creamware decorated with a resist pattern reserved in a 'silver' lustre ground. Mark: '*LEEDS*POTTERY*' impressed. Diameter 36.8 cm.* C.1064–1928.

The liquid platinum process which produces silver lustre was first used in England in 1805 by John Hancock, employed in Henry Daniel's enamelling workshop at the Spode factory in Stoke. The glazed ware was coated with a preparation composed of platinum dissolved in *aqua regia* (nitric and hydrochloric acids) suspended in a resinous medium, such as spirits of tar. During firing the resin burned away, leaving a thin film of untarnishable platinum on the surface. At first, lustre was steel-coloured and it was not until 1812–14 that a true silver was achieved by applying a second coating of platinum in the form of a powder mixed with water. Resist patterns, like the one on this dish, were produced by painting the design or background with gum or size which prevented the platinum from adhering to those areas.

It is not known when lustreware was introduced at Leeds, but it was probably a little before its first mention in the *Leeds Pottery Drawing Book* for 'Enamell'd Tea Ware' in 1819. Silver-lustred wares were also made in the Potteries, and in the north-east at Sunderland and Newcastle-upon-Tyne, as were copper, pink and purple lustres derived from gold.

The popularity of lustre stemmed partly from the desire of humble people to have tableware which looked like silver or other metals, and partly from the taste for opulent interiors and furnishing during the Regency period. Much of the finest English and Continental silver and porcelain was heavily gilt, and fashionable women carried small fans, set with cut steels or stamped gold and silver ornaments which glittered as they caught the light.

Further reading Leslie B. Hunt, 'The origin of English silver lustre', *The Connoisseur*, 200 (March 1979), pp. 185–9. Una des Fontaines, 'Shedding light on lustre', *Northern Ceramic Society Newsletter*, 70 (June 1988), pp. 41–3. Geoffrey A. Godden and Michael Gibson, *Collecting Lustreware*, 1991.

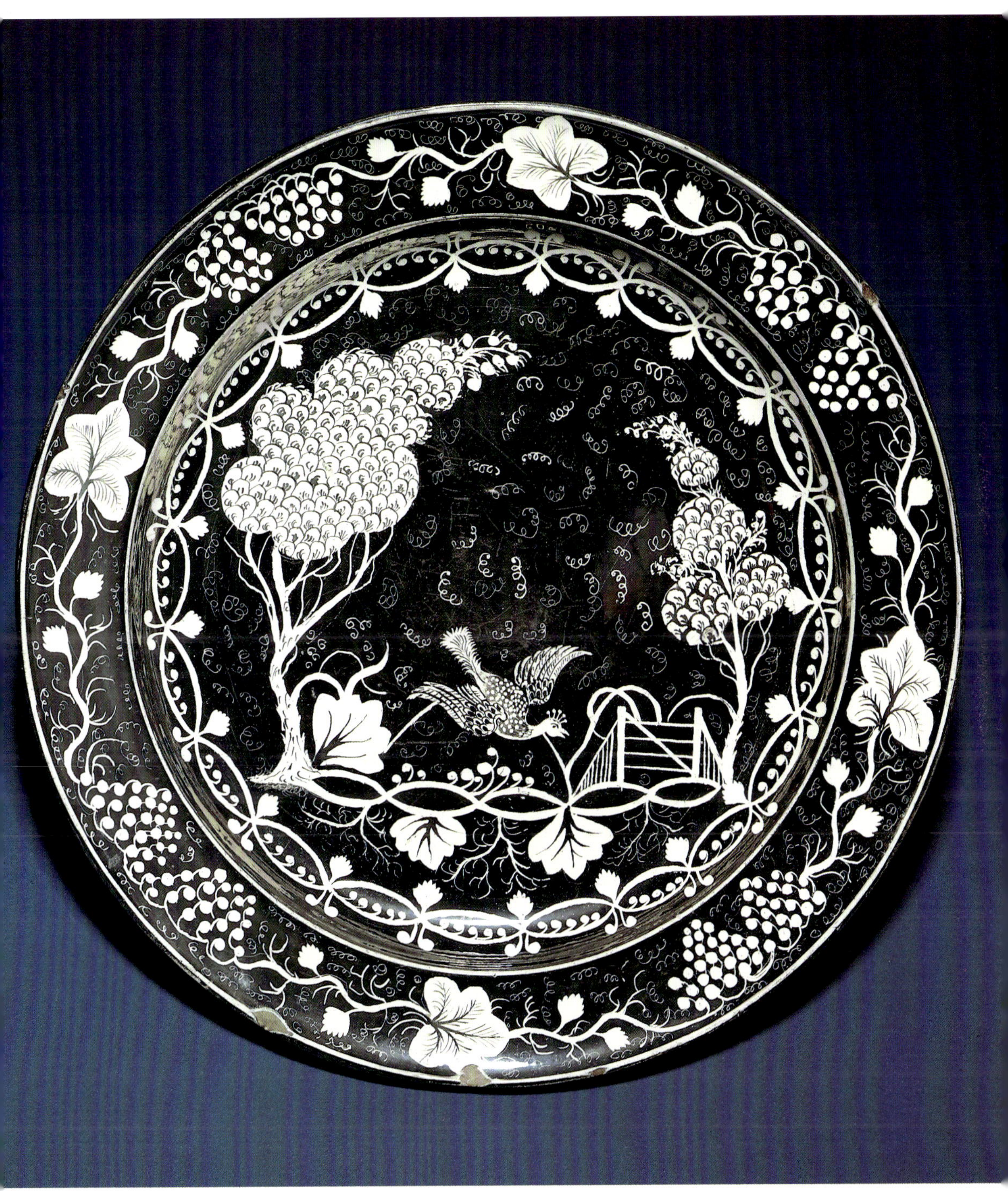

45

'PERSWAITION'

PROBABLY JOHN WALTON,
BURSLEM, c. 1815–25.

Pearlware decorated overglaze with enamels.
'PERSWAITION' *impressed on the front.*
Height 20 cm. C.957–1928.

'Perswaition' is a charming product of the realistic school of figure-making which developed in the Potteries between about 1800 and 1840. The couple are depicted in an unaffected manner, as if the young man had decided to propose on a stroll in the garden, or on their way home from church or chapel. The stylized tree behind them, known as *bocage* (a grove), was derived from eighteenth-century porcelain figures. It was a feature of figures by John Walton, who was christened in 1780, and was listed as a potter in local directories from 1818 to 1835. Some of his models, including examples of 'Perswaition' are marked 'WALTON' impressed or in relief on a raised scroll. Several other potters, such as Ralph Salt of Shelton, John Dale of Burslem and Charles Tittensor of Hanley, made figures in this rustic style but, as few were marked and plagiarism was rife, it is difficult to make firm attributions.

Further reading Reginald Haggar, *Staffordshire Chimney Ornaments*, 1955, pp. 71–6. Pat Halfpenny, *English Earthenware Figures 1740–1840*, 1991, pp. 215–60.

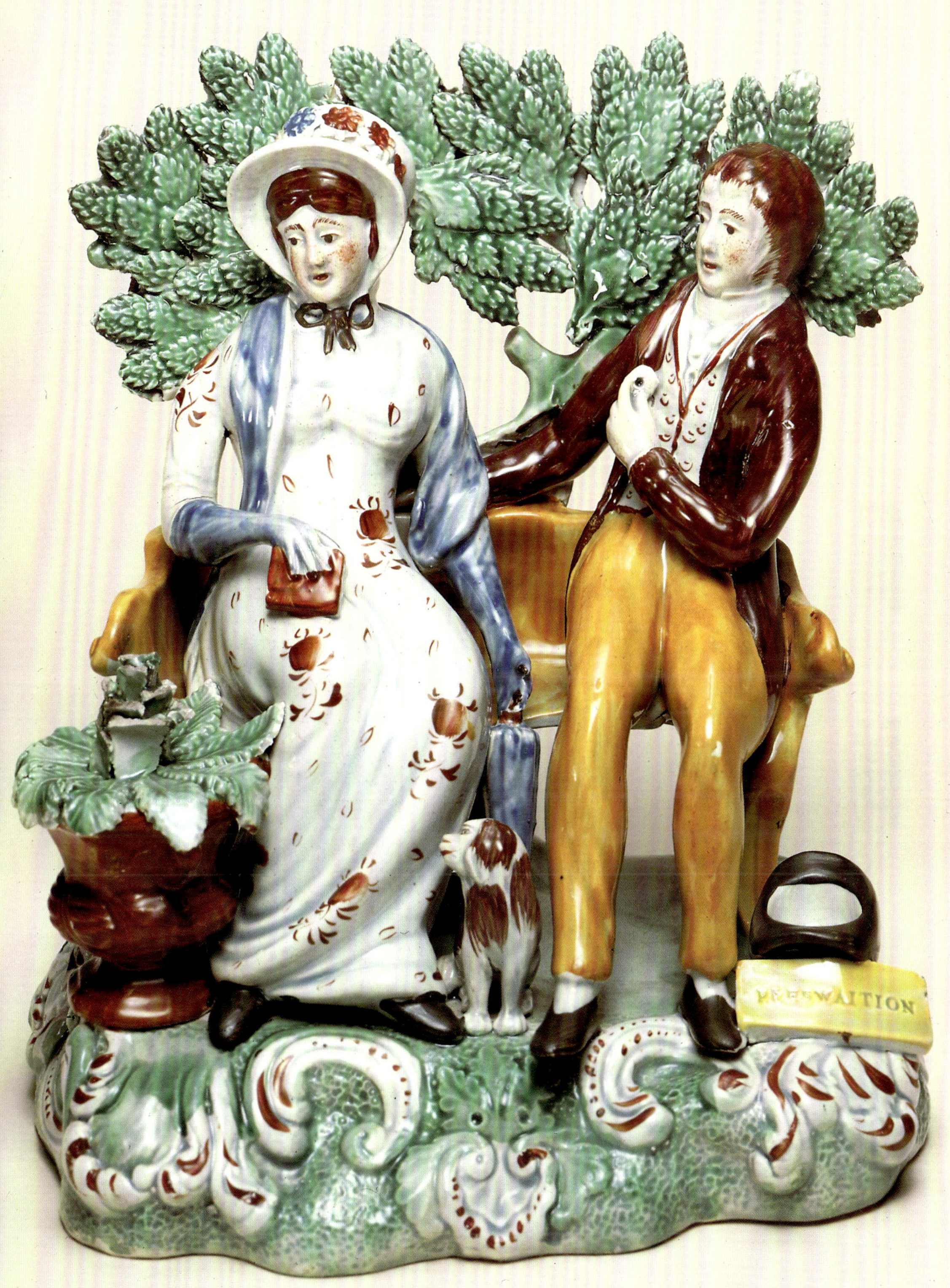

46

VASE AND COVER WITH PAGODA FINIAL

CHARLES JAMES MASON & CO.,
FENTON STONE WORKS, LANE DELPH,
FENTON, c. 1826–45.

Stone china, transfer-printed, painted in polychrome enamels and gilt. Mark: printed in black, a view of the factory and 'FENTON/ STONE WORKS/C.J.M. & C°/STAFFORDSHIRE POTTERIES GRANITE CHINA'. *Height 122 cm.* C.1280–1928.

Stone china was more durable than creamware or pearlware and closer to Oriental porcelain in appearance, although not translucent. The first patent for such a body was taken out by John and William Turner in 1800. Another patent, for what became known as 'Ironstone China', was granted to Charles James Mason (1791–1856) in 1813. In that year he and his two brothers purchased the Fenton Stone Works, which is illustrated in the mark on this vase. Mason remained there until 1848 when he was declared bankrupt, sold the works and moved to the Daisy Bank Pottery in Longton. He recovered sufficiently to exhibit at the Great Exhibition in 1851 and finally retired from business in 1853.

Mason's 'Ironstone' (sometimes referred to by the firm as 'granite china', quickly became fashionable and maintained its popularity despite competition from stone chinas introduced by Spode, Davenport and other manufacturers. Its strength made it particularly suitable for dinner services, jugs and large ornamental wares, a high proportion of which were decorated with brightly coloured 'Japan' or other Oriental patterns. Unfortunately mass production sometimes resulted in poor workmanship and this must have contributed to Mason's downfall. A close look at this immense hall or alcove vase reveals that the enamelling was applied rather carelessly. Nevertheless it is an eye-catching and rare survivor of the nineteenth-century taste for large ostentatious ceramics.

Further reading Reginald Haggar and Elizabeth Adams, *Mason Porcelain and Ironstone 1796–1853*, 1977. Geoffrey A. Godden, *Godden's Guide to Mason's China and the Ironstone Wares*, revised edn, 1991.

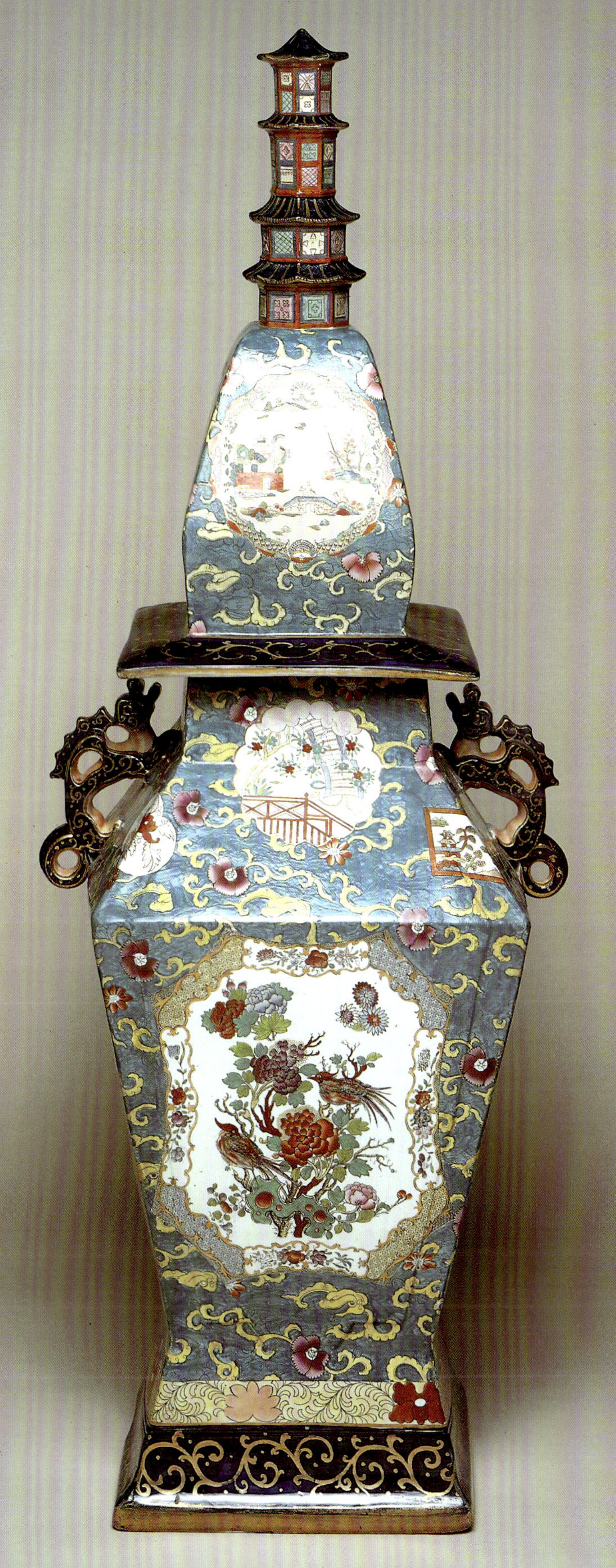

47

FLASK IN THE SHAPE OF A GIRL HOLDING A DOVE

JAMES BOURNE & CO.,
DENBY OR CODNOR PARK,
c. 1835–40.

Salt-glazed stoneware with brown dip on the upper part. Mark: 'DENBY & CODNOR PARK. BOURNE'S POTTERIES. DERBYSHIRE'.
Height 20.9 cm. C.1252–1928.

Bottle-making was an important aspect of the salt-glazed stoneware industry throughout the nineteenth century. Most bottles were utilitarian containers for drinks, ink or blacking, but several firms made novelty flasks for spirits and cordials. There were two basic types: flattened bottle shapes with relief decoration on one or both sides, and three-dimensional forms including human figures, pistols and boots. The name of the vendor, such as a publican or wine and spirit merchant, could be stamped on the back so that the flask served as an advertisement.

Prominent manufacturers in the London area included Doulton & Watts and Stephen Green of Lambeth, and in Derbyshire, James Bourne, who owned factories in Belper and Denby. This flask, which may represent Princess Victoria, was made after 1833 when Bourne took over the Codnor Park bottle-making factory. A similar example in a private collection is dated 1836.

Further reading Ivor Noël Hume, 'Stoneware gin flasks: legacy of the damned', *Antiques* (February 1975), reprinted in Paul Atterbury (ed.), *English Pottery and Porcelain, an Historical Survey*, 1980, pp. 253–62. Derek Askey, *Stoneware Bottles from Bellarmines to Ginger Beers 1500–1949*, 1981. Adrian Oswald, R.J.C. Hildyard and R.G. Hughes, *English Brown Stoneware 1670–1900*, 1982, pp. 178–84.

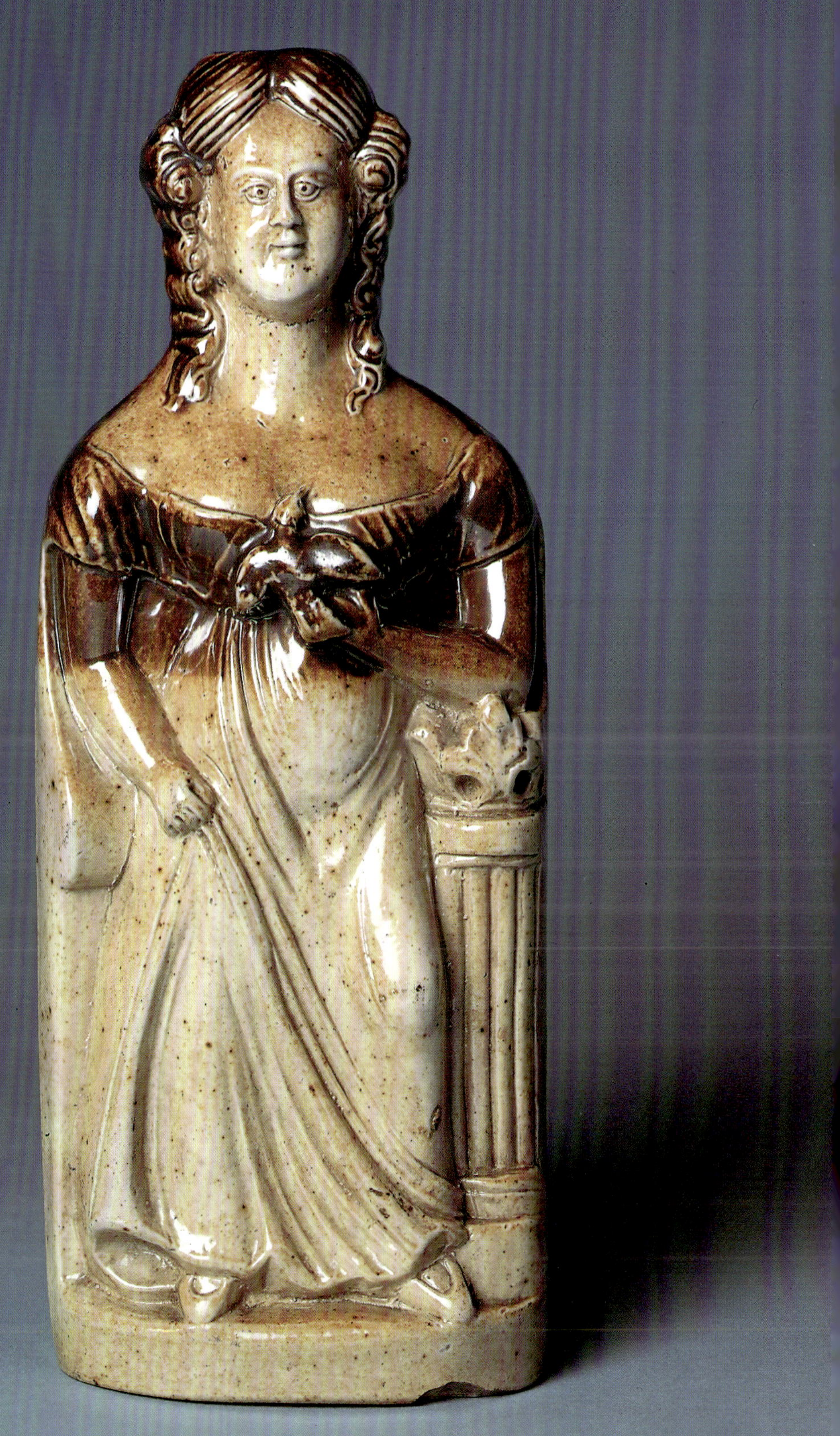

48

THE 'BULRUSH' WATER JUG

RIDGWAY & ABINGTON,
HANLEY, c. 1848–60.

Relief-moulded, smear-glazed grey stoneware with fully glazed interior. Patent registration mark for 7 March 1848. Height 16.4 cm. C.47–1981.

Throughout the nineteenth century there was a demand for jugs in which drinks could be served and stored. Relief-moulded stoneware jugs were ideal for these purposes, being both sturdy and attractive. They were also inexpensive because their decoration was formed in one process with the body by press-moulding or slip-casting. Introduced in about 1820, they had become popular by the 1830s, and for the rest of the century they were made in many shapes and sizes with decoration in every imaginable style.

William Ridgway and his partner, James Leonard Abington, made a name for relief-moulded ware with best-sellers such as the 'Tam O'Shanter' jug of 1835. In 1838 they were joined by Ridgway's son, Edward, who continued in partnership with Abington after his father's withdrawal from the firm in 1845.

The naturalistic and appropriate plant ornament of their 'Bulrush' jug may have been suggested by the water weeds on the 'Well Spring' glass carafe and jug, designed by Richard Redgrave R.A. (1804–88) for Felix Summerly's Art Manufactures in 1847. The simplicity of the jug's design is in marked contrast to some of its angular and heavily decorated contemporaries and it received a favourable review in *The Journal of Design and Manufactures* in 1849.

Further reading R.K. Henrywood, *Relief-Moulded Jugs 1820–1900*, 1984. Jill Rumsey, *Victorian Relief-Moulded Jugs*, 1987.

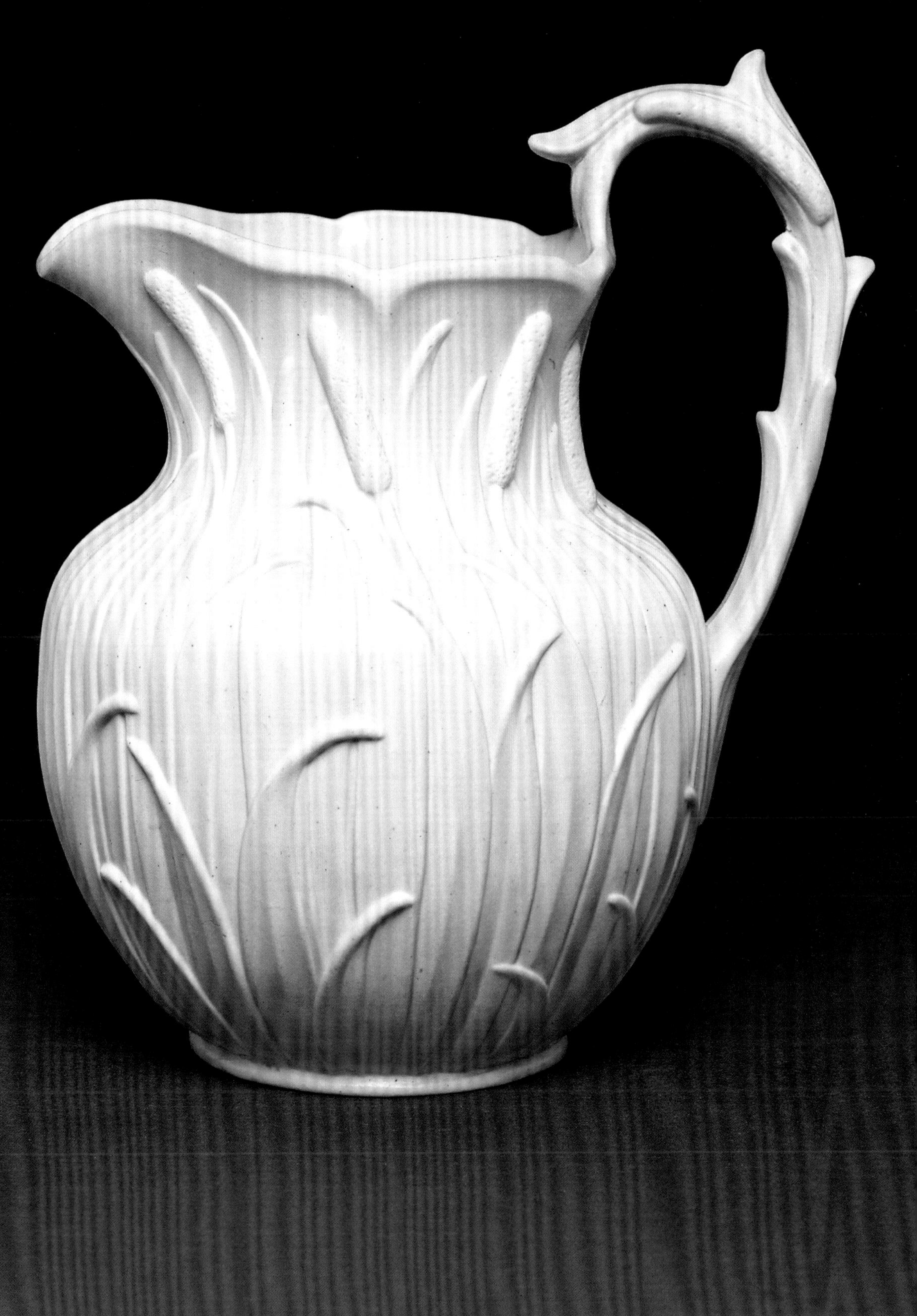

49

POT-LID

T.J. & J. MAYER,

DALE HALL POTTERY,

LONGPORT, BURSLEM,

1851.

White earthenware decorated underglaze with a multicolour transfer-print of the exterior of the Crystal Palace, inscribed 'THE GRAND INTERNATIONAL BUILDING OF 1851. *For the Exhibition of Art and Industry of all Nations'. Diameter 12.7 cm.* G.P.L.220–1928.

Lids for pots of bears' grease and various kinds of fish and meat paste were mass-produced from the 1840s. The earliest examples decorated with multicolour underglaze transfer-prints were probably made about 1847 by F. & R. Pratt of Fenton, who employed Jesse Austin (1806–79), the best-known engraver of pot-lid designs. T.J. & J. Mayer of Burslem must have adopted the technique by October 1850, when their customer Crosse & Blackwell patented this view of the Crystal Palace. By the time the Great Exhibition opened on 1 May 1851, both Pratt and Mayer had brought out commemorative pot-lids illustrating the interior and exterior of the building and the opening ceremony.

Multicolour underglaze transfer-printing enabled polychrome decoration to be executed without hand-painting. Separate line engravings were made for the black or brown outlines, and stipple engravings for each primary colour in the design. The transfers printed from them were placed on the once-fired lid one after the other with the 'keyplate' for the outlines last. Then the lid was glazed and fired again. The success of the finished product depended on the quality of the engraved plates and the degree of care exercised in aligning the transfers.

Further reading Cyril Williams-Wood, *Staffordshire Pot Lids and their Potters*, 1972. A. Ball, *The Price Guide to Pot-Lids and other Multicolour Prints on Ware*, 2nd edn, 1980, pp. 89–94.

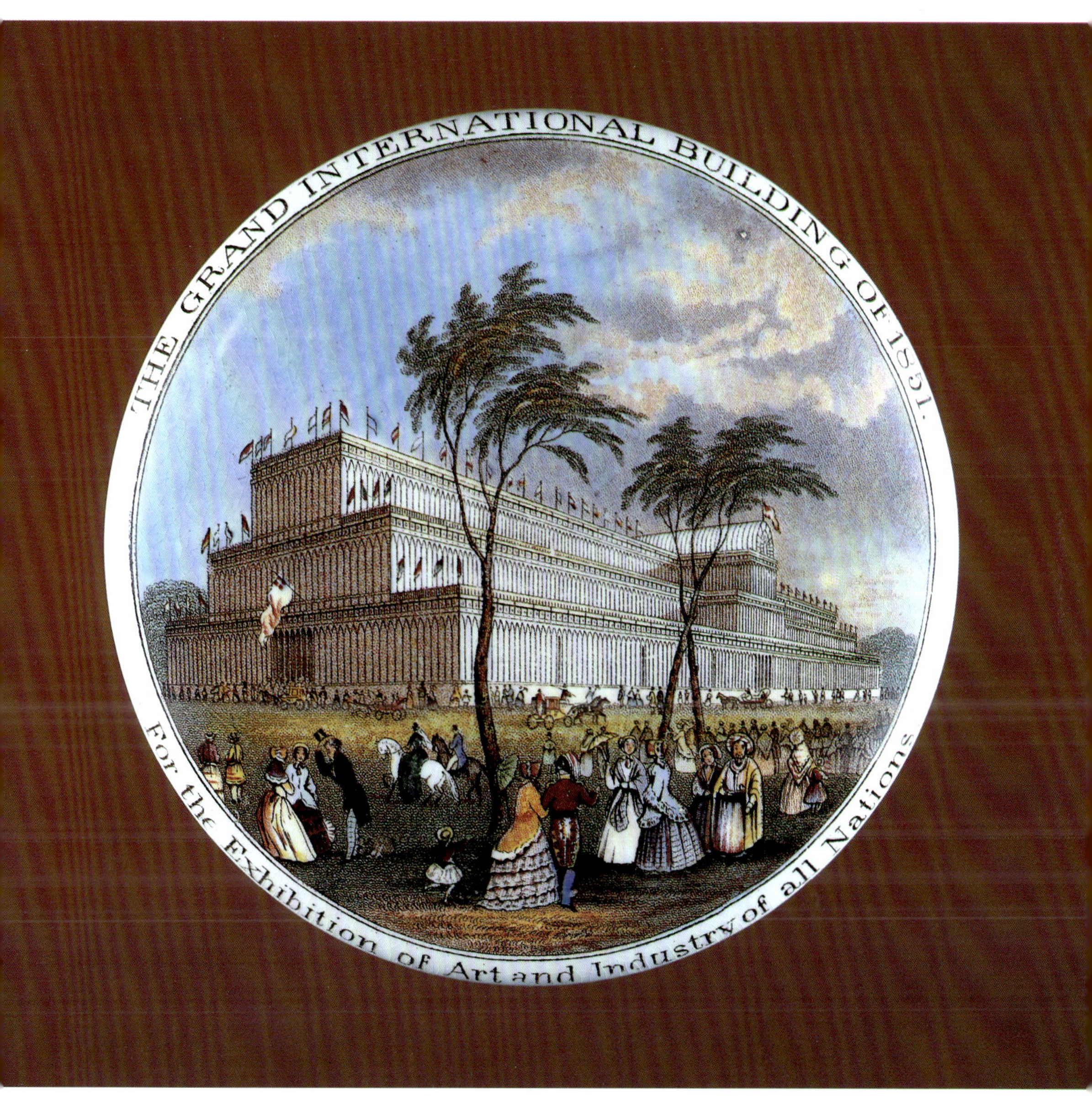
THE GRAND INTERNATIONAL BUILDING OF 1851.
For the Exhibition of Art and Industry of all Nations

50

EWER AND BASIN

MINTON, STOKE-ON-TRENT,
1856.

Earthenware, moulded and decorated with 'Majolica' glazes and blue enamel. Mark: impressed year cypher. Height of ewer 75 cm, length of basin 62.5 cm. C.40–1972.

Minton's 'Majolica' was developed at the end of the 1840s by Léon Arnoux, who served as the firm's Art Director from 1849 to 1892. Unlike Italian maiolica, which was tin-glazed earthenware with painted decoration, 'Majolica' was earthenware decorated with coloured lead glazes. First shown at the Great Exhibition of 1851, it was an immediate success, appealing to the Victorians' love of boldly modelled forms and vivid colouring. It was also extremely versatile, being as suitable for garden ornaments as it was for tablewares and figures.

The form of this massive ewer and basin, designed by Pierre Emile Jeannest (1813–57), reflects the widespread enthusiasm for Renaissance art during the mid-nineteenth century. The Great Exhibition had encouraged the manufacture of grandiose ornamental ceramics in revival styles, and Minton exhibited an elaborately painted ewer and basin of similar design at the London International Exhibition of 1862.

Many other English factories introduced versions of majolica, notably Wedgwood and George Jones, and it was also made on the Continent and in the United States.

Further reading Elizabeth Aslin and Paul Atterbury, *Minton 1798–1910*, 1976. Victoria Cecil, *Minton 'Majolica'*, 1982. Victoria Bergesen, Majolica, *British, Continental and American Wares*, 1989.

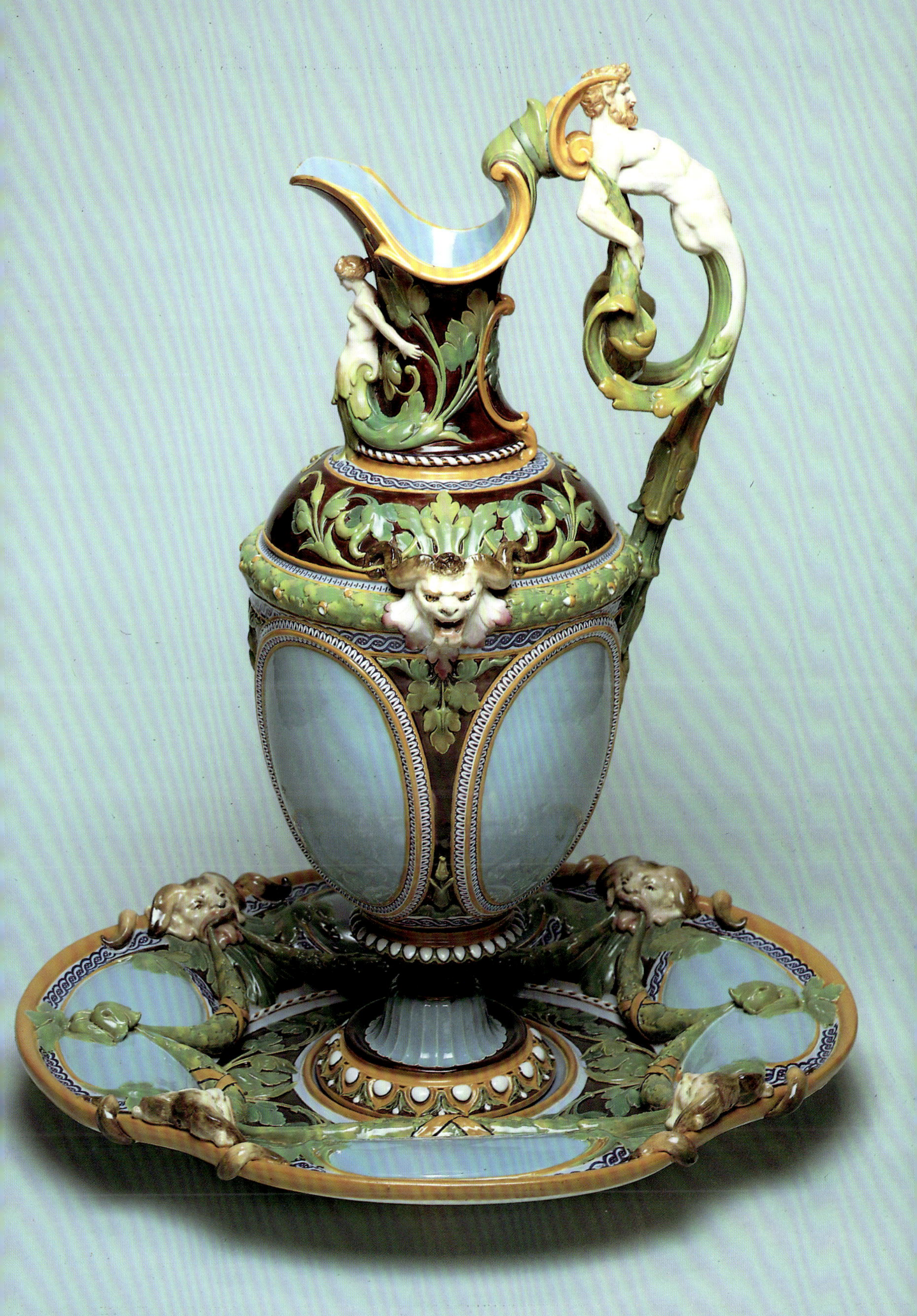

51

THE PRINCESS ROYAL AND PRINCE FREDERICK WILLIAM OF PRUSSIA

STAFFORDSHIRE, 1857.

Earthenware decorated with underglaze blue, onglaze enamels and gilding. The base is titled 'PRINCESS ROYAL & FR^{K}. OF PRUSSIA'. *Height* 40.2 *cm.* C.1011–1928.

Victorian Staffordshire portrait figures were cheaply made for the lower end of the market. Unlike most late eighteenth- and early nineteenth-century Staffordshire figures, which had been assembled from several moulded or modelled parts, they were usually made in three-piece moulds (front, back and base). Consequently they had simpler contours and integral pedestals, often titled in raised or indented letters. Early examples were gaily coloured in underglaze blue and onglaze enamels, but from the 1860s colour was applied more sparingly. By that date many of the figures had almost flat, undecorated backs. This helped manufacturers to reduce production costs and increase their output. The change did not deter potential customers because the figures were usually displayed on mantlepieces or dressers where the back was not visible.

Portraits of royalty were very popular. This group commemorates the announcement of the betrothal of Victoria, Princess Royal, to Prince Frederick William of Prussia in 1857. The couple first met in 1851, when the Prince and his parents visited the Great Exhibition, and he proposed while on holiday with the royal family at Balmoral in September 1855. After their marriage on 25 January 1858, the same group was re-issued with the words 'Pr & Prss.of.Prussia'. Like many other Staffordshire portrait groups, it presents a stereotyped view of the subjects. The Princess is scarcely recognizable as the intelligent young woman shown in Winterhalter's portrait which was issued as a print in 1856.

Further reading Gordon P.D. Pugh, *Staffordshire Portrait Figures of the Victorian Age*, revised edn, 1987. John Van der Kiste, *Queen Victoria's Children*, 1990.

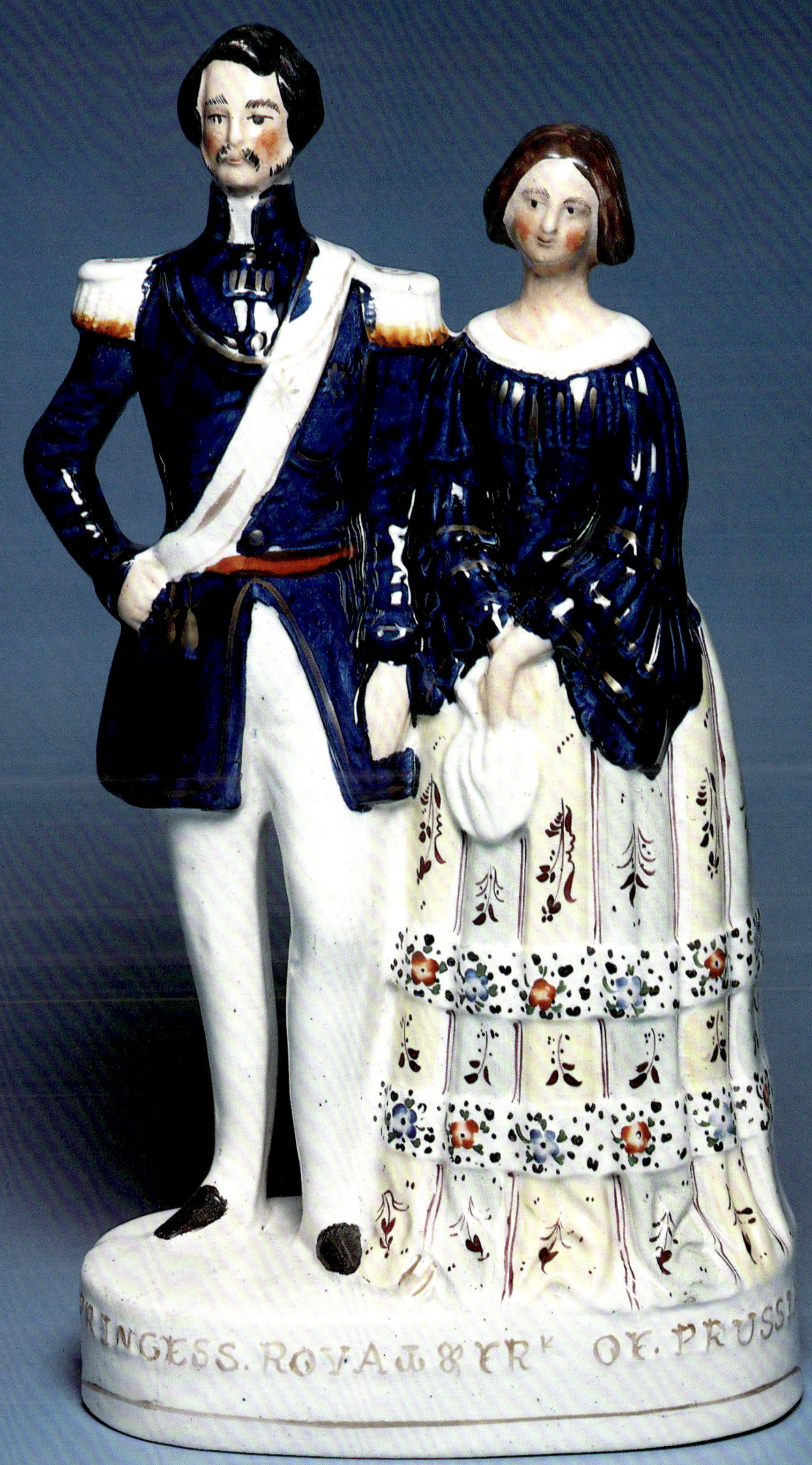
PRINCESS. ROYAL & FRK OF. PRUSSI

52

JUG

JOHN PHILLIPS HOYLE,
BIDEFORD, NORTH DEVON,
1857.

Slipware with sgraffito decoration;
inscribed, 'The Bucton Castle crossing the Line'
and 'From Rocks & Sands/& Every Ill/May God Protect
the Sailor/Still/John Phillips Hoyle/1857 Bideford'.
Height 27.4 cm. C.74–1928.

Incised or sgraffito decoration was a characteristic of North Devon slipware from the seventeenth to late nineteenth centuries. It involved coating a red–brown clay vessel with white slip, and incising a design through it to reveal the darker fabric beneath. After the vessel had been lead-glazed and fired, the design appeared red–brown against a yellow background. Alternatively the slip could be cut away to create a background for light-coloured motifs.

Large jugs, usually called harvest jugs, were the most accomplished products of Bideford and Barnstaple potters in the eighteenth and nineteenth centuries. Many of them bear inscriptions relating to ploughing and harvesting, but their decoration often reflects the importance of the sea in Devon life. Ships, mariners' compasses and ships' wheels were favourite motifs. Some examples, such as the one shown here, evidently had no connection with the harvest, but instead commemorated an event, such as a ship's maiden voyage, or crossing the Line. Another jug by John Hoyle (Fitzwilliam Museum, C.75–1928), bears the name of the *Sarah Newman*, a vessel of 1,220 tons which was built at Bideford.

Further reading R.H. Phillips, 'The Bideford pottery industry', *Devon Historian*, 2 (April 1971), pp. 11–14, and 3 (October 1971), pp. 3–6. Alison Grant, *North Devon Pottery: the Seventeenth Century*, 1983.

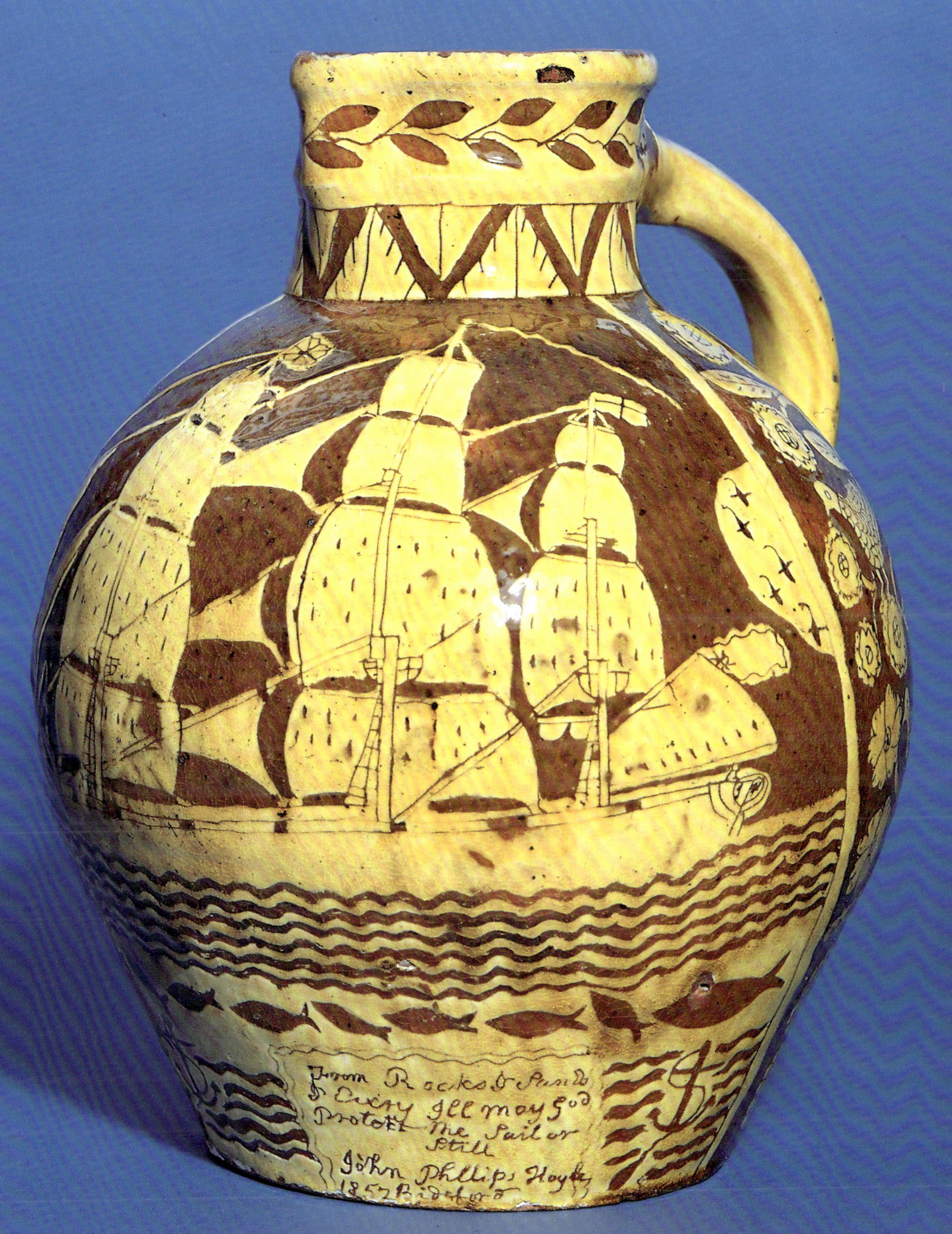
From Rocks & Sands
& Every Ill may God
Protect the Sailor
Still
John Phillips Hoyle
1857 Bideford

53

GIANT TEAPOT

PROBABLY CHURCH
GRESLEY OR WOODVILLE,
DERBYSHIRE, 1882.

Buff earthenware decorated with applied white reliefs coloured pink, blue and green under clear glaze, reserved in a brown glazed ground. One relief is impressed with 'A PRESENT FROM.J. SAY TO MRS BARNES 1882'. *Height 34.5 cm.* C.765–1928.

Brown 'Rockingham' glazed earthenware was made by several potteries at Church Gresley and Woodville in South Derbyshire during the late nineteenth and early twentieth centuries. It became known as 'Measham' or 'barge ware' because much of it was sold at Measham, Leicestershire, to bargees who called there when travelling along the Ashby-de-la-Zouche canal.

Giant teapots were the *pièces de resistance* and may have miniature teapots as knobs (for example, one in the Fitzwilliam Museum, C.766–1928). Other typical giftware included tobacco jars, jugs, kettles and chamber pots. Unlike most 'Rockingham' glazed earthenware, which was usually monochrome, Measham ware was decorated with applied sprigs of flowers and birds in white clay, coloured dark pink, green and blue. These stand out cheerfully from the shiny brown glaze which covers the rest of the surface. In addition some pieces have applied panels impressed in type with phrases, such as 'LOVE AT HOME', 'A PRESENT FROM A FRIEND' or 'A PRESENT FROM' followed by the donor and recipient's names and rarely, the date. This pot, like most Measham ware, is unmarked. It may have been made at Mason's pottery in Church Gresley, later Mason, Cash & Co. whose mark is occasionally found on Measham ware.

Further reading Griselda Lewis, *A Collector's History of English Pottery*, 4th revised edn, 1987, pp. 236–9.

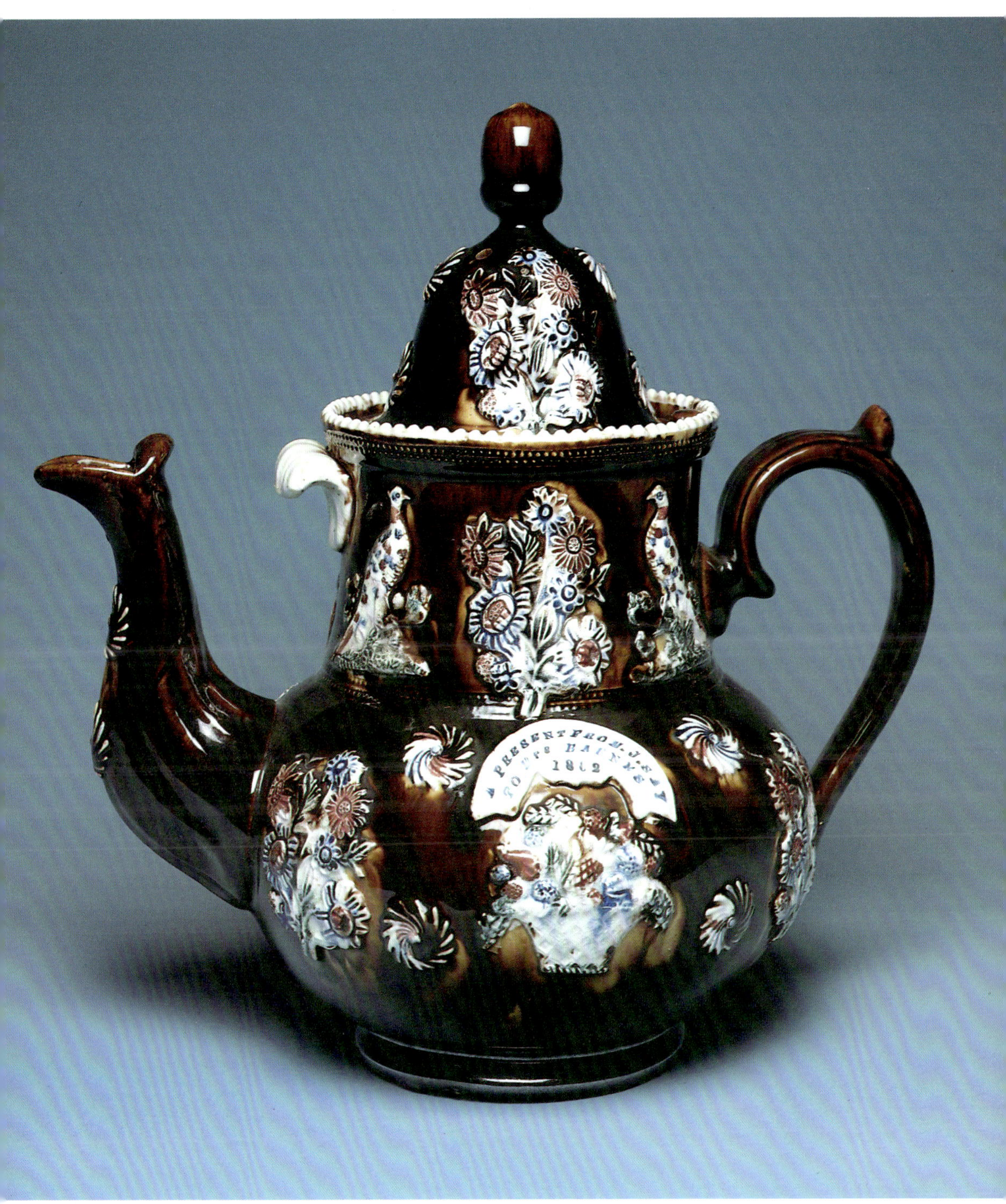
A PRESENT FROM

54

FLAGON

DOULTON & CO., LAMBETH; DECORATED BY GEORGE TINWORTH, 1874.

Salt-glazed stoneware with incised and applied decoration; silver mounts and cover, engraved with two crests and the motto 'FORCE AVEC VERTU'. *Marks:* 'DOULTON/1874/LAMBETH' *in oval seal; incised 'GT' monogram. Height 29 cm.* C.7–1971.

George Tinworth (1843–1913) took lessons in modelling at the Lambeth School of Art and the Royal Academy before joining Henry Doulton's Lambeth Pottery in 1866. During his first few years there he was responsible for the introduction of decorative salt-glazed stoneware. Appreciation of Tinworth's work at the Paris Exhibition of 1867 led to Doulton's engagement of other decorators, beginning with Hannah and Arthur Barlow in 1871. Their success and the long-lived popularity of 'Doulton Lambeth Ware' owed much to the firm's Art Director, Wilton P. Rix, who developed new bodies, pigments, coloured slips and glazes suitable for firing at the high temperatures required for stoneware.

Tinworth was a modeller and decorator, rather than a potter. Vessels were thrown to his instructions, and he added decoration, working extremely swiftly and often for hours on end in bursts of enthusiasm. The incised scrolling foliage, applied flower heads and beading on this flagon are typical of his style in the early 1870s. The silver cover, with London hallmarks for 1874–5, bears the crests of Egerton Leigh of West Hall, High Leigh, Cheshire, who was married in 1874 to Lady Elizabeth Mary, eldest daughter of the third Earl of Bantry.

Tinworth decorated thousands of pots during his long career at Doulton's, but this work was really an offshoot of his activity as a sculptor. He was better known for his unconventional terracotta and stoneware reliefs of religious subjects, some of which were exhibited at the Royal Academy. He also modelled lively and amusing figures of boy musicians, frogs and mice.

Further reading Richard Dennis, *Catalogue of an Exhibition of Doulton Stoneware and Terracotta 1870–1925*, 1971. Desmond Eyles, *The Doulton Lambeth Wares*, 1975. Peter Rose, *George Tinworth*, 1982.

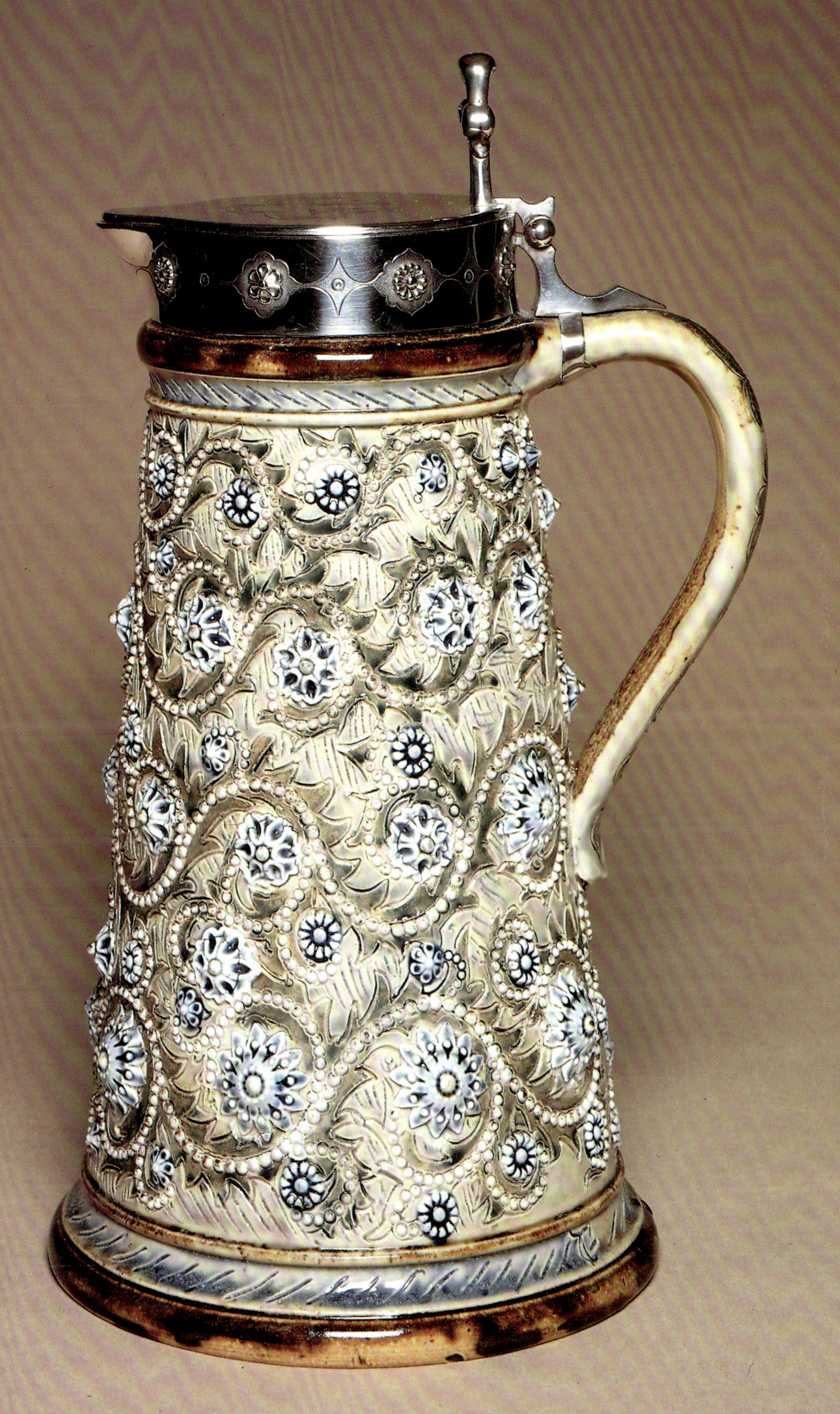

55

TILE PICTURE

WILLIAM DE MORGAN & CO.,
SANDS END POTTERY, FULHAM,
c. 1888–97.

Earthenware, coated with white slip and decorated underglaze in 'Persian colours'. Height 87.3 cm, width 51 cm. C.1–1976.

When William De Morgan (1839–1917) began to decorate tiles in about 1870, the Victorian boom in tile-manufacturing was at its height. Tiles were to be seen in almost every type of building and a immense repertoire of patterns was available. However, most tiles were mass-produced by industrial processes, and inevitably their decoration lacked spontaneity. William De Morgan, like William Morris, whom he first met in 1863, rejected mass production in favour of traditional methods adapted to modern conditions.

During the 1870s and 1880s he devised methods for hand-making and decorating tiles, the latter known as the 'Persian *faïence*' technique. This involved coating the fired tile with white slip to which a traced and hand-painted transfer was applied face down before glazing. During firing the transfer burned away, leaving the design under the glaze. The traced transfer technique permitted several tiles to be made to the same design, without sacrificing the handcraft element in production.

De Morgan's strongly linear designs were ideal for the decoration of flat tiled surfaces and their bright colouring stood out well from a distance. The brilliant turquoise and cobalt blues, green and aubergine used for this panel were described by De Morgan as 'Persian colours' although they were influenced as much by Damascus and Isnik tiles as by Persian prototypes.

Further reading William Gaunt and M.D.E. Clayton-Stamm, *William De Morgan*, 1971. Jon Catleugh, *William De Morgan Tiles*, 1983. Martin Greenwood, *The Designs of William De Morgan*, 1989.

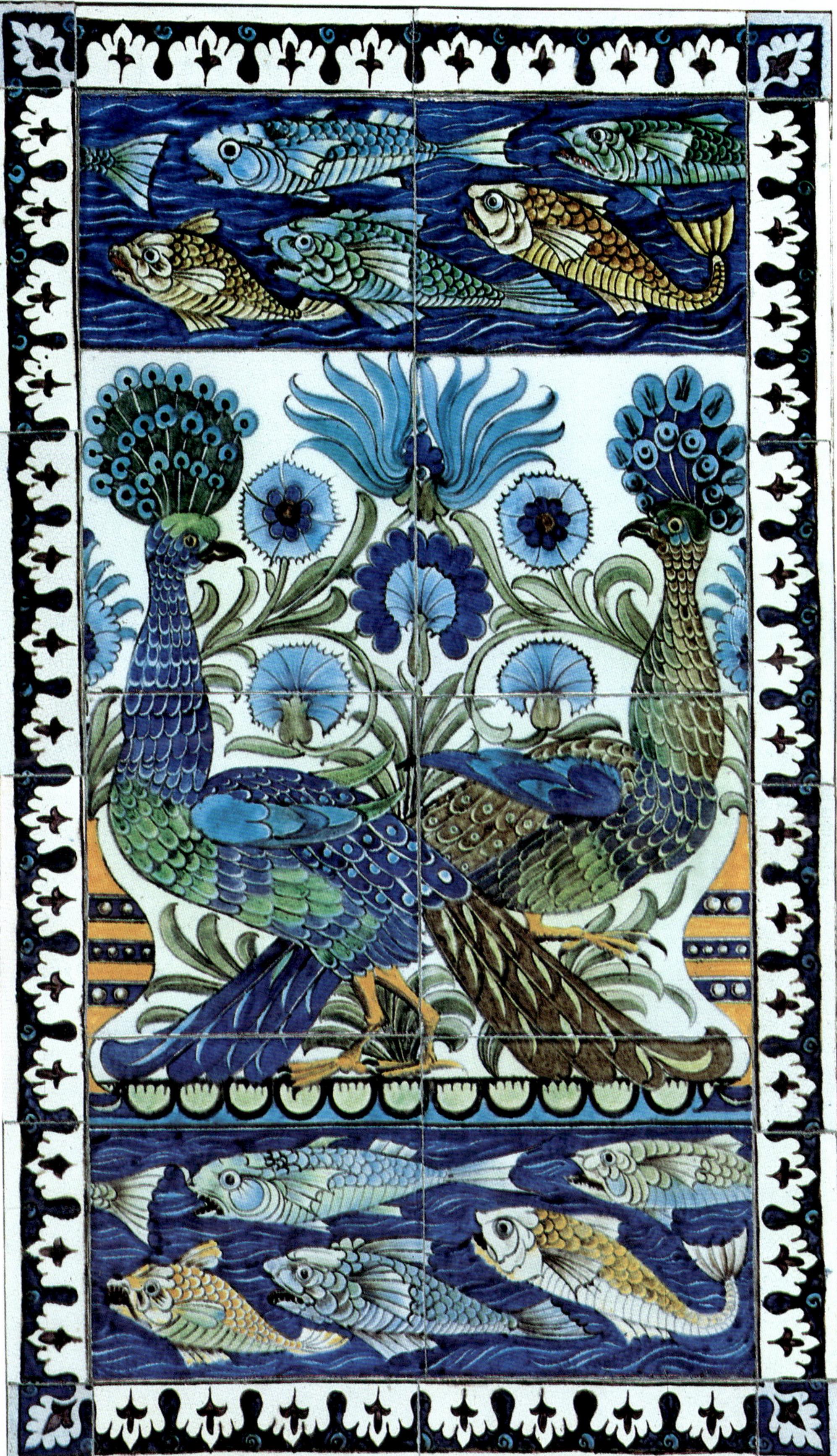

56

OWL

MARTIN BROTHERS, SOUTHALL, MODELLED BY ROBERT WALLACE MARTIN, SEPTEMBER 1903.

Salt-glazed stoneware decorated with blue, brown and sage-green slips. Marks: 'R.W. Martin. & Brothers. London & Southall. England' and 'R.W.M. S^c.' incised round the neck; '9 1903/R.W. Martin & Bros/London & Southall' incised on the base. Height 103 cm. C.41–1928.

Robert Wallace Martin (1843–1923) and his brothers Walter (1857–1912) and Edwin (1860–1915) set up a pottery at Pomona House, Fulham in 1873. At first they had their stoneware salt-glazed at the Fulham pottery, but after moving to Southall in 1877 they were able to make, decorate and fire their own work. Another brother, Charles (1846–1910), managed the business and sold their pottery at a shop and gallery in Brownlow Street, off Holborn in London.

Wallace Martin, who had trained as a sculptor, concentrated on modelling. He had a lively imagination which gave rise to a procession of grotesque and humorous creatures masquerading as jugs, spoon-warmers and toast-racks. His bird jars, known as 'Wally Birds', are vaguely rook-like and have curiously human expressions. His owls are truer to nature, and were probably inspired by earlier slipware and salt-glazed stoneware owls. Most of these birds are 20–35 cm high, but Martin also made a few giant owls, of which this example measuring 103 cm is the largest known.

In 1893 he is said to have made a punch bowl 'in the shape of a monster owl' for the Bohemian Club of San Francisco, a literary club founded in 1872 which has an owl as its emblem. According to the ceramic historian J. F. Blacker, Wallace's first model developed a firing crack and was not dispatched, but another arrived safely only to be destroyed in the 1906 earthquake. The Fitzwilliam Museum's owl also has a firing crack, and probably for that reason remained at the pottery until Wallace Martin's death in 1923.

Further reading Malcolm Haslam, *English Art Pottery 1865–1915*, 1975, pp. 48–54. Malcolm Haslam, *The Martin Brothers Potters*, 1978.

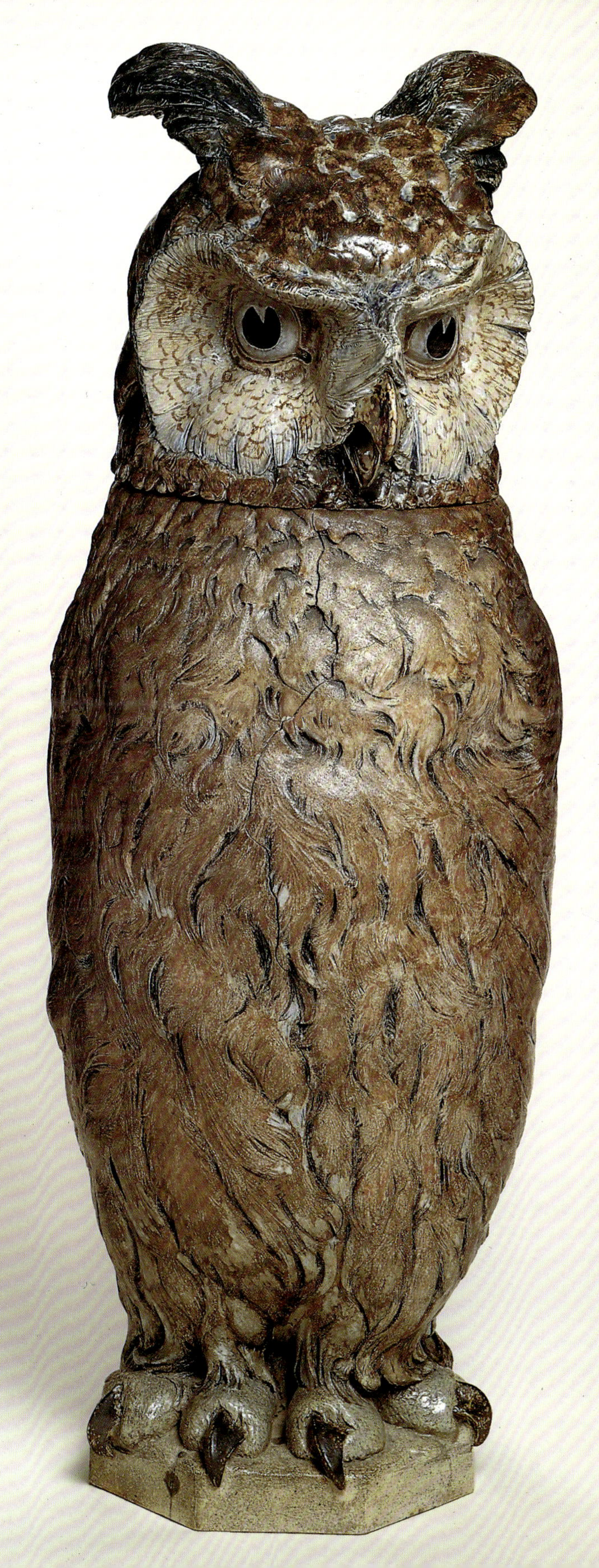

57

HOP JUG

BELLE VUE POTTERY,

RYE, SUSSEX,

1899.

Earthenware decorated with applied moulded hops and green and brown glazes. Inscribed on the neck 'J.W.L. Glaisher 1899'. Mark: 'Rye Pottery/F Mitchell/1899' incised into base. Height 22.1 cm. C.38B–1928.

The Belle Vue Pottery at Rye was one of several English country potteries which made 'Art Pottery' as well as traditional useful wares. It was founded in 1868 by Frederick Mitchell (1819–75) whose nephew, Frederick Thomas Mitchell (1864–1920), made this jug for Dr J.W.L. Glaisher, a fellow of Trinity College, Cambridge. In the 1870s the pottery became famous for pig-shaped flasks known as 'Sussex pigs', and 'hop wares' which were decorated with moulded and applied wreaths of hops and glazed green and brown. Unlike many green glazes which were derived from copper, this was coloured with brass dust produced in the manufacture of pins. When F.T. Mitchell took over the pottery in 1896 on the death of his uncle's widow, he revived these wares and continued to make them in the early twentieth century. A small puzzle jug decorated with a spray of oak leaves and acorns was purchased by Glaisher on another visit in 1912 (Fitzwilliam Museum, C.83C-1928).

Further reading Malcolm Haslam, *English Art Pottery 1865–1915*, 1975. John Manwaring Baines, *Sussex Pottery*, 1980, pp. 47–55.

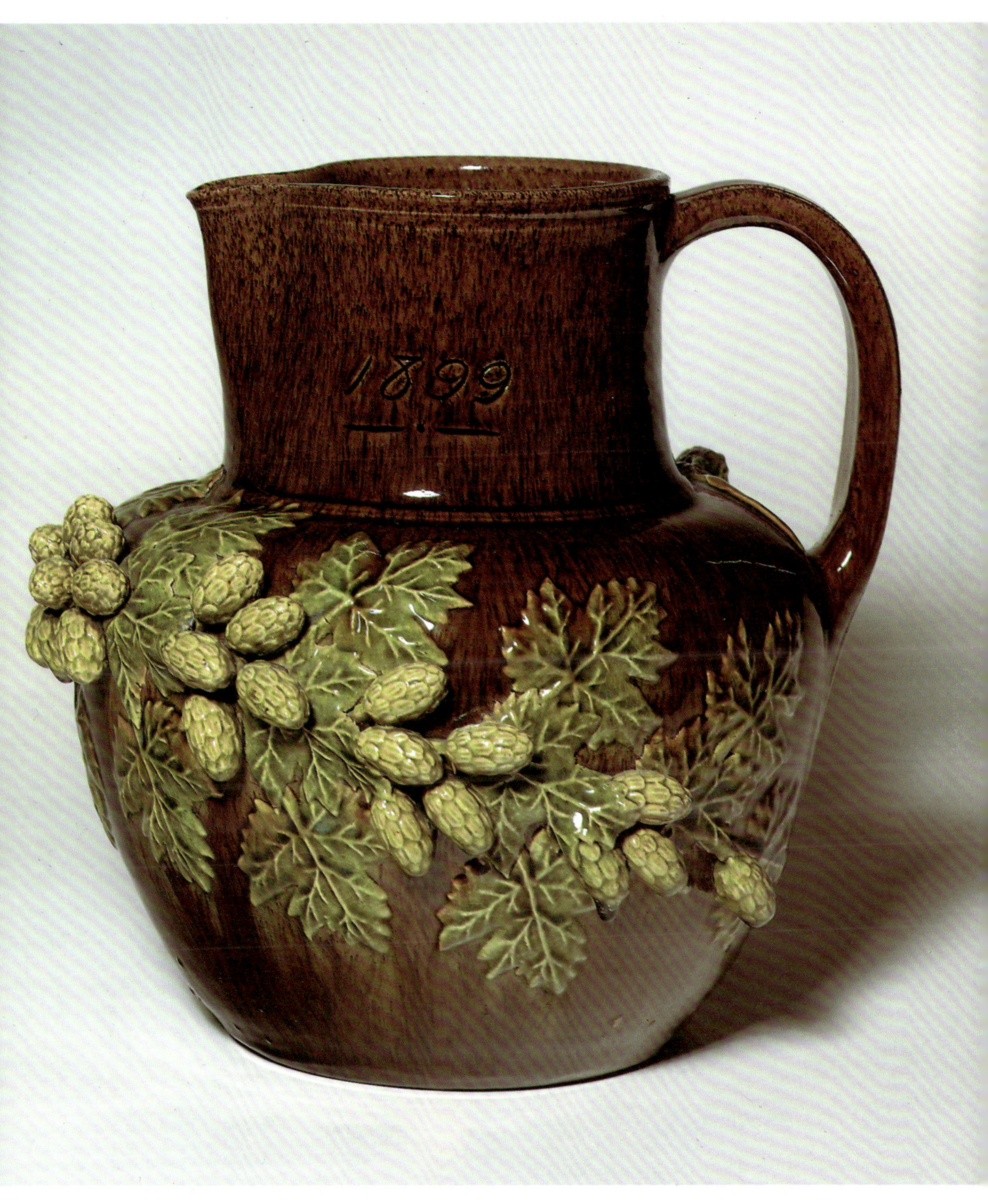
1899

58

VASE

DESIGNED BY WILLIAM MOORCROFT FOR JAMES MACINTYRE & CO., WASHINGTON WORKS, BURSLEM, AND MADE THERE OR AT COBRIDGE c. 1911–13.

*Cream porcellaneous body, the decoration outlined in slip and painted underglaze with 'Pomegranate' pattern. Marks: '*MADE FOR/LIBERTY*' printed in brown; 'W. Moorcroft' signed in green; '1398' impressed. Height 20 cm, diameter 20.3 cm.* C.27–1983.

William Moorcroft (1872–1945) studied art in Burslem, London and Paris before joining James Macintyre & Co. in 1897 as a designer. In 1898 he was appointed manager of the Ornamental Ware department and remained there until 1913, when it closed and he set up his own factory at Cobridge, which is still in existence.

Moorcroft's pottery had curvilinear hand-thrown forms and colourful decoration. The motifs, mainly based on plant forms, were carefully placed on each pot so as to enhance its contours and give an impression of growth. Outlines in raised slip were applied first by tube-lining or slip-trailing and these were painted in with pigments derived from metallic oxides. After firing, the pots were glazed and fired again to enhance the colours. At first Moorcroft used cool shades of blue, yellow and green often on a pale ground. Then from about 1902 gradually developed deeper shades of red, blue, purple and grey underglaze colours.

'Pomegranate' pattern, introduced in 1910, was one of Moorcroft's most popular designs and continued in production at his own factory after 1913. Initially it had a mottled yellowish ground which gave way to darker greens and blues at Cobridge. With several other patterns, it was supplied to Liberty's, the London department store, with a special printed 'MADE FOR LIBERTY & Co' mark in addition to Moorcroft's signature.

Further reading Paul Atterbury, *Moorcroft: a Guide to Moorcroft Pottery*, revised edn, 1990. Victoria Bergesen, *Encyclopaedia of British Art Pottery 1870–1920*, 1991, pp. 166–70 and 206–8.

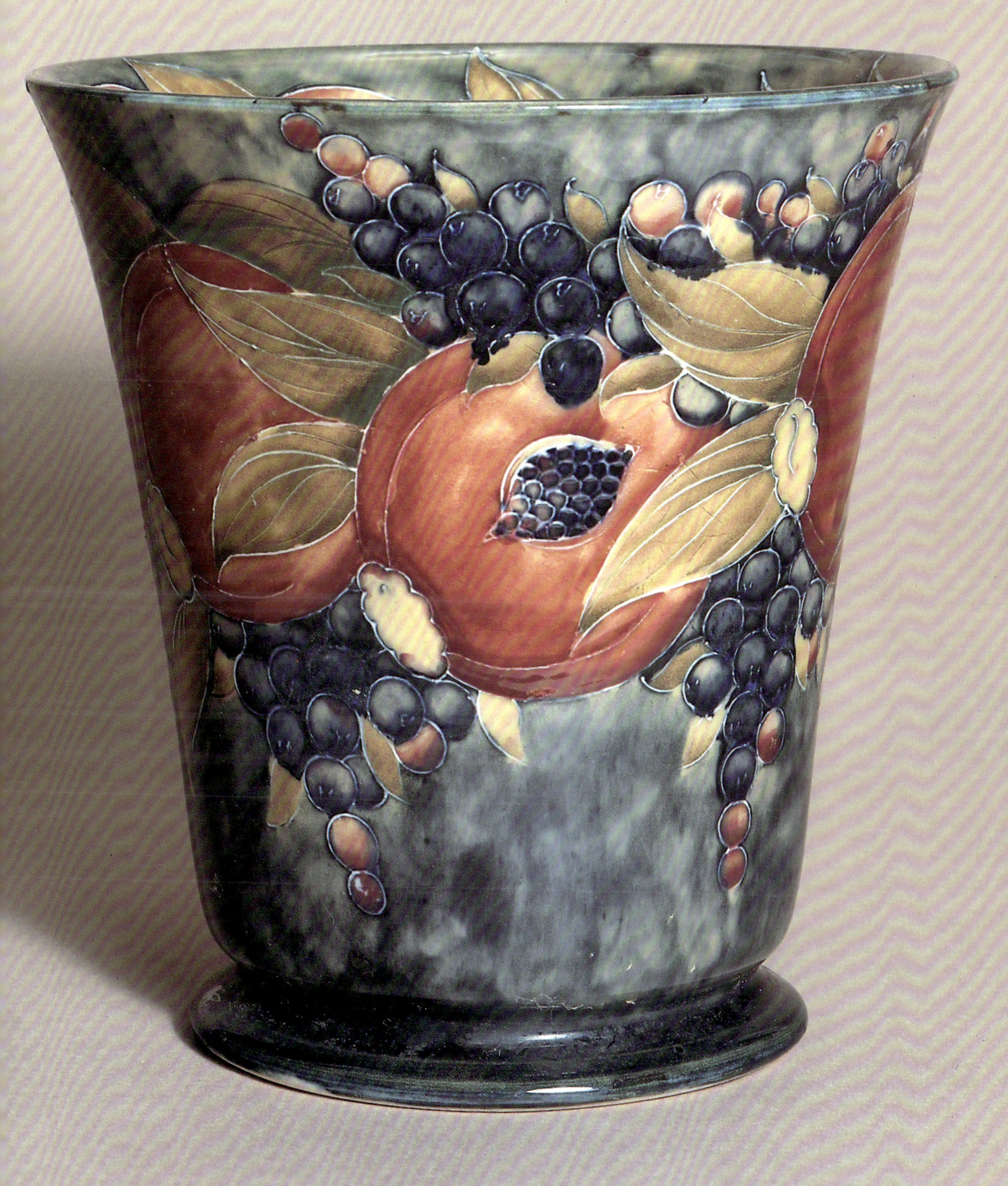

59

DISH

JOSIAH WEDGWOOD & SONS, ETRURIA;
DECORATED BY ALFRED POWELL, c.1908.

Cream-coloured earthenware painted underglaze with details overglaze in enamels. Marks: 'WEDGWOOD' impressed, AP monogram and '455' in black. Diameter 47 cm. C.49–1972.

By the late nineteenth century the increasing use of transfer-printed decoration had brought about a decline in free-hand painting on ceramics. A revival began at Wedgwood's in 1903 when Alfred Hoare Powell (1865–1960) began his long association with the firm as a designer and decorator. In 1906, in conjunction with Wedgwood, he set up a studio at 20 Red Lion Square, London, where he and his wife, Louise Lessore, decorated pottery sent from Etruria. They also made regular visits to the Etruria factory, where they trained paintresses and revived some late eighteenth-century hand-painted patterns.

In his youth Alfred Powell had been inspired by the ideals of the Arts and Crafts Movement and he always remained true to them.The influence of designs by William Morris and Sir Edward Burne-Jones is apparent in the decoration of this dish. The animals amid oak foliage and daisies in pots are reminiscent of the backgrounds of the medieval-style tapestries made by Morris and Company at Merton Abbey. A similar dish with a peacock in the centre is in the Zeitlin Collection.

Many of Powell's designs were based on plant and animal motifs, others incorporated architectural views and calligraphy. These were too intricate for repetition on a commercial scale, but both he and Louise Powell created simpler patterns which were adapted for factory production during the 1920s and 1930s.

Further reading Maureen Batkin, Wedgwood Ceramics 1846–1959, 1982, pp. 139–56. Robin Reilly, *Wedgwood*, vol. II, 1989, pp. 162–73. Cheltenham Art Gallery and Museums, *Alfred and Louise Powell: Good Workmanship with Happy Thoughts*, 1992, pp. 16–22.

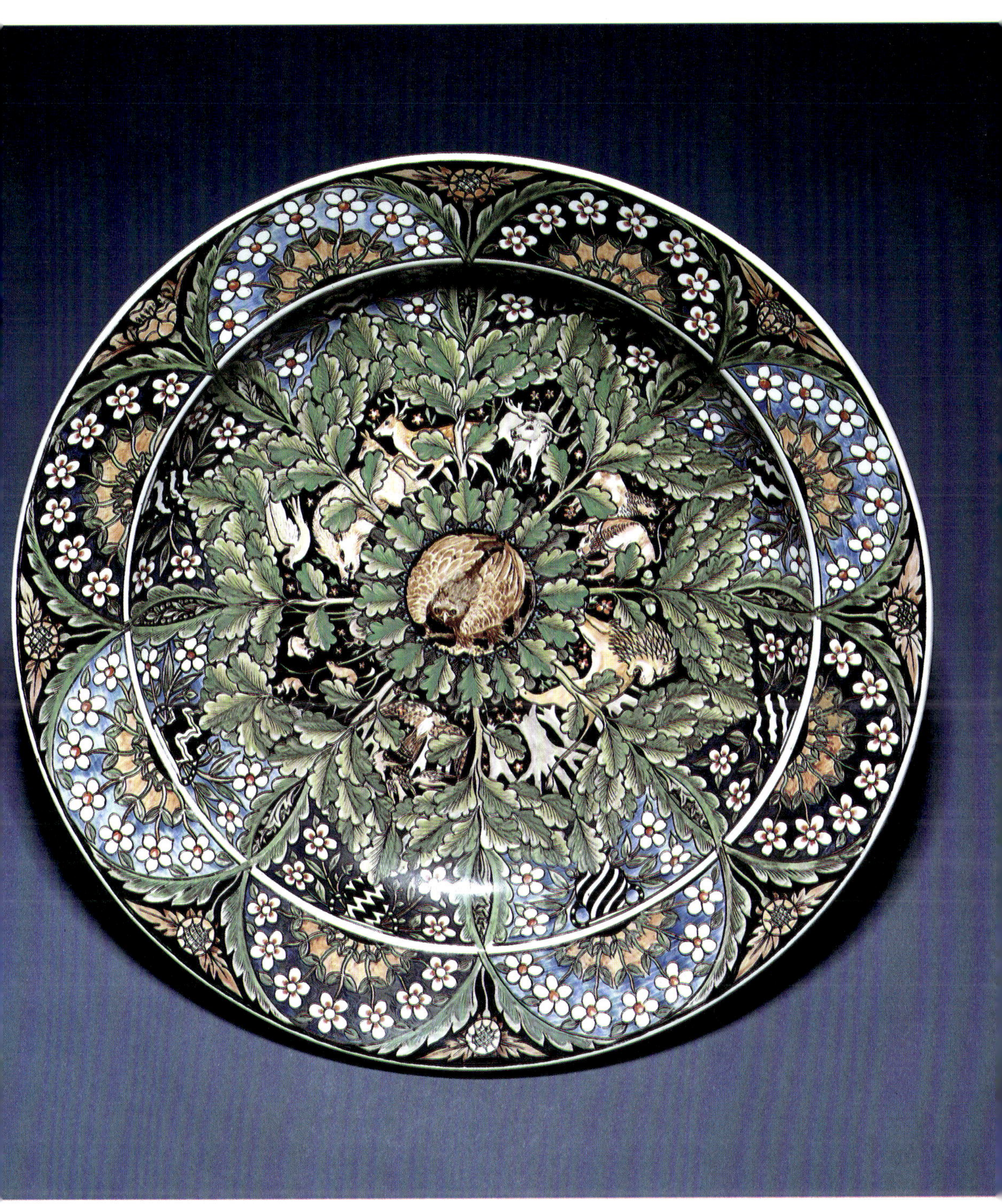

60

JUG

ROYAL DOULTON, BURSLEM,

c. 1930–40.

Earthenware, moulded and painted underglaze. 'Harvest' pattern. Marks: 'Designed by/Frank Brangwyn. R.A.' and 'ROYAL/DOULTON/ENGLAND' printed in dark green; 'D 5011' painted in dark green. Height 21.8 cm. C.12–1980.

'Harvest' pattern, introduced in 1930, was one of a range of designs for tableware and ornaments commissioned by Doulton's from Frank Brangwyn RA between 1928 and 1935. Brangwyn was best known as a mural painter, but had been involved in the design of furniture, textiles and interiors since the beginning of the century. His employment by Doulton's was an unusual step, because the Burslem factory had its own design studio and had rarely commissioned designs from outsiders.

Brangwyn's tablewares were intended for 'people of quite moderate means' and were priced accordingly. A teaset for twelve cost £3.15s.0d. They had simple forms which could be made by industrial processes and gained their individuality from lightly-incised and hand-painted decoration. 'Harvest' pattern was well-received by the critics, but it was not a commercial success and was withdrawn from production in 1940. This was probably because the design fell between two stools. It was very different from traditional tableware, but not sufficiently avant-garde to compete with the modernistic wares being produced by A.J. Wilkinson's Newport works, Gray's Pottery or Wood & Sons.

Further reading Paul Atterbury, 'Brangwyn and Royal Doulton', in *The Art of Frank Brangwyn*, catalogue of an exhibition at the Fine Art Society, London, 1980. Desmond Eyles, *The Doulton Burslem Wares*, 1980, pp. 120–1.

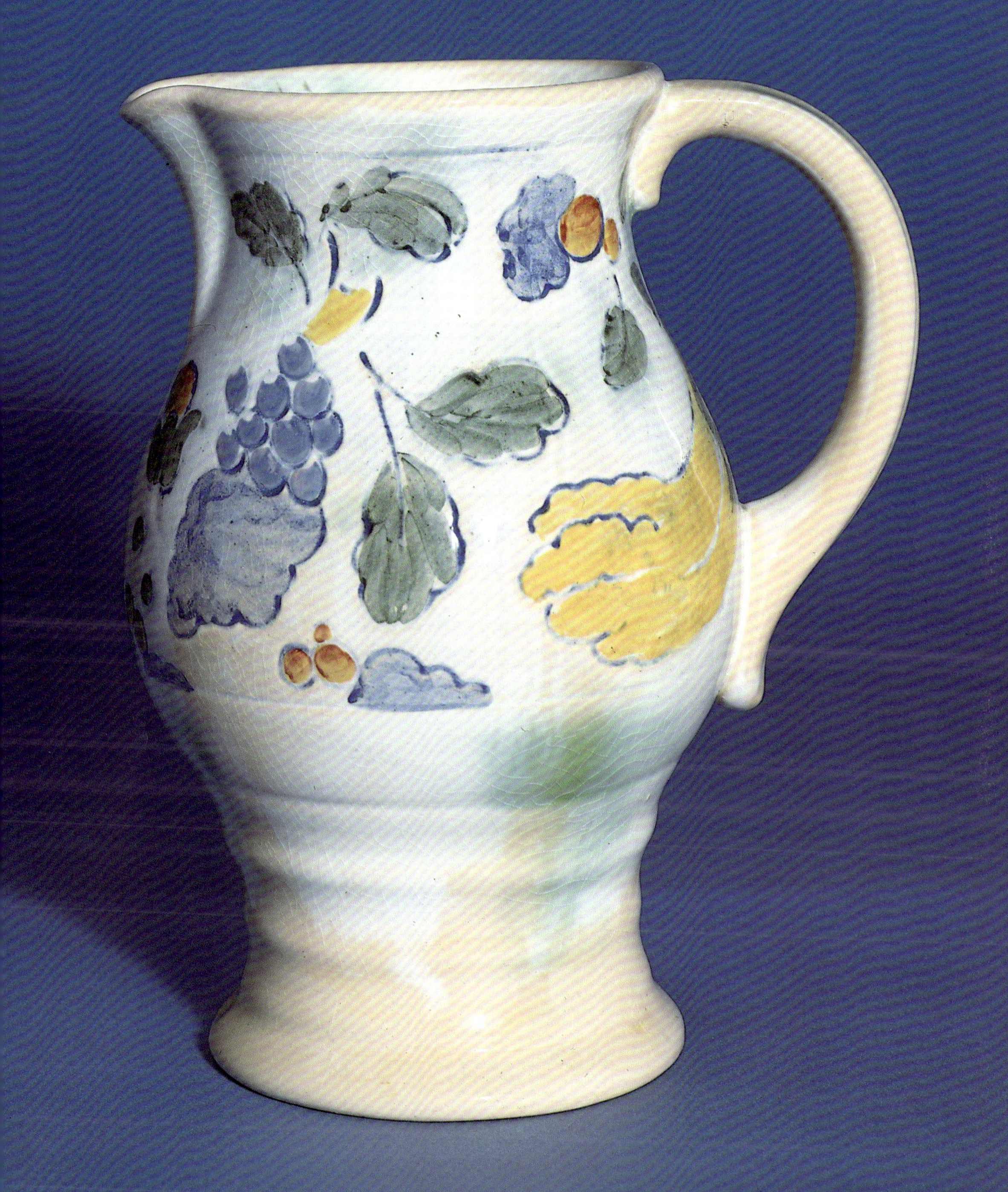

61

DINNER PLATE

JOSIAH WEDGWOOD & SONS,
BARLASTON, 1955.

Queen's Ware, printed in black and gilt.
Marks: 'WEDGWOOD/2 R 55' *impressed;*
circular printed Wedgwood mark; 'G 5558/2'
painted in red and '3' *printed in grey.*
Diameter 27.2 *cm.* C.2–1969.

In 1952 wartime restrictions on the making of decorated tableware for the home market were lifted, opening the way for the introduction of 'Contemporary' tableware with curving shapes and colourful patterns. This plate is not typically 'Contemporary' but it resembles many fifties tablewares in having bold linear motifs contrasting with a pale ground. The pattern was designed in 1952 by Richard Guyatt, Professor of Graphic Design at the Royal College of Art, for a service commissioned from Wedgwood for the high table of King's College, Cambridge. The central Tudor Rose made up of lovers' knots, encloses the ciphers of Henry VI, who founded the College in 1441, Henry VII and Henry VIII. The motif on the rim, an h formed by a dragon with its head in a cleft stake, was taken from windows in the College Chapel. Initially the service was made in Queen's Ware, but since 1971, when a larger service was ordered, it has been made in metallized bone china by Wedgwood's Hotelware Division.

Tableware for use in hotels and institutions has become an increasingly significant aspect of the ceramic industry during the second half of the twentieth century. Some of these 'hotelwares' are forms of bone china, while others, such as Steelite, have tough vitreous bodies strengthened by the addition of aluminium oxide.

Further reading Kathy Niblett, *Wedgwood of Etruria and Barlaston*, 1980, p. 126. Kathy Niblett, *Dynamic Design, the British Pottery Industry 1940–1990*, 1990.

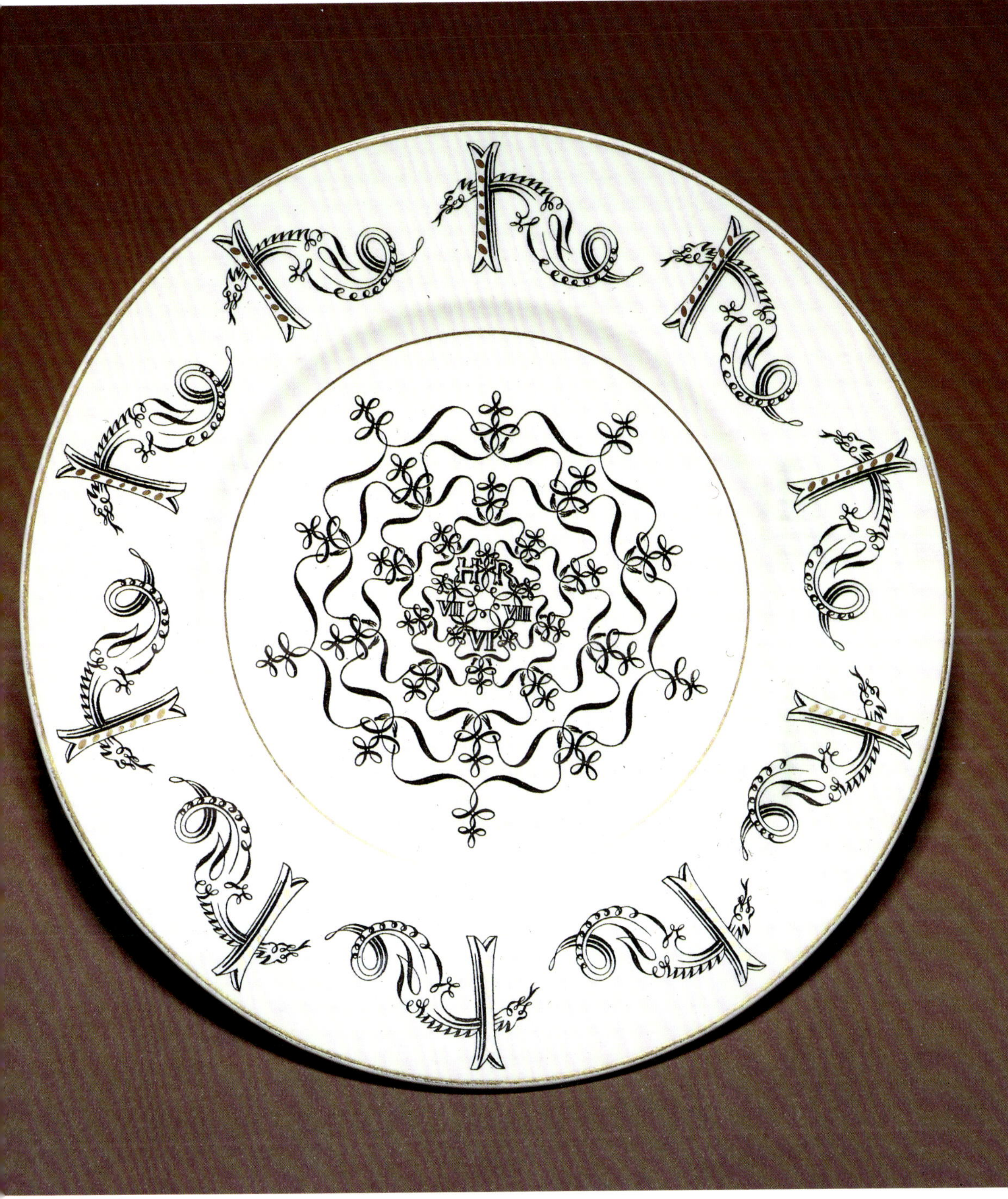

HR
VII VIII
VI

62

PAGODA-LIDDED BOWL

BERNARD LEACH, ST IVES,
CORNWALL, c. 1960–5.

Thrown and turned stoneware with brown glaze and incised decoration. Marks: square seal with 'BL' and circular seal with 'SI' impressed. Height 22.5 cm. C.22–1972.

Bernard Leach (1887–1979) went to Tokyo in 1909 to teach etching, then unknown in Japan, but was so impressed by *raku* earthenware that in 1911 he decided to become a potter. He studied in Tokyo under Ogata Kenzan VI, and later worked at kilns elsewhere in Japan before setting up his own. In 1920 he returned to England and with the help of Hamada Shoji (1892–1978) founded a pottery at St Ives, the first in the West to have an Oriental wood-fired climbing kiln. Japanese *raku* glazed ware, slipware and stoneware were made during the pottery's early years, but it was Leach's stoneware which had the greatest impact on the development of studio pottery during the mid-twentieth century. His philosophy and publications, such as *The Potter's Book*, were also immensely influential.

Although he greatly admired Oriental ceramics, Leach also drew inspiration from traditional English pottery, such as medieval jugs and seventeenth- and eighteenth-century slipwares. He deplored the 'inappropriateness of decoration and tawdriness of form' of many early twentieth-century factory-made ceramics, and stressed the importance of creating each pot as a whole which had an expressive and satisfying balance between form, glaze and decoration. Rejecting the quest for novelty which dogged Western craftsmen, he concentrated on a few forms and decorative themes which he repeated with subtle modulations throughout his long career. This covered bowl is essentially functional, but its sweeping contours and simple incised decoration make it equally pleasing to the eye.

Further reading Carol Hogben (ed.), *The Art of Bernard Leach*, 1978. T. Birks and C.W. Digby, *Bernard Leach, Hamada and their Circle*, 1990. Oliver Watson, *British Studio Pottery, the Victoria and Albert Museum Collection*, 1990, pp. 199–208.

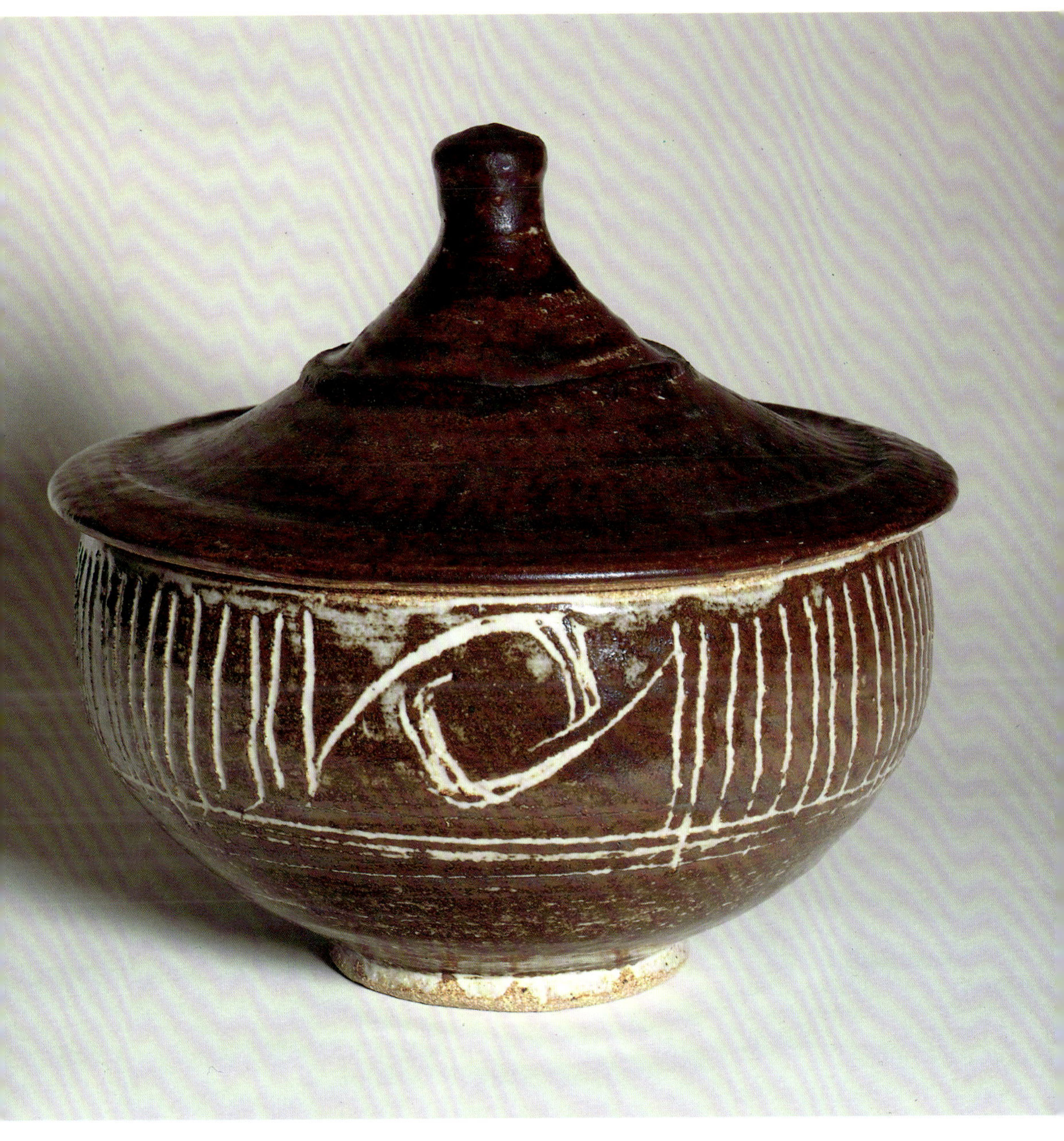

63

VASE

HANS COPER, c. 1966–70.

Thrown stoneware coated with white slip over manganese and sanded to create a textured surface before firing. Marks: impressed oval seal with 'HC' monogram. Height 27 cm. C.36–1972.

Hans Coper (1920–81) came to England as a refugee from Germany in 1939. After the war he went to work for Lucie Rie, an Austrian studio potter (b. 1902) who had been in London since 1938. On her advice he took lessons in throwing from Heber Mathews at Woolwich Polytechnic and quickly became adept. During the late 1940s and 1950s he and Lucie Rie produced tableware to support themselves while each evolved their own highly individualistic styles. In 1959 Coper moved to Digswell Arts Trust in Hertfordshire, and he later worked at Hammersmith and at Frome in Somerset.

Although Coper's pots have a sculptural quality, they were created mainly by the basic ceramic technique of throwing. Their striking forms, often made up of two or more sections, are enhanced by subtle texturing and shading of the surface. Coper's style owed nothing to Oriental or folk pottery but was influenced to some extent by that of Pre-Dynastic Egypt, the Cyclades and ancient Greece. Thoroughly modern and innovative, his work provided a new source of inspiration for studio potters, but stands austerely apart from the English ceramic tradition.

Further reading Tony Birks, *Hans Coper*, 1983. Norwich, Sainsbury Centre for the Visual Arts, *Lucie Rie, Hans Coper and their Pupils*, exhibition catalogue, 1990.

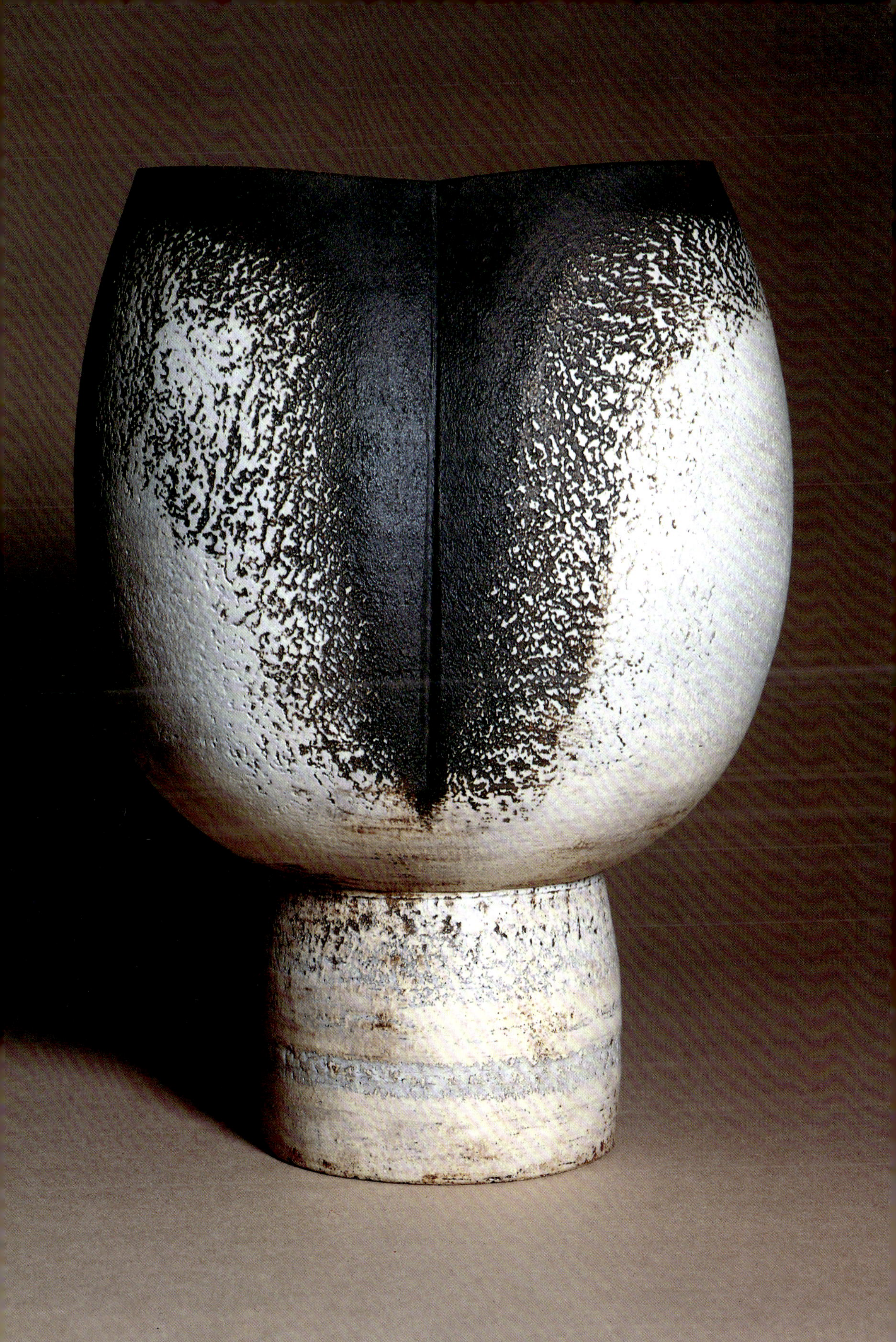

64

DEEP-SIDED BOWL ON A HIGH FOOT

ALAN CAIGER-SMITH,
ALDERMASTON POTTERY,
1981.

Tin-glazed earthenware decorated with lustre.
Mark: ACS monogram, date symbol, and 10 A.
Height 16.3 cm, diameter 44.4 cm.
C.39–1981.

This splendid bowl illustrates the calligraphic brush-stroke style which was the leitmotif of the Aldermaston Pottery, founded by Alan Caiger-Smith in 1955. During the 1960s it became famous for its tin-glazed earthenware with colourful inglaze decoration and overglaze reduced-lustre pigments, which contain compounds of silver and copper.

Unlike most contemporary studio potters who worked alone, Alan Caiger-Smith (b. 1930) established a workshop at Aldermaston in which he and one or more experienced potters, notably Edgar Camden, worked together with students who stayed for short periods. This traditional approach enabled the pottery to produce 'bread and butter' wares, such as mugs and jugs, while allowing individuals to develop a personal style for commissioned work. It also ensured that the tin-glaze and lustre techniques which Alan Caiger-Smith painstakingly revived and developed were passed on to younger potters. Unfortunately, despite his success, tin-glazed earthenware has remained an unfashionable technique in Britain, and the Aldermaston Pottery closed in 1993.

Further reading Alan Caiger-Smith, *Lustre Pottery*, 1985. Stoke-on-Trent, City Museum and Art Gallery, *Alan Caiger-Smith Tin-Glaze and Smoked Lustre Pottery by Alan Caiger-Smith and Aldermaston Pottery 1955–85*, 1985. Daphne Carnegie, *Tin-glazed Earthenware*, 1993.

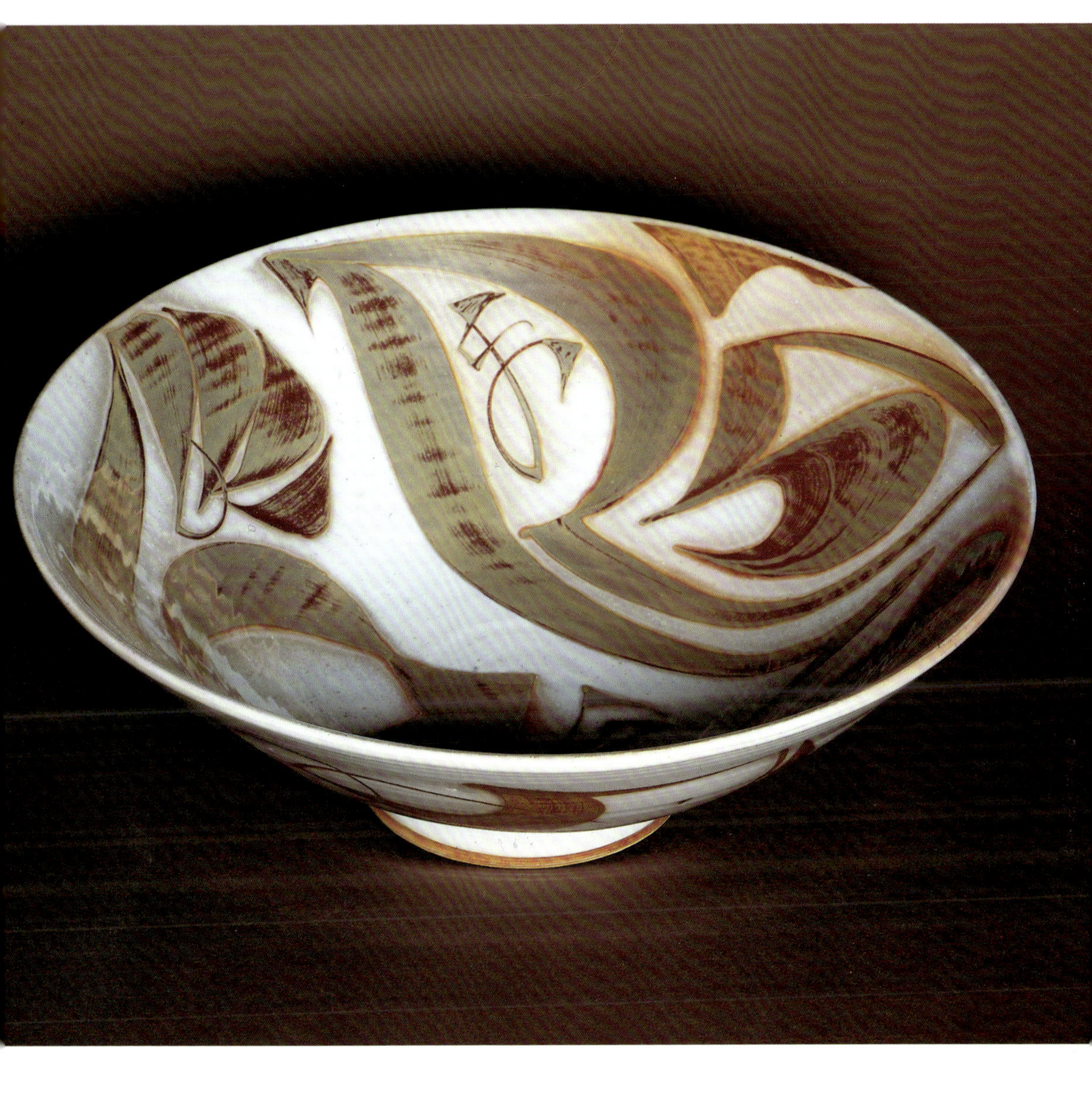

TABLEAUX
DES CONTRAVENTIONS
ET DES PEINES
EN MATIÈRE
DE CONTRIBUTIONS INDIRECTES.

DEUXIÈME ÉDITION,

AUGMENTÉE DES DISPOSITIONS CONCERNANT LE CONTENTIEUX DE LA RÉGIE ET CELUI DES OCTROIS,

AINSI QUE D'UNE COLLECTION DE MODÈLES A L'USAGE DES EMPLOYÉS DES DEUX ADMINISTRATIONS;

PAR D. GIRARD,

PREMIER COMMIS DE LA DIRECTION DES DROITS D'ENTRÉE DE PARIS.

Prix, 2 fr. 50 cent., et 3 fr. par la poste.

A PARIS,

Chez l'Auteur, rue des Francs-Bourgeois, n° 21.

DE L'IMPRIMERIE DE J. SMITH, RUE MONTMORENCY, N°. 16.

1818.

NOTA. Les articles des lois insérés en *lettres italiques* dans les tableaux, après chacun des cas de contravention, sont ceux que les Employés doivent citer dans les procès-verbaux.

ABRÉVIATIONS.

Adm. des Mon.	Administration des Monnaies.
Arr.	Arrêt de la Cour de cassation.
Art.	Article.
Circ.	Circulaire.
Coll.	Collection des Arrêts de la Cour de cassation.
D. A.	Décision du Conseil d'administration.
Mém.	Mémorial du Contentieux.
Rec.	Recueil des lois et instructions de la Régie.

TABLE

Des Lois et Réglemens cités dans cet ouvrage, avec indication de ceux qui sont insérés au Recueil général.

Loi du 13 fructidor an 5, *annexée à l'Instruction n° 45.*
— du 19 brumaire an 6, *Rec.*, *tom.* 1, *p.* 242.
Arrêté du 5 pluviôse an 6, — — *p.* 171.
—— du 19 floréal an 6, — — *p.* 174.
Loi du 6 frimaire an 7, — — *p.* 591.
— du 27 frimaire an 8, — *tom.* 2, *p.* 518.
Arrêté du 8 prairial an 11, *Rec.*, *tom.* 1, *p.* 424.
Décret du 14 fructidor an 12, — — *p.* 318.
— du 23 pluviôse an 13, *annexé à l'Instruction n° 45.*
— du 1er germinal an 13, *Rec.*, *tom.* 1, *p.* 18.
— du 4 prairial an 13, — — *p.* 107.
— du 13 fructidor an 13, — — *p.* 179.
Loi du 24 avril 1806, *Rec.*, *tom.* 3, *p.* 1.
Décret du 11 juin 1806, — — *p.* 102.
—— du 18 août 1807, *Mém.*, *tom.* 2, *p.* 559.
—— du 16 juin 1808, *Rec.*, *tom.* 4, *p.* 235.
—— du 9 février 1810, — *tom.* 5, *p.* 115.
Ordonnance du 9 décembre 1814.
Loi du 28 avril 1816.
— du 25 mars 1817.
— du 15 mai 1818, dont l'art. 84 proroge les deux lois précédentes jusqu'au 1er avril 1819.

Le principal motif qui a déterminé la publication de ces Tableaux a été de faciliter aux Employés l'application des lois et de faire cesser l'alternative dans laquelle ils se trouvaient placés, ou de se charger, lorsqu'ils s'éloignent de leur résidence, de collections trop volumineuses, ou d'opérer de mémoire dans beaucoup d'occasions.

Sans prétendre que ce travail ait complétement atteint ce but, qu'on ne pouvait se promettre d'un premier essai, on a du moins lieu de penser, d'après les soins dont il a été l'objet, qu'il sera facile de suppléer aux imperfections qui peuvent s'y rencontrer.

En trouvant réunies, dans des cadres resserrés, les dispositions législatives sur lesquelles repose la garantie des perceptions, MM. les Employés apprécieront l'étendue des moyens que la loi met entre leurs mains pour la répression de la fraude; mais en même temps ils ne sauraient considérer ces dispositions comme devant frapper sans distinction l'erreur ou la mauvaise foi; ils ne peuvent se méprendre à ce point sur les intentions de l'Administration dont ils connaissent tous l'esprit de justice et d'indulgence; ils savent que, se bornant aux mesures nécessaires à la sûreté des droits, elle réprouve tout ce qui va au-delà; et que, toujours disposée à excuser l'inexpérience, elle ne veut en général punir les contraventions que lorsqu'elles décèlent un caractère de fraude ou de résistance à la loi.

Ce n'est donc pas à eux que ces observations s'adressent; mais comme cet ouvrage pourrait tomber entre les mains de personnes étrangères à l'Administration, il importe peut-être de les prévenir contre l'impression que produiraient sur elles toutes ces dispositions, en apparence sévères ou minutieuses, et dont l'utilité ne peut être bien appréciée par des hommes peu familiarisés avec le système général de l'impôt, et qui ne sont pas à portée de connaître toutes les combinaisons de la cupidité pour en détourner le produit.

Ce qui doit principalement écarter toute fausse interprétation des intentions de la Régie, c'est l'application qu'elle fait constamment de la faculté qui lui est accordée de transiger sur les amendes et confiscations; cette faculté a cela de remarquable, qu'il ne peut jamais en être fait usage que dans l'intérêt des contrevenans. L'exercice en est délégué à MM. les Directeurs qui, placés dans le lieu même où siége le tribunal, sont ainsi à portée de discerner toutes les nuances des affaires; et on ne doit pas omettre de dire que les Magistrats chargés de prononcer sur les procès-verbaux et d'appliquer les peines, concourent fréquemment eux-mêmes aux bienfaits de la transaction. Leur intervention est toujours efficace, auprès de l'Administration ou de ses Employés supérieurs, lorsqu'ils recommandent à son indulgence ceux qu'ils en trouvent dignes.

Les arrêts cités, bien que nombreux et portant quelquefois sur des objets d'un faible intérêt, ne sauraient contredire ce qu'on vient d'avancer. La Régie ne pourrait, sans compromettre la perception, laisser prévaloir des doctrines erronées ; mais il suffit d'ouvrir le Mémorial du contentieux, où ces arrêts sont consignés, pour être convaincu que ce n'est que dans l'intérêt des principes, et par la nécessité de maintenir une jurisprudence uniforme, que les jugemens des premiers tribunaux sont déférés à la Cour de cassation. Ces arrêts ne servent jamais de prétexte pour imposer, dans la transaction, des conditions plus sévères que celles qui auraient été consenties avant le commencement de toute procédure.

On fera remarquer enfin, par la distribution même des tableaux, que, si les dispositions qu'ils renferment paraissent multipliées lorsqu'on les considère dans leur ensemble, il n'en est plus de même si elles sont prises isolément, puisqu'elles se trouvent divisées entre plusieurs assujétis d'états tout-à-fait distincts, et qui ne sont obligés qu'à celles qui leur sont propres. On fera remarquer surtout que, loin d'être gênantes et vexatoires, leur principal objet étant de suivre la matière imposable, et d'en faire rendre un compte exact, elles tendent à mettre dans le commerce des redevables l'ordre et la régularité que les négocians de bonne foi y établissent d'eux-mêmes.

Ces réflexions seront sans doute justifiées par la forme de cet ouvrage qui présente les lois de la Régie sous leur aspect le plus sévère.

Nos.	MOTIFS DES PROCÈS-VERBAUX.	OBJETS A SAISIR et peines encourues.
1	Enlèvement de vins, cidres, poirés (1, p. 29), eaux-de-vie, esprits et liqueurs (*) sans déclaration, et transport des mêmes boissons, sans qu'elles soient accompagnées d'une expédition de la Régie (2, p. 29). *Art.* 6 *de la loi du* 28 *avril* 1816.	
2	Défaut d'identité entre les boissons composant un ou plusieurs chargemens, et les expéditions représentées (3, p. 29). *Art.* 10 *id.*	
3	Transport des susdites boissons à une destination autre que celle portée dans les expéditions (4, p. 30) ou avec une expédition dont le délai est expiré (5, p. 30). *Art.* 13 *id.*	Saisie des boissons et des moyens de transport (a). *Art.* 17 *de la loi du* 28 *avril* 1816.
4	Refus de représenter lesdites expéditions à toute réquisition des Employés de la Régie, de ceux des douanes et des octrois (6, p. 30). *Art.* 17 *idem.*	Confiscation des boissons saisies et amende de 100 f. à 600 fr. *Art.* 19, *même loi.*
5	Séjour en route des susdites boissons, pendant plus de vingt-quatre heures, sans déclaration et sans avoir remis les expéditions aux employés de la Régie (7, p. 30). *Art.* 14 *idem.*	
6	Déchargement des mêmes boissons, pendant la route, sans déclaration (8, p. 31), *même article.*	
7	Refus de représenter, à toute réquisition des employés, les boissons déclarées en transit, *même article.*	

(*) S'il s'agit d'hydromel, outre l'article de la loi du 28 avril 1816, spécial à chaque espèce de contravention, il faudra encore citer l'art. 85 de la loi du 25 mars 1817.—Les fruits à l'eau-de-vie sont également compris dans le tarif.

(a) 1. Les Employés ne peuvent retenir les objets qui ne sont pas en fraude. *Art.* 17 *de la loi du* 28 *avril* 1816.

2. La confiscation des boissons emporte avec elle la confiscation des futailles qui les contiennent. *Arr. du* 4 *août* 1808; *Mém. tome* 4, *p.* 586.

3. Les Employés doivent toujours évaluer séparément, et de gré à gré, les moyens de transport, et en offrir la main-levée sous caution solvable, ou consignation du montant de l'évaluation, sans dépasser toutefois le maximum de l'amende.

Nos.	MOTIFS DES PROCÈS-VERBAUX.	OBJETS A SAISIR et peines encourues.
1	Introduction (*dans les villes où la perception est faite à l'entrée*) de vins, cidres, poirés, eaux-de-vie, esprits, liqueurs, vendanges et fruits (*) sans déclaration et paiement des droits (9, p. 31). *Art.* 24 *de la loi du* 28 *avril* 1816.	Saisie des boissons et des moyens de transport (a). *Art.* 27 *de la loi du* 28 *avril* 1816. Confiscation des boissons saisies et amende de 100 f. à 200 fr (b). *Art.* 46 *id.*
2	Déchargement ou introduction à domicile (*dans les villes où la perception est faite à bureau central*) des mêmes objets, sans déclaration et paiement des droits (10, p. 32). *Art.* 25 *idem.*	
3	Fausse déclaration pour les objets soumis aux droits d'entrée (11, p. 32). *Art.* 24 *idem.*	
4	Introduction des mêmes objets avant ou après les heures pendant lesquelles cette introduction est permise (12, p. 32). *Art.* 26 *idem.*	
5	Fabrication des boissons, sans déclaration, dans l'intérieur d'un lieu sujet, avec des matières pour lesquelles les droits n'auraient pas été acquittés à l'entrée (13, p. 33). *Art.* 20 *et* 24 *idem.*	Confiscation des boissons en fraude et amende de 100 fr. à 200 fr. *Art.* 46 *idem.*
6	Recel ou fausse déclaration, par un propriétaire récoltant, des boissons soumises à l'inventaire (14, p. 33). *Art.* 24 *idem.*	
7	Refus, par le même propriétaire, de souffrir l'inventaire de ses boissons, dans les communes où il est autorisé (15, p. 34). *Art.* 40 *idem.*	Amende de 100 francs à 200 francs. *Art.* 46 *idem.*
8	Refus, par un propriétaire récoltant, jouissant de l'entrepôt, de souffrir le recensement de ses boissons avant la récolte (16, p. 34). *Art.* 41 *idem.*	

(*) Pour l'hydromel, même observation qu'au Ier Tableau.

(a) Même observation qu'à la note (a), p. 1.

(b) 1. La fraude faite en voitures suspendues entraîne toujours une amende de 1000 fr. *Art.* 46 *de la loi du* 28 *avril* 1816.

2. Si elle est faite par escalade, par souterrain ou à main armée, la peine est de six mois de prison, outre l'amende et la confiscation. *Idem.* Dans ces derniers cas, les contrevenans doivent être constitués prisonniers et envoyés avec une copie du procès-verbal, par-devant un officier de police judiciaire. *Voy.* le procès-verbal no 4.

N^{os}	MOTIFS DES PROCÈS-VERBAUX.	OBJETS A SAISIR et peines encourues.
1	Vente en détail de boissons sans déclaration (17, p. 34). *Art.* 50 *de la loi du* 28 *avril* 1816.	Saisie des boissons trouvées en la possession des contrevenans. *Art.* 94 *de la loi du* 28 *avril* 1816.
2	Continuation de vente en détail de boissons après la déclaration de cesser, et même pendant les trois mois qui suivent cette déclaration (18, p. 35). *Art.* 67 *idem.*	Confiscation des boissons saisies, et amende de 300 f. à 1000 fr. (a). *Art.* 95 *id.*
3	Mise en activité ou continuation d'un débit de boissons sans que le débitant soit pourvu d'une licence pour cet établissement (19, p. 35). *Art.* 171 *idem.*	Amende de 300 fr. *Art.* 171 *idem.*
4	Fausse déclaration, ou déclaration incomplète, des boissons existant au pouvoir d'un débitant, chez lui ou ailleurs, au moment de l'établissement de son débit (20, p. 36). *Art.* 50 *id.*	Saisie des boissons non déclarées. *Art.* 94 *idem.* Confiscation des boissons saisies, et amende de 50 f. à 300 fr. (b). *Art.* 96 *id.*
5	Défaut, par un débitant, de placer une enseigne ou bouchon devant le lieu de son débit (21, p. 36). *Même article.*	Amende de 50 f. à 300 f. (b). *Art.* 96 *idem.*
6	Omission ou refus de retirer lesdits enseigne ou bouchon après la déclaration de cesser *Art.* 67 *idem.*	
7	Refus de déclarer les prix de vente en détail des boissons, ou fausse déclaration dans le prix de ces ventes (22, p. 37). *Art.* 48 *id.*	Saisie des boissons mises en vente. *Art.* 94 *idem.* Confiscation des boissons saisies, et amende de 50 f. à 300 fr. (b). *Art.* 96 *id.*
8	Omission ou refus d'afficher lesdits prix de vente (23, p. 37). *Idem.*	Amende de 50 francs à 300 fr. (b). *Art.* 96 *id.*
9	Refus de souffrir les exercices des Employés (24, p. 37). *Art.* 52 *idem.*	
10	Refus de laisser jauger, déguster et reconnaître les boissons introduites chez les débitans (25, p. 38). *Art.* 53 *idem.*	

(a) Les contrevenans peuvent obtenir la restitution des boissons saisies en payant une somme de 1000 fr., indépendamment de l'amende prononcée par le tribunal, *Art.* 95 *de la loi du* 28 *avril* 1816.

(b) L'amende est toujours de 500 fr. en cas de récidive. *Art.* 96 *idem.*

N[os]	MOTIFS DES PROCÈS-VERBAUX.	OBJETS A SAISIR et peines encourues.
11	Refus, par les débitans, d'ouvrir aux Employés leurs caves, celliers et autres parties de leurs maisons (26, p. 38). *Art.* 56 *de la loi du* 28 *avril* 1816.	Amende de 50 francs à 300 fr. (a). *Art.* 96 *de la loi du* 28 *avril* 1816.
12	Refus de souffrir les exercices et visites des Employés pendant les trois mois qui suivent la déclaration de cesser. *Art.* 67 *id.*	
13	Introduction de boissons dans le domicile, les caves ou celliers des débitans, sans expéditions de la Régie, ou avec des expéditions inapplicables (27, p. 39). *Art.* 53 *id.*	Saisie des boissons en fraude. *Art.* 94 *idem.* Confiscation des boissons saisies et amende de 50 à 300 fr. (a). *Art.* 96 *id.*
14	Défaut de représenter ledites expéditions pour les boissons introduites chez les débitans (28, p. 41). *Même article.*	
15	Défaut de représenter, dans les lieux sujets, les quittances des droits d'entrée pour les mêmes boissons, lorsqu'elles viennent du dehors ou qu'elles sortent de chez un entrepositaire (29, p. 41). *Même article.*	
16	Recelé de boissons, par les débitans, dans leur domicile ou ailleurs (30, p. 41). *Art.* 61 *idem.*	
17	Recelé ou dépôt chez un particulier, de boissons appartenant à un débitant, s'il n'y a bail authentique pour les lieux où sont placées les boissons (31, p. 42). *Idem.*	
18	Remplissage, hors la présence des Employés, sur les tonneaux marqués ou démarqués (32, p. 42). *Art.* 59 *idem.*	
19	Substitution d'eau, ou d'autres liquides, aux boissons prises en charge (33, p. 42). *Id.*	
20	Existence, sans autorisation, de boissons en vaisseaux d'une contenance inférieure à un hectolitre (34, p. 42). *Art.* 58 *idem.*	

(a) L'amende est toujours de 500 fr. en cas de récidive. *Article* 96 *de la loi du* 28 *avril* 1816.

N^os	MOTIFS DES PROCÈS-VERBAUX.	OBJETS A SAISIR et peines encourues.
21	Mise en vente ou en perse de plus de trois pièces à la fois de chaque espèce de boisson. *Art.* 58 *de la loi du* 28 *avril* 1816.	Saisie des boissons en fraude. *Art.* 94 *de la loi du* 28 *avril* 1816. Confiscation des boissons saisies, et amende de 50 f. à 300 fr. (a). *Art.* 96 *id.*
22	Mise en vente de boissons dans des vaisseaux d'une contenance supérieure à cinq hectolitres (35, p. 43). *Idem.*	
23	Enlèvement hors des caves, de pièces vides, avant qu'elles aient été démarquées par les Employés. *Art.* 59 *idem.*	Amende de 50 f. à 300 f. (a). *Art.* 96 *idem.*
24	Enlèvement de pièces pleines, sans qu'elles aient été démarquées, lors même qu'elles auraient été réellement vendues en gros (36, p. 43). *Art.* 57 *idem.*	
25	Existence de râpés prohibés (37, p. 44). *Art.* 60 *idem.*	Saisie des boissons en fraude. *Art.* 94 *idem.* Confiscation des boissons saisies, et amende de 50 f. à 300 fr. (a). *Art.* 95 *id.*
26	Remplissage hors la présence des Employés sur les râpés autorisés. *Idem.*	
27	Refus de sceller les communications intérieures entre la maison d'un débitant et les maisons voisines (38, p. 44). *Art,* 61 *id.*	Amende de 50 francs à 300 fr. (b). *Art.* 96 *id.*
28	Vente en détail de boissons par un bouilleur ou distillateur pendant la durée de la distillation, à moins d'une autorisation (39, p. 45). *Art.* 69 *idem.*	Saisie des boissons en fraude. *Art.* 94 *idem.* Amende de 50 f. à 300 f.
29	Vente en détail de boissons par des personnes non comprises dans la répartition, lorsque les débitans sont abonnés par corporation (40, p. 45). *Art.* 80 *idem.*	
30	Vente en détail par les débitans de boissons de leur cru et jouissant de la remise de 25 pour cent, d'autres boissons que celles indiquées par leur déclaration (41, p. 45). *Art.* 85 *idem.*	

(a) En cas de récidive, l'amende sera toujours de 500 fr. *Art.* 96 *de la loi du* 28 *avril* 1816.

(b) Même peine en cas de récidive.—S'il y avait des boissons recelées, elles seraient dans le cas de la saisie et de la confiscation. *Voyez* les n°s 16 et 17.

Nos	MOTIFS DES PROCÈS-VERBAUX.	OBJETS A SAISIR et peines encourues.
1	Établissement d'un commerce de boissons en gros sans déclaration (42, p. 45) ou continuation après déclaration de cesser (43, p. 46). *Art.* 97 *de la loi du* 28 *avril* 1816.	Saisie et confiscation des boissons que le contrevenant a en sa possession (a), et amende de 500 fr. à 2000 fr. *Art.* 106 *de la loi du* 28 *avril* 1816.
2	Vente habituelle de boissons en détail par un marchand en gros (44, p. 46). *Art.* 50 *id.*	
3	Exploitation d'un commerce en gros de boissons sans licence. (45, p. 46). *Art.* 171 *idem.*	Amende de 300 fr. *Art.* 171 *idem.*
4	Fausse déclaration, ou déclaration inexacte, des boissons existant au pouvoir d'un marchand en gros, chez lui ou ailleurs, au moment de l'établissement de son commerce (46, p. 47). *Art.* 97 *idem.*	Saisie et confiscation des boissons et amende de 50 f. à 300 fr. (b). *Art.* 106 *id.*
5	Introduction de boissons chez un marchand en gros sans expédition de la Régie ou avec des expéditions inapplicables (47, p. 47). *Art.* 100 *idem.*	
6	Refus de représenter lesdites expéditions pour les boissons reçues par un marchand en gros (48, p. 47). *Idem.*	
7	Refus de souffrir les vérifications des Employés (49, p. 47). *Art.* 101 *idem.*	Amende de 50 francs à 300 fr. (b). *Art.* 106 *id.*

(a) Le contrevenant pourra obtenir la main-levée des boissons en payant une somme de 2000 francs, indépendamment de l'amende prononcée par le tribunal. *Art.* 106 *de la loi du* 28 *avril* 1816.

(b) L'amende sera toujours de 500 fr. en cas de récidive. *Idem.*

Nos	MOTIFS DES PROCÈS-VERBAUX.	OBJETS A SAISIR et peines encourues.
1	Établissement d'une brasserie sans déclaration (50, p. 47). *Art.* 117 *de la loi du* 28 *avril* 1816.	Saisie et confiscation des bières trouvées en fraude, et amende de 200 f. à 600 f. *Art.* 129 *de la loi du* 28 *avril* 1816.
2	Fabrication de bière dans un lieu autre que celui ou ceux déclarés. *Idem.*	
3	Exploitation d'une brasserie sans licence (51, p. 48). *Art.* 171 *id.*	Amende de 300 fr. *Art.* 171 *idem.*
4	Défaut d'enseigne devant une brasserie en activité. *Art.* 124 *idem.*	Amende de 200 fr. à 600 fr. *Art.* 129 *idem.*
5	Usage dans une brasserie de chaudières, cuves et bacs, avant que leur contenance ait été reconnue et constatée par les Employés (52, p. 48). *Art.* 117 *idem.*	Saisie et confiscation des bières trouvées en fraude, et amende de 200 f. à 600 f. *Art.* 129 *idem.*
6	Changemens dans la contenance de ces ustensiles sans déclaration faite 24 heures d'avance (53, p. 48). *Art.* 118 *idem*	
7	Usage d'ustensiles dont la contenance a été changée, même lorsque la déclaration a été faite, avant que la nouvelle contenance ait été connue et constatée. *Idem.*	
8	Établissement de nouveaux ustensiles de l'espèce de ceux désignés nº 5, sans une déclaration faite 24 heures d'avance. *Idem.*	
9	Usage de nouveaux ustensiles, même lorsque la déclaration en a été faite, avant que leur contenance ait été reconnue et constatée. *Id.*	
10	Usage de chaudières d'une contenance inférieure à six hectolitres. *Art.* 116 *idem.*	
11	Usage de chaudières qui ne sont pas fixées à demeure et maçonnées. *Idem.*	Saisie et confiscation des bières trouvées en fraude, ainsi que des chaudières, et amende de 200 fr. à 600 fr. *Art.* 129 *idem.*
12	Usage, dans une brasserie, de tonneaux non revêtus de la marque des brasseurs. *Article* 124 *idem.*	Amende de 200 fr. à 600 fr. *Art.* 129 *idem.*

Nᵒˢ	MOTIFS DES PROCÈS-VERBAUX.	OBJETS A SAISIR et peines encourues.
13	Suppression ou altération des numéros et marques apposés par les Employés sur les vaisseaux indiqués nᵒ 5. *Art.* 117 *de la loi du* 28 *avril* 1816.	Amende de 200 fr. à 600 fr. *Art.* 129 *de la loi du* 28 *avril* 1816.
14	Mise de feu sous les chaudières pour un objet autre que pour la fabrication de la bière (54, p. 48). *Art.* 119 *idem.*	
15	Mise de feu sans déclaration pour fabrication de bière (55, p. 48). *Art.* 120 *idem.*	Saisie et confiscation des bières trouvées en fraude, et amende de 200 fr. à 600 fr. *Art.* 129 *idem.*
16	Mise de feu sous une chaudière avant l'heure indiquée par la déclaration. *Idem.*	
17	Mise de feu sous une chaudière autre que celle déclarée (54, p. 48). *Idem.*	
18	Défaut de représenter, à toute réquisition des Employés, l'ampliation de la déclaration de mise de feu, pendant la durée de la fabrication. *Idem.*	
19	Fabrication de bière d'une qualité différente de celle déclarée. *Idem.*	
20	Fabrication, avec la même drèche, d'un plus grand nombre de brassins que ceux portés dans la déclaration. *Idem.*	
21	Fabrication de plusieurs espèces de bières avec le même brassin. *Art.* 113 *idem.*	
22	Fabrication de petite bière sans déclaration (56, p. 49). *Art.* 120 *idem.*	
23	Décharge partielle des chaudières pendant la fabrication. *Art.* 113 *idem.*	
24	Entonnement de la bière pendant la nuit. *Art.* 112 *idem.*	

N°s	MOTIFS DES PROCÈS-VERBAUX.	OBJETS A SAISIR et peines encourues.
25	Entonnement à une heure autre que celle portée dans la déclaration. *Art.* 120 *de la loi du* 28 *avril* 1816.	Saisie et confiscation des bières trouvées en fraude, et amende de 200 à 600 fr. *Art.* 129 *de la loi du* 28 *avril* 1816.
26	Produit de fabrication excédant la contenance brute de la chaudière (57, p. 49). *Art.* 111 *id.*	
27	Excédant de plus du vingtième de la contenance de la chaudière dans le produit des trempes données pour un brassin (58, p. 49). *Art.* 109 *id.*	
28	Recelé de bières par un brasseur. *Art.* 125 *id.*	
29	Refus de laisser vérifier aux Employés le produit de la fabrication de chaque brassin. *Art.* 111 *id.*	Amende de 200 à 600 fr. *Art.* 129 *idem.*
30	Refus de souffrir les visites et vérification des commis, et de leur ouvrir, à toute réquisition, les maisons, brasseries, ateliers, magasins, caves et celliers des brasseurs (59, p. 49). *Art.* 125 *id.*	
31	Refus par les brasseurs de faire sceller toute communication des brasseries avec les maisons voisines autres que celle de leur habitation. *Id.*	
32	Exploitation d'une brasserie ambulante sans autorisation de la Régie. *Art.* 116 *id.*	Saisie et confiscation des bières trouvées en fraude, et amende de 200 à 600 fr. *Art.* 129 *idem.*
33	Augmentation des moyens de fabrication dans les villes où les brasseurs sont abonnés (60, p. 49). *Art.* 133 *id.*	
34	Mise de feu par un brasseur abonné sans l'avoir inscrit sur son registre (60, p. 49). *Art.* 135 *id.*	

Nos.	MOTIFS DES PROCÈS-VERBAUX.	OBJETS A SAISIR et peines encourues.
	DISTILLERIES DE GRAINS ET AUTRES SUBSTANCES FARINEUSES.	
1	Mise en activité d'une distillerie de grains et autres substances farineuses sans déclaration faite quatre heures d'avance dans les villes, et douze heures dans les campagnes. *Art.* 138 *et* 139 *de la loi du* 28 *avril* 1816.	Saisie et confication des eaux-de-vie trouvées en fraude, et amende de 200 à 600 fr. *Art.* 129 *et* 143 *de la loi du* 28 *avril* 1816.
2	Exploitation d'une distillerie sans licence (61, p. 50). *Art.* 171 *idem.*	Amende de 300 fr. *Art.* 171 *idem.*
3	Usage, dans une distillerie, de chaudières, cuves et bacs avant que leur contenance ait été reconnue et constatée par les Employés (*). *Art.* 117 *et* 140 *id.*	Saisie et confiscation des eaux-de-vie trouvées en fraude, et amende de 200 à 600 fr. *Art.* 129 *et* 143 *idem.*
4	Changemens dans la contenance de ces ustensiles sans déclaration faite vingt-quatre heures d'avance (53, p. 48). *Art.* 118 *et* 140 *id.*	
5	Usage des ustensiles dont la contenance a été changée, même lorsque la déclaration a été faite, avant que la nouvelle contenance ait été reconnue et constatée. *Id.*	
6	Établissement de nouveaux ustensiles de l'espèce de ceux désignés n° 3, sans une déclaration faite vingt-quatre heures d'avance. *Id.*	
7	Usage de nouveaux ustensiles, même lorsque la déclaration a été faite, avant que leur contenance ait été reconnue et constatée. *Id.*	
8	Mise de feu avant l'heure indiquée dans la déclaration. *Art.* 139, *id.*	
9	Prolongation du travail et du feu sous les chaudières au-delà du terme porté dans la déclaration. *Id.*	
10	Chargement des cuves de macération à une heure autre que celle indiquée par la déclaration. *Id.*	
11	Emploi d'une quantité de farine plus considérable que celle indiquée par la déclaration. *Id.*	

(*) *Voy.* le §. 1 de la note 52, qui est applicable aux distilleries.

N°	MOTIFS DES PROCÈS-VERBAUX.	OBJETS A SAISIR et peines encourues.
12	Recelé d'eaux-de-vie par un distillateur. *Art.* 138 *de la loi du* 28 *avril* 1816.	Les mêmes peines que pour les n°s 3 à 11. *Art.* 12[illegible] *et* 143 *de la loi du* 28 *avril* 1816.
13	Défaut de représenter l'ampliation de la déclaration à toute réquisition des Employés pendant la durée de la fabrication (*). *Id.*	Amende de 200 à 600 fr. *Idem.*
14	Suppression et altération des numéros et marques apposés par les Employés sur les vaisseaux indiqués n° 3. *Art.* 117 *et* 140 *id.*	
15	Refus de souffrir les visites et vérifications des Employés et de leur ouvrir, à toute réquisition, les maisons, distilleries, ateliers, magasins, caves et celliers des distillateurs (59, p. 49). *Art.* 125 *et* 140 *id.*	
	BOUILLEURS DE PROFESSION.	
16	Distillation de vins, cidres, poirés, marcs, lies, fruits ou mélasses sans déclaration faite quatre heures d'avance dans les villes et douze heures dans les campagnes. *Art.* 138 *et* 141 *id.*	Saisie et confiscation des eaux-de-vie trouvées en fraude, et amende de 200 à 600 fr. *Idem.*
17	Défaut de licence ou de renouvellement de licence (61, p. 50). *Art.* 171 *id.*	Amende de 300 fr. *Art.* 171 *idem.*
18	Prolongation du travail au-delà du nombre de jours indiqué par la déclaration. *Art.* 141 *id.*	Saisie et confiscation des eaux-de-vie trouvées en fraude, et amende de 200 à 600 fr. *Art.* 129 et 143 *idem.*
19	Mise en distillation d'une plus grande quantité de matière que celle indiquée par la déclaration. *Id.*	
20	Recelé d'eau-de-vie par un bouilleur de profession (62, p. 50). *Art.* 138 *id.*	
21	Défaut de représenter l'ampliation de la déclaration, à toute réquisition des Employés pendant la durée de la fabrication (*). *Id.*	Amende de 200 à 600 fr. *Idem.*
22	Refus de souffrir les exercices et vérifications des Employés. *Id.*	

(*) On suppose que la déclaration a eu lieu; car si elle n'avait pas été faite c'est conformément aux n°s 1 ou 16 qu'il faudrait opérer.

Nᵒˢ	MOTIFS DES PROCÈS-VERBAUX.	OBJETS A SAISIR et peines encourues.
1	Introduction (dans les villes où la perception a lieu aux entrées) d'huiles sans déclaration (63, p. 50). *Art.* 91 *de la loi du* 25 *mars* 1817.	
2	Déchargement ou introduction d'huiles à domicile (dans les lieux où la perception est faite à bureau central) sans déclaration. *Art.* 92 *id.*	Saisie de l'huile et des moyens de transport (a). *Art.* 94 *de la loi du* 25 *mars* 1817. Confiscation des huiles saisies, et amende de 100 à 200 fr. (b). *Art.* 109 *id.*
3	Fausse déclaration, ou déclaration inexacte, des huiles présentées à l'introduction (64, p. 50). *Art.* 91 *id.*	
4	Introduction d'huiles avant ou après les heures pendant lesquelles cette introduction est permise (*). *Art.* 93 *id.*	
5	Fabrication d'huiles, dans un lieu sujet, sans déclaration. *Art.* 98 *id.*	Saisie et confiscation des huiles fabriquées en fraude ou recelées, et amende de 100 à 200 f. *Art.* 109 *id.*
6	Recelé des huiles provenant des fabrications à l'intérieur. *Id.*	
7	Refus de souffrir les visites des Employés dans les moulins ou autres lieux de fabrication (65, p. 51). *Id.*	
8	Refus d'exercice par les entrepositaires d'huile (66, p. 51). *Art.* 101 *id.*	Amende de 100 fr. à 200 fr. *Art.* 109 *idem.*
9	Défaut de licence ou de renouvellement de licence par une personne jouissant de l'entrepôt à raison d'un commerce quelconque d'huile. *Art.* 107 *id.*	

(*) Ces heures sont les mêmes que celles indiquées note 12, p. 32.

(a) La saisie des moyens de transport n'est autorisée qu'à défaut, par le contrevenant, de consigner le *maximum* de l'amende ou de donner caution solvable. *Art.* 94 *de la loi du* 25 *mars* 1817.

(b) 1. La fraude faite en voiture suspendue entraîne toujours une amende de 1000 f. *Art.* 109 *idem.*

2. Si elle est faite par escalade, par souterrain ou à main armée, la peine est de six mois de prison, outre l'amende et la confiscation. *Idem.*— Dans ces derniers cas, les contrevenans doivent être constitués prisonniers, et envoyés, avec une copie du procès-verbal, par-devant un officier de police judiciaire.

Nos	MOTIFS DES PROCÈS-VERBAUX.	OBJETS A SAISIR et peines encourues.
1	Fabrication de cartes à jouer sans déclaration et sans autorisation de la Régie (67, p. 51). *Art.* 166 *de la loi du* 28 *avril* 1816.	Confiscation des objets de fraude, amende de 1000 à 3000 f. et un mois d'emprisonnement (a). *Art.* 166 *de la loi du* 28 *avril* 1816.
2	Défaut de licence ou de renouvellement de licence par un fabricant de cartes. *Art.* 164 *id.*	Amende de 300 fr. *Art.* 171 *idem.*
3	Fabrication de cartes à figures à portrait français, par un fabricant autorisé, avec d'autre papier que celui portant l'empreinte des moules de la Régie. *Art.* 1er *du décret du* 9 *février* 1810.	Saisie et confiscation des objets de fraude ou servant à la fraude, et amende de 1000 fr. (b). *Décret du* 4 *prairial an* 13.
4	Fabrication de cartes de points par un fabricant autorisé, sur du papier non filigrané. *Art.* 12 *du décret du* 1er *germinal an* 13.	
5	Fabrication de cartes par un fabricant autorisé, dans un local autre que celui déclaré. *Art.* 12 *de l'arrêté du* 19 *floréal an* 6.	
6	Défaut par le fabricant de mettre une enveloppe sur chaque jeu, ou emploi de fausses enveloppes (68, p. 51), *Art.* 4 *du décret du* 9 *février* 1810.	
7	Refus par un fabricant de classer dans ses magasins les papiers et cartons destinés à la fabrication. *Art.* 3 *du décret du* 13 *fructidor an* 13.	Amende de 1000 francs. *Décr. du* 4 *prairial an* 13.
8	Défaut par les fabricans de tenir un registre de vente. *Article* 10 *de l'arrêté du* 3 *pluviôse an* 6.	

(a) En cas de récidive, l'amende est toujours de 3000 fr. *Art.* 166 *de la loi du* 28 *avril* 1816.—Il y a lieu à constituer prisonniers les contrevenans, et à les renvoyer, avec une copie du procès-verbal, devant un officier de police judiciaire.

(b) Il y a également lieu à constituer prisonniers les contrevenans, mais seulement pour sûreté de l'amende. *Art.* 169 et 223 *idem.* — Ils doivent être conduits sur-le-champ devant un officier de police judiciaire, ou remis à la force armée, pour être conduits devant le juge compétent.—Si le prévenu offre bonne et suffisante caution de se présenter en justice et d'acquitter l'amende, ou s'il consigne le montant de ladite amende, il doit être mis en liberté s'il n'existe aucune autre charge contre lui. *Art.* 169 et 224 *idem.* *Voy.* Arrestation des vendeurs et colporteurs de tabacs, nomb. 97.

Nos	MOTIFS DES PROCÈS-VERBAUX.	OBJETS A SAISIR et peines encourues.
9	Contrefaçon ou imitation de moules, timbres et marques de la Régie. *Art.* 168 *de la loi du* 28 *avril* 1816.	Amende de 1000 fr. à 3000 fr. (a). *Art.* 168 *de la loi du* 28 *avril* 1816.
10	Emploi frauduleux des véritables moules, timbres et marques de la Régie. *Id.*	
11	Dépôt ou recelé de moules faux ou contrefaits. *Art.* 10 *du décret du* 9 *février* 1810.	Saisie et confiscation des objets de fraude ou servant à la fraude, et amende de 1000 fr. (b). *Décret du* 4 *prairial an* 13.
12	Dépôt ou recelé de moules à figures chez un fabricant. *Art.* 11 *du décret du* 1er *germinal an* 13.	
13	Dépôt ou recelé chez un particulier, de moules propres à imprimer les cartes. *Art.* 16 *de l'arrêté du* 19 *floréal an* 6.	
14	Fabrication de moules propres à imprimer les cartes à portraits français (*). *Art.* 2 *du décret du* 16 *juin* 1808.	
15	Défaut de déclaration par un graveur pour graver des moules de tarots et autres, dont la forme et la dimension diffèrent des cartes usitées en France (69, p. 51). *Art.* 13 *de l'arrêté du* 19 *floréal an* 6.	
16	Introduction ou usage de cartes fabriquées à l'étranger (70, p. 51). *Art.* 166 *de la loi du* 28 *avril* 1816.	Saisie et confiscation des cartes de fraude, amende de 1000 f. à 3000 f. et un mois d'emprisonnement. *Article* 166 *de la loi du* 28 *avr.* 1816.

(*) On suppose qu'il s'agit de moules différens de ceux de la Régie; car s'il y avait imitation de ces moules, c'est d'après le no 9 du tableau qu'il faudrait opérer.

(a) Les contrevenans doivent être constitués prisonniers. — Il est bien entendu que le corps du délit doit être saisi et mis sous le cachet des Employés et celui des parties (sauf leur refus constaté), afin qu'il ne puisse s'élever aucun doute sur l'identité des objets qui donnent lieu à verbaliser.—Outre l'amende, les contrevenans doivent être punis des peines portées par les articles 142 et 143 du Code pénal. *Art.* 168 *de la loi du* 28 *avril* 1816. — Ces peines sont la réclusion, pour le crime indiqué no 9 du tabl., *Art.* 142 *du Code pénal*, et le carcan pour celui indiqué no 10. *Art.* 143 *idem.*

(b) Même observation qu'à la note b, p. 13.

N°.	MOTIFS DES PROCÈS-VERBAUX.	OBJETS A SAISIR et peines encourues.
17	Vente, distribution ou colportage de cartes à jouer sans autorisation de la Régie (71, p. 51). *Art.* 166 *de la loi du* 28 *avril* 1816.	Saisie et confiscation des cartes de fraude, amende de 1000 f. à 3000 f. et un mois d'emprisonnement (a) *Art.* 166 *de la loi du* 28 *avril* 1816.
18	Usage de cartes prohibées dans les maisons où le public est admis (72, p. 52). *Art.* 167 *id.*	
19	Recoupe de cartes et vente, entrepôt ou colportage de cartes recoupées ou réassorties, qu'elles soient sous bandes ou sans bandes *Art.* 10 *du décret du* 16 *juin* 1808.	Saisie et confiscation des objets de fraude ou servant à la fraude, et amende de 1000 fr. *Décret du* 4 *prairial an* 13.
20	Vente, par un débitant commissionné, de cartes à portraits français autre que celles fabriquées avec les moulages de la Régie (73, p. 52). *Art.* 8 *idem*; *et art.* 2 *du décret du* 9 *février* 1810.	
21	Vente par un débitant commissionné, de cartes à portraits étrangers dépourvues de la légende *France* et du nom du fabricant. *Art.* 4 *du décret du* 16 *juin* 1808.	
22	Vente, par un débitant commissionné, de cartes quelconques dépourvues de bandes de contrôle. *Art.* 8 *du décret du* 13 *fructidor an* 13.	
23	Achat de cartes par un débitant, ailleurs que chez un fabricant commissionné. (*) *Art.* 11 *de l'arrêté du* 3 *pluviôse an* 6.	
24	Défaut, par un débitant, de tenir un registre d'achat et un registre de vente. (*) *Id.*	
25	Défaut par les entrepreneurs et directeurs de cafés, clubs et maisons où l'on donne à jouer, de tenir un registre d'achat. (*) *Art.* 12 *idem.*	Amende de 1000 francs.
26	Refus par les assujétis aux droits sur les cartes, de souffrir les exercices des Employés (74, p. 52). *Art.* 13 *id.*	*Idem.*

(*) On fera remarquer qu'on n'a indiqué ces contraventions qu'afin qu'elles ne soient pas omises si elles se rencontrent en même temps qu'une entreprise de fraude, et non pour en faire usage isolément, à moins que le Directeur ne le juge nécessaire, dans quelques circonstances, pour l'intérêt du service.

(a) Même observation qu'à la note a, p. 13.

N^os	MOTIFS DES PROCÈS-VERBAUX.	OBJETS À SAISIR et peines encourues.
	VOITURES A SERVICE RÉGULIER.	
1	Exploitation d'une entreprise de voitures publiques de terre ou d'eau, à service régulier, sans déclaration et sans licence (75, p. 53). *Art.* 115 *de la loi du* 25 *mars* 1817.	Saisie des voitures circulant sans estampille ou sans laissez-passer, ou avec un laissez-passer inapplicable, ainsi que des chevaux et harnais (a). *Art.* 120 *de la loi du* 25 *mars* 1817. Confiscation des objets saisis et amende de 100 fr. à 1000 f., dont le *minimum*, en cas de récidive, sera de 500 fr. *Art.* 122 *idem.*
2	Circulation de voitures sur une route non indiquée dans la déclaration. *Art.* 116 *id.*	
3	Fausse déclaration du nombre et du prix des places (76, p. 53). *Id.*	
4	Mise en circulation de voitures non revêtues de l'estampille de la Régie (77, p. 54). *Art.* 117 *idem.*	
5	Déplacement, sans déclaration, des estampilles pour les appliquer à de nouvelles voitures. *Idem.*	
6	Circulation d'une voiture sans laissez-passer ou avec un laissez-passer inapplicable (78, p. 54). *Idem.*	
7	Substitution d'une voiture à une autre sans déclaration (79, p. 54). *Idem.*	
8	Défaut de registre, ou défaut d'y porter les objets et les indications qui doivent y être inscrits (80, p. 54). *Art.* 3 *du décret du* 14 *fructidor an* 12.	Amende de 100 fr. à 1000 f., dont le *minimum*, en cas de récidive, sera toujours de 500 f. (b). *Art.* 122 *idem.*
9	Défaut par le conducteur d'être muni d'une feuille de route, ou défaut d'y porter les objets qui doivent y être inscrits (81, p. 55) *Art.* 5 *id.*	

(a) En cas de saisie des voitures en route, elles pourront continuer leur voyage au moyen de la main-levée qui en sera donnée sous caution suffisante, ou même sous la caution juratoire de l'entrepreneur ou du conducteur. — Dans aucun cas, les Employés ne peuvent arrêter les voitures sur les grandes routes, ailleurs qu'aux entrées et sorties des villes ou relais ; en cas de soupçon de fraude, ils ne peuvent faire leur vérification qu'à la première halte. *Art.* 120 *de la loi du* 25 *mars* 1817.

(b) Il y aurait lieu, en outre, à conclure au paiement des droits fraudés.

N^{os}.	MOTIFS DES PROCÈS-VERBAUX.	OBJETS A SAISIR et peines encourues.
10	Emploi de faux de registres, de fausses feuilles de route ou faux enregistremens (*). *Art.* 10 *du décret du* 14 *fructidor an* 12.	Amende de 100 f. à 1000 fr., dont le *minimum*, en cas de récidive, sera toujours de 500 fr. *Art.* 122 *de la loi du* 25 *mars* 1817.
11	Refus de représenter à toute réquisition des Employés le registre indiqué n° 8, ainsi que tous autres registres de contrôle et de receite établis pour le service de l'entreprise (**). *Art.* 4 *id.*	
12	Refus de représenter aux Employés la feuille de route indiquée n° 9, de leur en laisser prendre copie, et de leur permettre d'assister au chargement et déchargement des voitures. *Art.* 6 *id.*	
13	Voies de fait, résistance ou insulte envers les Préposés de la part des conducteurs, cochers, postillons et voituriers. *Art.* 11 *id.*	
	VOITURES D'OCCASION ET A VOLONTÉ.	
14	Mise en activité d'une entreprise de voitures publiques partant d'occasion et à volonté sans déclaration (82, p. 55). *Art.* 115 *de la loi du* 25 *mars* 1817.	Comme pour les n°s 1 à 7.
15	Mise en circulation de voitures non revêtues de l'estampille de la Régie (77, p. 54). *Art.* 117 *id.*	
16	Déplacement, sans déclaration, des estampilles pour les appliquer à de nouvelles voitures. *Id.*	
17	Circulation d'une voiture sans laissez-passer ou avec un laissez-passer inapplicable (78, p. 54). *Id.*	
18	Substitution d'une voiture à une autre sans déclaration (79, p. 54). *Id.*	

(*) Il y a lieu, outre les peines indiquées, aux poursuites extraordinaires pour crime de faux, suivant le cas. *Art.* 10 *du décret du* 14 *fructidor an* 12.

(**) La communication de ces registres doit être exigée sans déplacement. *Art.* 4 *id.*

Nos	MOTIFS DES PROCÈS-VERBAUX.	OBJETS A SAISIR et peines encourues.
1	Culture de tabacs sans déclaration (83, p. 55) et sans permission. *Art.* 180 *de la loi du* 28 *avril* 1816.	Amende de 50 fr. par 100 pieds de tabac (a). *Art.* 181 *de la loi du* 28 *avril* 1816.
2	Plantation d'une étendue de terre, ou d'un nombre de pieds de tabac, excédant de plus d'un cinquième la quantité déclarée (84, p. 56). *Art* 193 *id.*	Amende de 25 fr. par cent pieds de tabac plantés sur les terres excédant la déclaration (b). *Art.* 193 *idem.*
3	Dépôt chez un cultivateur, de tabacs destinés à être exportés, après les délais fixés par l'exportation (85, p. 56). *Art.* 207 *id.*	Saisie et confiscation des tabacs (c). *Art.* 207 *id.*
4	Dépôt de tabac en feuilles chez un particulier qui n'est pas cultivateur autorisé ou chez un cultivateur autorisé après l'époque fixée pour la livraison (86, p. 56). *Art.* 217 *id.*	Saisie et confiscation des tabacs, et amende de 10 f par kil. (d). *Art.* 218 *id.*
5	Circulation de tabacs en feuilles, en quelle quantité que ce soit, sans acquit-à-caution (87, p. 56). *Art.* 215 *id.*	Saisie et confiscation des tabacs, ainsi que des moyens de transport, et amende de 100 à 1000 f. *Art.* 216 *id.*
6	Fabrication de tabacs, par quelque particulier que ce soit, hors des manufactures royales (88, p. 57). *Art.* 172 *id.*	Saisie et confiscation des tabacs, ainsi que des moulins et ustensiles.—Amende de 1000 à 3000 f. (e). *Art.* 221 *id.*

(a) L'amende est de 150 fr. par cent pieds de tabac si le terrain est clos de murs. — Cette amende ne peut, dans aucun cas, excéder 3000 fr.— Les tabacs plantés en contravention doivent être détruits aux frais des cultivateurs, sur l'ordre du Sous-Préfet, à la réquisition du Directeur de la Régie. *Art.* 181 *de la loi du* 28 *avril* 1816.

(b) Cette amende ne pourra excéder 1500 fr., et sans préjudice de l'augmentation des charges au compte du cultivateur *Art.* 193 *idem.*

(c) Cette peine est sans préjudice des répétitions de la Régie contre le cultivateur et ses cautions pour raison des quantités manquantes. *Art.* 207 *idem.*

(d) Cette amende ne peut excéder 3000 fr. et être au-dessous de 100 f. *Art.* 218 *id.*

(e) En cas de récidive, l'amende sera double. *Art.* 221 *idem.*—Le *maximum* d'une amende établie pour la première contravention, est la base nécessaire de celle qui doit être prononcée en cas de récidive, lorsque la loi dit que, dans ce cas, l'amende sera double de la première. *Arr. du* 30 *décembre* 1813.—Aff. Meyer.

N^os^	MOTIFS DES PROCÈS-VERBAUX.	OBJETS A SAISIR et peines encourues.
7	Dépôt de tabacs fabriqués autres que ceux des manufactures royales (89, p. 57). *Art.* 217 *idem.*	Saisie et confiscation des tabacs, et amende de 10 f. par kil. (a). *Art.* 218 *de la loi du* 28 *avril* 1816.
8	Dépôt de tabacs fabriqués, même de ceux des manufactures royales, en quantité au-dessus de dix kil., s'ils ne sont revêtus des marques de la Régie. *Id.*	
9	Transport, colportage ou dépôt de tabacs de cantine dans les lieux où la vente n'en est pas autorisée (90, p. 57). *Art.* 219 *id.*	Saisie et confiscation des tabacs, et amende de 10 f. par kil. (a). *Art.* 219 *id.*
10	Circulation de tabacs fabriqués en quantité au-dessus de dix kil. sans acquit-à-caution. (*) *Art.* 215 *id.*	Saisie et confiscation des tabacs, ainsi que des moyens de transport, et amende de 100 fr. à 1000 fr. (b). *Art.* 216 *idem.*
11	Circulation des tabacs fabriqués en quantité de un à dix kil. sans laissez-passer ou sans être revêtus des marques de la Régie (91, p. 57). *Id.*	
12	Vente de tabac à domicile sans commission de la Régie (92, p. 57). *Art.* 172 *id.*	Saisie et confiscation des tabacs et des ustensiles servant à la vente, et amende de 300 à 1000 fr. — En cas de colportage, il y a lieu en outre à la saisie et confiscation des moyens de transport (c). *Art.* 222 *id.*
13	Vente ou colportage de tabacs en fraude (93, p. 58). *Art.* 222 *id.*	
14	Dépôt, chez quelque particulier que ce soit, de moulins, râpes, hache-tabacs, rouets et autres ustensiles de fabrication qui ne seraient pas sous les scellés de la Régie. *Art.* 220 *id.*	Saisie et confiscation des objets trouvés en contravention. *Art.* 220 *id.*
15	Falsification des tabacs des manufactures royales par les entreposeurs et débitans de la Régie (94, p. 58). *Art.* 227 *id.*	Amende de 300 à 1000 f. emprisonnement de trois mois à un an (d). *Art.* 125 *de la loi du* 27 *mars* 1817.

(*) Sont exceptés les tabacs levés par les débitans dans les entrepôts, pour lesquels le livret tient lieu d'expédition. *Circul.* n° 125.

(a) Cette amende ne peut excéder 3000 fr., ni être au-dessous de 100 fr. *Art.* 218 *de la loi du* 28 *avril* 1816.

(b) L'amende est de 1000 f. contre les personnes qui auraient fourni les tabacs saisis en fraude. *Art.* 216 *idem.*

(c) Il y a lieu, dans les deux cas, à arrêter les contrevenans pour sûreté de l'amende, comme il est expliqué note b, p. 13.

(d) Les contrevenans devraient être constitués prisonniers.

Nᵒˢ	MOTIFS DES PROCÈS-VERBAUX.	OBJETS A SAISIR et peines encourues.
1	Établissement d'une fabrique de sel à la chaudière sans déclaration (95, p. 58). *Art.* 51 *de la loi du* 24 *avril* 1806.	Saisie et confiscation des matières propres à la fabrication, et amende de 100 f. *Art.* 51 *de la loi du* 24 *avril* 1806.
2	Enlèvement et transport de sel, sans déclaration et sans congé ou acquit-à-caution, dans les trois lieues des côtes ou des fabriques et salines de l'intérieur et les quatre lieues frontières (96, p. 59). *Art.* 2 *du décret du* 11 *juin* 1806.	Saisie et confiscation des sels, ainsi que des moyens de transport (a). *Art.* 7 et 16 *du décr. du* 11 *juin* 1806.
3	Enlèvement et transport des sels dans le même rayon avant le lever du soleil ou après son coucher, à moins d'autorisation exprimée sur le congé ou l'acquit-à-caution. *Art.* 6 *idem.*	(Saisie et confiscation des sels, ainsi que des moyens de transport (a). *Art.* 7 et 16 *du décr. du* 11 *juin* 1806.)
4	Refus, dans les fabriques et salines de l'intérieur, de souffrir les exercices des Employés. *Art.* 8 *id.*	Amende de 100 fr. *Art.* 58 *de la loi du* 24 *avril* 1806.
5	Enlèvement de sel, des magasins du fabricant, sans qu'il se soit fait représenter le permis des Douanes ou des Contributions indirectes. *Art.* 20 *id.*	Condamnation au paiement du double droit du sel vendu. *Art.* 20 *du décret du* 11 *juin* 1806.
6	Enlèvement d'eaux salées dans les puits, sources, réservoirs, conduits et magasins des salines. *Art.* 1ᵉʳ *du décret du* 18 *août* 1807.	Comme pour le nᵒ 1.

(a) Si la fraude est commise par une réunion de trois individus et plus, il y aura lieu à l'arrestation des contrevenans et à leur traduction devant le tribunal correctionnel; et, indépendamment de la confiscation des sels et moyens de transport, et d'une amende individuelle qui ne pourra être moindre de deux cents francs ni excéder cinq cents francs, ils seront condamnés à un emprisonnement de quinze jours au moins et de deux mois au plus. *Art.* 30 *de la loi du* 17 *décembre* 1814, *sur les Douanes.*— Les mêmes peines seront prononcées contre tout individu qui sera reconnu coupable de récidive. *Art.* 31 *idem.*

N^os	MOTIFS DES PROCÈS-VERBAUX.	OBJETS A SAISIR et peines encourues.
	NAVIGATION.	
1	Défaut, par les conducteurs de bateaux, trains, etc. d'acquitter les droits à leur passage devant les bureaux (97, p. 59). *Art.* 23 *de l'arrêté du* 8 *prairial an* 11.	Amende de 50 fr. *Art.* 23 *de l'arrêté du* 8 *prairial an* 11.
2	Refus de représenter, à toute réquisition des Employés, les quittances des droits qui ont dû être acquittés. *Art.* 14 *id.*	
3	Insultes et violences envers les Employés. *Art.* 24 *id.*	Amende de 100 fr. (a). *Art.* 24 *idem.*
	BACS ET BATEAUX.	
4	Refus de payer les sommes portées au tarif par les personnes qui passent dans les bacs et bateaux (98, p. 59). *Art.* 48 *de la loi du* 6 *frimaire an* 7.	Amende de la valeur de trois journées de travail (b). *Art.* 56 *de loi du* 6 *frimaire an* 7.

(a) Cette amende est prononcée indépendamment des dommages et intérêts et des peines plus graves si le cas y échet, et ce, conformément aux dispositions du tit. 2 de la loi du 3 nivôse an 6, sur la taxe d'entretien des routes. *Art.* 24 *de l'arrêté du* 8 *prairial an* 11.

(b) 1. Cette amende est prononcée par le juge de paix qui, en cas de récidive, doit prononcer encore un emprisonnement d'un à trois jours, et l'affiche du jugement aux frais du contrevenant. *Art.* 56 *de la loi du* 6 *frimaire an* 7.

2. Si le refus est accompagné d'injures, menaces, violences ou voies de fait, les coupables doivent être traduits au tribunal de police correctionnelle, et condamnés à une amende qui pourra être de cent francs, et à un emprisonnement qui ne pourra excéder trois mois. *Art.* 57 *idem.*

3. Ceux qui auraient aidé ou favorisé la fraude, ou concouru à des contraventions, seront condamnés aux mêmes peines que les auteurs des fraudes et contraventions. *Art.* 58 *idem.*

4. A défaut, par ceux qui ont encouru lesdites amendes, d'en consigner le montant ou de fournir caution, leurs voitures et chevaux peuvent être mis en fourrière et leurs marchandises déposées à leurs frais.—La caution doit être reçue par le juge de paix ou l'un de ses assesseurs. *Art.* 59 *idem.*

5. Les fermiers ou leurs agens qui n'auraient pas qualité pour rédiger procès-verbal doivent se retirer devant le maire ou le juge de paix pour rendre leur plainte.

Nos.	MOTIFS DES PROCÈS-VERBAUX.	PEINES ENCOURUES.
	DISPOSITIONS GÉNÉRALES.	
1	Fabrication de poinçons servant à constater les titres et l'acquit des droits de marque, par d'autres que par le graveur des monnaies. *Art.* 17 *de la loi du* 19 *brumaire an* 6.	Saisie des faux poinçons, ainsi que des ouvrages qui en seraient marqués. *Art.* 101, *même loi.* Dix ans de fers et confiscation des ouvrages (a). *Art.* 19 *idem.*
2	Usage des poinçons de la garantie par d'autres personnes que les Employés de l'Administration préposés à cet effet (99, p. 60). *Art.* 110 *idem.*	Un an de détention. *Art.* 110 *idem;* et saisie des ouvrages. *Art.* 107 *idem.*
3	Mise en vente ou dépôt d'ouvrages sur lesquels les marques des poinçons seraient entées, soudées ou contre-tirées. *Art.* 108 *idem.*	Saisie et confiscation des ouvrages ainsi marqués, et en outre six ans de fers contre le possesseur *avec connaissance. Art.* 108 *id.*
4	Mise en vente ou dépôt d'ouvrages marqués de faux poinçons. *Art.* 109 *idem.*	Confiscation des ouvrages marqués de faux poinçons (b). *Art.* 109 *id.*
5	Présentation à l'essai d'ouvrages fourrés d'une matière étrangère (100, p. 60). *Art.* 65 *id.*	Saisie et confiscation, et amende de vingt fois la valeur. *Art.* 65 *idem.*
6	Défaut de présenter aux Employés des Douanes les ouvrages d'or et d'argent venant de l'étranger (101, p. 60). *Art.* 23 *id.*	Saisie et confiscation des objets en contravention. *Art.* 107 *idem.* Amende de 200 fr. pour la première fois, 500 f. pour la seconde, avec affiche du jugement, et pour la troisième fois amende de 1000 fr., avec interdiction de commerce. *Art.* 80. (s'applique aux nos 6, 7 et 8)
7	Mise en vente d'ouvrages venant de l'étranger qui n'auraient pas acquitté les droits et ne seraient pas marqués. *Art.* 24 *idem.*	
8	Mise en vente, dans les monts-de-piété et autres établissemens publics, d'ouvrages qui n'auraient pas été soumis aux droits et à la marque (102, p. 61). *Art.* 28 *idem.*	

(a) Ceux qui feraient usage de faux poinçons seraient condamnés aux mêmes peines. *Art.* 19.

(b) Ceux qui garderaient ces ouvrages ou les exposeraient en vente, *avec connaissance*, seraient en outre condamnés, la première fois, à une amende de 200 fr.; la seconde fois, l'amende sera de 400 fr., avec affiche de la condamnation dans tout le département; et la troisième fois, l'amende sera de 1000 fr., avec interdiction de tout commerce d'or et d'argent. *Art.* 109.

N^os.	MOTIFS DES PROCÈS-VERBAUX.	PEINES ENCOURUES.
9	Défaut par les orfévres et autres travaillant et fabriquant des ouvrages d'or et d'argent d'enregistrer à l'instant même (103, p. 61), jour par jour, par poids et espèce, les ouvrages vieux ou réputés vieux (104, p. 62), qu'ils reçoivent chez eux à quelque titre que ce soit. *Art.* 15 *de la déclaration du* 26 *janv.* 1749.	Comme aux n°s 6 à 8.
10	Mise dans le commerce de lingots et matières d'or et d'argent affinés, qui n'ont pas acquitté les droits et qui sont dépourvus de la marque. *Art.* 29 *de la loi du* 19 *brum. an* 6.	Confiscation des lingots dépourvus de marque, et amende de 500 francs (a). *Art.* 122.
	Des Fabricans et Marchands.	
11	Établissement d'une fabrique d'ouvrages d'or et d'argent sans déclaration à la préfecture et à la mairie, et sans y avoir fait insculper le poinçon du fabricant (105, p. 62). *Art.* 72, *même loi.*	Amende de 200 fr. pour la première fois; de 500 fr. la seconde, avec affiche du jugement; et pour la troisième fois, amende de 1000 fr., avec interdiction du commerce (b). *Art.* 80 *id.*
12	Établissement d'un commerce d'orfévrerie sans déclaration à la mairie (c). *Art.* 73 *id.*	
13	Défaut par les fabricans et marchands de tenir un registre et d'y inscrire les ouvrages d'or et d'argent qu'ils vendent et achètent (106, p. 62). *Art.* 74 *idem.*	
14	Refus par eux de représenter ledit registre à toute réquisition. *Art.* 76 *idem.*	
15	Achat par eux de personnes inconnues ou n'ayant pas de répondans connus. *Art.* 75 *id.*	
16	Défaut d'avoir, affiché dans leur magasin ou boutique, le tableau énonçant les articles de la loi relatifs au titre et à la vente des ouvrages d'or et d'argent (107, p. 63). *Art.* 78 *idem.*	
17	Refus de remettre aux acheteurs le bordereau énonciatif du titre et du poids des ouvrages vendus (108, p. 63). *Art.* 79 *idem.*	

(a) L'amende doit être prononcée contre l'affineur qui aurait délivré les lingots. *Même article.*

(b) Il y aurait lieu, en outre, à la saisie de tous les ouvrages non marqués, pour contravention à l'art. 77, et à leur confiscation. *Art.* 107, *même loi.*

(c) Ceux qui se bornent à faire le commerce d'orfévrerie sans entreprendre la fabrication, sont dispensés d'avoir un poinçon. *Même art.* 73.

N^os^.	MOTIFS DES PROCÈS-VERBAUX.	PEINES ENCOURUES.
18	Défaut de marque sur les ouvrages achevés existant chez eux (109, p. 63). *Art.* 77 *de la loi du* 19 *brumaire an* 6.	Comme aux n°s 6 à 8.
	Des Fabricans et Marchands de galons, tissus, broderies et autres ouvrages en fil d'or et d'argent.	
19	Établissement de ces fabricans et marchands sans déclaration à la mairie. *Art.* 73 *et* 81 *idem.*	
20	Défaut par eux de tenir un registre et d'y inscrire leurs achats et ventes (106, p. 62). *Art.* 74 *et* 81.	Les mêmes peines que pour les numéros 12 à 17. *Art.* 80 *et* 81.
21	Refus par eux de représenter ledit registre à toute réquisition (*). *Art.* 76 *et* 81 *idem.*	
22	Achat par eux de personnes inconnues ou n'ayant pas de répondant connu. *Art.* 75 *et* 81 *idem.*	
23	Défaut d'avoir, affiché dans leur magasin ou boutique, le tableau indiqué n° 16 (a). *Art.* 78 et 81 *idem.*	Les mêmes peines que celles indiquées aux n°s 11, 12 et 13. *Art.* 80 *et* 81.
24	Refus de remettre aux acheteurs le bordereau énonciatif indiqué n° 18 (b). *Art.* 79 *et* 81 *id.*	
25	Vente pour fins d'ouvrages en or et argent faux. *Art.* 81 *idem.*	Amende de 200 f., outre la restitution à la personne qui a été trompée (c). *Art.* 81.
	Des Joailliers (110, p. 63).	
26	Défaut de la tenue d'un registre et d'y inscrire jour par jour les ventes et achats (106, p. 62). *Art.* 86 *idem.*	Les mêmes peines que celles indiquées aux n°s 11, 12 et 13. *Art.* 88 *idem.*

(*) Un assujéti qui représenterait tardivement son registre n'en serait pas moins en contravention et dans le cas de l'amende pour ne l'avoir pas représenté à la première réquisition.

(a, n°. 23) *Voyez* §. 2, note 107.

(b, n°. 24) *Voy.* note 108.

(c) Pour la seconde fois, l'amende sera de 400 fr., avec affiche de la condamnation; la troisième fois, l'amende sera de 1000 fr., avec interdiction de tout commerce d'or et d'argent; dans tous les cas, il y aura lieu à la restitution envers la personne qui aura été trompée. *Même article* 81.

Nos.	MOTIFS DES PROCÈS-VERBAUX.	PEINES ENCOURUES.
27	Refus de remettre aux acheteurs le bordereau énonciatif de la nature et de la forme de chaque ouvrage, ainsi que de la qualité des pierres (a). *Art.* 87 *de la loi du* 19 *brumaire an* 6.	Comme au n° 26.
28	Mélange de pierres fausses avec les fines sans le déclarer aux acheteurs. *Art.* 89 *idem.*	Restitution de la valeur des pierres, et amende de 300 fr. (b). *Art.* 89 *idem.*
	Des Marchands ambulans des ouvrages d'or et d'argent (c).	
29	Mise en vente d'objets d'or et d'argent dans une commune sans que le marchand se soit présenté à la mairie. *Art.* 92 *idem.*	Les mêmes peines que pour le n° 18. *Art.* 94 *id.*
30	Défaut de représenter au maire ou à son adjoint le bordereau des orfévres qui ont vendu aux marchands les ouvrages dont ils sont porteurs (111, p. 63). *Même article.*	Les mêmes peines que celles indiquées pour les nos 11, 12 et 13. *Art.* 94 *id.*
31	Défaut de marques sur ces ouvrages. *Art.* 94 *idem.*	
	Des Fabricans de Plaqué et Doublé d'or et d'argent sur métaux.	
32	Établissement d'une fabrique de plaqué sans en avoir fait la déclaration à la mairie, à la préfecture et à l'administration des monnaies (d). *Art.* 95 *idem.*	La même peine que pour le n° 12.
33	Défaut par le Fabricant d'apposer son poinçon sur chacun de ses ouvrages, et d'y ajouter le chiffre indicatif de la quantité d'or et d'argent ainsi que le mot *doublé* (112, p. 64). *Art.* 97 *idem.*	Saisie des objets en contravention; confiscation de ces objets, et amende de dix fois leur valeur (e). *Art.* 99 *idem.*

(a, n°. 27) *Voy.* note 108.

(b) L'amende sera triple la seconde fois, avec affiche de la condamnation; et la troisième fois, le contrevenant sera déclaré incapable d'exercer la joaillerie, et les effets composant son magasin seront confisqués. *Art.* 89.

(c) Quoique la loi ait placé les marchands ambulans sous la surveillance spéciale des maires, les Employés de la Régie n'en ont pas moins qualité pour constater les contraventions indiquées sous les numéros 29, 30 et 31, la loi du 5 ventôse an 12, et le décret du 28 floréal an 13 ne faisant aucune distinction.

(d, n° 32) *Voy.* la note 105, §§. 6 et 7.

(e) La seconde fois, l'amende sera double, avec affiche de la condamnation; enfin, la troisième fois, l'amende sera quadruple, avec interdiction; celle-ci sous peine de la confiscation de tous les objets du commerce des contrevenans. *Art.* 99 *idem.*

Nos	MOTIFS DES PROCÈS-VERBAUX.	PEINES ENCOURUES.
34	Défaut de la tenue d'un registre et d'y inscrire jour par jour les ventes faites par le Fabricant (a). *Art.* 98 *de la loi du* 19 *brumaire an* 6.	Comme au nº 33.
35	Refus de remettre aux acheteurs le bordereau énonciatif de l'ouvrage vendu (b). *Même article.*	Comme au nº 33.
36	Achat de matières et ouvrages d'or et d'argent de personnes inconnues ou n'ayant pas de répondant connu. *Art.* 100 *idem.*	Les mêmes peines que pour le nº 15. *Art.* 100.
	Des Affineurs.	
37	Travail pour le commerce sans déclaration à la mairie, à la préfecture et à l'administration des monnaies (c). *Art.* 113 *idem.*	Les mêmes peines que celles pour les numéros 12, 13 et 17. *Art.* 121 *idem.*
38	Réception de matières qui n'auraient pas été essayées et titrées par un essayeur public autre que celui qui doit juger le lingot affiné. *Art.* 114 *idem.*	Les mêmes peines que celles pour les numéros 12, 13 et 17. *Art.* 121 *idem.*
39	Refus de délivrer au porteur de ces matières la reconnaissance indicative de leurs nature, poids, titre et numéro (d). *Art.* 115 *idem.*	Les mêmes peines que celles pour les numéros 12, 13 et 17. *Art.* 121 *idem.*
40	Défaut de la tenue d'un registre (e) et d'y inscrire jour par jour, et par ordre de numéros, les matières apportées aux affineurs, et celles qu'ils rendent après l'affinage. *Art.* 116 *idem.*	Les mêmes peines que celles pour les numéros 12, 13 et 17. *Art.* 121 *idem.*
41	Défaut par les affineurs d'insculper leur nom en toutes lettres sur les lingots affinés. *Art.* 117 *idem.*	Les mêmes peines que celles pour les numéros 12, 13 et 17. *Art.* 121 *idem.*
42	Défaut de faire marquer au bureau de garantie les lingots affinés avant de les rendre aux propriétaires (113, p. 64). *Art.* 29 *et* 117 *idem.*	Amende de 500 francs contre l'affineur, et saisie et confiscation des lingots s'ils sont trouvés dans le commerce. *Art.* 122 *id.*

(a, nº 34) Ce registre doit être coté et paraphé par le Maire. *Même art.* 98. *Voy.* le nº. 9 du tableau et la note qui s'y rapporte.
(b, n. 35) *Voy.* n. 108.
(c, nº. 37) *Voy.* la note 105, §. 7.
(d, nº. 39) *Voy.* note 108.
(e, nº. 40) Ce registre doit être coté et paraphé par le Préfet. *Art.* 116.

Nos.	MOTIFS DES PROCÈS-VERBAUX.	OBJETS A SAISIR et peines encourues.
	POUDRES.	
1	Fabrication de poudre à tirer par quelque particulier que ce soit (114, p. 64). *Art.* 24 *de la loi du* 13 *fructidor an* 5.	Saisie et confiscation de la poudre, des matières et ustensiles, et amende de 3000 f. – Détention pendant trois mois (a) des ouvriers employés à la fabrication. *Art.* 27 *de la loi du* 13 *fructidor an* 5.
2	Vente de poudre à tirer par quelque particulier que ce soit s'il n'a une commission de l'Administration (115, p. 65). *Même article.*	Saisie et confiscation de la poudre, et amende de 500 fr. *Art.* 28 *idem.*
3	Dépôt de poudre à tirer, en quantité au-dessus de cinq kilogrammes chez un particulier non autorisé. *Même article.*	Saisie et confiscation de la poudre, et amende de 100 fr. *Même article.*
4	Vente de poudre de contrebande par un débitant commissionné, ou dépôt de la même poudre dans son domicile (116, p. 65). *Art.* 36 *de la même loi.*	Saisie et confiscation des matières prohibées, et amende de 1000 f. (b). *Art.* 36 *id.*
5	Dépôt de poudre de guerre en quelque quantité et chez quelque particulier que ce soit (117, p. 65). *Art.* 4 *du décret du* 23 *pluviôse an* 13.	Saisie et confiscation de la poudre; et amende de 3000 f. (c). *Art.* 27 *idem* *et art.* 4 *du décr. du* 23 *pluviôse an* 13.
6	Transport de poudres en quantité au-dessus de cinq kil. sans un passeport de l'autorité compétente, visé à la municipalité du lieu du départ (118, p. 65). *Art.* 30 *de la loi du* 13 *fructidor an* 5.	Saisie et confiscation de la poudre, ainsi que des chevaux et voitures, et amende de 10 fr. par livre de poudre saisie (20 fr. 40 c. par kil.). *Art.* 30 *de la loi du* 13 *fructidor an* 5.
7	Introduction dans le royaume, de poudres étrangères. *Art.* 21 *idem.*	Mêmes peines qu'au n° 6, à moins que l'introduction ne soit faite par la voie de mer, alors l'amende est double. *Art.* 21, *même loi.*

(a) En cas de récidive, la détention sera d'un an. *Art.* 27 *de la loi du* 13 *fruct. an* 5.
(b) Le débitant perdrait en outre sa commission. *Art.* 36 *idem.*
(c) Le prévenu est dispensé de cette amende s'il prouve qu'il a acheté la poudre d'un marchand patenté ou domicilié, ou s'il met le vendeur sous la main des tribunaux. *Art.* 4 *du décret du* 23 *pluviôse an* 13.

Nos.	MOTIFS DES PROCÈS-VERBAUX.	PEINES ENCOURUES.
	SALPÊTRES.	
8	Fabrication de salpêtres ou exploitation de matériaux salpêtrés naturellement ou par des nitrières artificielles, sans l'autorisation du gouvernement (119, p. 66). *Art.* 1er *de la loi du* 13 *fructidor an* 5.	Saisie et confiscation des matières et des ustensiles de fabrication (a). *Art.* 15 *de la loi du* 13 *fructidor an* 5.
9	Livraisons de salpêtres, par un salpêtrier commissionné, à d'autres qu'à l'administration des poudres et salpêtres (120, p. 66). *Art.* 12 *idem.*	Abolition de l'atelier, confiscation des matières détournées, et amende de 500 f. *Art.* 12 *idem.*
10	Dépôt de salpêtre chez un particulier (non salpêtrier) qui ne pourrait justifier que le salpêtre trouvé chez lui provient d'achats dans les magasins de l'administration ou de l'importation autorisée par l'arrêté du 27 pluviôse an 8. *Art.* 2 *du décret du* 16 *mars* 1813.	Les mêmes peines que pour le n° 8. *Art.* 2 *du décret du* 16 *mars* 1813.
11	Vente de salpêtre, par quelque particulier que ce soit (121, p. 66). *Art.* 12 *de la loi du* 13 *fructidor an* 5, *et art.* 12 *de l'arrêté du* 27 *pluviôse an* 8.	Les mêmes peines que pour le n° 8. *Art.* 12 *de la loi du* 13 *fructidor an* 5.
12	Circulation de salpêtres sans être accompagnés de passeports délivrés par les commissaires des poudres et salpêtres, visés par les autorités du lieu du départ ou d'un acquit-à-caution des douanes (122, p. 66). *Art.* 7 *de l'arrêté du* 10 *prairial an* 11.	Confiscation du salpêtre. *Art.* 7 *de l'arrêté du* 10 *prairial an* 11.

(a) En cas de récidive, il y a lieu à une amende de 300 fr. outre la confiscation. *Art.* 15 *de la loi du* 13 *fructidor an* 5.

NOTES.

1. (N.° 1 du 1.er Tableau, pag. 1).

1. L'obligation de déclarer l'enlèvement et de prendre des expéditions n'est pas applicable aux vendanges et fruits. *Art.* 11 *de la loi du* 28 *avril* 1816.

2. Ne sont pas considérés comme fruits en nature, les raisins écrasés, foulés et transportés dans des tonneaux ; c'est alors du vin moût qui doit être accompagné d'expéditions. *Arr. des* 5 *et* 13 *févr.* 1807, *Mém., tom.* 1, *p.* 268.

2. (N.° 1 du 1.er Tableau, pag. 1.)

1. Une seule expédition suffit pour plusieurs voitures ayant la même destination et marchant ensemble. *Art.* 6 *de la loi du* 28 *avril* 1816.

2. Les voyageurs ne sont pas tenus de se munir d'expéditions pour les vins destinés à leur usage pendant la route et moyennant qu'ils n'excèdent pas trois bouteilles par personne. *Art.* 18 *idem.*—Cette exception n'est pas applicable à des voituriers, pour des boissons qu'ils transportent à une destination quelconque. *Arr. du* 25 *juin* 1813, *affaire Vanderven.*

3. En cas de changement de destination pour des boissons en cours de transport, on doit prendre une nouvelle expédition ; à défaut, les boissons doivent être saisies, lors même que l'ancienne expédition aurait été revêtue du visa des Employés. *Arr. du* 30 *juillet* 1807, *Mém., tom.* 2, *p.* 385.

4. Les vins sortant des pressoirs pour être conduits dans les caves des propriétaires, ne peuvent circuler sans déclaration préalable et sans être accompagnés de passavans. *Arr. du* 11 *septembre* 1807, *Mém., tom.* 2, *page* 582.

5. Les boissons, quelque faible qu'en soit la quantité, ne peuvent circuler sans expédition, même lorsqu'elles sortent d'un débit exercé. *Arr. du* 7 *mai* 1809, *Mém., tom.* 5, *pag.* 330; *autre du* 5 *octobre suivant, tom.* 6, *pag.* 534; *autre du* 6 *avril* 1810, *tom.* 6, *pag.* 603; *autre du* 14 *août* 1812, *tom.* 7, *pag.* 347.

6. Une expédition n'est pas valable, si elle indique pour conducteur un voiturier autre que celui qui accompagne le chargement pour lequel les expéditions ont été délivrées. *Arr. du* 21 *juill.* 1809, *Mém., tom.* 6, *page* 467.

7. L'article 57 de la loi du 5 ventôse an 12 étant abrogé, les boissons faites avec de l'eau passée sur les marcs de raisins, pommes et poires, sont soumises à toutes les obligations imposées par les lois, lorsqu'elles sont mises dans la circulation ou en vente. *Arr. du* 2 *avril* 1813, *Mém., tom.* 8, *page* 129; *autre du* 21 *nov.* 1817. Aff. Lévêque.

3. (N.° 2 du 1.er Tableau, p. 1).

1. Les Employés doivent avoir égard aux changemens survenus pendant la route, soit pour la conservation des boissons, soit à la suite d'un accident, lorsque néanmoins ces changemens sont légalement constatés, dans le premier cas, par les Employés de la Régie, et, dans le second, à défaut des Employés, par le Maire ou par l'Adjoint de la commune la plus voisine du lieu où l'accident est arrivé. *Art.* 15 *de la loi du* 28 *avril* 1816.

2. Il y a lieu, d'après l'article 16, à accorder pour coulage de route des déductions calculées suivant les usages de commerce; ainsi, quand les différences reconnues n'ont pas d'autre cause, on ne doit pas verbaliser pour défaut d'identité.

2. Si le nombre de sacs, caisses ou futailles ne concorde pas avec les expéditions, il y a contravention, lors même qu'il y aurait identité pour les objets énoncés auxdites expéditions. *Arr. du* 31 *juill.* 1806, *Mém.*, *tom.* 2, *p.* 620.

3. S'il n'y a pas identité entre un chargement de boissons et l'expédition, celle-ci est inapplicable, et il y a lieu à saisir le chargement. *Arr. du* 23 *avril* 1808, *Mém.*, *tom.* 3, *pag.* 329; *autre du* 11 *novembre* 1808, *Mém.*, *tom.* 4, *p.* 718.

4. La preuve par témoins ne peut remplacer le certificat de l'autorité locale pour constater un accident de force majeure. *Arr. du* 21 *avril* 1809, *Mém.*, *tom.* 6, *p.* 394; *autre du* 7 *décembre* 1810, *tom.* 7, *p.* 63.

4. (N°. 3 du 1er Tableau, p. 1).

1. L'expédition qui contient de fausses indications sur le lieu de la destination et le nom du destinataire, est nulle, et les boissons pour lesquelles elle est représentée sont saisissables. *Arr. du* 29 *juillet* 1808, *Mém.*, *tom.* 4, *pag.* 705.

2. La déclaration d'un prévenu, consignée au procès-verbal, suffit pour fournir la preuve d'une fausse destination lorsque cette déclaration dément les énonciations contenues dans l'expédition. *Arr. du* 23 *avril* 1808, *Mém.*, *tom.* 3, *p.* 329.

5. (N°. 3, 1er Tableau, p. 1).

1. Les Employés de la Régie peuvent, en délivrant des expéditions, déterminer le délai pendant lequel le transport des boissons doit être effectué, et, passé ce délai, le transport doit être considéré comme fait sans expédition. *Arr. du* 3 *juin* 1808, *Mém.*, *tom.* 4, *p.* 449. — *Le droit de fixer un délai résulte d'ailleurs de l'article* 13 *de la loi du* 28 *avril* 1816.

2. L'expédition dont le délai est expiré n'est plus valable. *Arr. du* 21 *avril* 1809, *Mém.*, *tom.* 5, *p.* 394.

6. (N.° 4 du 1.er Tableau, p. 1).

1. Il y a contravention lorsqu'un conducteur de boissons ne représente pas, à la première réquisition des Employés, l'expédition dont il doit être porteur. — La représentation tardive, même avant la rédaction du procès-verbal, la preuve que l'expédition a été délivrée avant l'enlèvement, l'allégation qu'elle a été oubliée dans une maison voisine, ou qu'elle a été perdue, ne sauraient affranchir des peines de cette contravention. *Arr. des* 26 *juin*, 31 *juillet*, 30 *octobre* 5 *et* 13 *novembre* 1807, *Mém.*, *tom.* 2, *pag.* 399, 393, 710, 705 et 719; *autre du* 21 *juillet* 1809, *Mém.*, *tom.* 6, *p.* 460.

2. Un conducteur de boissons divisées en plusieurs chargemens, marchant séparés, ne serait pas admis à se justifier du défaut de représentation d'expéditions, sous le prétexte qu'il n'a qu'un seul congé qui accompagne un des chargemens qui faisait partie du même transport. *Arr. du* 7 *décembre* 1810, *Mém.*, *tom.* 7, *p.* 63.

7. (N° 5, 1er Tableau, p. 1).

1. Lorsque les Employés trouvent un voiturier dont le transport est interrompu, ils doivent s'informer du motif de son séjour et l'engager, s'il doit le prolonger, à faire sa déclaration de transit; ce n'est que dans le cas où cet avertissement aurait été sans résultat, qu'il y aurait bien réellement lieu à verbaliser, attendu que le procès-verbal, pour être concluant, doit établir que le voiturier est stationnaire depuis vingt-quatre heures accomplies.

8. (N° 6, 1er Tableau, p. 1).

1. Il faut néanmoins excepter le cas où un accident occasionnerait le prompt déchargement d'une voiture ou d'un bateau ; mais alors l'accident devra être constaté par les Employés, ou, à leur défaut, par le Maire ou par l'Adjoint de la commune la plus voisine. *Art.* 15 *de la loi du* 28 *avril* 1816.

9. (N° 1, 2e Tableau, p. 2).

1. Outre les objets dénommés au tableau, les fruits secs, ainsi que les eaux-de-vie et esprits, altérés par un mélange quelconque, sont soumis à la déclaration et aux droits à l'entrée. *Art.* 23 *de la loi du* 28 *avril* 1816. — Les fruits à l'eau-de-vie sont également soumis à la déclaration, étant compris dans le tarif des droits d'entrée.

2. Les Employés sont nécessairement autorisés à faire la visite des personnes et des chargemens ; il n'y a d'exceptions que celles ci-après :
1° Pour les voyageurs à pied ou à cheval, ou en voitures particulières et suspendues. *Art.* 44 *de la loi du* 28 *avril* 1816.
2° Pour les courriers ; ils ne peuvent être arrêtés à leur passage. *Art.* 45 *id.* Mais les voyageurs ne sont pas moins tenus de faire la déclaration prescrite, en raison des boissons qu'ils transportent, et suivant la destination de ces boissons. La même obligation est imposée aux courriers, et l'art. 45 précité donne à cet effet le droit aux Employés d'accompagner les malles et d'assister à leur déchargement.

3. Dans tous les lieux ayant un octroi, les réglemens particuliers et l'ordonnance du 9 décembre 1814 doivent être invoqués avec la loi du 28 avril, lorsqu'il s'agit d'objets compris dans les deux tarifs : alors les saisies sont communes, elles se constatent par un seul procès-verbal dressé à la requête des deux Administrations.

On indiquera, dans les paragraphes suivans, et toutes les fois que cela sera nécessaire, les dispositions prescrites en matière d'octroi, et dont on devra faire usage pour ces sortes de saisies.

4. Tout porteur ou conducteur d'objets assujétis à l'octroi est tenu, avant de les introduire, d'en faire la déclaration au bureau. *Art.* 28 *de l'ordonnance du* 9 *décembre* 1814.

5. Ils sont également tenus de souffrir, sur les bateaux, voitures et autres moyens de transport, les visites, recherches et perquisitions des Employés, et même de faciliter toutes les opérations nécessaires à ces vérifications. *Idem.* — L'opposition à l'exercice des fonctions des Préposés serait punie d'une amende de 50 francs. *Art.* 15 *de la loi du* 27 *frimaire an* 8.

6. Tout objet soumis à l'octroi qui, nonobstant l'interpellation faite par les Préposés, serait introduit sans avoir été déclaré, ou sur une déclaration fausse ou inexacte, doit être saisi. *Art.* 29 *de l'ordonnance du* 9 *décemb.* 1814.

7. Les personnes voyageant à pied ou à cheval, ou en voitures particulières suspendues, ne peuvent être arrêtées, questionnées ou visitées sur leurs personnes ou en raison de leurs malles ou effets, à peine, par les Préposés, d'être poursuivis correctionnellement comme pour acte de violence. *Art.* 30 *idem.* — Mais en cas de soupçon de fraude, ces personnes peuvent être conduites devant un officier de police ou devant le Maire pour y être interrogées, et la visite de leurs effets autorisée s'il y a lieu. *Art.* 31 *idem.*

8. Les diligences, fourgons, fiacres, cabriolets et autres voitures de louage sont soumis aux visites des Préposés. *Art.* 32 *idem.*

9. Les courriers sont soumis aux mêmes dispositions déjà indiquées au §. 2 ci-dessus. *Art.* 33 *idem.*

10. Il est défendu aux Employés de faire usage de la sonde dans la visite des caisses, malles et ballots annoncés contenir des objets susceptibles d'être endommagés. *Art.* 35 *idem.*

10. (N° 2, 2ᵉ Tableau, p. 2).

1. La même contravention est prévue en matière d'octroi par l'art. 34 de l'ordonnance du 9 décembre 1814, qu'il faudrait citer en cas de saisie commune.

11. (N° 3, 2ᵉ Tableau, p. 2).

1. Lorsqu'il y a fausse déclaration, on ne doit saisir que l'excédant reconnu; mais ceci n'est applicable qu'aux objets dont la circulation peut avoir lieu sans expédition, tels que les fruits et les vendanges; car, lorsqu'il s'agit de boissons pour lesquelles ces expéditions sont prescrites, s'il n'y a pas identité entre lesdites expéditions et les quantités présentées à l'entrée, on doit saisir la totalité du chargement, en vertu de l'art. 10 de la loi du 28 avril 1816.

2. Les fraudes aux droits d'entrée que l'on tenterait de commettre, à l'abri d'une déclaration de passe-debout, de transit ou d'entrepôt, deviendraient une contravention à l'art. 24 ou 25, et devraient être constatées et poursuivies en conséquence.

3. Il y a contravention si les boissons déclarées en transit dans un lieu sujet, sont présentés à la sortie dans un état différent de celui dans lequel elles étaient à l'entrée, et lors même qu'elles seraient en quantité plus forte. *Arr. du* 30 *frimaire an* 13, *Mém., tom.* 1, *p.* 176.

4. Des boissons destinées à traverser, en passe-debout, un lieu sujet, ne peuvent être déchargées chez un particulier, sans contravention. *Arr. du* 21 *juill.* 1809, *Mém., tom.* 6, *p.* 467.

5. Un voiturier qui traverse, en passe-debout, une ville sujette aux droits d'entrée, ne peut se justifier de n'avoir pas fait la déclaration de ses boissons, en prétextant qu'elles sont constamment restées sous la surveillance des Employés. *Arr. du* 7 *décembre* 1810, *Mém., tom.* 7, *p.* 63.

6. Un particulier qui déclare des objets à l'entrée, doit attendre que la vérification en ait été faite par les Préposés; à défaut, il est en contravention, quoiqu'il ait déposé sur le bureau le montant présumé du droit. *Arr. du* 14 *mars* 1817. — Aff. Sicard.

7. Lorsqu'un réglement relatif à l'octroi établit la nécessité de faire une déclaration à des bureaux extérieurs, l'omission de cette déclaration est une contravention suffisante pour exiger l'application de l'amende, quoique les objets soumis à l'octroi n'aient point encore été introduits dans la ville. *Arr. du* 5 *brumaire an* 12, *Mém., tom.* 1, *p.* 107.—On ne peut connaître la déclaration qui a été faite au bureau de l'octroi que par le laissez-passer et l'acquit des droits qui sont représentés. Toute différence entre les quantités énoncées dans ces pièces et celles introduites, quel qu'en soit le motif, fait supposer une fausse déclaration. *Arr. du* 27 *février* 1807, *Mém., tom.* 2, *p.* 547.—La substitution de tonneaux remplis d'eau à des tonneaux remplis de bière qu'un brasseur a déclaré expédier au-dehors à l'effet d'obtenir l'exemption du droit d'octroi, constitue une fausse déclaration qui entraîne une amende égale à la valeur de la bière déclarée pour la sortie. *Arr. du* 7 *janvier* 1814.—Aff. Beck.

12. (N° 4, 2ᵉ Tableau, p. 2).

1. Les heures pendant lesquelles l'introduction est permise, sont :

Pendant les mois de janvier, février, novembre et décembre, de sept heures du matin à six heures du soir.—Pendant les mois de mars, avril, septembre et octobre, de six heures du matin à sept du soir. — Pendant les mois de mai, juin, juillet et août, de cinq heures du matin à huit du soir.

13. (N° 5, 2e Tableau, p. 2).

1. Cette disposition ne concerne pas les eaux-de-vie dont la fabrication est soumise à des règles particulières, indiquées dans le 6e Tableau.

Elle ne concerne également pas les propriétaires récoltans pour les boissons qu'ils fabriquent *à l'époque ordinaire de la vendange et du pressurage des fruits*, ces propriétaires n'étant assujétis alors qu'à souffrir l'inventaire et le recensement indiqués aux numéros 7 et 8 du tableau.

Mais elle est applicable; 1° DANS LES COMMUNES OÙ LES DROITS SUR LES VENDANGES ET FRUITS SONT PERÇUS AU MOMENT DE L'INTRODUCTION: Aux particuliers non récoltans qui, n'importe à quelle époque de l'année, fabriqueraient des vins, cidres ou poirés, avec des raisins ou fruits récoltés dans l'intérieur, ou qui auraient été affranchis à l'entrée, tels que les fruits à couteau, les raisins destinés à être mangés à la main et les raisins secs.

2° DANS LES MÊMES COMMUNES: Aux propriétaires récoltans qui fabriqueraient, *à une autre époque que celle où les inventaires sont autorisés*, des vins, cidres ou poirés, avec des raisins ou des fruits de la même origine que ceux désignés ci-dessus.

3° DANS LES COMMUNES OUVERTES OU LA PERCEPTION SUR LES VENDANGES ET FRUITS N'EST PAS OPÉRÉE AU MOMENT DE L'INTRODUCTION: A toutes les fabrications de vins, cidres ou poirés faites avant ou après l'époque pendant laquelle les inventaires peuvent avoir lieu, avec des raisins et fruits ayant la même origine.

2. La déclaration préalable étant le seul moyen par lequel les personnes qui confectionnent des boissons peuvent, dans les cas ci-dessus, acquitter les droits dont le paiement est prescrit par l'art. 20, ces personnes sont en contravention à défaut de cette formalité, sans qu'elles puissent invoquer le bénéfice de l'art. 40, qui n'est applicable qu'aux propriétaires récoltans, pour les boissons fabriquées à l'époque ordinaire de la vendange, puisque d'ailleurs, passé cette époque, les Employés n'ont plus le droit de se présenter chez aucun particulier sans être accompagnés d'un officier de police.

Dans les communes ayant un octroi, cette déclaration est de rigueur pour tous les cas (excepté celui indiqué §. 5 de la note suivante); elle est prescrite par l'article 36 de l'ordonnance du 9 décembre 1814, qu'il faudra citer si la saisie est commune, et qui est ainsi conçu: « Toute personne qui récolte, » prépare ou fabrique, dans l'intérieur d'un lieu sujet, des objets compris » au tarif, est tenue, sous peine de l'amende prononcée par l'article 28, » d'en faire la déclaration, et d'acquitter immédiatement le droit, si elle ne » réclame l'entrepôt. — Les Préposés de l'octroi peuvent reconnaître à domi- » cile les quantités récoltées, préparées ou fabriquées, et faire toutes les » vérifications nécessaires pour prévenir la fraude. »

14. (N° 6, 2e Tableau, p. 2).

1. Dans celles des villes ouvertes où la perception des droits d'entrée sur les vendanges, pommes ou poires, ne peut être opérée au moment de l'introduction, la Régie est autorisée à faire faire, après la récolte, chez tous les propriétaires récoltans, l'inventaire des vins ou cidres fabriqués. Il en est de même à l'égard des vendanges et fruits récoltés dans l'intérieur d'un lieu sujet. Tout propriétaire qui ne réclame pas l'entrepôt, ou qui n'aura pas récolté (au moins 9 hectol. de vin, ou 18 hectol. de cidre ou poiré), sera tenu de payer immédiatement les droits d'entrée sur les vins ou cidres inventoriés. *Art. 40 de la loi du 28 avril 1816.* — Ces droits sont recouvrables par voie d'avertissement et de contrainte.

2. Les boissons dites *piquettes*, faites par les propriétaires récoltans avec de l'eau jetée sur de simples marcs sans pression, ne sont pas inventoriées chez eux, et sont exemptes du droit, à moins qu'elles ne soient déplacées pour être vendues en gros ou en détail. *Art.* 42 *idem.* — Cette exception ne peut s'entendre des cidres de seconde qualité, quoiqu'il entre de l'eau dans leur confection, et on ne doit l'appliquer qu'aux boissons provenant de l'eau passée simplement sur les marcs. *Arr. du* 17 *janvier* 1810, *Mém.*, *tom.* 6, *p.* 641.

3. Les piquettes (*voy.* §. 7, note 2, p. 29) ne pouvant être déplacées sans déclaration, ni circuler sans expédition, le droit d'entrée, lorsqu'elles en sont passibles, doit être perçu au moment même de la déclaration d'enlèvement.

4. Dans les communes où la perception du droit d'entrée est renvoyée après la récolte, l'habitant est tenu, quand les Employés se présentent à son domicile, de faire la déclaration exacte de ses boissons, à peine, en cas de fausse déclaration, de l'amende et de la confiscation prononcées pour les fausses déclarations à l'entrée. *Arr. du* 6 *août* 1813. —Aff. Hentz.

5. Dans les mêmes villes, les droits d'octroi, s'il y en a d'établis, se perçoivent de la même manière, et l'on doit citer, en cas de saisie commune, l'art. 46 de l'ordonnance du 6 décembre 1814.

15. (N° 7, 2e Tableau, p. 2).

1. L'absence volontaire d'un particulier qui laisse ses caves fermées pendant le temps des inventaires, doit être considérée comme un refus d'en faire l'ouverture, et donne lieu à l'application de l'amende. *Arr. du* 17 *mai* 1806, *Mém.*, *tom.* 1, *p.* 65.

2. Après avoir constaté l'opposition, il convient que les Employés se fassent assister d'un officier de police pour établir l'inventaire en sa présence.

16. (N° 8, 2e Tableau, p. 2).

1. Cette disposition n'est applicable qu'aux propriétaires qui ont eu entrepôt des boissons de leur récolte seulement; car s'ils avaient en même temps des boissons d'achat, ils seraient assujétis à toutes les obligations imposées par l'art. 37 de la loi du 28 avril 1816.

2. Les propriétaires ne sont soumis, outre l'inventaire, qu'à un recensement avant la récolte suivante.—Ils sont obligés de payer le droit d'entrée au fur et à mesure de leurs ventes à l'intérieur.—Lors du recensement ils doivent acquitter le même droit sur les manquans non justifiés, déduction faite de la quotité allouée pour coulage. *Art.* 41 *idem.*

3. Dans le premier cas, le droit doit être perçu au moment de la déclaration d'enlèvement; dans le second, il est recouvrable par voie d'avertissement et de contrainte.

17. (N° 1, 3e Tableau, p. 3).

1. Sont exempts les cantiniers des troupes établis dans les camps, forts et citadelles, pourvu qu'ils ne reçoivent que des militaires, et qu'ils aient une commission du Ministre de la guerre. *Art.* 51 *de la loi du* 18 *avril* 1816.— Plusieurs décisions ministérielles ont été rendues au sujet de cette disposition qui existait déjà dans l'ancienne législation sur les boissons; elles ont toutes eu pour objet de faire cesser des oppositions élevées pour des casernes et autres établissemens militaires auxquels l'exception n'était pas applicable.

Il serait superflu de rapporter ici ces décisions, attendu que les Employés, lorsqu'ils rencontrent des difficultés pareilles, doivent se borner à constater le refus qu'ils éprouvent, et à en rendre compte immédiatement à leur directeur, qui seul a qualité pour en informer l'Administration ou pour agir auprès des autorités compétentes, suivant le cas.

2. Un particulier qui vend en détail des boissons sans déclaration ne peut se soustraire aux peines prononcées par la loi, sous prétexte qu'il ne vend qu'à ses amis, et des boissons provenant d'un débitant qui en a acquitté les droits de détail. *Arr. du* 26 *août* 1808, *Mém.*, *tom.* 6, *p.* 548.

3. Un particulier ne peut, sans contravention, débiter des boissons qui lui ont été cédées en paiement, lorsqu'il n'a pas fait sa déclaration, et les juges ne peuvent se fonder sur un certificat du maire pour déclarer qu'un prévenu ne fait pas le commerce des boissons. *Arr. du* 13 *déc.* 1810, *Mém.*, *tom.* 7, *p.* 332.

4. Les chefs d'établissemens dont les ouvriers reçoivent, outre leur salaire, la nourriture et la boisson, doivent être considérés comme détaillans; mais on doit, autant que possible, les abonner. *D. A. n°* 66.

18. (N° 2, 3e Tableau, p. 3).

1. Les débitans doivent être contraints, outre les peines résultant de la contravention, au paiement des droits pour tout le temps écoulé depuis la déclaration de cesser, proportionnellement aux sommes constatées à leur charge pendant le trimestre précédent. *Art.* 67 *de la loi du* 28 *avril* 1816.

2. Les manquans reconnus par les exercices qui ont lieu chez les débitans pendant les trois mois qui suivent la déclaration de cesser ne doivent pas être soumis au droit de détail. *D. A. n°* 386.

19. (N° 3, 3e Tableau, p. 3).

1. Le défaut de déclaration pour l'établissement d'un débit de boissons est nécessairement accompagné d'une contravention aux droits de licence; alors les peines prononcées pour ces deux contraventions se confondent, ou, pour mieux dire, il n'y a qu'une seule et même peine, d'après l'art. 144, celle qui est prononcée par l'art. 95; mais si l'on verbalisait pour défaut de licence seulement, c'est d'après l'art. 171 qu'il faudrait procéder. *D. A. n°* 291.

2. Au commencement de l'année, époque du renouvellement des licences, les Employés, après avoir averti les redevables d'aller en acquitter le droit au bureau, doivent, à l'expiration d'un délai raisonnable, au 15 janvier, par exemple, rapporter procès-verbal (fondé alors sur l'art. 171) contre tous ceux qui n'auront pas satisfait à cette obligation. *Circ. n°* 22.—*Voy.* nomb. 30, §. 7, p. 85.

3. Le débitant qui porte des boissons dans les foires et marchés doit deux licences; mais le débitant forain ne doit qu'une licence s'il n'a pas d'établissement. §. 4 *de la Circ. n°* 11, *timbrée divisions territoriales.*

4. Le propriétaire débitant le vin de son cru n'est pas exempt de la licence; mais il n'est pas tenu à en prendre une seconde pour les ventes accidentelles qu'il peut faire successivement dans les foires de différentes communes. §. 5 *id.* —Il doit jouir, sur le prix de la licence, de la remise de 25 pour cent accordée par l'art. 85 de la loi du 28 avril. §. 27 *idem.*

5. Les débitans abonnés sont soumis à la licence, même dans le cas d'abonnement général. §. 6 *idem.*

6. Les débitans sont soumis à prendre autant de licences qu'ils ont d'établissemens, même lorsque ces établissemens sont fixés dans la même commune. §. 7 *id.*

7. Un débitant qui a pris licence dans une commune où il est établi, et qui va demeurer dans une autre, doit prendre, pour le nouveau débit qu'il a ouvert, une nouvelle licence. §. 10 *id.*

8. Le droit de licence est dû par un débitant chaque fois qu'il change de local, même sans quitter la commune. On peut cependant ne pas l'exiger des débitans qui ne font que déplacer leur établissement, sans interruption, *dans la même commune*, à moins qu'il n'y ait un changement notable dans le genre de commerce. §. 11 *id.*

9. Un débitant qui a cessé son débit dans le cours de l'année, et qui le reprend avant qu'elle soit expirée, n'est pas assujéti à une nouvelle licence, s'il n'y a pas changement de domicile et de personne. §. 12 *id.*

10. Lorsqu'un marchand en gros renonce à cette qualité pour prendre celle de débitant, il doit se munir d'une licence. §. 23 *id.*

11. Dans les communes où l'on prend les eaux, les personnes qui, pendant la saison, louent leurs appartemens à des étrangers, et les prennent en pension pour la nourriture seulement, ne doivent pas être assujéties à la licence. § 24 *id.*

12. Les débitans de bière sont tenus de prendre une licence. § 25 *idem.*

20. (N° 4, 3e Tableau, 3).

1. Les débitans sont obligés de faire la déclaration de toutes les boissons qu'ils ont en leur possession, sans distinction de celles qui sont l'objet de leur débit et de celles qui pourraient être destinées à leur consommation personnelle. *Arr. du* 13 *avril* 1809, *Mém.*, *tom.* 5, *p.* 264.—Cette question a encore été décidée par deux autres arrêts insérés au Mémorial, tom. 6, p. 656, et tom. 7, p. 263. Elle ne peut plus se reproduire, d'après l'art. 66 de la loi du 28 avril 1816, qui accorde aux débitans une remise de trois pour cent pour tous déchets et pour consommation de famille.

2. Dans les villes où les débitans sont exempts des exercices, ils ne sont pas moins obligés de déclarer les boissons qu'ils entreposent dans leurs magasins situés hors desdites villes. *Arr. du* 25 *mai* 1810, *Mém.*, *tom.* 6, *p.* 724; *autre du* 24 *août* 1811, *Mém.*, *tom.* 7, *p.* 187.

3. Un tribunal civil ne peut annuler une contrainte sous le prétexte que la boisson pour laquelle les droits sont demandés n'est que de la piquette. *Arr. du* 16 *janvier* 1816.—Aff. Noël.

4. Dès qu'une nouvelle déclaration aura été reçue par un buraliste, les Employés se transporteront au domicile du débitant pour y dresser l'inventaire de toutes les boissons en sa possession.—S'ils reconnaissent une différence en moins entre les quantités déclarées et celles représentées, ils tireront en produit le manquant; s'ils trouvent au contraire un excédant de quelque importance, ils exigeront qu'il leur soit exhibé des expéditions pour la quantité formant cet excédant. *Observations insérées dans le modèle de portatif de détail.*—Il résulte de ces observations qu'on ne doit pas faire de procès-verbal pour les différences reconnues dans un premier inventaire, lorsque ces différences portent sur les boissons mises en évidence par le débitant, qui ne peut être soupçonné, dans ce cas, d'aucune intention de fraude.—Il n'en serait pas de même si l'on découvrait chez lui des boissons cachées, soit à l'époque de cet inventaire, soit dans les exercices suivans.

21. (N° 5, 3e Tableau, p. 3).

1. Les débitans ne peuvent se dispenser d'établir le bouchon ou l'enseigne, sous prétexte que leur qualité est connue d'ailleurs par les Employés. *Arr. du* 25 *février* 1808, *Mém.*, *tom.* 3, *p.* 157.

2. Un débitant est en contravention toutes les fois qu'il n'a pas une enseigne ou bouchon pour indiquer son débit, même lorsqu'il est abonné, ou que son enseigne a été déplacée, et que c'est un accident qui l'a détruite. *Arr. du* 7 *avril* 1809, *Mém.*, *tom.* 5, *p.* 193.

22. (Nº 7, 3e Tableau, p. 3).

1. Les débitans abonnés à l'hectolitre sont dispensés de l'obligation de déclarer les prix de vente. *Art. 71 de la loi du* 28 *avril* 1816.

2. En cas de contestation relativement à l'exactitude des prix de vente, il en sera référé au Maire de la commune, lequel prononcera sur le différend, sauf le recours au Préfet.—Le droit sera provisoirement perçu d'après la décision du Maire, sauf rappel ou restitution. La décision ne pourra s'appliquer aux boissons vendues antérieurement à la contestation. *Art.* 49 *idem.*
Les Employés ne doivent avoir recours à cette disposition que dans le cas où ils n'auraient pas acquis la preuve que le débitant vend ses boissons, ou partie de ses boissons, à un prix plus élevé que celui indiqué par la déclaration ; car, lorsque cette preuve est établie, il y a lieu à verbaliser pour fausse déclaration, en contravention à l'art. 48. *D. A. n°* 409.—Il y aura encore lieu à verbaliser si le prix de vente était supérieur à celui fixé par le Maire.

3. Les débitans ne peuvent changer le prix de vente de leurs boissons sans faire une nouvelle déclaration. *Arr. du* 8 *février* 1810, *Mém., tom.* 6, *p.* 648.

23. (Nº 8, 3e Tableau, p. 3).

1. Cette affiche doit être apposée par le débitant dans le lieu le plus apparent de son domicile. *Art.* 48 *de la loi du* 28 *avril* 1816.

2. Ces affiches doivent être fournies aux débitans par la Régie. Le prix en est fixé à dix centimes. *Ordonnance du* 19 *juin* 1816.

24. (Nº 9, 3e Tableau, p. 3).

1. Les exercices peuvent avoir lieu chez les débitans pendant tout le temps où les lieux de débit sont ouverts au public. *Art.* 235 *de la loi du* 28 *avril* 1816.

2. Ils sont également permis, même les jours de fêtes et dimanches, à l'exception seulement des heures où, en raison du service divin, les débits sont fermés, en exécution des lois et ordonnances. *Art.* 56 *idem.*

3. Les abonnemens individuels, et par corporation, ne dispensent pas des exercices, ils ne sont supprimés, d'après l'art. 76, qu'à la suite des abonnemens généraux par commune.

4. Les procès-verbaux pour refus d'exercice doivent être présentés dans les vingt-quatre heures au Maire de la commune, et soumis à son visa. *Art.* 68 *id.* —En cas de refus du Maire, ou de son adjoint, si le Maire est empêché, les Employés devraient constater ce refus par un procès-verbal qui, alors, tiendrait lieu du visa exigé par la loi.

5. Les débitans qui auront refusé l'exercice seront contraints, nonobstant les suites à donner aux procès-verbaux, au paiement du droit de détail sur toutes les boissons restant en charge lors du dernier exercice. Ils seront tenus d'acquitter en outre le même droit, pendant tout le temps que les exercices seront suspendus, au prorata de la somme la plus élevée qu'ils auront payée pour un trimestre pendant les deux années précédentes.—Ceux qui n'auraient pas été soumis précédemment aux exercices, seront obligés d'acquitter une somme égale à celle payée par le débitant le plus imposé du même canton de justice de paix. *Idem.*

6. Lorsque les redevables refusent de se soumettre aux exercices, les Employés ne doivent pas se borner à constater ce refus ; mais ils doivent, autant que cela est possible, requérir l'officier de police pour effectuer leur visite, autrement on doit concevoir que les redevables, pour éviter d'être surpris dans une fraude, souvent très-considérable, ne manqueraient pas de faire

usage de ce moyen, afin de se ménager le temps de soustraire les objets de fraude. *Mém.*, *tom.* 3, *p.* 269.—Cette précaution aurait d'ailleurs l'avantage de rendre très-difficiles les inscriptions de faux, auxquelles les procès-verbaux pour refus d'exercice sont plus exposés, parce qu'ils ne portent que sur des objets matériels de fraude.

7. L'opposition aux exercices par une personne qui se trouve dans la maison d'un débitant, et qui agit en son nom, est une contravention dont le débitant est responsable, et dont il ne peut se justifier en alléguant que cette personne lui est étrangère. *Arr. du* 9 *mai* 1807, *Mém.*, *tom.* 2, *p.* 410.

8. Un assujéti qui refuse l'exercice, sous prétexte d'une inscription de faux qu'il a déclaré contre un procès-verbal précédemment rendu par les Employés qui se présentent chez lui, commet une contravention. *Arr. du* 11 *février* 1808, *Mém.*, *tom.* 3, *p.* 265.

9. Les injures verbales, l'opposition à la dégustation des boissons, constituent des refus d'exercice. *Arr. du* 8 *juillet* 1808, *Mém.*, *tom.* 4, *p.* 513.

10. Lorsque la femme d'un débitant de boissons, en l'absence de son mari, s'oppose aux exercices des Employés, le mari est responsable de cette contravention, et les poursuites peuvent être dirigées contre lui seulement. *Arr. du* 10 *novembre* 1809, *Mém.*, *tom.* 6, *p.* 528; *autre du* 12 *août* 1813. —Aff. Koger.

11. La simple opposition verbale aux exercices des Employés, constitue une contravention. *Arr. du* 16 *novembre* 1810, *Mém.*, *tom.* 7, *p.* 28.

12. Les injures et menaces, ou les emportemens contre les Employés, par les personnes que la loi assujétit à leurs exercices, constituent une opposition que la loi défend, et les tribunaux ne peuvent se dispenser de le reconnaître, en prétextant que les injures et menaces n'étaient pas de nature à intimider les Employés. *Arr. du* 7 *mai* 1813.—Aff. Petit-Didier.

25. (N° 10, 3e Tableau, p. 3).

1. L'opposition qu'un débitant met à ce que les Employés fassent usage de la sonde pliante, est un refus d'exercice, et c'est à l'Administration que les assujétis doivent s'adresser lorsqu'ils présument que les moyens de vérification mis en usage par les Employés peuvent être préjudiciables à leurs marchandises et à leurs ustensiles. *Arr. du* 4 *novembre* 1809, *Mém.*, *tom.* 6, *p.* 522; *autre du* 24 *janvier* 1812, *Mém. tom.* 7, *p.* 195.

2. L'opposition verbale à la dégustation des boissons est un refus d'exercice. *Arr. du* 6 *août* 1813.—Aff. Tamisier.

26. (N° 11, 3e Tableau, p. 4).

1. La demande de l'assistance d'un officier de police par un débitant, pour permettre la visite de ses appartemens, doit être considérée comme un refus d'exercice qui entraîne la condamnation à l'amende, lors même que le débitant aurait, immédiatement après, souffert l'exercice en présence de l'officier de police appelé par les Employés. *Arr. du* 27 *mai* 1808, *Mém.*, *tom.* 4, *p.* 385.

2. Il y a refus d'exercice de la part d'un débitant chez lequel on trouve des caisses ou des armoires qu'il ne veut ouvrir, prétextant qu'il n'en a pas les clefs et qu'elles ne lui appartiennent point. *Arr. du* 30 *mars* 1810, *Mém.*, *tom.* 6, *p.* 598.

3. Le retard qu'un débitant met à ouvrir une partie de ses appartemens, est un refus d'exercice. *Arr. du* 29 *juillet* 1813, *Mém.*, *tom.* 8, *p.* 142.

4. Le droit que les Employés ont de faire des visites chez un débitant de

boissons est général et illimité. La contravention résultant du refus d'ouvrir un meuble, sur la demande des Employés, ne peut être couverte par l'offre que le débitant a faite de l'ouvrir en présence d'un commissaire de police. *Arr. du 27 décembre* 1817.—Aff. Rouillé-Hutinot.

27. (N° 13, 3ᵉ Tableau, p. 4).

1. Le débitant ne peut être renvoyé de la contravention qui résulte du défaut d'identité entre l'expédition et les boissons, sous le prétexte que l'inexactitude de l'expédition provient du fait du vendeur qui a fait la déclaration. *Arr. du* 5 *novembre* 1806, *Mém.*, *tom.* 1, *p.* 193.

2. Les aubergistes ne peuvent recevoir, dans les cours de leurs maisons, des charrettes chargées de boissons non accompagnées d'expéditions. *Arr. du* 30 *janvier* 1807, *Mém.*, *tom.* 1, *p.* 326.

3. Un débitant ne peut être absous de la contravention qui résulte du défaut d'expédition pour des boissons introduites chez lui, lors même que l'omission proviendrait de la négligence de l'expéditeur. *Arr. du* 9 *mai* 1807, *Mém.*, *tom.* 2, *p.* 521.

4. Des boissons introduites chez un débitant avec une expédition sur laquelle il n'est pas indiqué comme destinataire, sont saisissables, et le débitant est en contravention. *Arr. du* 22 *mai* 1807, *Mém.*, *tom.* 2, *p.* 458.

5. Il n'y a pas lieu à exiger d'expédition pour les raisins égrappés ou foulés achetés par un débitant avant l'égrappage, à moins que les Employés ne soient en état de contester ce fait, et d'empêcher le débitant d'en faire la preuve. *Arr. des* 12 *et* 27 *février* 1808, *Mém.*, *tom.* 3, *p.* 210 *et* 346.

6. Il en est de même pour les boissons provenant de la récolte des débitans, et fabriquées chez eux. *Arr. du* 5 *mars* 1808, *Mém.*, *tom.* 3, *p.* 141.

7. L'irrégularité d'une expédition ne peut être excusée par la déclaration que fait l'expéditeur qu'il a commis une erreur dans sa déclaration. *Arr. du* 10 *juin* 1808, *Mém.*, *tom.* 4, *p.* 392.

8. Lorsque l'on trouve chez un débitant des pièces non marquées renfermant des boissons, elles sont présumées avoir été introduites en fraude chez le débitant, si le portatif énonce qu'à l'époque du dernier exercice, toutes les pièces prises en charge étaient marquées. *Arr. du* 8 *juillet* 1808, *Mém.*, *tom.* 4, *p.* 667.

9. La déclaration faite par la femme d'un débitant que la boisson lui a été vendue par un particulier autre que celui énoncé sur l'expédition, ne peut compromettre l'expéditeur, mais elle constitue le débitant en contravention. *Arr. du* 3 *novembre* 1808, *Mém.*, *tom.* 4, *p.* 710.

10. Lorsque l'expédition qui accompagne des boissons n'est pas précisément celle qui est prescrite par la loi, il y a contravention, malgré l'existence d'une autre pièce équivalente qui exclut toute idée de fraude et qui constate le paiement des droits. *Arr. du* 2 *mars* 1809, *Mém.*, *tom.* 5, *p.* 129.

11. Un débitant ne peut, sans contravention, introduire des boissons dans son domicile en vertu d'expéditions prises au nom de divers particuliers pour le compte desquels il prétend que les boissons sont destinées. *Arr. du* 1ᵉʳ *septembre* 1809, *Mém.*, *tom.* 6, *p.* 513.

12. Un débitant ne peut se dispenser de représenter les expéditions de quelques pièces de vin trouvées dans son domicile, sous prétexte que le vin est gâté, et que, d'ailleurs, il a déjà fait sa déclaration de cesser. *Arr. du* 10 *novembre* 1809, *Mém.*, *tom.* 6, *p.* 528.

13. La déclaration des Préposés qui reconnaissent avoir commis une erreur

dans la rédaction d'une expédition, ne peut absoudre le débitant de la contravention qui résulte de l'irrégularité de cette expédition. *Arr. du 8 février 1810, Mém., tom.* 6, *p.* 672.

14. Lorsque l'on trouve chez un débitant un excédant au nombre des bouteilles prises en charge, pour lequel il ne représente aucune expédition, cet excédant doit être considéré comme introduit en fraude, et le débitant est dans le cas de l'amende et de la confiscation, quoiqu'il prétendit que cet excédant provient de la transvasion d'une pièce en charge. *Arr. du 15 juin* 1810, *Mém., tom.* 6, *p.* 714.

15. Lorsqu'on trouve dans une cruche, chez un débitant, des boissons différentes de celles prises en charge, il y a contravention, si ces boissons, quelque foible qu'en soit la quantité, n'ont pas été déclarées aux Employés. *Arr. du 9 février* 1812, *Mém., tom.* 8, *p.* 14.

16. Un débitant qui fait sortir de son domicile une pièce de vin accompagnée d'une expédition régulière, pour en faire la vente à une foire, ne peut faire rentrer chez lui le reste de cette boisson qu'il n'a pas vendue, sans se munir d'une nouvelle expédition pour la quantité restée. *Arr. du* 1er *mai* 1812, *Mém., tom.* 7, *p.* 358.—*Voy.* le § 20 ci-après.

17. Une très-petite quantité de boissons trouvée chez un débitant, pour laquelle il ne peut représenter d'expédition, est réputée introduite en fraude, et la confiscation, ainsi que l'amende, doivent être prononcées contre le débitant, quoique les boissons eussent été réclamées par une personne qui est présente et qui en demande la restitution. *Arr. du 22 janvier* 1813, *Mém., tom.* 8, *p.* 65.

18. Le débitant qui n'a plus de boissons à ses charges au portatif, et chez lequel on trouve une bouteille de vin pour laquelle il ne peut représenter d'expédition, est en contravention, et ne peut être dispensé de l'amende et de la confiscation, quoique le vin eût été apporté par une personne avec laquelle il s'est trouvé à boire chez lui. *Arr. du 3 juin* 1813. Aff. Revol.

19. Lorsqu'il est constaté par un procès-verbal qu'il existe une différence de qualité entre du vin trouvé dans un broc servant à la vente chez un débitant et les vins contenus dans la pièce prise en charge, il s'ensuit nécessairement que le vin trouvé dans le broc a été introduit sans expédition, et il y a lieu à prononcer la confiscation dudit vin, ainsi que l'amende de 50 fr. à 300 fr. L'allégation que la différence reconnue par les Employés doit être attribuée au séjour du vin dans le broc et au contact de l'air, plutôt qu'à une diversité de nature, est inadmissible. *Arr. du 22 août* 1817. — Aff. Gissot et Massonnier.

20. Les boissons transportées sur un champ de foire en quantité inférieure à un hectolitre doivent être accompagnées d'un passavant s'il s'agit de vin ou de cidre, ou d'un acquit-à-caution s'il s'agit d'eaux-de-vie ou liqueurs; le compte du débitant n'est déchargé que sur la représentation de la quittance du droit de détail payé sur le champ de foire : la quantité invendue peut rentrer au moyen d'une simple autorisation des Employés au dos du passavant. *D. A. n*° 165.

21. Il peut arriver que le jaugeage des pièces, lors de la prise en charge, fasse reconnaître une différence en plus ou en moins, entre les contenances réelles et celles exprimées aux expéditions. Les Employés doivent, dans l'un et l'autre cas, rapporter procès-verbal, si cette différence est d'une certaine importance; si elle est peu considérable, ils se borneront à prendre en charge les vaisseaux pour les quantités reconnues par le jaugeage. Mention des différences sera faite au dos des congés. *Observations insérées dans le modèle de portatif de détail.* — *Voy.* §. 2, note 3, p. 29.

28. (N° 14, 3e Tableau, p. 4).

1. Le défaut de représenter une expédition au moment des exercices est une contravention, lors même que le congé serait représenté après le procès-verbal. *Arr. du* 11 *mars* 1808, *Mém.*, *tom.* 3, *p.* 204; *autre du* 17 *février* 1809, *Mém.*, *tom.* 5, *p.* 199.

2. Les débitans sont tenus de déclarer toutes les boissons qu'ils ont en leur possession au moment de l'exercice, et de representer les expéditions qui ont dû accompagner ces boissons; à défaut, ils sont en contravention et ne peuvent s'en excuser en prétendant que les Préposés ont pu voir toutes leurs boissons, et qu'ils doivent s'imputer de ne les avoir pas prises en charge. *Arr. du* 4 *août* 1809, *Mém.*, *tom.* 6, *p.* 473.

3. La contravention résultant du défaut de représentation d'un congé pour des nouvelles venues chez un débitant, ne peut être justifiée, quand même il serait prouvé que l'expédition existait réellement lors de l'enlèvement des boissons. *Arr. du* 30 *mars* 1810, *Mém.*, *tom* 6, *p.* 598; *autre du* 3 *septembre* 1813. —Aff. Lehaire.

4. La contravention que commet un débitant lorsqu'il ne peut produire ni l'expédition pour le transport qui a dû accompagner les boissons introduites chez lui, ni la quittance du droit d'entrée, ne peut être couverte sous prétexte que le buraliste a mis du retard dans la vérification des boissons à l'entrée, et que le débitant lui a déposé au passage l'expédition, ainsi que la valeur présumée du droit d'entrée. *Arr. du* 14 *mars* 1817.—Aff. Sicard.

29. (N° 15, 3e Tableau, p. 4).

1. Les débitans sont également tenus de représenter les quittances des droits d'octroi ou de banlieue lorsqu'ils y sont soumis. *Art.* 53 *de la loi du* 28 *avril* 1816.

2. On doit considérer comme étant communes à l'octroi et à la Régie, les saisies faites chez les débitans par défaut de représentation d'expédition de l'octroi dans le cas prévu par l'article 53 précité. *Circulaire timbrée Contentieux*, n° 17.—Le défaut d'expédition d'une quittance de droits d'octroi rend la saisie commune, lors même que le débitant ne serait pas soumis aux droits d'entrée. *D. A. n°* 63.

3. Le débitant, dans un lieu sujet, est en contravention par le fait seul de l'introduction, dans son domicile, de boissons pour lesquelles les droits d'entrée n'ont pas été acquittés, sans qu'il puisse être affranchi des suites de cette contravention, sous prétexte que le voiturier doit seul être poursuivi, comme étant chargé par la loi de faire ce paiement. *Arr. du* 26 *décembre* 1811, *Mém.*, *tom.* 7, *p.* 338. Voy. §. 4, note 28.

30. (N° 16, 3e Tableau, p. 4).

1. Toutes les boissons trouvées chez un débitant sont censées lui appartenir, quoiqu'elles soient dans des caves qu'il prétend avoir données à loyer, si la location n'est pas prouvée par un bail authentique. *Arr. du* 6 *juin*, 1807, *Mém.*, *tom.* 1, *p.* 338.

2. Le propriétaire d'un local est légalement présumé le propriétaire des boissons qui y sont renfermées, dès qu'on ne représente aucun bail qui puisse justifier que ces boissons appartiennent à une autre personne. *Arr. du* 21 *avril* 1809, *Mém.*, *tom.* 5, *p.* 206.

3. Les boissons trouvées chez un débitant dans un lieu qui n'est pas destiné à les recevoir, sont réputées avoir été recélées, quelque faible qu'en soit la

quantité, et le débitant ne peut se justifier de la contravention en alléguant que le vin saisi n'était pas bon et marchand. *Arr. du 16 novembre* 1810, *Mém., tom.* 7, *p.* 28.

4. Il y a contravention lorsque des boissons qui doivent, d'après les expéditions, être transportées au domicile d'un débitant, sont déposées dans un autre local, quand même le débitant serait propriétaire de ce local. *Arr. du 24 août* 1811, *Mém., tom.* 7, *p.* 187.—*Voy.* note 38, §§. 5, 6 et 7.

31. (N° 17, 3e Tableau, p. 4).

1. Les maisons, caves ou celliers donnés à loyer par les débitans, sont toujours censés leur appartenir, quoique séparés de leur habitation, si la location n'est pas prouvée par un bail authentique, et les boissons trouvées dans ces maisons, caves ou celliers sont saisissables, quoique arrivées avec des expéditions au nom du prétendu locataire. *Arr. du 9 novembre* 1810, *Mém., tom.* 7, *p.* 75.

2. Un débitant qui habite seul une maison dans laquelle il fait son débit est censé occuper toute la maison, s'il n'est prouvé par un bail authentique qu'une partie qu'il prétend ne pas occuper a été réservée par le propriétaire ou louée à un tiers. *Arr. du* 11 *juillet* 1817.—Aff. Maugé.

3. Il résulte de l'art. 61 que, toutes les fois que des boissons appartenant à un débitant sont trouvées dans le domicile, les caves ou celliers d'un particulier, elles sont saisissables, tant sur lui que sur le débitant, s'il n'y a pas bail authentique pour les lieux où les boissons sont déposées, et qu'ils sont l'un et l'autre passibles de l'amende; mais que quand il y a un bail authentique, les boissons doivent être saisies sur le débitant seulement si elles n'ont pas été déclarées aux Employés.—*Voy.* note 38, §§. 5, 6 et 7.

32. (N° 18, 3e Tableau, p. 4).

1. Le procès-verbal doit porter saisie de la quantité de boissons existant au moment de la découverte de la fraude; les dixièmes reconnus manquans dans les précédens exercices doivent être tirés en produit, on doit faire la décharge, par un acte motivé, de la quantité restant dans la pièce lors du dernier exercice; enfin si la pièce saisie est laissée à la garde du contrevenant, elle doit être reprise en charge à son compte pour la quantité qu'elle contient réellement. *D. A.* nos 423 et 496.

33. (N° 19, 3e Tableau, p. 4).

1. Le débitant qui cherche à soustraire aux Employés la connaissance du débit de partie de ses boissons, en substituant de l'eau à celles prises en charge, et vendues en détail, est en contravention, et doit être condamné à l'amende et à la confiscation des boissons débitées furtivement. *Arr. du 15 juin* 1810, *Mém.*; *tom.* 6, *p.* 714.

2. La substitution de tonneaux remplis d'eau à des tonneaux renfermant des boissons prises en charge chez un débitant, est une contravention qui nécessite l'application de l'amende et de la confiscation des vins manquans. *Arr. du* 18 *novembre* 1813.—Aff. Faugère.

34. (N° 20, 3e Tableau, p. 4).

1. Il y a exception pour la mise en bouteille des vins, qui est autorisée, pourvu que la transvasion ait lieu en présence des Employés; alors les bouteilles doivent être cachetées du cachet de la Régie, et, à cet effet, le débitant doit fournir la cire et le feu. *Art.* 58 *de la loi du* 28 *avril* 1816.

2. La défense faite aux débitans par l'art. 58 de la loi du 28 avril, s'applique

non seulement aux vaisseaux renfermés dans leurs caves, mais encore à ceux qui peuvent se trouver dans leur domicile et dans les chambres qui servent à leur habitation personnelle. *Arr. du* 16 *juin* 1808, *Mém.*, *tom.* 4, *p.* 460.

3. Le débitant qui a des boissons dans des vases d'une contenance inférieure à un hectolitre ne peut excuser cette contravention en alléguant que ces boissons n'étaient que du vin de rebut et non destiné à la vente. *Arr. du* 16 *novembre* 1810, *Mém.*, *tom.* 7, *p.* 28.

4. Il suffit qu'il y ait des boissons dans un vaisseau d'une contenance inférieure à l'hectolitre, quelque faible qu'en soit la quantité, pour constituer le débitant en contravention. *Arr. du* 9 *février* 1812, *Mém.*, *tom.* 8, *p.* 14.

5. Le débitant chez lequel on trouve des boissons dans un vaisseau d'une contenance inférieure à un hectolitre, ne peut se disculper en prétendant que le vaisseau ne lui appartient pas, qu'il a été laissé chez lui par un inconnu à qui il a vendu la boisson qu'il contient, et qui doit venir le reprendre dans peu d'instans. *Arr. du* 25 *juillet* 1812, *Mém.*, *tom.* 7, *p.* 268.

6. Les tribunaux ne peuvent admettre l'excuse donnée par un débitant qui prétend, pour s'opposer au cachetage des bouteilles, que les vins qu'elles contiennent sont des vins vieux qui ne peuvent supporter sans dépréciation le mouvement que le cachetage occasionnerait. *Arr. du* 9 *avril* 1813.—Aff. Bêcu.

7. Un débitant chez lequel les Employés trouvent et saisissent un vaisseau d'une contenance inférieure à un hectolitre, est en contravention à l'art. 58 de la loi du 28 avril 1816, lorsqu'il ne justifie pas d'une autorisation spéciale et individuelle pour faire usage de ces sortes de vaisseaux, et les tribunaux ne peuvent se dispenser de prononcer l'amende et la confiscation, sous la considération que le vase saisi est d'une trop faible capacité pour être assimilé aux vaisseaux prohibés par la loi, et que le débitant ne s'en servait qu'afin de s'éviter la peine de descendre à chaque instant à sa cave. *Arr. du* 21 *mars* 1817.—Aff. Martineau.

8. Il n'est pas nécessaire, lorsque l'on trouve du vin dans un vase de petite dimension caché chez un débitant, qu'un remplissage frauduleux soit prouvé pour lui appliquer l'amende et prononcer la confiscation, puisque l'existence seule du vin en vaisseau d'une contenance au-dessous de l'hectolitre constitue une contravention. *Arr. du* 27 *décembre* 1807.—Aff. Poulvert.

35. (N° 22, 3ᵉ Tableau, p. 5).

1. Les débitans de boissons de leur cru, jouissant de la remise de 25 pour cent, sont libres d'établir leur vente en détail sur des vaisseaux d'une contenance supérieure à cinq hectolitres. *Art.* 86 *de la loi du* 28 *avril* 1816.

2. On pourra user de tolérance à l'égard des futailles dont la contenance surpasse de peu de chose cinq hectolitres. §. 78, *Instruction n°* 36.

36. (N° 24, 3ᵉ Tableau, p. 5).

1. Le droit de détail doit être constaté sur la contenance des futailles enlevées sans démarque. *Art.* 57 *de la loi du* 28 *avril* 1816.

2. Si un débitant, en représentant une quittance, demandait la décharge de boissons qu'il aurait enlevées sans que les futailles eussent été démarquées, et qu'il prétendrait avoir vendues en gros, elle lui serait refusée, et la quantité manquante serait tirée en produit. Les Employés relateraient dans l'acte, *qu'ils n'ont eu aucun égard à la quittance représentée, le débitant ne s'étant point conformé aux formalités prescrites par l'art.* 57 *de la loi du* 28 *avril* 1816. —*Observations insérées dans le portatif de détail.*

3. On ne doit pas considérer la déclaration de vente en gros que le débitant

fait chez le buraliste, afin d'obtenir une expédition, comme emportant réquisition aux Employés de démarquer; et, malgré cette déclaration, le débitant ne peut enlever ni livrer la pièce qu'elle n'ait été démarquée. *Arr. du* 27 *février* 1808, *Mém.. tom* 3, *p.* 193.

37. (N° 25, 3e Tableau, p. 5).

1. Cet article ne permet qu'un seul râpé de raisin d'une contenance de trois hectolitres pour les débitans qui ont en cave au moins trente hectolitres de vin. Ainsi il y a lieu à verbaliser, 1° contre les débitans qui, n'ayant pas en cave la quantité de vin prescrite, auraient chez eux un ou plusieurs râpés, de quelque nature que ce soit; 2° contre les débitans ayant plus de trente hectolitres de vin qui auraient chez eux plus d'un râpé de raisin, ou un râpé de raisin d'une contenance supérieure à trois hectolitres, ou un râpé d'une autre substance que le raisin.

38. (N° 27, 3e Tableau, p. 5).

1. S'il y a impossibilité d'interdire les communications, il n'y a pas lieu à dresser procès-verbal, mais le voisin du débitant peut être soumis aux exercices et au paiement des droits de détail lorsque sa consommation apparente est évidemment supérieure à ses facultés et à la consommation réelle de sa famille, d'après les habitudes du pays. *Art.* 62 *de la loi du* 28 *avril* 1816.

2. Avant de procéder à aucune opération, les Employés feront, par écrit, un rapport à leur Directeur, et ne pourront commencer les exercices sans exhiber l'arrêté du Préfet qui l'aura autorisé. *Art.* 63 *idem.*

3. Les Employés doivent adresser le résultat de cet exercice au Directeur, qui leur fera connaître la quantité de boissons allouée pour consommation et celle assujétie au paiement des droits. *Art.* 64 *idem.*

4. L'existence de portes de communications avec des maisons voisines constitue le débitant en contravention, quoique les Employés n'aient point exigé qu'elles soient scellées. *Arr. du* 23 *octobre* 1807, *Mém., tom.* 2, *p.* 649; *autre du* 4 *février* 1808, *Mém., tom.* 3, *p.* 79.

5. Les boissons trouvées dans les caves qui communiquent avec le domicile d'un débitant, sont réputées recelées, soit par le fait de l'existence d'une porte de communication, soit par l'identité des boissons recelées avec celles qui sont en charge au compte du débitant. — Le droit que les Employés ont d'exiger la fermeture des portes de communication, n'est qu'un mode d'exécution qui n'empêche pas la saisie des boissons recelées. — Les portes de communication avec les caves ou maisons voisines ne sont pas permises à un débitant, quoique la communication ait lieu dans un local qu'il tient à loyer, et dans lequel il n'exerce pas son débit. *Arr. du* 7 *décembre* 1810, *Mém., tom.* 7, *p.* 84.

6. Lorsqu'il n'y a pas de communication intérieure entre la cave d'un débitant et le domicile d'un particulier, mais que la porte de l'un et de l'autre sont contiguës et placées dans la même cour, on doit considérer comme recelées et appartenant au débitant, les boissons trouvées dans le domicile de ce particulier, surtout lorsque d'autres circonstances, comme la faiblesse du débit ostensible, fortifient la présomption du recelé. *Arr. du* 24 *mars* 1811, *Mém., tom.* 7, *p.* 281.

7. Les boissons trouvées dans un lieu qui communique au domicile d'un débitant sont censées lui appartenir, quoiqu'un particulier non débitant s'en déclare le propriétaire, et ces boissons peuvent être saisies, quoiqu'il n'existe pas de preuve positive que le débitant en fait usage pour alimenter son débit. *Arr. du* 19 *février* 1813, *Mém., tom.* 8, *p.* 23.

39. (N° 28, 3ᵉ Tableau, p. 5).

1. Cette vente pourra toutefois être autorisée si le local où se tient le débit est totalement séparé de l'atelier de distillation. *Art.* 69 *de la loi du* 28 *avril* 1816.

40. (N° 29, 3ᵉ Tableau, p. 5).

1. Les procès-verbaux, dans ce cas, sont dressés à la requête des débitans ou de leurs syndics, et les poursuites sont exercées par eux. *Art.* 82 *de la loi du* 28 *avril* 1816.—La Régie doit rester étrangère à ces poursuites. *D. A.* n° 151. Mais si on verbalise pour introduction, à domicile, de boissons sans expéditions, on doit suivre les règles ordinaires quant aux poursuites et à la répartition du produit de l'amende et de la confiscation. *D. A. n°* 259.

2. Lorsqu'un nouveau débitant remplace un débitant compris dans la répartition, il n'y a pas contravention. *Art.* 80 *idem.*

3. Il en est de même pour les personnes auxquelles les débitans abonnés ou leurs syndics auraient accordé le droit de vendre en détail des boissons. *Art.* 83 *idem.*

41. (N° 30, 3ᵉ Tableau, p. 5).

1. Ces débitans doivent encore faire la vente de leurs boissons par eux-mêmes, ou par des domestiques à leurs gages, dans des maisons à eux appartenant, ou qu'ils auront louées par bail authentique. *Art.* 85 *de la loi du* 28 *avril* 1816.

2. Ils ne peuvent fournir aux buveurs que les boissons déclarées, avec des bancs et des tables. *Art.* 86 *id.*

3. Les visites et exercices des commis n'auront pas lieu dans l'intérieur de leur domicile, pourvu que le local où les boissons sont vendues en détail en soit séparé. *Même article.*

4. Le propriétaire qui fait la déclaration de vendre en détail les boissons de son cru est tenu de faire, comme les débitans ordinaires, la déclaration de toutes les boissons qu'il a en sa possession, même de celles placées ailleurs que dans son domicile et le lieu de son débit. — Il ne peut imputer aux Préposés de la Régie l'omission qui se trouve dans sa déclaration. *Arr. du* 2 *janvier* 1809, *Mém., tom.* 5, *p.* 73.

5. Ces débitans sont, comme les débitans ordinaires, soumis aux visites et exercices des commis, pendant les trois mois qui suivent la déclaration de cesser. *Arr. du* 11 *janvier* 1810, *Mém.*, *tom.* 6, *p.* 577.

6. Ils n'ont pas droit à la remise de 25 pour cent sur les eaux-de-vie qu'ils distillent et qu'ils vendent en détail. *D. A. n°* 1.

42. (N° 1. 4ᵉ Tableau, p. 6).

1. Tout particulier qui reçoit ou expédie, soit pour son compte, soit pour le compte d'autrui, des boissons, soit en futaille d'un hectolitre au moins, ou en plusieurs futailles, qui, réunies, contiendraient plus d'un hectolitre, soit en caisses et paniers de vingt-cinq bouteilles et au-dessus, doit être considéré comme marchand en gros. *Art.* 98 *de la loi du* 28 *avril* 1816.

2. Sont exceptés néanmoins : 1° les particuliers recevant accidentellement une pièce, une caisse ou un panier de vin, pour le partager avec d'autres personnes, pourvu que, dans la déclaration, l'expéditeur ait énoncé, outre le nom et le domicile du destinataire, ceux des copartageans, et la quantité destinée à chacun : 2° les personnes qui, dans le cas de changement de domicile, veudraient les boissons qu'elles auraient reçues pour leur consommation ;

3° les personnes qui vendraient, immédiatement après le décès de celle à qui elles auraient succédé, les boissons dépendant de la succession et provenant de sa récolte et de ses provisions, pourvu qu'elle ne soit ni marchand en gros, ni débitant, ni fabricant de boissons. *Art.* 99 *id.*

43. (N° 1, 4e Tableau, p. 6).

1. Les marchands en gros ne peuvent faire une déclaration de cesser tant qu'ils conservent en leur possession des boissons qu'ils auraient reçues en raison de ce commerce, excepté toutefois lorsque la quantité n'excède pas celle reconnue nécessaire pour leur propre consommation. *Art.* 105 *de la loi du* 28 *avril* 1816.—A moins d'une exagération évidente et hors de mesure, on doit se montrer facile sur les quantités restantes au moment où un marchand en gros déclare cesser son commerce. *D. A.* n° 385.

44. (N° 2, 4e Tableau, p. 6).

1. Toute vente de boissons en quantité au-dessous de l'hectolitre si elles sont en futailles, ou au-dessous de 25 litres si elles sont en bouteilles, est considérée comme vente en détail. *Art.* 102 *de la loi du* 28 *avril* 1816.

2. Les marchands en gros peuvent faire accidentellement des ventes de cette nature, pour lesquelles ils sont tenus de payer le droit de détail. *Art.* 102 *id.* —Ce droit est perçu par le buraliste au moment où il reçoit la déclaration.

45. (N° 3, 4e Tableau, p. 6).

1. Si cette contravention est constatée en même temps que celle pour défaut de déclaration, il n'y a également lieu qu'à une seule peine, celle prononcée par l'art. 106. *Voy.* §§. 1 et 2, note 19, p. 35.

2. Les marchands en gros ne sont assujétis qu'à une seule licence pour tous leurs magasins situés sur le territoire de la commune où ils ont fait leur déclaration. §. 8, *Circ. n°* 11, *Divisions territoriales.*—Tout magasin situé dans une autre commune donne ouverture au paiement d'une autre licence. § 9 *id.*

3. Les colporteurs ne sont tenus qu'à une licence s'ils n'ont pas un établissement fixe, autrement ils doivent en avoir deux. §. 13 *id.*

4. Un entrepositaire dont le compte n'est chargé que de liqueurs étrangères déposées dans les magasins de la Douane, et qu'il est tenu de réexporter, n'est pas soumis à la licence s'il ne fait aucun commerce de boissons. §. 14 *id.*

5. Les fournisseurs de subsistances militaires et leurs agens, qui fournissent des boissons au gouvernement, doivent prendre autant de licences qu'ils ont d'établissemens particuliers situés dans différentes communes. §. 15 *id.*—Cette décision a été modifiée et rétablie par les circulaires n°s 14 et 19.

6. Un marchand en gros dans une commune, et en même temps propriétaire dans une autre, n'est pas obligé de prendre une licence dans la commune où il est simplement propriétaire, lorsqu'il ne dépose dans les caves de ses vignobles que les vins de sa récolte. §. 16 *id.*

7. Les commissionnaires de roulage ne sont tenus de prendre une licence qu'autant qu'ils font le commerce des boissons, et qu'ils sont désignés dans les expéditions comme vendeurs, acheteurs, expéditeurs ou destinataires.—Ils n'y sont pas soumis s'ils ne reçoivent des boissons qu'en transit. §. 17 *id.*

8. Les négocians et armateurs qui reçoivent des boissons pour la consommation de leurs équipages ou pour le commerce extérieur, doivent le droit de licence. § 18 *id.*

9. Il est également dû par les personnes qui reçoivent des boissons destinées à être expédiées soit en France, soit hors du royaume. §. 19 *id.*

10. Les étapiers qui reçoivent des boissons en dépôt d'un marché à l'autre, ne sont pas soumis à la licence s'ils ne vendent pas des boissons dans l'intervalle du marché, pour le compte des propriétaires; dans le cas contraire, ils doivent le droit. §. 20 *id.*

11. Les personnes qui, d'un marché à l'autre, placent des boissons dans des magasins loués en leur nom, ne sont pas assujéties à la licence, si ces boissons proviennent de leur récolte; le droit est exigible si ces boissons proviennent d'achat. §. 21 *id.*

12. Les propriétaires jouissant de l'entrepôt dans leur domicile pour les boissons provenant de leur récolte, dans les lieux sujets, ne sont pas tenus de se munir d'une licence. §. 22 *id.*

13. Tout vinaigrier qui reçoit chez lui des boissons dans l'état où il les achète, doit prendre une licence de marchand en gros; il en sera cependant dispensé s'il se soumet à verser sur son vin, avant de l'introduire chez lui, une quantité suffisante de vinaigre pour qu'il cesse d'être potable. §. 26 *id.*

46. (N° 4, 4e Tableau, p. 6).

1. Les marchands en gros doivent faire la déclaration de toutes les boissons qu'ils possèdent, à quel titre que ce soit, même celles provenant de leur récolte, et déposées dans une autre commune que celle où ils ont fait leur déclaration de marchands en gros. *Arr. du* 21 *juillet* 1808, *Mém.*, *tom.* 4, *p.* 577.

47. (N° 5, 4e Tableau, p. 6).

1. On doit saisir tout excédant de vin ou de cidre, trouvé sans expédition, chez un marchand en gros, lors même que celui-ci prétendrait que cet excédant provient de coupages ou de mélanges faits hors la présence des Employés. *D. A.* n° 179.

48. (N° 6, 4e Tableau, p. 6).

1. Les commissionnaires doivent représenter les expéditions pour les boissons qu'ils placent dans les entrepôts publics, comme pour celles qu'ils reçoivent dans leurs magasins particuliers. *Arr. du* 26 *mars* 1808, *Mém.*, *tom.* 3, *p.* 278.

49. (N° 7, 4e Tableau, p. 6).

1. Les vérifications des Employés ne peuvent avoir lieu que dans les magasins, caves et celliers des marchands en gros, et seulement depuis le lever jusqu'au coucher du soleil. *Art.* 101 *de la loi du* 28 *avril* 1816.

2. Les Employés pourraient néanmoins faire des visites dans l'intérieur des habitations des marchands en gros, en cas de soupçon de fraude; mais alors ils devraient se faire accompagner par un officier de police, en se conformant à l'art. 237 de la loi précitée.

50. (N° 1, 5e Tableau, p. 7).

1. Les brasseurs sont tenus de faire au bureau de la Régie la déclaration de leur profession, et du lieu où sont situés leurs établissemens. *Art.* 117 *de la loi du* 28 *avril* 1816.

2. Les particuliers qui ne brassent que pour leur consommation, les colléges, maisons d'instruction et autres établissemens publics, sont assujétis aux mêmes taxes que les brasseurs, et tenus aux mêmes obligations.—Néanmoins il doit être établi pour les hôpitaux un droit proportionnel à la qualité de la bière qu'ils font fabriquer pour leur consommation intérieure. — Ce droit est réglé par des experts. *Art.* 128 *idem.*

3. Les brasseurs doivent déposer au bureau, en même temps qu'ils font leur déclaration, une empreinte de la marque dont leurs tonneaux doivent être revêtus. *Art.* 124 *idem.*

4. Les bières destinées à être converties en vinaigre, sont assujéties aux mêmes droits de fabrication que les autres bières. *Art.* 115, *idem.* Les brasseurs qui veulent faire, pour la fabrication du vinaigre, un ou plusieurs brassins par infusion, doivent déclarer la contenance de la cuve dans laquelle les trempes doivent être réunies pour fermenter. *Art.* 120, *idem.* En cas d'excédant pour la bière faite par infusion, il doit être procédé suivant les n°s 26 et 27 du tableau. *Art.* 115 *idem.*

51. (N° 3, 5e Tableau, p. 7).

1. Si cette contravention est constatée en même temps que celle pour défaut de déclaration, il n'y a lieu qu'à une seule peine, celle portée à l'art. 129. *Art.* 144 *de la loi du* 28 *avril* 1816. — *Voy.* §§. 1 et 2, note 19, pag. 35.

2. Sont exceptés du paiement de la licence, les particuliers qui ne brassent que pour leur consommation, les colléges, maisons d'éducation et autres établissemens publics. *Art.* 128 *idem.*

52. (N° 5, 5e Tableau, p. 7).

1. Les brasseurs doivent fournir l'eau et les ouvriers nécessaires pour vérifier, par l'empotement, la contenance des ustensiles déclarés. — Cette opération doit être dirigée en leur présence par les Employés de la Régie, et il en est dressé procès-verbal. *Art.* 117 *de la loi du* 28 *avril* 1816.

2. Ils sont autorisés à se servir de hausses mobiles qui ne sont pas comprises dans l'épalement, pourvu qu'elles n'aient pas plus d'un décimètre de hauteur, qu'elles ne soient placées sur les chaudières qu'au moment de l'ébullition de la bière, et qu'on ne se serve point de mastic ou autre matière pour les soutenir et les élever. *Art.* 122 *idem.*

3. Toutes constructions en charpente, maçonnerie ou autrement, fixées à demeure sur les chaudières, et qui s'étendent sur plus de la moitié de leur contour, doivent être comprises dans l'épalement, ou enlevées par les brasseurs. *Art.* 123 *idem.*

53. (N° 6, 5e Tableau, p. 7).

1. Une simple réparation faite à une chaudière lorsqu'elle n'a pas pour objet d'en changer la capacité, n'oblige pas les brasseurs à faire cette déclaration. *Mém.*, *tom.* 5, *p.* 213.

54. (N°s 14 et 17, 5e Tableau, p. 8).

1. La Régie peut autoriser la mise de feu sous une chaudière supplémentaire, pourvu qu'elle ne serve qu'à chauffer les eaux nécessaires à la confection de la bière et au lavage des ustensiles de la brasserie. Le feu doit être éteint sous cette chaudière, et elle doit être vidée aussitôt que l'eau destinée à la dernière trempe en a été retirée. *Art.* 121 *de la loi du* 28 *avril* 1816.

55. (N° 15, 5e Tableau, p. 8).

1. Cette déclaration doit être faite au moins quatre heures d'avance dans les villes, et douze heures dans les campagnes *Art.* 120 *de la loi du* 28 *avril* 1816.

2. La prolongation du feu de la chaudière au-delà du terme fixé pour fabriquer un brassin déclaré, constitue à elle seule une contravention, quoique le

procès-verbal ne constate pas une fabrication frauduleuse. *Art. du* 25 *prairial an* 13, *Mém.*, *tom.* 1, *p.* 140.

Voyez, pour la mise de feu par les brasseurs abonnés, le n° 34 du tableau.

56. (N° 22, 5e Tableau, p. 8).

1. La petite bière dont il est question dans ce numéro, est celle qui est exempte de tout droit; elle doit être fabriquée sans ébullition; elle est le produit d'eau froide versée dans la cuve matière sur les marcs qui ont servi à la fabrication des brassins déclarés; elle ne peut être fabriquée que de jour; elle ne doit pas excéder le huitième des bières assujéties aux droits pour un des brassins précédens; enfin elle doit, en sortant de la cuve matière, être livrée de suite à la consommation. A défaut de l'une de ces conditions, toute la petite bière fabriquée doit être soumise aux droits, indépendamment des peines encourues pour fausse déclaration. *Art.* 114 *de la loi du* 28 *avril* 1816.

57. (N° 26, 5e Tableau, p. 9).

1. Si l'excédant de fabrication reconnu et saisi excède de plus d'un dixième la contenance brute de la chaudière, indépendamment de l'amende, il y aura lieu à percevoir le droit pour un brassin entier supposé fabriqué sans déclaration. — Les excédans à la quantité imposable sont seulement soumis aux droits lorsqu'ils sont de plus du dixième de cette quantité, soit qu'on le constate sur les bacs, ou à l'entonnement. *Art.* 111 *de la loi du* 28 *avril* 1816.

58. (N° 27, 5e Tableau, p. 9).

1. La Régie est autorisée à régler l'emploi de l'excédant de vingtième et au-dessous, de manière à ce qu'il n'en résulte aucun abus. *Art.* 109 *de la loi du* 28 *avril* 1816.

59. (N° 30, 5e Tableau, p. 9, et n° 15, 6e Tableau, p. 11).

1. Ces visites ne peuvent avoir lieu dans les maisons non contiguës aux brasseries (et distilleries), ou non enclavées dans la même enceinte. *Art.* 125 *et* 140 *de la loi du* 28 *avril* 1816.

2. Les visites et exercices des Employés ne peuvent être faits que de jour, pendant les heures indiquées par la note 12, p. 32, à moins qu'il ne résulte des déclarations que ces établissemens sont en activité pendant la nuit. *Art.* 235 *et* 236 *idem.*

3. Un distillateur qui exige la présence d'un officier de police pour les visites que les Employés demandent à faire dans son domicile pendant le jour, commet un refus d'exercice. *Arr. du* 5 *août* 1813, *Mém.*, *tom.* 8, *p.* 151.

60. (Nos 33 et 34, 5e Tableau, p. 9).

1. A Paris et dans les villes au-dessus de 30,000 ames, les brasseurs peuvent être abonnés. *Art.* 130 *de la loi du* 28 *avril* 1816.

2. Au moyen de l'abonnement, les brasseurs sont dispensés de la déclaration avant chaque mise de feu; mais ils doivent les inscrire, au moment où elles ont lieu, sur un registre coté et paraphé.—Les commis doivent se borner à s'assurer, par la vérification des quantités de bière existant dans la brasserie, qu'il n'a été fait de brassin qui n'ait été inscrit sur le registre du fabricant. *Art.* 135, *idem.*

3. L'augmentation des moyens de fabrication peut d'ailleurs être un motif pour résilier l'abonnement. *Art.* 134, *idem.*

61. (Nos 2 et 17, 6e Tableau, p. 10 et 11).

1. Si cette contravention est constatée en même temps que celle pour défaut de déclaration, il n'y a lieu qu'à une seule peine, celle portée à l'art. 129. *Art. 144 de la loi du 28 avril* 1816. *Voy.* §§. 1 et 2, note 19, p. 35.

2. Les bouilleurs de cru ne sont assujétis à prendre une licence qu'autant qu'ils profitent du bénéfice de l'art. 90 de la loi du 28 avril, en se soumettant aux exercices pour les eaux-de-vie qu'ils transportent dans les magasins séparés de leurs brûleries. §. 1, *Circ. n° 11, Divisions territoriales.*

3. Un bouilleur de profession doit prendre, indépendamment de sa licence comme bouilleur, une licence de marchand en gros s'il vend des vins ou s'il achète des eaux-de-vie. §. 2 *id.*

4. On ne peut considérer comme distillateur de profession que celui qui achète des vins pour les distiller, et qui vend les eaux-de-vie qu'il obtient de la distillation. — Le propriétaire d'un appareil distillatoire ambulant n'est qu'un loueur d'alambic, et cette profession ne l'oblige ni à la déclaration ni à la licence.—Si ceux qui emploient son alambic ne distillent que les vins de leur cru, ils ne sont pas tenus à la licence; mais ils y deviennent sujets s'ils distillent des vins d'achat, ou si, domiciliés dans un lieu sujet aux entrées, ils jouissent de l'entrepôt pour les produits de leur distillation. *D. A.* n° 229.

5. La décision précédente ne s'applique pas au bouilleur de profession qui va distiller hors de chez lui avec ses alambics, et qui doit faire les déclarations voulues par les art. 138 et suivans de la loi du 28 avril, dans quelque lieu qu'il exerce sa profession. *Idem n°* 478.

62. (N° 20, 6e Tableau, p. 11).

1. Les bouilleurs de profession doivent déclarer par approximation la quantité et le degré de l'eau-de-vie qui devra être fabriquée. *Art. 141 de la loi du 28 avril* 1816.

2. Les directeurs sont autorisés à convenir, de gré à gré, d'une base d'évaluation des vins, cidres, poirés, lies, marcs ou fruits en eaux-de-vie, ou esprits. *Art.* 142, *idem.*—Si la quantité d'eau-de-vie représentée n'atteint pas le minimum établi par la base de conversion adoptée avec le bouilleur, on ne doit pas moins prendre en charge ce minimum; la différence doit être tirée immédiatement en produit, parce qu'elle est censée avoir été consommée ou vendue.—Si, au contraire, il y a un excédant, on doit se borner à le prendre en charge, à moins qu'il ne fût caché; dans ce cas, il serait saisi comme provenant de vins ou de cidres introduits sans expédition. *D. A.* nos 453 et 498.

63. (N° 1, 7e Tableau, p. 12).

1. Les dispositions indiquées par le §. 2, de la note 9, p. 51, relativement aux voyageurs et aux courriers, sont prescrites pour le droit sur les huiles, par les art. 110 et 111 de la loi du 25 mars 1817.—Si les huiles sont imposées au tarif de l'octroi, voyez les paragraphes suivans de la même note.

2. Les fruits, graines et autres substances destinées à faire de l'huile, ne sont pas imposés à l'entrée.

64. (N° 3, 7e Tableau, p. 12).

1. S'il y avait différence dans la quantité seulement, il n'y aurait lieu à saisir que l'excédant non déclaré; mais si l'on présentait de l'huile d'olive sous une autre dénomination, la totalité de l'huile faussement déclarée serait alors saisissable. *Voyez* les §§. 2 et suivans de la note 11, p. 52.

65. (N° 7, 7° Tableau, p. 12).

1. Les visites des Employés chargés de constater les produits de la fabrication, peuvent être faites de nuit et de jour, et sans l'assistance d'un officier public, dans les moulins ou autres établissemens où l'huile est fabriquée pendant le moment de la fabrication. *Art.* 98 *de la loi du* 25 *mars* 1817.

66. (N° 8, 7° Tableau, p. 12).

1. Les entrepositaires d'huile sont soumis à toutes les obligations imposées aux marchands en gros de boissons, par la loi du 28 avril 1816. *Art.* 101 *de la loi du* 25 *mars* 1817.

67. (N° 1, 8° Tableau, p. 13).

1. Les fabricans de cartes ne peuvent s'établir hors des chefs-lieux de direction de la Régie. *Art.* 10 *du décret du* 1er *germinal an* 13.—Les fabriques qui existaient dans les autres villes à l'époque où le décret a été rendu, doivent être conservées. *Circulaire timbrée*, 1re *division*, n° 15.—Elles peuvent être autorisées dans tous les chefs-lieux des directions actuelles. *D. A.* n° 302.

2. Il est défendu à toutes personnes de tenir dans ses maisons et domicile aucun moule propre à imprimer les cartes; d'y retirer, ni laisser travailler à la fabrique et recoupe des cartes et tarots aucuns cartiers, ouvriers et fabricans qui ne seraient pas pourvus d'une commission de la Régie. *Art.* 16 *de l'arrêté du* 19 *floréal an* 6.

3. Lorsque la maison dans laquelle on découvre une fabrique clandestine de cartes est le domicile commun du père et du fils, celui-ci ne peut se prétendre exempt des peines de la contravention, à raison de sa qualité de fils de famille, s'il est majeur et s'il exerce une profession particulière pour son propre compte. *Arr. du* 25 *mai* 1809, *Mém.*, *tom.* 5, *p.* 215.

68. (N° 6, 8° Tableau, p. 13).

1. Les enveloppes doivent indiquer les noms, demeures, enseignes et signature en forme de griffe des fabricans qui ont dû en déposer une empreinte, tant au greffe du tribunal de première instance que dans les bureaux de la Régie. — Les fabricans ne peuvent en changer la forme sans déclaration et sans faire de nouveaux dépôts.—Tout emploi et entrepôt de fausses enveloppes est prohibé. — Sont réputées fausses les enveloppes non conformes à celles déposées, ou qui seraient trouvées chez des fabricans autres que ceux indiqués. — Les cartiers qui font des enveloppes par sixains, ne peuvent les employer qu'en forme de bandes, de manière à laisser apparentes celles de contrôle apposées par la Régie sur chaque jeu. *Art.* 4 *du décret du* 9 *février* 1810.

69. (N° 15, 8° Tableau, p. 14).

1. L'usage de ces moules est conservé, mais ils doivent rester déposés dans les bureaux de la Régie. *Art.* 3 *du décret du* 16 *juin* 1808. — Il n'y a donc lieu à verbaliser pour leur fabrication, que dans le cas où le graveur n'aurait pas fait la déclaration indiquée n° 7 du tableau.

70. (N° 16, 8° Tableau, p. 14).

1. La réimportation des cartes fabriquées en France, et sorties en franchise du droit, constituerait une fraude pareille à celle indiquée par ce numéro, et devrait être constatée de la même manière.

71. (N° 17, 8e Tableau, p. 15).

1. La prohibition faite par l'article 166 de la loi du 28 avril 1816 pour la vente des cartes sans autorisation, comprend non seulement les commis, concierges ou domestiques des clubs, réunions et maisons où l'on donne à jouer, dénommés dans l'art. 11 de l'arrêté du 19 floréal an 6, mais encore toute autre personne quelconque qui n'a pas une commission de la Régie, n'importe qu'il s'agisse de cartes de fraude ou de cartes légales, avec bandes ou sans bandes.

2. Le transport de jeux de cartes par un individu faisant le métier de colporteur, et non autorisé par la Régie, constitue le délit de colportage prévu par l'article 166 de la loi du 28 avril 1816, attendu que la loi a attaché à ce transport la présomption légale de la destination de vente, et l'a assimilé à la vente qu'elle prohibe; et le prévenu ne peut être renvoyé des peines prononcées par ledit article 166, sur le fondement qu'on a trouvé sur lui, éparses dans ses poches, beaucoup de cartes de la même espèce que celles saisies entières, qu'il a allégué qu'elles étaient destinées à faire des étiquettes et des adresses, et que le fait de la vente n'est pas prouvé. *Arr. du* 28 *novembre* 1817. — Aff. Dupont.

72. (N° 18, 8e Tableau, p. 15).

1. On doit considérer comme cartes prohibées, *chez tous les assujétis aux droits sur les cartes :* 1° les cartes à portrait étranger qui sont dépourvues de la légende *France*, et du nom du fabricant. *Art.* 4 *du décret du* 16 *juin* 1808. — 2° Toutes les cartes à portrait français fabriquées avec d'autre papier que celui imprimé sur les moules de la Régie, puisque des délais ont été successivement fixés pour l'écoulement des cartes d'ancienne fabrication. — Voir à ce sujet les articles 14 et 16 de l'arrêté du 3 pluviôse an 6; les art. 9 et 15 de l'arrêté du 19 floréal suivant; les art. 7 et 8 du décret du 16 juin 1808; l'art. 2 du décret du 9 février 1810, et enfin la décision du ministre des finances du 3 juillet 1810.—*Voy.* quels sont ces assujétis, note 74.

2. Il y aurait lieu aux mêmes peines contre le propriétaire de l'établissement, lors même que les cartes auraient été apportées par les joueurs. *Art.* 67 *de la loi du* 28 *avril* 1816.

3. L'existence de cartes de fraude chez un cabaretier suffirait seule pour établir qu'il en permet l'usage. *D. A.* n° 435. — *Voy.* l'arrêt indiqué §. 2, note 71.

73. (N° 20, 8e Tableau, p. 15).

1. Les débitans de cartes ne peuvent avoir en leur possession, chez eux ou ailleurs, d'autres cartes à portraits français, que celles fabriquées avec les moulages de la Régie, et revêtues des bandes du contrôle. — Il y a lieu par conséquent à saisir toute autre espèce de cartes, même celles des fabrications précédemment autorisées, attendu qu'à l'expiration des délais fixés pour leur écoulement, celles qui ont pu leur rester ont dû être mises hors de la consommation en restituant les droits.—*Voyez* la note 72.

74. (N° 26, 8e Tableau, p. 15).

1. Les Employés sont autorisés à se présenter, toutes les fois qu'ils le trouvent convenable, chez les fabricans et marchands de cartes, ainsi que dans les lieux de bals, fêtes champêtres, réunions, clubs, billards, cafés et autres maisons où l'on donne à jouer. *Art.* 13 *de l'arrêté du* 3 *pluviôse an* 6.

2. Les Employés peuvent entrer en tout temps chez les individus sujets aux droits sur les cartes. *Art.* 81 *de la loi du* 5 *ventôse an* 12.

3. Ceux qui tiennent des cafés, des auberges, des débits de boissons, et en général des établissemens où le public est admis, sont tenus de souffrir les visites des préposés de la Régie. *Art* 167 *de la loi du* 28 *avril* 1816.

4. Les membres d'une assemblée dans laquelle on joue aux cartes, sont obligés de souffrir les exercices des Préposés dans le local où la société se réunit. —Les procès-verbaux font foi en justice contre les membres de cette société, sous le rapport des obstacles et des troubles qu'ils ont pu susciter pour empêcher l'exercice des Préposés. *Arr. du* 13 *mai* 1809. *Mém., tom.* 6, *p.* 555.

75. (N° 1, 9e Tableau, p. 16).

1. Sont considérées comme voitures à service régulier, toutes celles qui font le service d'une même route ou d'une ville à une autre, lors même que les jours et heures varieraient. *Art.* 112 *de la loi du* 25 *mars* 1817.

2. Les entrepreneurs chargés du transport des dépêches, en vertu de traités avec l'administration des postes, jouissent d'une indemnité pour places vides de moitié du prix total des places. *Art.* 114, *idem.* — M. le Directeur-Général fait connaître, particulièrement aux directeurs, les voitures qui ont droit à cette indemnité. *Circulaire n°* 17. — Les entrepreneurs ne peuvent substituer une voiture à une autre sans déclaration. *Arr. du* 10 *avril* 1807. *Mém.*, *tom.* 1, *p.* 313.

3. Tout changement dans les heures de départ, ou dans le prix des places, doit être constaté par un acte au portatif des Employés, et sans qu'il soit besoin d'une nouvelle déclaration. *Circ. n°* 17.

4. Les malles servant au transport des dépêches qui sont conduites par des courriers en titre, ne doivent pas être assujéties au paiement du droit, à raison des voyageurs qu'elles transportent. *Décision du ministre des finances du* 14 *messidor an* 7, *Rec.*, *tom.* 1, *p.* 331.

5. Le droit de 10e du prix des places est dû pour tous les voyages, soit en allant à la destination déclarée, soit pour le retour. *Arr. du* 14 *brumaire an* 13, *Mém.*, *tom.* 1, *p.* 184.

6. La fixité de la destination d'une voiture publique suffit pour l'assujétir à la déclaration et au paiement du droit proportionnel. *Arr. du* 10 *prairial an* 13. *Mém.*, *tom.* 1, *p.* 247; *autre du* 30 *brumaire an* 14, *Coll.*, *p.* 63.

7. Si les selliers, carrossiers, louent des voitures à des particuliers qui voyagent pour leur propre compte, et qui ne font point la profession de transporter des voyageurs à prix convenu, ils ne sont sujets à aucune des obligations de la loi sur les voitures publiques; mais ils y deviennent assujétis, s'ils louent leurs voitures à des entrepreneurs qui, ayant des chevaux, soit en propre, soit d'emprunt ou de louage, transportent avec lesdites voitures des voyageurs à prix d'argent. *Décis. du Ministre des finances du* 30 *fructidor an* 13, *Rec.*, *tom.* 1, *p.* 368.

8. Un loueur de chevaux qui conduit une voiture particulière n'est pas soumis aux droits. *D. A.* n° 444.

76. (N° 3, 9e Tableau, p. 16).

1. Un entrepreneur ne peut, sous le prétexte d'un abonnement avec la Régie, recevoir dans sa voiture un nombre de voyageurs plus grand que celui fixé dans sa déclaration. *Arr. du* 11 *mai* 1810. *Mém.*, *tom.* 6, *p.* 631.

2. Le conducteur peut céder sa place à un voyageur, à condition que celui-ci soit inscrit sur la feuille de route. *D. A.* n° 90.—Il ne peut même y avoir exception lorsque la personne qui excéderait le nombre des voyageurs serait attachée à l'entreprise à titre d'inspecteur. *Idem n°* 415.

3. Un entrepreneur est en contravention s'il exige séparément des voyageurs soit une rétribution pour le conducteur, soit le remboursement de l'indemnité de 25 cent. établie en faveur des maîtres de poste. *D. A.* n° 351 et n° 418.

77. (Nos 14 et 15, 9e Tableau, p. 16).

1. Le prix des estampilles est fixé à 2 fr., qui doivent être remboursés par les entrepreneurs. *Art.* 117 *de la loi du* 25 *mars* 1817. — Quand une estampille devra être apposée, elle le sera avant la délivrance du laissez-passer, et le prix de 2 fr. sera perçu par le buraliste qui en sera comptable. *Circulaire n°* 17. —Les estampilles qui deviennent hors d'usage doivent être retirées, à moins que l'entrepreneur ne consente à ce que leur empreinte soit biffée. *D. A.* n° 486.

2. A Paris, les numéros que la police fait apposer sur les voitures de place tiennent lieu de l'estampille. *D. A.* n° 349.

3. Le numéro de l'estampille est remplacé, pour les voitures des grandes messageries, par les lettres MR. *Idem*, n° 350.

78. (Nos 6 et 17, 9e Tableau, p. 16 et 17).

1. Le laissez-passer est inapplicable si le signalement qu'il indique n'est pas conforme à celui de la voiture, ou si la voiture circule sur une autre route que celle indiquée.

2. S'il existait un laissez-passer, mais dont la représentation n'aurait pas eu lieu à la demande des Employés, la représentation tardive n'effacerait pas la contravention, puisqu'aux termes de l'art. 8 du décret du 14 fructidor an 12, cette représentation doit avoir lieu à la première réquisition des Employés.

3. Il y aurait également lieu à saisir les voitures pour lesquelles on délivre des laissez-passer à chaque voyage, si elles circulaient avec des voyageurs, et un laissez-passer dont le délai serait expiré. *Circulaire n°* 17, *nouv. série.*

79. (Nos 7 et 18, 9e Tableau, p. 16 et 17).

1. La mise en circulation d'une voiture, autre que celle déclarée et estampillée, est une contravention, quoiqu'il ne soit pas prouvé que l'entrepreneur a fait circuler un plus grand nombre de voitures que celles pour lesquelles il paie les droits. *Arr. du* 10 *prairial an* 13, *Coll., p.* 62.

2. La substitution d'une voiture à celle déclarée qui se trouve accidentellement en réparation, ne peut avoir lieu sans déclaration. *Arr. du* 21 *février* 1806, *Coll., p.* 67.

80. (N° 8, 9e Tableau, p. 16).

1. Le registre doit être tenu sur papier timbré, et coté et paraphé par le Sous-Préfet ou tout autre officier public désigné par le Préfet. — Il est visé par les Préposés de la Régie. — Les entrepreneurs doivent y inscrire, jour par jour, toutes les personnes et marchandises dont ils entreprennent le transport, ainsi que le prix des places, la nature, le poids et le prix des paquets et marchandises. *Art.* 3 *du décret du* 14 *fructidor an* 12.

2. La perception du droit de dixième du prix du transport des marchandises s'établit sur le vu de ces registres, contrôlés par les feuilles de route remises aux conducteurs. *Art.* 75 *de la loi du* 5 *ventôse an* 12, *et Instruction n°* 10.

3. Sont considérés comme marchandises sujettes aux droits, tous les objets qui donnent lieu à une perception au profit de l'entreprise. *Art.* 4 *du décret du* 14 *fructidor an* 12.

4. Les espèces transportées par les voitures qui conduisent les voyageurs, sont sujettes au droit de dixième du prix de leur transport. *Circulaire n°* 3, *Rec., tom.* 1, *p.* 344.

5. Les objets que les entrepreneurs prétendraient transporter *gratis*, n'en sont pas moins soumis aux droits du dixième du prix du transport, établi au taux ordinaire fixé par l'entrepreneur. *Circulaire n°* 14, *Rec.*, *tom.* 1, *p.* 352.

6. Le dixième du prix du transport des marchandises doit être perçu sur la totalité du prix payé aux entrepreneurs, sans distraction de la somme due à la Régie pour le droit de dixième. *Id.*, et *D. A. n°* 173.

7. Les fourgons qui suivent les diligences, mais qui ne transportent que des marchandises, ne sont pas assujétis aux droits. *Avis du Conseil-d'Etat du 1er complémentaire an* 12, *Rec.*, *tom.* 1, *p.* 320.

81. (N° 9, 9ᵉ Tableau, p. 16).

1. Cette feuille de route doit être remise, au moment du départ, au conducteur, cocher, postillon ou voiturier, certifiée de l'entrepreneur ou d'un de ses commis. — Elle doit indiquer le n° de l'estampille, le nom de l'entrepreneur, celui du conducteur, ainsi que le nombre des places de la voiture. — Enfin elle doit présenter littéralement, article par article, les enregistremens, ainsi que le prix des places et du port des objets portés au registre. — Les chargemens faits pendant la route, doivent également y être inscrits, et reportés au registre du bureau d'arrivée. *Art.* 5 *du décret du* 14 *fructidor an* 12.

82. (N° 14, 9ᵉ Tableau, p. 17).

1. Les entrepreneurs de voitures partant d'occasion et à volonté, doivent déclarer l'espèce et le nombre des voitures, le nombre de places dans chaque voiture, tant à l'intérieur qu'à l'extérieur, et le genre de service auquel elles sont destinées. *Art.* 116 *de la loi du* 25 *mars* 1817.

2. Tous ceux qui ont des carrosses de remise, des fiacres, des cabriolets de louage qui circulent dans Paris, ainsi que dans les autres villes, sont des entrepreneurs de voitures partant d'occasion et à volonté, et sont par conséquent compris dans les termes de la loi. *Décision du Ministre des finances du* 7 *frimaire an* 6, *Rec.*, *tom.* 1, *p.* 329. — *Arrêts des* 24 *nivôse an* 13 *et* 11 *avril* 1806, *Mém.*, *tom.* 1, *p.* 186 *et* 244.

3. La déclaration faite par un conducteur dans un procès-verbal, que la voiture qu'il conduit fait un service d'occasion, est une preuve suffisante de contravention, si la voiture n'a pas été déclarée et estampillée. *Arr. du* 12 *août* 1808, *Mém.*, *tom.* 4, *p.* 631. *Voyez*, pour les selliers-carrossiers, §. 7, note 75, p. 51.

4. Celui qui loue au public des voitures partant à volonté est soumis aux droits, et ne peut être renvoyé des peines résultant du défaut de déclaration, sous le prétexte que l'état de loueur de voiture n'est pas compris dans la loi, et qu'elle n'oblige que les entrepreneurs. *Arr. du* 18 *déc.* 1817. Aff. Barillon.

83. (N° 1, 10ᵉ Tableau, p. 18).

1. La culture du tabac n'est permise que dans les départemens où elle était autorisée, à l'époque de la loi du 28 avril 1816. *Art.* 180. — Ces départemens sont ceux du *Bas-Rhin*, des *Bouches-du-Rhône*, d'*Ille-et-Vilaine*, du *Lot*, de *Lot-et-Garonne*, du *Nord*, du *Pas-de-Calais* et du *Var*.

2. On ne peut admettre de déclaration pour moins de 20 ares en une seule pièce. *Id.*

3. Les cultivateurs qui auraient fait des plantations sans déclaration, doivent être privés pour l'avenir du droit de planter des tabacs. *Art.* 195, *id.*

4. Les cultivateurs sont tenus d'arracher et de détruire, immédiatement après la récolte, les tiges et souches de leur plantation; à défaut, sur leur

refus, il y sera procédé à leurs frais sur l'ordre du Sous-Préfet donné à la réquisition du Directeur. *Art.* 196, *idem.*— Les tiges et souches de tabac ne peuvent, sans contravention, être mises dans le commerce ou en circulation, et elles doivent être saisies partout où elles peuvent être trouvées. *D. A. n°* 443.

5. Le propriétaire du terrain sur lequel on trouve du tabac en culture, est présumé l'auteur de la plantation, sans qu'il puisse, si la Régie s'y refuse, mettre en cause un individu qu'il désigne comme ayant fait cette plantation. — Les tribunaux doivent prononcer les peines déterminées par la loi, contre le propriétaire, sauf son recours contre qui de droit. *Arr. du* 30 *avril* 1813, *Mém.*, *tom.* 8, *p.* 182.

6. Le propriétaire d'un terrain sur lequel les Employés constatent qu'il existe une plantation de tabacs en fraude, et qui prétend que la plantation est du fait de son fermier, doit fournir la preuve de l'affermement; à défaut, il est réputé l'auteur des plantations et ensemencemens qui existent sur son terrain, et il est responsable personnellement des délits qui peuvent résulter de son exploitation. *Arr. du* 3 *juin* 1813. Aff. Van Brabau.

84. (N° 2, 10ᵉ Tableau, p. 18).

1. En cas de contestation sur le mesurage des terres plantées en tabac, ou sur le nombre des pieds de tabac, le Préfet doit en ordonner d'office la vérification, aux frais de celle des parties dont l'estimation aura présenté la différence la plus forte, avec la contenance réelle. *Art.* 194 *de la loi du* 28 *avril* 1816.

2. Les cultivateurs qui auraient fait des plantations excédant de plus d'un cinquième leur déclaration, doivent être privés pour l'avenir du droit de planter des tabacs. *Art.* 195, *id.*

85. (N° 3, 10ᵉ Tableau, p. 18).

1. Le délai pour l'exportation expire le 1ᵉʳ août de l'année qui suit la récolte; il peut être prorogé par le Préfet, sur l'avis du Directeur, jusqu'au 1ᵉʳ septembre; et si le cultivateur préfère déposer ses tabacs dans les magasins de la Régie, ils peuvent y rester en entrepôt jusqu'au moment de l'exportation. *Art.* 206 *de la loi du* 28 *avril* 1816.

2. Le cultivateur qui aurait soustrait tout ou partie de sa récolte à l'exportation, serait privé pour l'avenir du droit de planter du tabac. *Art.* 195, *id.*

86. (N° 4, 10ᵉ Tableau, p. 18).

1. Pour les cultivateurs autorisés, le mode de surveillance, contrôle et livraison des tabacs, est déterminé par le Préfet. *Art.* 188 *et* 191 *de la loi du* 28 *avril* 1816.

2. Les pharmaciens, les propriétaires de bestiaux et les artistes vétérinaires, peuvent avoir des tabacs en feuilles, mais seulement lorsqu'ils proviennent des ventes que la Régie est autorisée à leur faire. *Art.* 178, *id.*

3. Les cultivateurs de tabac sont en contravention à l'art. 217 de la loi du 28 avril, comme les simples particuliers, pour les tabacs qu'ils ont chez eux après l'époque fixée pour la livraison. *D. A. n°* 139.

4. On ne peut saisir que les quantités de tabac de la récolte qu'un cultivateur est surpris à vendre en fraude. *Idem n°* 382.

87. (N° 5, 10ᵉ Tableau, p. 18).

1. Sont exceptés de la formalité de l'acquit-à-caution : 1° les tabacs destinés à l'exportation, enlevés de chez les cultivateurs pour être transportés au bureau

établi près le magasin le plus voisin. *Art.* 208 *de la loi du* 28 *avril* 1816. — 2° Les tabacs transportés du domicile du cultivateur au magasin de réception de la Régie ; mais, dans les deux cas, les tabacs doivent être accompagnés d'un laissez-passer, à défaut duquel ils sont dans le cas d'être saisis et confisqués, ainsi que les moyens de transport. *Art.* 215 *et* 216, *id.*

88. (N° 6, 10ᵉ Tableau, p. 18).

1. Sont considérés comme fabricans frauduleux, les personnes chez lesquelles on trouve des ustensiles, machines ou mécaniques propres à la fabrication ou à la pulvérisation, et en même temps des tabacs en feuilles ou en préparation, quelle qu'en soit la quantité, ou plus de 10 kil. de tabacs fabriqués, non revêtus des marques de la Régie. *Art.* 221 *de la loi du* 28 *avril* 1816.

89. (N° 7, 10ᵉ Tableau, p. 19).

1. Si les tabacs n'étaient qu'en quantité de 10 kil. et au-dessous, ils ne seraient saisissables qu'autant qu'ils seraient revêtus de marques autres que celles de la Régie, ou qu'autant qu'il résulterait de l'aveu des prévenus, ou de toute autre preuve, que ce sont des tabacs de fraude.

2. Un particulier qui loge dans sa maison des individus qui y introduisent des tabacs de fraude, peut être poursuivi personnellement comme coupable du dépôt frauduleux, quoique les objets soient trouvés dans la chambre où logent les étrangers, et que ceux-ci déclarent qu'ils leur appartiennent. — Le mari, en cette matière, est responsable du fait de sa femme. *Arr. du* 9 *novembre* 1810, *Mém.*, *tom.* 7, *p.* 56.

90. (N° 9, 10ᵉ Tableau, p. 19).

1. Les tabacs de cantine, vendus par la Régie, doivent être saisis comm étant en fraude, lorsqu'ils sont trouvés dans les lieux où la vente n'en est pas autorisée. *Art.* 219 *de la loi du* 28 *avril* 1816.

2. Une ordonnance royale du 14 août, même année, autorise la Régie à faire fabriquer des tabacs en poudre et à fumer, à des prix inférieurs à ceux du tarif, et lui laisse le droit de déterminer dans quels lieux la vente en sera permise. — Ces tabacs doivent être considérés comme tabacs de fraude dans les arrondissemens où la vente n'en est pas autorisée, et doivent être saisis chez les débitans et sur les colporteurs qui s'en trouveraient munis. *Circulaire timbrée tabacs n°* 9, *nouvelle série.*

91. (N° 11, 10ᵉ Tableau, p. 19).

1. Les laissez-passer sont délivrés par les débitans ; ils doivent indiquer le numéro et la date sous lesquels la vente est enregistrée au livret, le nom de l'acheteur, la quantité vendue, et le lieu de la destination. — Ils ne valent qu'à raison d'un jour pour cinq lieues de distance à parcourir. — Il faut, autant que possible, les soumettre au *visa* des Employés. *Circulaire timbrée tabacs n°* 7, *nouvelle série.*

92. (N° 12, 10ᵉ Tableau, p. 19).

1. Il y aurait également contravention, lors même que les tabacs proviendraient des manufactures royales.

2. Quand les tabacs de fraude sont découverts dans un lieu quelconque, sans qu'il soit constaté par qui ils y sont déposés, c'est le propriétaire de ce local ou celui qui le tient à loyer qui doit être réputé l'auteur du délit. *Arr. du* 13 *mai* 1808, *Mém.*, *tom.* 4, *p.* 560.

3. Un aubergiste chez lequel on découvre du tabac de fraude, est passible des peines de la contravention, sauf son recours contre ceux qu'il prétendrait avoir, à son insu, introduit les tabacs dans son domicile. *Arr. du* 22 *décembre* 1809, *Mém.*, *tom.* 6, *p.* 503.

4. Une vente frauduleuse de tabac peut ressortir des circonstances rapportées au procès-verbal, telles que la découverte, dans le lieu de la vente, d'un particulier tenant du tabac qu'il déclare avoir acheté du marchand, et qui insiste pour qu'on lui remette ou son tabac ou l'argent qu'il en a donné. — Le prévenu, lorsque ces circonstances ne sont pas déniées en justice, ne peut être renvoyé des peines qu'il a encourues, sous le prétexte qu'il ne vendait pas le tabac, mais qu'il en avait cédé quelquefois au particulier trouvé chez lui. *Arr. du* 6 *août* 1813. Aff. Taque.

93. (N° 13, 10e Tableau, p. 19).

1. Les marchands ambulans seraient dans le cas de contravention prévu par cet article, lors même que les tabacs dont ils feraient la vente proviendraient des manufactures royales.

2. La contrebande avec attroupement et à main armée doit être poursuivie et punie comme en matière de douanes. *Art.* 226 *de la loi du* 28 *avril* 1816. — La loi du 13 floréal an 11 détermine les caractères de la contrebande avec attroupement et port d'armes, en matière de douanes; mais il y a lieu à appliquer les peines prononcées par le Code pénal. *Instructions de Monseigneur le Chancelier, du* 21 *novemb.* 1814. — La contrebande est avec attroupement et port d'armes, lorsqu'elle est faite par trois personnes ou plus, et que dans le nombre une ou plusieurs sont porteurs d'armes en évidence ou cachées, telles que fusils, pistolets et autres armes à feu, sabres, épées, poignards, massues, et généralement tous instrumens tranchans, perçans ou contondans. — Ne sont pas réputées armes, les cannes ordinaires sans dards ni ferremens, ni les couteaux fermant et servant habituellement aux usages de la vie. *Art.* 3 *de la loi du* 13 *floréal an* 11. — Les peines sont : *Les travaux forcés à temps*, s'il y a réunion de plus de vingt personnes armées. *Art.* 210 *du Code pénal*, ou *la réclusion*, si la réunion est de trois personnes jusqu'à vingt inclusivement. *Art.* 211 *idem.* — En cas de meurtre, il y a lieu à appliquer l'art. 304 du même Code, qui prononce la peine de mort. — Les prévenus doivent être arrêtés et livrés à M. le Procureur du Roi de l'arrondissement qui est chargé de les faire constituer prisonniers et d'exercer contre eux les fonctions de son ministère. — Les Directeurs doivent adresser immédiatement l'original du procès-verbal à ce magistrat. — Ils doivent intervenir dans la procédure pour requérir les condamnations civiles au profit de l'administration.

3. Les tribunaux ne peuvent se dispenser de prononcer les condamnations contre un individu surpris avec un transport de tabac de fraude, en prétextant que cet individu n'avait été que le simple guide ou conducteur du cheval chargé des tabacs, et qu'il ignorait la nature de cette charge. *Arr. du* 30 *novembre* 1811, *Mém.*, *tom.* 7, *p.* 176.

94. (N° 15, 10e Tableau, p. 19).

1. Il y aurait encore lieu à verbaliser pour contravention à l'art. 222, contre les débitans de la Régie qui vendraient des tabacs de fraude, et ces débitans sont dans le cas d'être arrêtés s'ils ne fournissent caution. *Circulaire timbrée tabacs n° 7, nouvelle série.*

95. (N° 1, 11e Tableau, p. 20).

1. La recherche des fabriques clandestines et la rédaction des procès-verbaux de contravention sont exclusivement réservées aux Employés des douanes

dans les trois lieues des côtes. — Hors ce rayon, la surveillance est exercée par les mêmes Employés, par ceux des contributions indirectes, par la gendarmerie, les gardes champêtres et forestiers. *Art. 7 de l'ordonnance du 19 mars* 1817.

2. C'est au plus prochain bureau des douanes que doit être faite la déclaration pour l'établissement d'une fabrique de sel à la chaudière, si elle est située dans les trois lieues des côtes, ou les quatre lieues des frontières de terre; celles situées dans l'intérieur doivent être déclarées au plus prochain bureau de la Régie des Contributions Indirectes. *Art.* 15 *du décret du* 11 *juin* 1806

3. Il doit être tenu, par les Fabricans et les Préposés, des registres en doubles sur lesquels sont portées les quantités de sel fabriquées, celles en magasin et celles vendues. *Art.* 19, *idem.*

4. Tous les sels sont soumis aux droits, quelle que soit la matière dont ils ont été extraits, et sans exception de l'usage auquel ils sont destinés. *Arr. du* 7 *mars* 1808, *Mém.*, *tom.* 3, *p.* 314.

96. (N° 2, 11ᵉ Tableau, p. 20).

1. S'il n'y avait pas identité pour la quantité de sel, ou si l'expédition indiquait une autre route que celle sur laquelle le transport serait rencontré, il y aurait lieu à saisir le chargement comme s'il n'était pas accompagné d'expédition, et pour contravention à l'article 3 du décret du 11 juin 1806.

2. Il en serait de même si le délai était expiré. *Art.* 6, *même décret.*

3. Les conducteurs sont tenus de représenter l'expédition dont ils doivent être porteurs, à toute réquisition des Employés, lorsqu'ils circulent dans l'étendue du rayon indiqué n° 2 du tableau. *Art.* 2, *id.*

4. Si la limite du rayon était contestée, son étendue devrait être mesurée par une ligne droite la plus courte possible, et prise par conséquent dans un plan parfaitement horizontal. *Arr. du* 28 *juillet* 1806, *Mém.*, *tom.* 1, *p.* 166.

97. (N° 1, 12ᵉ Tableau, p. 21).

1. Il est de principe général que la navigation qui s'exécute entre deux bassins, c'est-à-dire, qui commence et qui finit sur des points intermédiaires, n'est pas soumise aux droits. *Circ. n°* 41 *et* 42, *Rec.*, *tom.* 4, *p.* 296 et 302.

2. Mais les ports de navigation doivent être marqués aux deux extrêmités par des poteaux formant les limites, dans l'enceinte desquels le droit est exigible. *Lettre du Ministre des finances du* 2 *février* 1808, *jointe à la Circulaire n°* 41 *précitée.* — Ces limites sont déterminés par des arrêtés des Préfets.

3. Les bateaux employés au transport des troupes, ne sont pas sujets aux droits de navigation lorsqu'ils ne sont chargés que de troupes, armes, havresacs et porte-manteaux des officiers. *Avis du Conseil d'état du* 16 *février* 1807, *Mém.*, *tom.* 1, *p.* 143.

4. Les bâtimens de la marine royale ne sont pas exempts du droit de navigation. *Lettre du Min. des finances du* 26 *janvier* 1808, *Mém.*, *tom.* 5, *p.* 91.

5. Des réglemens spéciaux ont fixé les tarifs des droits à percevoir pour chaque arrondissement de navigation, et déterminé diverses exemptions qui n'ont pu être rapportées ici, attendu qu'elles varient suivant les localités.

98. (N° 4, 12ᵉ Tableau, p. 21).

1. La perception des droits de bacs et passages d'eau est affermée à l'enchère publique, d'après les ordres et instructions du Ministre des finances, et à la diligence des Préfets. *Art.* 1ᵉʳ *de l'arrêté du* 8 *floréal an* 12.

2. La Régie est chargée de faire le recouvrement du prix des baux d'adjudication. *Art.* 4 *de l'arrêté du* 5 *germinal an* 12.

3. C'est à ce recouvrement que se bornent les fonctions des Employés ; tout ce qui tient à l'établissement ou la suppression des bacs et bateaux, à leur matériel ainsi qu'à la police d'exécution, est dans les attributions de la Direction générale des ponts-et-chaussées, ou réunis à la surveillance administrative des Préfets. *Instruction n° 26, Rec., tom. 1, p. 117.*

4. Aux termes de l'art. 3 du Cahier des charges, les Employés de la Régie, dans l'exercice de leurs fonctions, sont exempts de payer aux fermiers le droit dû au passage des bacs. *Circulaire n° 45, Rec., tom. 5, p. 136.*

99. (N° 2, 13e Tableau).

1. Les poinçons destinés à marquer les ouvrages d'or et d'argent, sont désignés par les art. 10, 11, 12, 13, 15 et 16 de la loi du 19 brumaire an 6.

Ils sont fabriqués par le graveur des Monnaies, sous la surveillance de l'Administration des Monnaies qui les fait parvenir dans les bureaux de garantie. *Art. 17 de la loi du 19 brumaire an 6.*

2. Lorsqu'on ne fait point usage des poinçons, ils sont enfermés dans une caisse à trois serrures dont l'Essayeur, le Receveur et le Contrôleur ont chacun une clef. *Art. 18 et 45 idem.*

3. Lorsqu'il y a lieu de faire usage des poinçons, c'est le Contrôleur du bureau qui, conjointement avec l'Essayeur et le Receveur, les retire de la caisse à trois serrures et les applique sur les ouvrages en présence des propriétaires. *Art. 55 idem.*

4. Les Employés des bureaux qui calqueraient les poinçons ou qui en feraient usage sans observer les formalités prescrites par la loi, seraient destitués et condamnés à un an de détention. *Art. 46 idem.*

100. (N° 5, 13e Tableau, p. 22).

1. Si l'Essayeur soupçonne aucun des ouvrages d'or, de vermeil ou d'argent, d'être fourré de fer, de cuivre ou de toute autre matière étrangère, il le fera couper en présence des propriétaires : si la fraude est reconnue, l'ouvrage sera saisi et confisqué, et le délinquant sera dénoncé aux tribunaux et condamné à une amende de vingt fois la valeur de l'objet ; mais, dans le cas contraire, le dommage sera payé sur-le-champ au propriétaire, et passé en dépense comme frais d'Administration. *Art. 65 de la loi du 19 brumaire an 6.*

2. Lorsqu'il est reconnu, par l'Administration des Monnaies, que des ouvrages saisis comme étant fourrés, sont seulement trop chargés de soudure, il y a lieu à restituer les objets saisis, après toutefois qu'ils ont été dénaturés. — Aff. Moulinier, Baute et comp., *Mém., tom. 5, p. 85.*

101. (N° 6, 13e Tableau, p. 22).

1. Les ouvrages ainsi présentés aux Employés des Douanes, doivent être pesés, plombés et envoyés au bureau de garantie le plus voisin pour être marqués du poinçon ET, et payer des droits égaux à ceux qui sont perçus sur les ouvrages d'or et d'argent fabriqués en France.

Sont exceptés de cette disposition :

1.° Les objets d'or et d'argent appartenant aux ambassadeurs et envoyés des puissances étrangères.

2.° Les bijoux d'or à l'usage personnel des voyageurs, et les ouvrages en argent servant également à leur personne, pourvu que leur poids n'excède pas en totalité 5 hectogrammes. *Art. 23 de la loi du 19 brumaire an 6.*

2. Les ouvrages exceptés en vertu des dispositions ci-dessus ne peuvent être mis dans le commerce sans être marqués du poinçon et sans avoir acquitté les droits. *Art. 24 idem.*

3. Une ordonnance du 3 mai 1815 détermine les bureaux de garantie auxquels les ouvrages venant de l'étranger doivent être envoyés par les Employés des Douanes, qui se conforment pour cet effet aux instructions particulières qui leur sont données par leur Administration.

4. Lorsqu'un marchand venant de l'étranger est porteur d'objets d'or et d'argent dépourvus de marques, et qu'il ne les a pas déclarés à la douane au moment de l'introduction, ni au Maire dans la commune de l'intérieur où il en fait la vente, il est en contravention aux art. 23 et 92 de la loi du 19 brumaire an 6, et passible des peines portées par les art. 80, 94 et 107 de la même loi. *Arr. du 7 décembre* 1815.—Aff. Reusille.

102. (N° 8 13e Tableau, p. 22).

1. L'art. 28 de la loi du 19 brumaire an 6 est applicable aux ouvrages mis en vente publique chez les particuliers. *Rec., p.* 213, *tom.* 3.

2. L'action, en cas de contravention, doit être intentée contre l'officier public qui préside à la vente, sauf son recours personnel contre le propriétaire ou les vendeurs qu'il représente. *Id.*

3. Lorsque des propriétaires ou héritiers déclarent vouloir réserver pour leur usage et retirer de la vente des objets d'or et d'argent, on doit s'abstenir de dresser procès-verbal de contravention, et surtout d'opérer la saisie de ces objets. *Déc. du Conseil d'Adm.*, *Mém., p.* 19, *tom.* 1.

4. Les Officiers ministériels sont dans l'obligation de faire marquer les ouvrages d'or et d'argent qui se vendent publiquement, et d'acquitter les droits de garantie de ces ouvrages avant de les exposer en vente. *Circ. de l'Adm. des Monn. du* 16 *juin* 1806.

103. (N° 9, 13e Tableau, p. 23).

1. L'exécution de l'art. 13 de la déclaration du 26 janvier 1749 a été ordonnée par l'arrêté du 16 prairial an 7.

2. Les orfèvres, joailliers, fourbisseurs, merciers, graveurs et autres travaillant et fabriquant des ouvrages d'or et d'argent, sont obligés d'inscrire tous les ouvrages vieux ou réputés vieux qu'ils achètent pour leur compte ou pour les revendre, ou qui leur sont portés pour raccommoder, ou donnés en nantissement, pour modèles ou dépôts, ou sous quelque prétexte que ce puisse être.—Ils doivent aussi faire mention, dans leur enregistrement, de la nature et qualité des ouvrages, des armes qui y sont gravées, des noms et demeures des personnes à qui ils appartiennent, sans qu'ils puissent travailler aux ouvrages qui leur auraient été donnés à raccommoder, qu'ils ne les aient portés sur leurs registres.—Ces enregistremens doivent être faits à l'instant même, jour par jour, par poids et espèces. *Art.* 13 *de la déclaration du* 26 *janvier* 1749.

3. Les horlogers sont également tenus d'enregistrer les montres qui leur sont données à raccommoder lorsqu'elles ne sont pas dûment marquées. *Circ. de l'Adm. des Mon. du* 1er *prairial an* 8, *Rec., p.* 299, *tom.* 1.

4. Les montres données à raccommoder sont confiscables à défaut de marques, si l'horloger ne les a pas inscrites sur son registre. *Arr. du* 2 *janvier* 1806, *Coll.*, *p.* 18; *autre du* 30 *janvier* 1808, *Mém.*, *tom.* 3, *p.* 350.

5. L'horloger, ne fût-il que raccommodeur de montres, doit, à peine d'amende, comme tout autre marchand d'or et d'argent, tenir registre sur lequel il est obligé d'inscrire même les montres qui lui sont données pour les réparer; à défaut de cette inscription, ces montres sont dans le cas de la confiscation, si elles ne sont point revêtues du poinçon déterminé par la loi. *Arr. du* 24 *avril* 1807, *M.*, *tom.* 1, *p.* 285.

6. L'ouvrier horloger qui ne fait que raccommoder les montres, n'est obligé

qu'à la tenue du registre prescrit par la déclaration de janvier 1749. *Arr. du* 3 *mars* 1808, *Mém.*, *tom.* 3, *p.* 145.

7. Les fabricans et marchands ne sont pas tenus d'inscrire sur leur registre le titre des ouvrages d'or et d'argent dont ils n'ont pas acquis la propriété, et qui ne sont chez eux que comme dépôts ou pour raccommoder. *Arr. du* 10 *mars* 1809, *Mém.*, *p.* 148, *tom.* 5.

8. L'impossibilité de produire des registres sur lesquels se trouvent inscrits les ouvrages vieux d'or et d'argent trouvés chez un fabricant, est une preuve suffisante de la contravention. *Arr. du* 20 *août* 1813.—Aff. Orings.

9. Un orfévre est en contravention, quoiqu'il ait un registre, s'il n'y inscrit pas les ouvrages d'or et d'argent qu'il achète. *Arr. du* 15 *février* 1817.—Aff. Griffe.

104. (N° 9, 13ᵉ Tableau, p. 23).

1. Les ouvrages vieux ou réputés vieux, trouvés chez les fabricans et marchands, quoique marqués des anciens poinçons, doivent être considérés comme n'ayant aucune marque légale, s'ils ne sont en même temps revêtus du poinçon de récense ou du poinçon en usage, et cette contravention entraîne la confiscation et l'amende, à moins qu'il ne soit prouvé par des registres régulièrement tenus, que le marchand a acheté ces ouvrages depuis trop peu de temps, pour avoir pu les présenter au bureau avant la saisie. *Arr. du* 8 *frimaire an* 14, *Coll.*, *p.* 12; *autre du* 15 *avril* 1808, *Mém.*, *tom.* 4, *p.* 469; *autre du* 23 *novembre* 1810, *Mém.*, *tom.* 7, *p.* 151.

105. (N° 11, 13ᵉ Tableau, p. 23).

1. Le poinçon du fabricant peut être gravé par tel artiste qu'il lui plaît de choisir, et en observant les formes et les proportions établies par l'Administration des Monnaies. *Art.* 9 *de la loi du* 19 *brumaire an* 6.

2. Le poinçon doit être invariablement formé en losange et dans la proportion établie par chaque fabricant, en raison du genre d'ouvrage qu'il fabrique. *Art.* 1 *et* 2 *de l'arrêté de l'Adm. des Mon. du* 17 *nivôse an* 6.

3. Les ouvrages ne peuvent être reçus à l'essai que revêtus du poinçon du fabricant. *Art.* 48 *de la loi du* 19 *brumaire an* 6.

4. A la mort d'un orfévre, son poinçon doit être remis, dans le délai de cinquante jours, au bureau de garantie, pour y être brisé de suite.—Pendant ce temps, le dépositaire des poinçons sera responsable de l'usage qui en aura été fait. *Art.* 90 *idem.*

5. Un fabricant ou orfévre, lorsqu'il quitte le commerce, doit remettre son poinçon au bureau de garantie pour y être également biffé; s'il veut s'absenter plus de six mois, il doit déposer son poinçon au bureau, et le Contrôleur fera poinçonner les ouvrages fabriqués chez lui en son absence. *Art.* 91 *idem.*

6. On ne doit reconnaître pour ouvriers en orfévrerie, et comme exempts de la déclaration, que ceux qui travaillent chez le maître; tous ceux qui travaillent dans leur domicile, pour leur compte ou pour celui d'autrui, sont réputés fabricans, et, en cette qualité, soumis à toutes les obligations que contient la loi du 19 brumaire an 6. *Circ. de l'Adm. des Mon. du* 1ᵉʳ *prairial an* 8, *Rec.*, *p.* 299, *tom.* 1.

7. Un orfévre, quoiqu'il ait fait insculper son poinçon à la mairie, n'en est pas moins en contravention s'il a omis de remplir la même formalité à la Préfecture. *Arr. du* 30 *mai* 1806, *Mém.*, *tom.* 2, *p.* 664.

106. (Nᵒˢ 13, 20 et 26, 13ᵉ Tableau, p. 23 et 24).

1. Ce registre doit être coté et paraphé par le maire: les fabricans et

marchands doivent y inscrire la nature, le nombre, le poids et le titre des matières et ouvrages, avec les noms et demeures des vendeurs. *Art.* 74, 81 *et* 86 *de la loi du* 19 *brumaire an* 6.—*Voyez* le n° 9 du tabl. et la note 104.

107. (N° 16, 13e Tableau, p. 23).

1. Le défaut de tableau dans la boutique d'un bijoutier constitue une contravention qui doit entraîner l'amende prononcée par l'art. 80 de la loi du 19 brumaire an 6. *Arr. du* 10 *janvier* 1806, *Coll.*, *p.* 21.

2. Un orfévre, chez qui on ne trouve point affiché le tableau prescrit, est en contravention, quoiqu'il offre de prouver qu'il avait précédemment affiché ce tableau qui a été momentanément enlevé par accident. *Arr. du* 1er *octobre* 1807, *Mém.*, *tom.* 3, *p.* 40.

108. (N° 17, 13e Tableau, p. 23).

1. Ce refus ou cette omission ne sont pas classés au nombre des contraventions, par la circulaire de l'Administration des Monnaies du 1er prairial an 8, *Rec.*, *p.* 289, *tom.* 1. Cependant l'obligation de faire cette remise et les peines sont formellement exprimées; on doit en conclure qu'il n'y aurait lieu à dresser procès-verbal que dans le cas où l'on aurait à constater en même temps d'autres contraventions, ou sur la plainte formelle de l'acheteur, ou enfin, dans les cas extraordinaires, si l'intérêt du service rendait cette mesure nécessaire.

109. (N° 18, 13e Tableau, p. 24).

1. Les ouvrages que les orfévres déclarent être à leur usage personnel ne peuvent être dispensés de l'essai, de la marque et des droits. *Circ. de l'Adm. des Mon. du* 1er *prairial an* 8, *Rec.*, *p.* 298, *tom.* 1.

2. Les ouvrages de coutellerie garnis de viroles et de médaillons d'or et d'argent sont soumis à l'essai et à la marque, à peine de confiscation et d'amende. *Arr. du* 4 *août* 1806, *Coll.*, *p.* 27.

110. (Des Joailliers, 13e Tableau, p. 24).

1. Les joailliers sont assujétis à faire la déclaration indiquée par le n° 12 du tableau et sous les mêmes peines. *Circ. de l'Adm. des Mon. du* 1er *floréal an* 8, *Rec.*, *tom.* 1, *p.* 291.

2. Ils sont dispensés de l'essai, de la marque et des droits, pour tous les ouvrages montés en pierres fines ou fausses et en perles, et pour ceux émaillés dans toutes les parties ou auxquels sont adaptés des cristaux. *Art.* 86 *de la loi du* 19 *brumaire an* 6.

3. Cependant cette dispense n'est applicable qu'aux ouvrages de joaillerie qui ne pourraient supporter l'empreinte du poinçon sans déterioration. *Arrêté du* 1er *messidor an* 6, *Rec.*, *tom.* 1, *p.* 265.

4. Les joailliers sont tenus de se conformer aux dispositions de la loi du 19 brumaire an 6, pour tous les ouvrages qui sont susceptibles de recevoir les marques sans détérioration; il y a lieu, en cas de contravention, à leur appliquer les peines prononcées par les articles 80 et 107 de ladite loi. *Arr. du* 26 *octobre* 1810, *Mém.*, *tom.* 7, *p.* 137.

111. (N° 30 13e Tableau, p. 25).

1. Le (Maire ou son adjoint, ou le commissaire de police), fera examiner les marques de ces ouvrages par des orfévres, ou, à défaut, par des personnes connaissant les marques et poinçons, afin d'en constater la légitimité. *Art.* 93 *de la loi du* 19 *brumaire an* 6.

2. Il fera saisir et remettre au tribunal de police correctionnelle de l'arron-

dissement les ouvrages d'or et d'argent qui ne seraient pas accompagnés du bordereau, et ne seraient pas marqués de vieux ou de recense, ou les ouvrages dont les marques paraîtraient contrefaites, ou enfin qui ne lui auraient pas été déclarés. *Art.* 94 *idem.*

112. (N° 33, 13e Tableau, p. 25).

1. Les fabricans de plaqué peuvent employer l'or ou l'argent dans telle proportion qu'ils le jugent convenable. *Art.* 96 *de la loi du* 19 *brumaire an* 6.

2. L'Administration des Monnaies a un poinçon spécial pour les ouvrages doublés et plaqués d'or et d'argent. *Art.* 8 *idem.*

3. Le poinçon de chaque fabricant a une forme particulière déterminée par l'Administration. *Art.* 14 *id.*

4. La forme du poinçon de chaque fabricant de doublé ou de plaqué doit être un carré parfait. *Art.* 3 *de la délibération de l'Adm. des Mon. du* 17 *nivôse an* 6.

5. L'obligation imposée aux fabricans d'ajouter sur chacun de leurs ouvrages les chiffres indicatifs de la quantité d'or et d'argent qu'ils contiennent, est encore prescrite par l'art. 14 de la loi du 19 brumaire an 6.

113. (N° 42, 13e Tableau, p. 26).

1. Tous les anciens lingots ont dû être présentés au bureau de garantie, dans le délai de deux mois, pour y recevoir l'empreinte des poinçons de recense ou ceux de garantie. *Arrêté du* 19 *messidor an* 9.

2. Il y a près de l'Administration des Monnaies un affineur pour le service des monnaies; le public a la faculté d'y faire affiner ou départir les matières d'or et d'argent contenant or; le service en est déterminé par la sect. 2, tit. 9 de ladite loi.

3. Les lingots non affinés apportés à l'Essayeur du bureau de garantie pour être essayés, ne sont soumis qu'aux frais d'essai. Avant d'être remis au propriétaire, ils doivent être marqués du poinçon de l'Essayeur qui doit en outre insculper son nom des chiffres indicatifs du vrai titre, et d'un numéro particulier. *Art.* 66 *et* 67 *idem.*

4. Les tireurs d'or et d'argent sont obligés de porter leurs lingots aux argues établies près de l'Administration des Monnaies pour y être dégrossis, marqués et tirés. *Art.* 137 *idem.*

5. Aucun particulier ne peut avoir en sa possession des outils ou instrumens propres au service de l'argue royale, sous peine de confiscation et d'une amende de trois mille francs applicables, lors même que les outils ou instrumens pourraient avoir un autre usage.—Les tireurs d'or et d'argent ne peuvent, sous les mêmes peines, faire forger, dégrossir et tirer leurs lingots dans d'autres lieux que l'argue royale, lors même que le lingot, dans l'état où il est saisi, pourrait subir des opérations étrangères à l'argue. *Arr. du* 12 *juillet* 1817. — Aff. Martin et Duchamp.

114. (N° 1, 14e Tableau, p. 27).

1. En cas de procès-verbal pour fabrication illicite de poudre, les Employés doivent saisir non seulement la poudre fabriquée, mais encore les matières servant à la fabrication, ainsi que les ustensiles; ils requerront, en outre, l'arrestation des ouvriers employés à cette fabrication. §. 10 *de l'Instruction n°* 45.

2. L'individu surpris à fabriquer de la poudre pour son propre compte ne peut être dispensé de l'amende et condamné seulement à l'emprisonnement,

sous le prétexte que fabriquant lui-même il doit être condamné comme ouvrier. —On ne peut qualifier ouvrier que celui qui travaille pour salaire et pour le compte d'autrui. *Arr. du* 29 *juillet* 1813.—Aff. Frezia.

115. (N° 2, 14ᵉ Tableau, p. 27).

1. Il est défendu aux militaires, ouvriers et employés des poudres, de vendre, donner ou échanger de la poudre à peine de destitution, et d'une détention de trois mois pour les gardes-magasins et militaires, et d'un an pour les ouvriers et employés des poudreries. *Art.* 29 *de la loi du* 13 *fructidor an* 5.

2. A dater du 1er juin 1818, la vente des poudres de chasse, de mine ou de commerce, sera exclusivement exploitée par la Régie des contributions indirectes.—Il en sera de même des poudres de guerre destinées aux armemens du commerce maritime et à la consommation des artificiers. *Ord. du* 25 *mars* 1818, *art.* 1.

3. A dater de la même époque, il n'y aura plus d'autres débitans que ceux commissionnés par la Régie, et on devra verbaliser contre tout particulier qui vendrait de la poudre (1). *Art.* 13 *idem.*

4. Le livret des débitans de tabac servira à inscrire les levées et les ventes de poudres faites par les débitans.

5. Les poudres de guerre, de mine et de commerce ne seront pas vendues par les débitans. *Circ. n°* 22, *tabacs, nouv. série.*—L'Administration désignera les magasins ou entrepôts dans lesquels la vente de poudres de cette qualité aura lieu.

116. (N° 4, 14ᵉ Tableau, p. 27).

1. Les débitans ne pourront s'approvisionner ailleurs que dans les magasins qui leur seront désignés par l'Administration, ni vendre d'autres poudres que les poudres de chasse. *Circ. n°* 22, *Tabacs, nouv. série.*

2. Un tableau du prix des poudres doit être affiché dans chaque bureau, et les débitans ne peuvent les vendre à un prix plus élevé, sous peine de révocation et d'être poursuivis suivant la rigueur des lois. *Idem.*

3. A dater du 1er octobre 1818, les poudres de chasse ne seront vendues qu'en rouleaux ou paquets revêtus de vignettes. *Ord. du* 25 *mars* 1818, *art.* 5.

117. (N° 5, 14ᵉ Tableau, p. 27).

1. L'administration pourra toutefois faire délivrer aux artificiers patentés la poudre de guerre dont ils justifieront avoir besoin, en s'engageant à produire à toute réquisition le certificat d'achat de ladite poudre. *Art.* 5 *du décret du* 23 *pluviôse an* 13.

2. Les artificiers doivent être porteurs d'un livret, sur lequel doivent être enregistrées les levées faites par eux dans les magasins de la Régie. Ce livret doit être représenté à toute réquisition. §. 15 *de l'Instruction n°* 45.

118. (N° 6, 14ᵉ Tableau, p. 27).

1. Si le conducteur n'a pas connaissance du chargement, il aura son recours contre le chargeur qui l'aura trompé. *Art.* 30 *de la loi du* 13 *fructidor an* 5.

2. Dans les deux lieues frontières, le transport de la poudre reste soumis à tout ce qui est prescrit par la loi pour la circulation dans cette étendue. *Même art.*

---

(1) Le même article autorise néanmoins les anciens débitans non conservés à débiter, jusqu'au 1er août 1818, les poudres qui leur restent de leurs achats.

3. La poudre dont s'approvisionnent les débitans, est enregistrée sur un livret qui leur tient lieu de passeport. §. 13 *de l'Instruction n° 45.*

4. Tout transport supérieur à cinq kilogrammes, doit être accompagné d'un passeport délivré par le commissaire des poudres et salpêtres. §. 17, *idem.*— Ou d'un acquit-à-caution de la Régie des contributions indirectes.

119. (N° 8, 14e Tableau, p. 28).

1. Nul ne peut exercer la profession de salpêtrier s'il n'est commissionné du ministre de la guerre. *Art.* 6 *de l'arrêté du 27 pluviôse an* 11.

2. Les possesseurs des nitrières existantes, et qui voudraient en former de nouvelles, sont autorisés à les exploiter, à la condition expresse d'en livrer tous les salpêtres dans les magasins de l'État. *Art.* 14 *de la loi du* 13 *fruct. an* 5.

120. (N° 9, 14e Tableau, p. 28).

1. Il y a contravention, soit que la livraison ait lieu par suite de vente ou d'échange. *Art.* 12 *de la loi du* 13 *fructidor an* 5.

2. Les ouvriers des raffineries et ateliers nationaux de salpêtres qui en détourneront les produits, encourront les mêmes peines que les ouvriers des poudreries. *Art.* 29 *idem.*—*Voy.* note 15, §. 1.

121. (N° 11, 14e Tableau, p. 28).

1. L'administration des poudres a seule le droit de vendre le salpêtre brut ou raffiné aux fabricans qui font usage de cette matière dans leur fabrication. §. 2 *de l'Instruction n°* 45.

122. (N° 12, 14e Tableau, p. 28).

1. Les salpêtres ne peuvent être transportés de l'atelier des salpêtriers dans les magasins de l'administration qu'accompagnés d'un livret signé du commissaire, ou d'un magasin à un autre qu'accompagnés d'un passeport de l'administration ou laissez-passer du commissaire.—A l'égard des petites quantités de salpêtre mises en circulation pour les besoins des fabriques d'acide, eaux-fortes, etc., elles doivent être accompagnées d'un bulletin de levée dans l'un des magasins de l'administration des poudres. §. 2 *de l'Instruction n°* 45.

2. Tout fabricant qui emploie des salpêtres comme matière première dans ses opérations, pourra en importer par les seuls ports de........ le salpêtre ne pourra être introduit dans l'intérieur qu'au moyen d'un acquit-à-caution délivré par les Employés des douanes. *Art.* 11 *de l'arrêté du* 27 *pluviôse an* 8.

3. Il est défendu à ces fabricans, ou à tous autres particuliers, de vendre du salpêtre, sous les peines portées par les lois. *Art.* 12 *idem.*

FIN DE LA PREMIÈRE PARTIE.

DEUXIÈME PARTIE.

CONTENTIEUX.

CHAPITRE PREMIER.

Des Procès-Verbaux de saisies et contraventions.

1. Les Employés de la Régie seront âgés au moins de vingt-un ans accomplis : ils seront tenus, avant d'entrer en fonctions, de prêter serment (a) devant le juge de paix ou le tribunal civil (b) de l'arrondissement dans lequel ils exercent ; ce serment sera enregistré au greffe et transcrit sur leur commission (c), sans autres frais que ceux d'enregistrement (d) et de greffe, et sans qu'il soit besoin d'employer le ministère d'avoué. *Décret du 1er germinal an 13, art. 20.*

(a) *Serment des Employés.*

1. En cas de changement de résidence, il n'est pas nécessaire que les Employés prêtent un nouveau serment. *Instruction n° 27, Rec., tom. 1, p. 122. Lettre commune du 18 juin 1816, n° 1579.*

2. L'Employé qui passe à de nouvelles fonctions par sa nomination à un grade supérieur à celui qu'il occupait, est soumis à une nouvelle prestation de serment. *Circ. timbrée contentieux, n° 19, nouv. série.*

3. Les débitans de tabac, quel que soit leur sexe, sont soumis à la prestation de serment. *Idem.*

4. Les Employés ne sont pas obligés de faire mention de l'acte de leur prestation de serment dans les procès-verbaux qu'ils rédigent. *Arr. du 25 fructidor an 13, coll., p. 5.*

5. Les Employés de la garantie ne sont pas obligés de renouveler leur serment lorsqu'ils changent de résidence et qu'ils sont appelés à exercer leurs fonctions dans un autre département que celui où ils ont rempli cette formalité. *Arr. du 1er mai 1806, Coll., p. 24.*

6. Il suffit, pour la validité des actes des préposés, que leur prestation de serment soit transcrite au pied de leur commission : l'omission que le greffier aurait faite de l'enregistrer ne peut priver les procès-verbaux de la foi qui leur est due. *Arr. du 1er avril 1808, Mém., tom. 3, p. 295.*

(b) *Réception du serment.*

7. Le serment des Employés de la Régie doit être prêté devant le tribunal civil de l'arrondissement. *Circ. de Monseigneur le Chancelier, du 20 novembre 1816.*

(c) *Commission des Employés.*

8. Dans l'exercice de leurs fonctions, les Employés doivent toujours être porteurs de leur commission pour être en état de la représenter à la première réquisition. *Instr. n° 7, Rec., tom. 1, p. 109.*

(d) *Droits exigibles pour les prestations de serment.*

9. Par frais d'enregistrement et de greffe, on ne doit entendre que les droits appartenant au gouvernement tels qu'ils sont perçus par la Régie de l'enregistrement. Il n'est dû aucune vacation au juge qui reçoit le serment et au greffier qui en transcrit l'acte sur la commission. *Inst. n° 27, Rec., tom. 1, p. 122.*

10. Le droit d'enregistrement est de trois francs en principal pour les surnu-

méraires, les buralistes, les débitans de tabac et les élèves des manufactures. *Circ. n° 19, contentieux, nouv. série.*—Il est de 15 francs en principal pour tous les autres Employés, conformément à l'article 68 de la loi du 22 fructidor an 7. *Même circ.*

2. Les procès-verbaux énonceront la date (a) et la cause de la saisie, la déclaration qui en aura été faite au prévenu (b), les noms, qualités et demeures (c) des saisissans et de celui chargé des poursuites; l'espèce, poids et mesure des objets saisis (d); la présence de la partie à leur description, ou la sommation qui lui aura été faite d'y assister; le nom et la qualité du gardien (e) s'il y a lieu; le lieu de la rédaction (f) du procès-verbal, et l'heure de la clôture. *Décret du 1er germinal an 13, art. 21.*

(a) *Date des procès-verbaux.*

1. Lorsqu'un procès-verbal ne peut être clos le jour même où il a été commencé, il doit énoncer les motifs qui ont fait suspendre ou prolonger l'opération. — Les Employés doivent toujours, autant que possible, rédiger de suite et clore leur procès-verbal sous une seule et même date. *Mém., tom. 3, p. 92.*

2. Lorsque la copie d'un procès-verbal ne porte pas la même date que l'original, l'incertitude qui résulte de cette différence rend le procès-verbal nul. *Arr. du 31 juillet 1807, Mém., tom. 2, p. 449.*

(b) *Saisie réelle des objets de fraude.*

3. Il suffit que la saisie d'un objet trouvé en contravention soit déclarée pour donner lieu à la confiscation et à l'amende, quoique les Employés, à raison de la résistance opposée par le contrevenant, n'aient pu effectuer la saisie réelle de cet objet *Arr. du 19 février 1807, Mém., tom. 1, p. 263.*

(c) *Qualités et demeure des Employés saisissans.*

4. Les préposés ne sont pas obligés, à peine de nullité, d'énoncer, dans leurs procès-verbaux de saisie, leur demeure individuelle, il suffit qu'ils indiquent la ville dans laquelle ils résident. *Arr. de la cour d'appel de Paris, du 26 juillet 1806, Mém., tom. 1, p. 163.*

5. Des Employés qui indiquent leur grade et leur résidence dans un procès-verbal fait à la requête de l'Administration des Contributions indirectes, indiquent suffisamment qu'ils appartiennent à cette Administration. *Arr. du 7 mars 1813.*—Aff. Howels.

(d) *Désignation des objets saisis.*

6. L'obligation d'énoncer l'espèce, poids et mesure des objets saisis, n'emporte pas la nécessité de désigner en détail le poids ou la mesure de chacun des objets soumis à la saisie lorsqu'ils sont de même nature. *Arr. du 6 floréal an 11, Mém., tom. 3, p. 99; autre du 3 septembre 1813.*—Aff. Lehaire.

7. Le défaut de pesée des objets saisis n'est pas un motif de nullité, si le contrevenant a mis obstacle à l'accomplissement de cette formalité. *Arr. du 22 août 1806, Mém., tom. 1, p. 239.*

8. Les Employés, lorsqu'ils font chez un débitant de boissons la saisie d'une futaille, ne sont pas obligés de la marquer pour en assurer l'identité. *Arr. du 29 décembre 1808, Mém., tom. 4, p. 723.*

9. La déclaration d'un prévenu portant qu'il conduit une quantité de boisson différente de celle indiquée par l'expédition, n'entraîne pas la preuve de la contravention, si les Employés omettent dans le procès-verbal de constater l'espèce et la mesure des objets saisis. *Arr. du 21 avril 1809, Mém., tom. 6, p. 394.*

10. Dans les saisies de tabacs faites à domicile, on doit soigneusement énoncer le poids net des tabacs, autrement les tribunaux n'ayant pas de base suffisante pour déterminer l'amende, se trouveraient dans la nécessité d'ordonner des vérifications qui retarderaient la marche des procédures.

11. Dans les saisies de cartes, outre l'indication du nombre de jeux ou de sixains, il est essentiel de faire connaître si elles sont ou non revêtues de bandes de contrôle; si elles sont fabriquées en papier filigrané ou en papier libre, et enfin la nature du moulage des cartes à figures.

(e) *Gardien.—Dépôt des objets saisis.*

12. Un procès-verbal est nul s'il n'énonce pas le nom et la qualité du gardien des objets saisis. *Arr. du 23 octobre 1807, Mém., tom. 2, p. 619.*

13. Le dépôt des objets saisis peut être fait régulièrement chez un des préposés saisissans qui s'en constitue gardien. *Arr.*

du 23 *avril* 1808, *Mém.*, *tom.* 3, *p.* 329.

14. Le gardien des objets saisis est suffisamment indiqué dans un procès-verbal qui énonce que ces objets ont été déposés chez le (Directeur) de l'arrondissement, quoique le nom de ce fonctionnaire ne soit pas indiqué. *Arr. du* 5 *octobre* 1809, *Mém.*, *tom.* 6, *p.* 534.

15. Le moyen d'assurer l'identité des objets saisis et mis en dépôt, est de les réunir sous une enveloppe, ficelée et cachetée par les saisissans d'un cachet dont ils rapportent l'empreinte en marge de leur procès-verbal, ainsi que celle du cachet du prévenu, lorsqu'il consent à y apposer le sien : s'il s'y refuse, après avoir été sommé de le faire, la sommation et le refus doivent être constatés.—Le lieu du dépôt, qui doit, autant que possible, être le bureau le plus voisin de la saisie, sera indiqué au prévenu par le procès-verbal; il faut avoir la plus grande attention à ce que le dépôt soit en lieu sûr, et tel que les marchandises ne puissent y dépérir ou s'avarier. *Instr. n*° 27, *Rec.*, *tom.* 1, *p.* 122.

(f) *Lieu de rédaction des procès-verbaux.*

16. Les Employés ne sont pas tenus, à peine de nullité, de rédiger leurs procès-verbaux sur le lieu même de la saisie, surtout lorsque des causes légitimes y mettent obstacle. *Arr. du* 29 *décembre* 1808, *Mém.*, *tom.* 4, *p.* 723. — Il convient cependant que le procès-verbal soit, autant que possible, rédigé sur le lieu même du délit; et que, en cas d'obstacle, il en soit fait mention. *Instr. n*° 27.

3. Dans le cas où le motif de la saisie portera sur le faux et l'altération des expéditions, le procès-verbal énoncera le genre de faux, les altérations ou surcharges; lesdites expéditions, signées et paraphées des saisissans, *ne varietur*, seront annexées au procès-verbal, qui contiendra la sommation faite à la partie de les parapher, et sa réponse. *Décret du* 1er *germinal an* 13, *art.* 22.

4. Il sera offert main-levée (a), sous caution solvable ou en consignant la valeur des navires, bateaux, voitures, chevaux et équipages saisis pour autre cause que pour importation d'objets dont la consommation est défendue, et cette offre, ainsi que la réponse de la partie, sera mentionnée au procès-verbal. *Idem*, *art.* 23.

(a) *Main-levée des objets saisis.*

1. En cas de fraude simple, la remise provisoire des objets saisis, sous caution solvable, sera offerte après estimation modérée et de gré à gré; il est même des cas où la main-levée provisoire doit être accordée, toujours après estimation faite, sous la simple caution juratoire du prévenu, lorsque les objets ou instrumens de fraude compris dans la saisie ne peuvent être déplacés sans inconvénient. *Instr. n*° 27.

2. Lorsque la saisie est motivée sur l'état de prohibition des objets qu'elle comprend, tels que les tabacs de fraude, les cartes non timbrées, les marchandises d'orfèvreries dépourvues de poinçons, les poudres, on ne peut, sous aucun prétexte, accorder la main-levée et laisser à la disposition du prévenu des objets dont la loi interdit la circulation. *Instr. n*° 27.

5. Si le prévenu est présent, le procès-verbal énoncera qu'il lui en a été donné lecture (a) et copie (b); en cas d'absence du prévenu (c), la copie sera affichée dans le jour (d) à la porte de la maison commune du lieu de la saisie.—Ces procès-verbaux et affiches pourront être faits tous les jours (e) indistinctement. *Décret du* 1er *germinal an* 13, *art.* 24.

(a) *Lecture des procès-verbaux.*

1. Lorsque le prévenu n'est pas présent à la rédaction et à la clôture d'un procès-verbal, et que la copie lui en a été signifiée à son domicile, il n'y a pas nullité si on ne lui donne pas lecture du procès-verbal. *Arr. du* 10 *août* 1810, *Mém.*, *tom.* 6, *p.* 744; *autre du* 26 *août* 1813. — Aff. Ybos.

2. Le défaut de lecture d'un procès-

verbal en matière de garantie n'est pas une nullité. *Arr. du* 25 *février* 1813. — Aff. Holtz.

(b) *Copie des procès-verbaux.*

3. Les vices de forme dont la copie d'un procès-verbal est entachée entraînent la nullité du procès-verbal. *Arr. du* 1er *brumaire an* 13, *Mém., tom.* 2, *p.* 493.

4. Un procès-verbal est nul s'il n'établit pas qu'il en a été remis copie au prévenu. *Arr. du* 14 *frimaire an* 14, *Coll., p.* 51; *autre du* 25 *octobre* 1807, *Mém., tom.* 2, *p.* 649.

5. La femme d'un assujéti a qualité pour recevoir la copie d'un procès-verbal dressé contre son mari. *Arr. du* 25 *juin* 1807, *Mém., tom.* 1, *p.* 375.

6. On ne peut faire résulter la nullité d'un procès-verbal, de ce que l'énonciation qu'il en a été donné copie ne se trouve pas dans la copie même, lorsque cette énonciation se trouve dans l'original. *Arr. du* 18 *mars* 1818, *Mém., tom.* 3, *p.* 305.

7. Lorsqu'un procès-verbal énonce que les Employés se sont transportés chez le prévenu pour lui en donner lecture et copie, ces expressions ne suffisent pas pour constater que la copie a été réellement donnée. *Arr. du* 2 *décembre* 1808, *Mém., tom.* 5, *p.* 233.

(c) *Affiche. — Notification des procès-verbaux.*

8. La signification d'un procès-verbal faite à domicile est valable, quoique le prévenu ne soit pas présent au moment de la rédaction. *Arr. du* 6 *septembre* 1806, *Mém., tom.* 1, *p.* 223; *autre du* 26 *mars* 1807, *tom.* 3, *p.* 369; *autre du* 23 *juin* 1808, *tom.* 4, *p.* 490.

9. La copie d'un procès-verbal rédigé contre un gendarme absent au moment de la rédaction, est légalement remise à son brigadier. *Arr. du* 30 *juillet* 1807, *Mém., tom.* 2, *p.* 478.

10. Quand le prévenu ayant un domicile connu dans le lieu de la saisie, n'est pas présent à la rédaction du procès verbal, on peut indifféremment lui en faire la notification à domicile ou par affiche à la porte de la maison commune. *Arr. du* 5 *novembre* 1807, *Mém., tom.* 2, *p.* 735.

11. La notification d'un procès-verbal faite à la femme d'un assujéti, dans le domicile de celui-ci, est valable, quoique l'absence du mari soit reconnue. *Arr. du* 4 *décembre* 1807, *Mém., tom.* 3, *p.* 25.

12. Les Employés ont légalement trois voies ouvertes pour faire la signification du procès-verbal, quand le prévenu n'est pas présent au moment de la rédaction : ils peuvent, ou afficher une copie à la porte de la maison commune, ou faire la notification au domicile naturel du prévenu, ou enfin la faire en parlant à sa personne, partout où il peut être trouvé, chez lui ou ailleurs. *Arr. du* 23 *août* 1816. — Aff. Favier.

(d) *Délai pour l'affiche des procès-verbaux.*

13. Le délai d'un jour fixé pour l'affiche ou la notification d'un procès-verbal en cas d'absence du prévenu, doit s'entendre de vingt-quatre heures, à partir de celle de la clôture. *Arr. du* 4 *décembre* 1806, *Mém., tom.* 1, *p.* 225; *autre du* 26 *mars* 1807, *tom.* 3, *p.* 369.

(e) *Jours fériés.*

14. Les actes de procédure en matière correctionnelle peuvent être faits et signifiés tous les jours indistinctement. *Arr. du* 27 *août* 1807, *Mém., tom.* 3, *p.* 154.

15. Les contraintes, significations, saisies, contraintes par corps, ventes et exécutions judiciaires ne peuvent avoir lieu le dimanche ou autres jours fériés. *Mém., tom.* 2, *p.* 609. — *Voy.*, pour les exercices chez les débitans de boissons, le §. 2, note 24.

6. Les procès-verbaux seront affirmés (a) au moins par deux des saisissans (b) dans les trois jours (c) devant le juge de paix ou l'un des suppléans (d); l'affirmation énoncera qu'il en a été donné lecture (e) aux affirmans. *Décret du* 1er *germinal an* 13, *art.* 25.

(a) *Affirmation.*

1. Un procès-verbal est nul à défaut d'affirmation. *Arr. du* 25 *frimaire an* 14, *Mém., tom.* 1, *p.* 10.

2. En matière de garantie, l'affirmation n'est pas nécessaire, la saisie et le procès-verbal étant faits en présence et avec le concours d'un officier public. *Arr. du* 1er *mai* 1806, *Mém., tom.* 1, *p.* 44. — Quoique

cet arrêt soit rendu en termes généraux, et qu'on peut le considérer comme applicable à tous les cas où les procès-verbaux sont rédigés avec l'assistance d'un officier de police, on ne doit jamais négliger l'affirmation. *Mém., tom.* 1, *p.* 46.—*Voy.* §. 4 ci-après.

3. Lorsqu'un procès-verbal ne peut être rédigé dans une seule séance, l'affirmation faite par un préposé qui n'aurait pas assisté aux premières séances est valable, s'il a assisté à la séance dans laquelle la saisie a été prononcée. *Arr. du* 22 *août* 1806, *Mém., tom.* 1, *p.* 239.

4. Les procès-verbaux en matière de garantie ne sont pas soumis à l'affirmation. *Arr. du* 2 *janvier* 1806, *Mém., tom.* 1, *p.* 44; *autre du* 26 *janvier* 1809, *tom.* 5, *p.* 222.

5. Il n'est pas nécessaire que l'acte d'affirmation énonce les noms et prénoms des Employés affirmans. *Arr. du* 7 *avril* 1809, *Mém., tom.* 5, *p.* 193.

6. Les tribunaux ne peuvent annuller un procès-verbal sous prétexte que la date de l'affirmation est antérieure à celle du procès-verbal, lorsqu'il est évident, d'après toutes les circonstances, que l'affirmation est régulière et que la date qu'elle porte est le résultat d'une erreur matérielle. *Arr.* 28 *août* 1812.

7. Il suffit, pour la régularité d'un acte d'affirmation, que l'acte et les renvois qu'il pourrait contenir soient signés par le juge de paix. *Arr. du* 26 *août* 1813. — Aff. Ybos.

(b) *Signature des procès-verbaux.—Nombre d'Employés affirmans.*

8. Il suffit qu'un procès-verbal soit signé et affirmé par deux des saisissans, quoiqu'un plus grand nombre d'Employés ait coopéré à la saisie. *Arr. du* 18 *janvier* 1809, *Mém., tom.* 5, *p.* 40.

(c) *Délai pour l'affirmation.*

9. Les trois jours que la loi accorde pour l'affirmation doivent être composés de soixante-douze heures, à compter de celle de la clôture du procès-verbal. *Arr. du* 7 *octobre* 1809, aff. Ricouard, *Mém., tom.* 6, *p.* 623.—Afin d'éviter toute incertitude, il convient, lorsque l'affirmation est faite le troisième jour, de faire indiquer l'heure à laquelle elle a eu lieu. *Mém., tom.* 6, *p.* 627.

10. Si, pendant les trois jours que la loi accorde pour l'affirmation, le juge de paix et son suppléant se trouvaient absens, les Employés devraient dresser procès-verbal de cette absence, et la faire constater par le maire ou son adjoint; ils feraient alors l'affirmation devant le juge de paix le plus voisin résidant dans le même arrondissement. *Mém., tom.* 1, *p.* 358.

(d) *Juge de paix qui doit recevoir l'affirmation.*

11. Les procès-verbaux doivent, à peine de nullité, être affirmés devant le juge de paix du lieu où les saisies sont faites. *Arr. du* 24 *avril* 1807, *Mém., tom.* 1, *p.* 351.

12. Dans les villes où il existe plusieurs juges de paix, l'affirmation faite devant l'un d'eux est valable. *Arr. du* 24 *mars* 1811, *Mém., tom.* 7, p. 281.

(e) *Lecture du procès-verbal aux affirmans.*

13. Ces termes employés par le juge de paix dans un acte d'affirmation, *après lecture faite en leur présence*, fournissent la preuve que, suivant le vœu de la loi, il a été donné aux affirmans lecture du procès-verbal. *Arr. du* 10 *avril* 1807, *Mém., tom.* 2, *p.* 473; *autre du* 26 *août* 1813. — Aff. Ybos.

14. Le juge de paix doit donner aux Employés lecture du procès-verbal seulement; il n'est pas nécessaire qu'il leur donne lecture de l'acte d'affirmation. *Arr. du* 11 *février* 1808, *Mém., tom.* 3, *p.* 265; *autre du* 7 *avril* 1809, *tom.* 6, *p.* 430.

7. Les procès-verbaux ainsi rédigés et affirmés, seront crus (a) jusqu'à inscription de faux.—Les tribunaux ne pourront admettre contre lesdits procès-verbaux d'autres nullités (b) que celles résultant de l'omission des formalités prescrites par les articles précédens. *Décret du* 1er *germinal an* 13, *art.* 26.

(a) *Foi due aux procès-verbaux.*

1. On ne peut admettre en justice la preuve de faits qui, sans être absolument contraires à l'énoncé des procès-verbaux, tendent néanmoins à détruire la foi qui leur est due. *Arr. du* 7 *nivôse an* 12, *Mém., tom.* 1, *p.* 88.

2. On ne peut, par un jugement prépa-

ratoire, admettre en preuve des faits contraires au contenu d'un procès-verbal. *Arr. du* 30 *messidor an* 12, *Mém., tom.* 1, *p.* 174.

3. Les procès-verbaux en matière de garantie font foi pour les aveux qui y sont consignés, et lorsque ces aveux fournissent la preuve d'une contravention, les tribunaux ne peuvent se dispenser de prononcer les peines et d'appliquer strictement la loi. *Arr. du* 30 *mai* 1806, *Mém., tom.* 2, *p.* 664.

4. Un procès-verbal régulier et non attaqué par une inscription de faux, dans lequel il est fait mention que le prévenu a avoué le délit, suffit pour constater cet aveu, et faire condamner le prévenu, malgré la dénégation qu'il fait ensuite devant le tribunal. *Arr. du* 20 *juin* 1806, *Mém., tom.* 2, *p.* 752; *autre du* 23 *avril* 1807, *tom.* 2, *p.* 462; *autre du* 13 *décembre* 1810, *tom.* 7, *p.* 332.

5. Les procès-verbaux dressés par des préposés temporaires nommés par l'Administration, et assermentés, font foi en justice comme ceux dressés par les préposés ordinaires. *Arr. du* 22 *octobre* 1807, *Mém., tom.* 2, *p.* 641.

6. Lorsque le prévenu appelle en garantie d'autres particuliers, les tribunaux peuvent ordonner la preuve testimoniale, si elle n'a pour objet que de fixer la légitimité de la demande en garantie sans attaquer la foi due au procès-verbal. *Arr. du* 22 *janvier* 1808, *Mém., tom.* 3, *p.* 133.

7. Lorsque les Employés se fondent sur la notoriété publique pour établir une contravention, on ne peut empêcher le prévenu d'opposer la preuve testimoniale. *Arr. du* 18 *février* 1808, *Mém., tom.* 3, *p.* 185.

8. Un procès-verbal doit faire foi en justice, quoique toutes les formalités prescrites à peine de nullité n'aient pas été remplies, si la résistance du contrevenant a mis obstacle à l'accomplissement de ces formalités. *Arr. du* 7 *avril* 1808, *Mém., tom.* 3, *p.* 257.

9. Lorsque la Régie consent à une vérification par expert ou à une audition de témoins sur un fait justificatif allégué par le prévenu, elle ne renonce pas pour cela au procès-verbal. *Arr. du* 20 *mai* 1808, *Mém., tom.* 5, *p.* 161.

10. Un procès-verbal suffit pour constater des injures et menaces envers les Employés et pour déterminer la compétence du tribunal correctionnel, lorsque ces injures ont pour objet ou pour résultat d'empêcher les exercices. *Arr. du* 8 *juillet* 1808, *M., tom.* 4, *p.* 513; *autre du* 27 *décembre* 1810, *tom.* 7, *p.* 100.

11. Les aveux du prévenu, quoiqu'il n'ait pas signé le procès-verbal dans lequel ils sont énoncés, suffisent pour établir une contravention, malgré la déclaration contraire faite postérieurement par le même prévenu. *Arr. du* 12 *août* 1808, *Mém., tom.* 4, *p.* 631.

12. Un procès-verbal ne fait pas foi pour les aveux d'un prévenu lorsqu'il n'est rédigé que le lendemain du jour où ces aveux ont eu lieu, et lorsqu'au moment de la rédaction le prévenu a rétracté ses premières déclarations. *Arr. du* 20 *octobre* 1808, *Mém., tom.* 5, *p.* 257.

13. On ne peut admettre la preuve testimoniale contre des faits établis par un procès-verbal. *Arr. du* 3 *mars* 1809, *Mém., tom.* 5, *p.* 183.

14. Un fait bien antérieur, rapporté dans un procès-verbal, peut être contesté par le prévenu et déclaré inexact par le tribunal. *Arr. du* 10 *mars* 1809, *M., tom.* 5, *p.* 148.

15. Une contravention peut être établie par les propos et aveux des parties, et le procès-verbal fait foi en justice pour cet objet comme pour les faits matériels de la fraude et des contraventions. *Arr. du* 9 *novembre* 1810, *Mém., tom.* 7, *p.* 20.

16. Les aveux et déclarations faits par la femme d'un assujéti, et constatés au procès-verbal, fournissent la preuve de la contravention, malgré le désaveu que le mari fait à l'audience. *Arr. du* 7 *décembre* 1810, *Mém., tom.* 7, *p.* 84.

17. Les procès-verbaux dressés par des gendarmes, pour constater des fraudes sur les tabacs, doivent avoir foi en justice jusqu'à la preuve contraire. Ces procès-verbaux ne sont pas soumis aux formalités prescrites pour ceux des Employés de la Régie *Arr. du* 20 *mars* 1812, *Mém., tom.* 7, *p.* 304; *autre du* 4 *septembre* 1813.—Aff. Durand.

18. Les procès-verbaux rendus par les Employés de la garantie des matières d'or et d'argent font foi en justice jusqu'à inscription de faux. *Arr. du* 25 *février* 1813, *Mém., tom.* 8, *p.* 87.

19. On ne peut, sans s'inscrire en faux, induire de la différence d'encre qui existe entre un renvoi et le corps de l'acte, que ce renvoi a été ajouté après coup. *Arr. du* 26 *août* 1813.—Aff. Holtz.

20. Un jugement préparatoire qui ordonne la dégustation par experts de l'échantillon qui a été pris sur une boisson saisie, méconnaît la foi qui est due au

procès-verbal, lorsque les Employés ont constaté l'espèce et la qualité de la boisson saisie. *Arr. du* 21 *novembre* 1817.—Aff. Lévêque.

21. Un procès-verbal qui constate une différence en moins dans le degré des eaux-de-vie prises en charge chez un débitant, doit faire foi en justice, si aucune inscription de faux n'est déclarée contre le portatif sur lequel le degré des eaux-de-vie prises en charge est constaté —Cet affaiblissement dans le degré de l'eau-de-vie ne peut avoir d'autre cause qu'une introduction d'eau, faite dans la futaille sans avoir appelé les Employés, ou une substitution d'eau-de-vie d'un degré inférieur à celles prises en charge, et dans l'un ou l'autre cas le débitant est en contravention et passible de l'amende et de la confiscation. *Arr. du* 17 *janv.* 1818, aff. Bonchereau.

(b) *Nullité des procès-verbaux.*

22. Les tribunaux ne peuvent admettre contre les procès-verbaux des nullités résultantes des lois générales relatives aux actes des procédures. *Arr. du* 16 *fructidor an* 11, *Mém.*, *tom.* 3, *p.* 47.

23. L'omission, dans la copie d'un procès-verbal, d'une formalité prescrite à peine de nullité, entraîne la nullité du procès-verbal, lors même qu'il contiendrait l'énonciation de la formalité omise dans la copie. *Arr. du* 1er *brumaire an* 13, *Mém.*, *tom.* 2, *p.* 193.

24. Les vices de forme qui emportent la nullité des procès-verbaux ne pourraient être proposés devant la cour de cassation lorsqu'ils ne l'auraient pas été devant les premiers tribunaux. *Arr. du* 8 *frimaire an* 14, *Coll.*, *p.* 12.

25. Les vices de forme qui emportent la nullité des procès-verbaux peuvent être proposés en appel, quoiqu'ils ne l'aient pas été en première instance. *Arr. du* 10 *avril* 1807, *Mém.*, *tom.* 2, *p.* 421.

26. Un procès-verbal étant par lui-même le titre de l'action, les nullités qui le vicient ne sont pas en général susceptibles d'être couvertes, elles sont absolues. —L'observation des formes dans la rédaction des procès-verbaux dressés pour constater une contravention, est donc d'une grande importance. *Mém.*, *tom.* 5, *p.* 238.

CHAPITRE II.

Poursuites judiciaires des Fraudes et Contraventions.

8. Les contraventions qui...... entraînent la confiscation ou l'amende seront poursuivies par-devant les tribunaux de police correctionnelle (a) qui prononceront les condamnations (b). *Loi du* 5 *ventôse an* 12, *art.* 90.

(a) *Avoués.*

1. Le ministère des avoués n'est pas nécessaire dans les instances qui concernent une administration, et les préposés de cette administration sont autorisés à prendre des conclusions devant les tribunaux. *Arr. du* 1er *germinal an* 10, *Mém.*, *tom.* 2, *p.* 679.

2. L'obligation de constituer un avoué n'est applicable qu'aux affaires entre particuliers, et non point à celles qui concernent le gouvernement *Arr. du* 29 *thermidor an* 10, *Mém.*, *tom.* 2, *p.* 490.

3. La Régie n'est pas tenue de constituer un avoué, même dans les affaires qui ont pour objet le recouvrement des revenus publics d'une autre nature que la perception des impôts indirects. *Arr. du* 13 *pluviôse an* 11, *Mém.*, *tom.* 2, *p.* 616.

4. L'Administration est dispensée de constituer un avoué dans les assignations qu'elle donne en validité d'une saisie-arrêt, comme dans toutes les autres instances relatives à la perception des droits. *Arr. du* 28 *juillet* 1812, *Mém.*, *tom.* 8, *p.* 60.

5. Dans des affaires relatives à des délits qui n'entraînent pas la peine d'emprisonnement, le prévenu peut se faire représenter par un avoué. *Art.* 185 *du Code d'Instruction criminelle.*

9. L'assignation à fin de condamnation sera donnée dans la huitaine, au plus tard, de la date du procès-verbal (a); elle pourra être donnée par les commis. *Décret du* 1er *germinal an* 13, *art.* 28.

(a) *Assignation.*

1. L'assignation n'est pas nulle et n'entraîne pas la déchéance des poursuites, quoiqu'elle soit donnée après le délai de huitaine de la date du procès-verbal. *Arr. du 4 brumaire an* 14, *Mém., tom.* 1, *p.* 35; *autre du* 25 *juillet* 1812, *tom.* 7, *p.* 288; *autre du* 23 *août* 1816.—Aff. Favier.

2. Quand une saisie est faite sur deux associés, le procès-verbal commencé en présence de l'un et fini en présence de l'autre, ne peut être attaqué de nullité sous ce prétexte; ce qui est fait contre l'un vaut contre l'autre : il suffit que l'assignation soit donnée à un seul. *Arr. du* 29 *mai* 1806, *Mém., tom.* 1, *p.* 160.

3. Lorsqu'un objet saisi a été laissé à la garde du contrevenant, la prise en charge qui en serait faite par d'autres préposés que ceux qui ont opéré la saisie, ne pourrait être considérée comme un abandon du procès-verbal. *Arr. du* 23 *octobre* 1806, *Mém. tom.* 1, *p.* 235.

4. L'assignation donnée pour comparaître, après le délai de trois jours francs, à la première audience du tribunal de police, et en tant que de besoin, aux audiences suivantes, est régulière. *Arr. du* 5 *février* 1808, *Mém., tom.* 3, *p.* 241.

10. Si le tribunal juge la saisie mal fondée, il pourra condamner la Régie, non seulement aux frais du procès-verbal et à ceux de fourrière, le cas échéant, mais encore à une indemnité proportionnée à la valeur des objets dont le saisi aurait été privé pendant le temps de la saisie, jusqu'à leur remise ou l'offre qui en aura été faite; mais cette indemnité ne pourra excéder un pour cent par mois de la valeur desdits objets (a). *Décret du* 1er *germinal an* 13, *art.* 29.

(a) *Dommages-intérêts.*

1. Les tribunaux ne peuvent condamner la Régie à une indemnité de déplacement envers un particulier qui, par erreur de nom et par une fausse déclaration faite par le véritable contrevenant, a été mal à propos poursuivi en vertu d'un procès-verbal qui ne le concernait pas. *Arr. du* 28 *décembre* 1809, *Mém., tom.* 6, *p.* 683.

2. Lorsque la remise des objets saisis a été faite ou offerte au prévenu, il ne peut lui être accordé d'indemnité, en supposant que la saisie soit reconnue mal fondée. *Arr. du* 27 *février* 1813.—Aff. Bazorque.

11. Si, par l'effet de la saisie et leur dépôt dans un lieu et à la garde d'un dépositaire qui n'aurait pas été choisi ou indiqué par le saisi, les objets saisis avaient dépéri avant leur remise ou les offres valables de les remettre, la Régie pourra être condamnée à en payer la valeur ou l'indemnité de leur dépérissement. *Décret du* 1er *germinal an* 13, *art.* 30.

12. Dans le cas où, la saisie n'étant pas déclarée valable, la Régie interjetterait appel du jugement (a), les navires, voitures et chevaux saisis, et tous les objets sujets à dépérissement ne seront remis que sous caution solvable, après estimation de leur valeur. *Idem, art.* 31.

(a) *Déclaration d'appel.*

1. Lorsqu'un jugement interlocutoire a admis le prévenu à faire une preuve, la Régie n'est plus recevable à appeler de ce jugement après que la preuve a été faite. *Arr. du* 27 *floréal an* 13, *Mém., tom.* 1, *p.* 30.

2. La Régie n'est pas obligée de joindre à sa déclaration d'appel une requête indicative de ses moyens. *Arr. du* 7 *nivôse an* 14, *Mém., tom.* 1, *p.* 152.

3. Lorsqu'une cour royale trouve un appel irrégulier dans sa forme, elle doit se borner à le déclarer non recevable, et elle n'a pas le droit de confirmer le jugement dont est appel. *Arr. du* 11 *mars* 1807, *Mém., tom.* 3, *p.* 300.

4. Lorsque le ministère public appelle seul d'un jugement qui intéresse la Régie, celle-ci aurait le droit de former opposition à l'arrêt sur l'appel, comme rendu par défaut, s'il blessait ses intérêts. *Arr. du* 22 *juillet* 1808, *Mém., tom.* 4, *p.* 744.

5. Le Code de procédure civile, quoique promulgué postérieurement au décret du 1er germinal an 13, n'a porté aucune atteinte aux formes prescrites pour les instances qui intéressent la Régie. *Arr. du* 23 *novembre* 1810, *Mém., tom.* 7, *p.* 167.

6. La Régie peut attaquer par la voie de l'appel les jugemens rendus contre elle par défaut, sans être obligée d'employer la voie de l'opposition. *Arr. du* 12 *avril* 1811, *Mém., tom.* 7, *p.* 212. — On doit néanmoins préférer ce dernier moyen pendant que les délais ne sont pas expirés. *Mém., tom.* 7, *p.* 218.

7. On doit considérer comme rendu par défaut un jugement rendu sans que l'Administration ait formé aucune défense. — L'audition du ministère public ne peut, dans aucun cas, donner au jugement le caractère d'un jugement contradictoire. — Le ministère public n'est pas le défenseur nécessaire de l'Administration, mais seulement le défenseur naturel de la loi. *Arr. du* 11 *mars* 1812. — Aff. Cazals.

13. L'appel devra être notifié dans la huitaine de la signification du jugement (a) sans citation préalable au bureau de paix et conciliation; après ce délai, il ne sera point recevable, et le jugement sera exécuté purement et simplement. La déclaration d'appel contiendra assignation (b) à trois jours, devant le tribunal criminel du ressort de celui qui aura rendu le jugement; le délai de trois jours sera prorogé d'un jour par chaque deux myriamètres de distance du domicile du défendeur au chef-lieu du tribunal (c). *Décret du* 1er. *germinal an* 13, *art.* 32.

(a) *Délai pour l'appel.*

1. Le Code d'instruction criminelle est inapplicable pour déterminer les délais d'appel en matière de contributions indirectes. *Arr. du* 29 *frimaire an* 14, *Coll., p.* 30; *autre du* 13 *août* 1813. — Aff. Nieweg.

2. Lorsque la partie n'a pas fait signifier le jugement de police correctionnelle rendu en sa faveur, la Régie n'est pas obligée à le faire signifier elle-même, afin de faire courir le délai pour l'appel, qu'elle a toujours le droit de déclarer pendant que la signification ne lui a pas été faite. *Arr. du* 17 *mars* 1806, *Mém., tom.* 1, *p.* 99; *autre du* 19 *janvier* 1810, *tom.* 6, *p.* 665.

3. La signification d'un jugement n'a d'autre effet que de faire courir le délai de l'appel; et, quoiqu'elle soit faite sans réserve, elle ne peut être considérée comme un acquiescement qui interdit à la Régie la voie de l'appel. *Arr. du* 6 *juin* 1806, *Mém., tom.* 1, *p.* 79.

4. La nullité de l'appel d'un jugement de police correctionnelle qui n'a pas été signifié par la partie, n'emporte pas la déchéance, et la Régie est recevable à former un nouvel appel régulier. *Arr. du* 11 *mars* 1807, *Mém., tom.* 3, *p.* 300.

5. Les dispositions du Code civil ne sont pas applicables en matière de contravention aux contributions indirectes, et la partie à qui la Régie fait signifier un arrêt rendu en appel par défaut n'est plus recevable à y former opposition après le délai de huitaine de la signification. *Arr. du* 24 *août* 1810, *Mém., tom.* 7, *p.* 95.

6. Lorsque la Régie a déclaré appel d'un jugement de police correctionnelle, la signification qu'elle a faite de ce jugement en tête de l'appel ne fait pas courir le délai contre elle: si l'appel est annullé, elle a toujours le droit d'en former un nouveau, attendu que le délai ne court que du jour de la signification du jugement par la partie. *Arr. du* 10 *février* 1814. — Aff. Clerici.

(b) *Assignation sur appel.*

7. L'assignation sur appel, pour être valable, doit être donnée à la personne ou à son domicile réel; elle serait nulle si elle était donnée au domicile élu par la partie. *Arr. du* 4 *déc.* 1806, *Mém., tom.* 1, *p.* 299.

8. L'assignation sur appel est nulle si elle n'est signifiée à personne ou à domicile; cependant, si la partie assignée de son côté sans opposer de cette nullité, elle est couverte, et elle ne peut plus être proposée devant la cour d'appel. *Arr. du* 14 *janvier* 1807, *Mém., tom.* 4, *p.* 477.

9. Le décret du 1er germinal an 13 règle exclusivement le mode d'instruction et les délais de citation sur appel. *Arr. du* 22 *juillet* 1808, *Mém., tom.* 4, *p.* 744.

10. L'assignation sur l'appel dans une instance commune à plusieurs parties, n'est pas nulle envers toutes les parties, parce que la copie donnée à l'une d'elles est irrégulière. *Arr. du* 8 *décembre* 1808, *M., tom.* 4, *p.* 755.

11. L'assignation donnée en vertu de la déclaration d'appel au nom de la Régie n'est pas nulle, quoiqu'elle indique un délai plus long que celui de trois jours. *Arr. du* 15 *décembre* 1808, *Mém., tom.* 5, *p.* 34.

12. La notification d'appel serait régulièrement faite au domicile élu par la partie, s'il était prouvé que celle-ci a eu connaissance de l'appel. *Arr. du* 23 *mars* 1809, *Mém., tom.* 5, *p.* 341.

13. Une contravention aux contributions indirectes, quoique commise par plusieurs individus, n'en est pas moins personnelle et entière vis-à-vis chacun d'eux, et une nullité commise dans la signification d'appel, à l'égard de l'un d'eux, ne doit pas influer sur la régularité des poursuites à l'égard des autres. *Arr. du* 23 *novembre* 1810, *Mém., tom.* 7, *p.* 167.

14. La peine de déchéance n'est relative qu'à la première disposition de l'art. 32 du décret du 1er germinal, qui veut que l'appel soit interjeté dans la huitaine de la signification du jugement. — Elle n'est pas applicable à la citation en appel qui peut être donnée pour comparaître à la première audience dans le délai de trois jours francs. *Arr. du* 8 *avril* 1813.

(c) *Pourvoi en cassation en matière correctionnelle.*

15. Le pourvoi en cassation s'exerce en matière correctionnelle ou de simple police contre les arrêts ou jugemens rendus en dernier ressort. *Art.* 177 *et* 216 *du Code d'instruction criminelle.*—Il n'est ouvert contre les arrêts préparatoires et d'instruction, ou les jugemens en dernier ressort qui ont cette qualité, qu'après l'arrêt ou jugement définitif : l'exécution volontaire de tels arrêts ou jugemens ne peut, en aucun cas, être opposée comme fin de non recevoir. *Art.* 416 *idem.*

16. La partie civile, le prévenu, la partie publique et les personnes civilement responsables du délit, peuvent se pourvoir en cassation. *Art.* 177 *et* 216 *idem.*— La partie civile ne peut se pourvoir que quant à ses intérêts civils. *Art.* 373 *idem.*

17. Le pourvoi se forme au moyen d'une déclaration faite au greffe même du tribunal qui a rendu le jugement, par la partie, ou par son avoué, ou par un fondé de pouvoirs. —Elle est inscrite par le greffier sur un registre; toute personne a le droit de s'en faire délivrer des extraits. *Art.* 417 *idem.*

18. Cette déclaration doit être faite dans le délai de trois jours francs après celui où le jugement a été rendu. *Art.* 373 *idem.*— Dans ce délai, le jour de la prononciation de l'arrêt, et celui de la déclaration de pourvoi, ne sont pas comptés; en sorte que cette déclaration peut être valablement faite le cinquième jour. *Arr. du* 21 *février* 1806, *Mém., tom.* 1, *p.* 97.—Si elle était faite le sixième jour, elle serait hors du délai et ne serait plus recevable. *Arr. du* 7 *janvier* 1808, *Mém., tom.* 3, *p.* 235.

19. La partie civile qui se pourvoit en cassation est tenue de joindre aux pièces une expédition authentique de l'arrêt ou jugement attaqué. *Art.* 419 *du Code d'instruction criminelle.*— La Régie des Contributions indirectes ne peut se dispenser de lever une expédition des jugemens ou arrêts contre lesquels elle exerce le pourvoi en cassation. *Décis. du Ministre de la justice, du* 20 *janvier* 1818.

20. Le recourant, soit en faisant sa déclaration, soit dans les dix jours suivans, peut déposer au greffe une requête contenant ses moyens de cassation. *Art.* 422 *du Code d'instruction criminelle.*—Le Directeur doit informer aussitôt l'Administration de ce qu'il aura fait, afin qu'elle puisse fournir un mémoire supplémentaire si elle le juge convenable. *Circ. n°* 147, *Rec., tom.* 4, *p.* 183.

21. Le pourvoi en matière criminelle, correctionnelle et de simple police est suspensif. *Art.* 373 *du Code d'instruction criminelle.*— On ne peut procéder à l'exécution d'un jugement ou arrêt attaqué par la voie de cassation. *Arr. du* 30 *brumaire an* 14, *Coll., p.* 63.—Il est également suspensif pour les exécutoires de frais accordés aux parties contre la Régie. *Arr. du* 2 *avr.* 1812.—Aff. Vanhamme.

14. Si la saisie est jugée bonne, et qu'il n'y ait pas d'appel dans la huitaine de la signification, le neuvième jour le préposé au bureau indiquera la vente des objets confisqués, par une affiche signée de lui, et apposée, tant à la porte de la maison commune qu'à celle de l'auditoire du juge de paix, et procédera à la vente cinq jours après. *Décret du* 1er *germinal an* 13, *art.* 33.

15. Dans le cas où le procès-verbal portant saisie d'objets prohibés

serait annullé par vice de forme (a), la confiscation desdits objets sera néanmoins prononcée sans amende, sur les conclusions du poursuivant, ou du procureur du Roi. — La confiscation des objets saisis en contravention sera également prononcée, nonobstant la nullité du procès-verbal, si la contravention se trouve suffisamment prouvée par l'instruction (b). *Idem, art.* 34.

(a) *Second procès-verbal.*

1. Un procès-verbal étant déclaré nul, on ne peut, après le jugement, rapporter un second procès-verbal pour constater la même contravention. *Arr. du* 23 *prairial an* 9, *Mém., tom.* 1, *p.* 156.

(b) *Instruction des procédures malgré la nullité des procès-verbaux.*

2. Lorsqu'un procès-verbal est déclaré nul, le tribunal doit, si la Régie le demande, continuer l'instruction, pour savoir si le prévenu est en contravention, et pour appliquer la peine de la confiscation dans le cas de l'affirmative. *Arr. du* 26 *mars* 1807, *Mém. tom.* 3, *p.* 369.

3. Lorsqu'un procès-verbal est déclaré nul, la confiscation ne peut être refusée qu'autant qu'il a été vérifié, et par suite déclaré qu'il ne résulte de l'instruction aucune preuve de la contravention. *Arr. des* 26 *et* 31 *décembre* 1807, *Mém., tom.* 3, *p.* 84.

4. Les tribunaux doivent rechercher et admettre, lors de l'instruction, toutes les preuves tendantes à établir la vérité des faits portés dans les procès-verbaux, lorsque, par quelques expressions équivoques ou obscures, ils se croient fondés à en prononcer la nullité. *Arr. du* 8 *septemb.* 1808, *Mém., tom.* 4, *p.* 603.

5. On ne doit pas appeler d'un jugement dans lequel le tribunal, après avoir annulé le procès-verbal par un motif quelconque et fondé, déclare que la contravention n'est pas justifiée par d'autres preuves. *Arr. du* 19 *janvier* 1810, *Mém., tom.* 6, *p.* 690.

6. Lorsqu'un procès-verbal est annullé pour vice de forme, le tribunal ne peut refuser au procureur du Roi la faculté de faire la preuve de la contravention, si ce magistrat requiert d'office d'être admis à faire cette preuve. *Arr. du* 28 *août* 1812. —Aff. Gen.

16. Les propriétaires des marchandises seront responsables du fait de leurs facteurs, agens ou domestiques (a), en ce qui concerne les droits, confiscations, amendes et dépens. *Décret du* 1er *germinal an* 13, *art.* 35.

(a) *Responsabilité des propriétaires.*

1. Celui qui occupe un appartement dans lequel on trouve des marchandises prohibées, est passible des peines encourues, quoiqu'il n'existe aucune preuve qu'il ait effectué lui-même ce dépôt. *Arr. du* 7 *floréal an* 12, *Mém. tom.* 1, *p.* 92.

2. Lorsque l'absence d'un assujéti est reconnue, sa femme, qui habite dans sa maison, et qui suit son commerce, le représente légalement dans toutes les relations que ce commerce nécessite avec la Régie. *Arr. du* 4 *décembre* 1807, *Mém., tom.* 3, *p.* 25.

3. La femme d'un assujéti est le préposé naturel de son mari. *Arr. du* 11 *février* 1808, *Mém., tom.* 3, *p.* 265.

4. Un particulier qui se trouve dans la maison d'un propriétaire absent, pendant le temps des inventaires, qui répond aux interpellations des commis, est censé représenter légalement le propriétaire, quoiqu'il ne soit ni son agent ni son domestique; et les fausses déclarations que fait ce particulier, établissent une contravention dont le propriétaire absent est responsable, quoiqu'il prétende n'avoir donné ni mission ni pouvoir d'agir en son nom. *Arr. du* 18 *mars* 1808, *Mém., tom.* 3, *p.* 270.

5. Lorsque les objets de fraude sont découverts dans un lieu quelconque, sans qu'il soit constaté par qui ils ont été déposés, c'est le propriétaire ou le locataire du local qui doit être considéré comme le véritable auteur de la fraude, quoiqu'il ne soit pas dénommé au procès-verbal. *Arr. du* 13 *mai* 1808, *Mém., tom.* 4, *p.* 560.

6. Un redevable ne peut contester la déclaration faite par sa femme pendant son absence. *Arr. du* 10 *août* 1808, *Mém., tom.* 5, *p.* 251.

7. Les déclarations que fait la femme d'un assujéti en l'absence de son mari, ont

la même force que si c'était le mari qui les eût faites. *Arr. du 3 novembre* 1808, *Mém.*, *tom.* 4, *p.* 710.

7. Les propriétaires de marchandises soumises aux droits étant responsables du fait de leurs domestiques, ceux-ci ont qualité pour représenter leur maître en tout ce qui tient à l'exécution des formalités prescrites par la loi en cas de saisie. — Les poursuites peuvent être dirigées contre les propriétaires qui sont soumis, dans ce cas, non seulement à la confiscation, mais encore aux amendes résultant des contraventions. *Arr. du* 13 *mai* 1809, *Mém.*, *tom.* 6, *p.* 417.

9. Un aubergiste chez lequel on trouve des tabacs de fraude, est passible des peines de la contravention, sauf son recours contre ceux qui auraient, à son insu, introduit les tabacs dans son domicile. *Arr. du* 22 *décembre* 1809, *Mém.*, *tom.* 6, *p.* 503.

10. Un particulier qui loge dans sa maison des individus qui y introduisent des objets de fraude, peut être poursuivi personnellement comme coupable du dépôt frauduleux, quoique les objets soient trouvés dans la chambre où logent les étrangers, et que ceux-ci déclarent qu'ils leur appartiennent. *Arr. du* 9 *novembre* 1810, *Mém.*, *tom.* 7, *p.* 56.

11. Le particulier entre les mains duquel les Employés saisissent des objets en contravention, ne peut être absous, quoiqu'il amène en cause l'expéditeur, et sauf son recours contre lui. *Arr. du* 28 *décembre* 1810, *Mém.*, *tom.* 7, *p.* 118.

12. Lorsqu'une saisie est faite sur un agent ou sur un ouvrier porteur des objets en contravention, et que toutes les formalités qui constituent la régularité du procès-verbal ont été remplies vis-à-vis de lui, les Employés ne sont pas obligés de réitérer ces formalités vis-à-vis le propriétaire des objets saisis, et le procès-verbal est régulier contre lui. *Arr. du* 4 *septembre* 1813. Aff. Thietens.—*Voy.* note 83, §§ 5 et 6.

17. La confiscation des objets saisis pourra être prononcée contre les conducteurs (a) sans que la Régie soit tenue de mettre en cause les propriétaires, quand même ils lui seraient indiqués, sauf si les propriétaires intervenaient (b) ou étaient appelés par ceux sur lesquels les saisies auraient été faites, à être statué, ainsi que de droit, sur leur intervention ou réclamation. *Décret du* 1er *germinal an* 13, *art.* 36.

(a) *Conducteurs d'objets de fraude.*

1. Les préposés peuvent régulièrement dresser procès-verbal contre les conducteurs des boissons non accompagnées d'expédition, quoique le propriétaire de ces boissons soit présent à la saisie. *Arr. du* 7 *mai* 1808, *Mém.*, *tom.* 3, *p.* 340.

2. Les tribunaux, en prononçant la confiscation d'objets transportés en fraude, ne peuvent se dispenser de condamner, sans distinction, le conducteur contre lequel les poursuites sont dirigées. *Arr. du* 30 *novembre* 1811, *Mém.*, *tom.* 7, *p.* 176.

(b) *Intervention des propriétaires.*

3. Les propriétaires d'objets saisis sur un conducteur ne peuvent se pourvoir par voie de tierce-opposition contre le jugement qui condamne ce conducteur, et leur intervention, s'ils veulent l'exercer, doit avoir lieu pendant l'instance et avant le jugement. *Arr. de la Cour de justice criminelle du Cantal, du* 10 *juin* 1808, *Mém.*, *tom.* 3, *p.* 364.

4. Une partie intervenant dans une instance dirigée contre un individu, peut être condamnée pour une contravention qui lui est personnelle et que sa propre défense fait découvrir, quoiqu'il n'en soit fait aucune mention dans le procès-verbal. *Arr. du* 25 *mai* 1810, *Mém.*, *tom.* 6, *p.* 724.

18. Les condamnations pécuniaires (a) entre plusieurs personnes pour un même fait de fraude sont solidaires (b). *Décret du* 1er *germinal an* 13, *art.* 37.

(a) *Recouvrement des amendes. — Contrainte par corps en matière correctionnelle.*

1. L'exécution des condamnations à l'amende, aux restitutions, aux dommages-intérêts et aux frais, pourra être poursuivie par la voie de la contrainte par corps. *Art.* 52 *du Code pénal.*—Si le condamné prouve son absolue insolvabilité, la durée de l'emprisonnement (pour les amendes, les confiscations et les frais) doit être réduite à six

mois, sauf à reprendre la contrainte par corps s'il survient au condamné quelques moyens de solvabilité. *Art.* 53 *idem.*

2. La contrainte par corps pour le recouvrement des condamnations prononcées en police correctionnelle, doit être exécutée suivant les règles tracées par le Code d'instruction criminelle, et n'est pas soumise aux dispositions prescrites par lesCodes civil et de procédure civile. *Lettre du Ministre de la justice, du* 12 *septembre* 1807, *Mém., tom.* 2, *p.* 677.

3. C'est à la Régie à poursuivre le recouvrement des amendes, même par la voie de la contrainte par corps.— Cependant, si l'insolvabilité du condamné est légalement constatée, l'emprisonnement devient une peine, et c'est au procureur du Roi à faire la diligence nécessaire pour la faire subir. *Décis. du Ministre de la justice du* 15 *nivôse an* 10, *Mém., tom.* 2, *p.* 607.

4. Le recouvrement des amendes prononcées pour rebellion ou pour injures et insultes envers les préposés de la Régie, dans l'exercice de leurs fonctions, appartient exclusivement à l'Administration. *Décis. du Minist. des finances, du* 30 *mai* 1809, *Rec., tom.* 5, *p.* 64.

5. Il y a lieu à exercer la contrainte par corps dans les cas où elle est autorisée par la loi, lors même qu'elle n'aurait pas été prononcée par le jugement de condamnation. *Arr. du* 2 *janv.* 1807, *Mém., tom.* 3, *p.* 161.

6. Le paiement des frais faits pour le recouvrement des amendes doit précéder la mise en liberté des condamnés. *Mém., tom.* 2, *p.* 671.

(b) *Solidarité des condamnés.*

7. La solidarité des condamnations pécuniaires en matière correctionnelle est confirmée par l'art. 55 du Code pénal.

8. Lorsque plusieurs individus sont condamnés, comme auteurs d'un délit correctionnel, chacun au *maximum* de l'amende, les tribunaux ne doivent pas moins prononcer la solidarité contre eux. *Arr. du* 11 *septembre* 1807, *Mém., tom.* 3, *p.* 157.

19. Les objets, soit saisis pour fraude ou contravention, soit confisqués, ne pourront être revendiqués par les propriétaires, ni le prix, soit qu'il soit consigné ou non, réclamé par aucun créancier, même privilégié, sauf leurs recours contre les auteurs de la fraude. *Décret du* 1er *germinal an* 13, *art.* 38.—*Voy.* nomb. 17, §§ 3 et 4.

20. Les juges ne pourront, à peine d'en répondre en leur propre et privé nom, modérer les confiscations et amendes (a), ni en ordonner l'emploi au préjudice de la Régie. *Idem, art.* 39.

(a) *Modération des peines.*

1. L'art. 29, tit. 2 de la loi du 22 août 1791, n'est plus applicable, et les tribunaux ne peuvent se dispenser de prononcer la confiscation des chevaux et voitures des entreprises de messageries lorsqu'elle est encourue pour transport d'objets de fraude. *Arr. du* 7 *brumaire an* 14, *Mém., tom.* 3, *p.* 60.

2. L'attribution des tribunaux est étroitement circonscrite dans l'exécution de la loi, à laquelle ils contreviennent en voulant apprécier les circonstances atténuantes d'un délit constaté par un procès-verbal. *Arr. du* 21 *février* 1806, *Coll., p.* 67; *autre du* 29 *mars* 1806, *Coll., p.* 56.

3. Les juges doivent, indépendamment de toutes conclusions de la Régie, suppléer d'office aux moyens qui auraient été omis par elle, et prononcer les condamnations qu'elle aurait négligé de demander. *Arr. du* 5 *novembre* 1806, *Mém., tom.* 1, *p.* 193.

4. Lorsque la loi exige qu'une déclaration soit inscrite sur un registre, le redevable ne peut suppléer à cette inscription, en prouvant qu'il a fait la déclaration contestée, ni se fonder sur le refus ou la négligence du receveur, qu'autant qu'il l'a fait constater légalement et en temps utile. *Arr. du* 7 *novembre* 1806. *Mém., tom.* 1, *p.* 200; *autre du* 26 *avril* 1808, *tom.* 5, *p.* 97.

5. Un prévenu ne peut être absous par les tribunaux, d'une contravention légalement constatée, sous le prétexte de son ignorance des lois et de sa bonne foi. *Arr. du* 30 *juillet* 1807, *Mém., tom.* 2, *p.* 385; *autre du* 7 *mai* 1808, *tom.* 3, *p.* 510.

6. Il n'appartient pas aux tribunaux de décider des circonstances, quelles qu'elles soient, qui peuvent rendre la contravention plus ou moins excusable. Simples applicateurs de la loi, ils doivent se conformer rigoureusement à sa disposition; l'Administration seule a le droit de remettre

les peines encourues, et les juges commettent un véritable excès de pouvoir quand ils se permettent d'acquitter un contrevenant par des considérations prises de son intention et de sa bonne foi. *Arr. du* 5 *novembre* 1807, *Mém., tom.* 2, *p.* 735.

7. La Régie peut, dans l'assignation, se prévaloir d'une contravention différente de celle mentionnée au procès-verbal, lorsque cette nouvelle contravention dérive implicitement de l'exposé du procès-verbal, et le tribunal ne peut se dispenser de prononcer les peines encourues. *Arr. du* 27 *février* 1808, *Mém., tom.* 5, *p.* 193.

8. Les tribunaux ne doivent pas se borner à prononcer sur la contravention constatée par un procès-verbal; ils sont obligés, au contraire, de prononcer sur toutes les contraventions résultant de l'instruction. *Arr. du* 20 *mai* 1808, *Mém., tom.* 5, *p.* 161.

9. Des allégations d'erreurs commises au moment d'une déclaration et la bonne foi des contrevenans ne peuvent être admises pour excuse par les tribunaux. *Arr. du* 10 *juin* 1808, *Mém., tom.* 4, *p.* 392.

10. Les tribunaux doivent prononcer sur toutes les contraventions constatées par un procès-verbal, lorsque la citation a été donnée aux fins de ce procès-verbal, et quoiqu'il n'ait pas été pris des conclusions directes sur toutes ces contraventions. *Arr. du* 17 *février* 1809, *Mém., tom.* 5, *p.* 199.

11. Le décret du 5 germinal an 12 ayant donné à la Régie seule le droit de transiger sur les amendes et confiscations, il s'ensuit nécessairement que, quand la contravention existe, les tribunaux ne peuvent, en aucune manière, faire remise de la peine. *Arr. du* 1er *sept.* 1809.—Aff. Podesta.

12. Lorsqu'une contravention est matériellement établie, les tribunaux ne peuvent absoudre le contrevenant d'après les déclarations orales des préposés qui reconnaissent avoir commis une erreur dans la rédaction des expéditions qu'ils ont délivrées. *Arr. du* 8 *février* 1810, *Mém., tom.* 6, *p.* 672.

13. Une expédition délivrée par les Employés de la Régie, l'apposition même par eux des plombs et autres marques, ne peuvent couvrir une contravention.—Le fait de ces préposés n'est pas celui de la Régie; ils ne peuvent modifier l'exécution de la loi ni rendre légitime ce qu'elle prohibe. *Arr. du* 28 *décembre* 1810, *Mém., tom.* 7, *p.* 118.

14. Les tribunaux ne peuvent déclarer en principe qu'il n'y a point de contravention lorsqu'elle ne porte que sur de très-petites quantités d'objets soumis aux droits. *Arr. du* 9 *févr.* 1812.—Aff. Alesch.

15. Dans les matières qui sont réglées par des lois spéciales, on ne peut faire l'application de l'art. 66 du Code pénal et décharger le contrevenant des peines encourues, par le motif qu'il est âgé de moins de seize ans et qu'il a agi sans discernement. —Les pères sont civilement responsables des délits commis par leurs enfans mineurs. *Arr. du* 2 *juillet* 1813.

16. Le décès d'un prévenu de contravention, avant que la condamnation ait été prononcée, éteint l'action pour l'amende, mais les tribunaux ne peuvent se dispenser de prononcer la confiscation des objets de fraude. *Arr. du* 9 *décemb.* 1813, aff. Vanbraban. *Voy.* nomb., 44, § 2.

17. Les tribunaux doivent prononcer sur toutes les contraventions résultant du procès-verbal, même sur celles pour lesquelles la Régie n'aurait pas pris des conclusions, ni devant le tribunal, ni dans l'assignation. — Une cour d'appel ne peut refuser de prononcer sur une contravention résultant d'un procès-verbal, sous prétexte que la Régie n'a pas pris de conclusions en première instance sur cette contravention. *Arr. du* 18 *décembre* 1817.—Aff. Philibert.

CHAPITRE III.

De l'inscription de faux.

21. Celui qui voudra s'inscrire en faux contre un procès-verbal, sera tenu d'en faire la déclaration par écrit en personne, ou par un fondé de pouvoirs spécial, passé devant notaire, au plus tard à l'audience indiquée pour l'assignation à fin de condamnation (a). Il devra, dans les trois jours suivans, faire au greffe dudit tribunal le dépôt (b) des moyens de faux et des noms et qualités des témoins (c) qu'il voudra faire entendre, le tout à peine de déchéance de l'inscription de faux (d).

—Cette déclaration sera reçue par le président et le greffier, dans le cas où le déclarant ne saurait écrire ni signer (e). *Décret du 1er germinal an 13, art.* 40.

(a) *Délai pour la déclaration.*

1. Lorsque des premières assignations, quoique régulières, ont été mal à propos abandonnées par la Régie, le prévenu peut être admis à s'inscrire en faux contre le procès-verbal, à l'audience indiquée par la dernière assignation. *Arr. du* 19 *janvier* 1809, *Mém., tom.* 5, *p.* 291.

2. Le prévenu qui ne s'est pas inscrit en faux à l'audience fixée par l'assignation, ne peut plus être admis à le faire à une audience suivante, lorsque la cause a été renvoyée. *Arr. du* 30 *novembre* 1811, *Mém., tom.* 7, *p.* 226.

3. Le prévenu qui n'a pas paru à la première audience indiquée par l'assignation, et contre lequel il a été rendu un jugement par défaut, ne peut plus être admis à s'inscrire en faux contre le procès-verbal.—Le délai dont il est fait mention dans l'art. 41 n'est relatif qu'au dépôt des moyens de faux qui doit être fait au greffe quand l'inscription a été déclarée dans les limites de l'art. 40, et non point à la déclaration de faux elle-même, qui doit être faite dans le temps qui s'écoule depuis le procès-verbal jusqu'à la première audience indiquée par l'assignation. *Arr. du* 7 *mai* 1813, aff. Leperche.

4. Quand l'assignation est donnée pour la première audience qui sera tenue trois jours francs après sa date, cette audience est le dernier terme où la déclaration d'inscription de faux puisse être valablement faite, encore que, n'importe par suite de quelle circonstance la cause n'ait été ni appelée à cette audience, ni même inscrite sur le rôle, ou qu'il y soit intervenu une sentence de condamnation par défaut.—La déclaration d'inscription de faux peut être valablement faite ailleurs qu'à l'audience dans le temps qui s'écoule depuis le procès-verbal jusqu'à l'audience indiquée par l'assignation. *Arr. du* 20 *mai* 1813.—Aff. Douchez et Piteux.

(b) *Dépôt au greffe des moyens de faux.*

5. L'acte de dépôt des moyens de faux qui doit être fait au greffe ne peut être suppléé par une requête présentée au tribunal. *Arr. du* 23 *novembre* 1810, *Mém., tom.* 7, *p.* 44.

Voy. le § 10 ci-après.

(c) *Désignation des témoins.*

6. La partie qui s'inscrit en faux contre un procès-verbal doit, à peine de déchéance, en fournissant ses moyens, en offrir la preuve, et indiquer les noms et prénoms des témoins à l'aide desquels elle prétend la faire. *Arr. du* 19 *avril* 1811, *Mém., tom.* 7, *p.* 127.

(d) *Nullités des inscriptions de faux.*

7. Les nullités d'une déclaration d'inscription de faux ne peuvent être couvertes ni par le silence ni par le consentement soit des parties intéressées, soit du ministère public; elles peuvent être proposées en tout état de cause comme exception préjudicielle éteignant l'instance; il est même du devoir des juges de suppléer au silence des parties. *Arr. du* 18 *novembre* 1813.—Aff. Saquebouille et autres.

(e) *Signature du déclarant.*

8. La déclaration d'inscription de faux faite devant le tribunal doit être signée, à peine de déchéance, si le déclarant sait écrire, ou même lorsqu'il ne saurait que signer. *Arr. du* 14 *août* 1807, *Mém., tom.* 3, *p.* 232.

9. La déclaration d'inscription de faux qui doit être reçue et signée par le président et le greffier, lorsque le prévenu ne sait pas signer, ne peut être suppléée par un jugement qui donne acte à ce prévenu de la déclaration verbale qu'il a faite à l'audience de vouloir s'inscrire en faux. *Arr. du* 29 *juin* 1810, *Mém., tom.* 7, *p.* 37.

10. Une déclaration d'inscription de faux faite à la première audience est nulle si elle n'a été faite par écrit.—Elle est encore nulle si l'acte contenant les moyens de faux et le nom des témoins n'est signé que par l'avoué du prévenu, quoique celui-ci soit présent au dépôt qui en est fait au greffe. *Arr. du* 18 *novembre* 1813.—Aff. Saquebouille et autres.

22. Le délai pour s'inscrire en faux contre le procès-verbal ne commencera à courir que du jour de la signification de la sentence,

si elle a été rendue par défaut. *Décret du* 1er. *germinal an* 13, *art.* 41.

Ce délai n'est relatif qu'au dépôt des moyens de faux. *Voy.* §§ 3 et 4, nomb. 21.

23. Les moyens de faux proposés, dans le délai et dans la forme réglés par l'art. 41 ci-dessus, par les prévenus contre les procès-verbaux des préposés de la Régie, ne seront admis qu'autant qu'ils tendront à justifier les prévenus de la fraude ou des contraventions qui leur sont imputées (a). *Idem, art.* 43.

(a) *Admission des moyens de faux.*

1. Les tribunaux inférieurs, même les juges de paix, ne peuvent se dispenser de prononcer en première instance sur les inscriptions de faux déclarées à l'occasion des contestations portées devant eux, et les tribunaux supérieurs, malgré le renvoi qui leur est fait par les premiers juges, ne peuvent prononcer sur l'inscription de faux avant qu'elle ait été jugée admissible en première instance. *Arr. du* 13 *frimaire an* 12, *Mém., tom.* 2, *p.* 667.

2. Lorsque le tribunal devant lequel a été déclarée une inscription de faux a examiné les moyens, et jugé qu'ils étaient admissibles, il doit surseoir au jugement de la contravention, et renvoyer l'affaire sur le faux aux juges qui doivent en connaître. *Arr. du* 6 *janvier* 1809, *Mém., tom.* 5, *p.* 107.

3. Dans le cas où une inscription de faux est déclarée dans les formes légales, les tribunaux ne peuvent procéder à la preuve des faits avant d'avoir jugé si les moyens de faux peuvent détruire l'existence de la fraude. *Arr. du* 19 *janvier* 1809, *Mém., tom.* 5, *p.* 46.

4. Un procès-verbal qui constate une contravention en matière d'octroi, ou toute autre matière, ne peut être attaqué par l'inscription de faux que quand les moyens de faux, en les supposant prouvés, justifient le prévenu de la contravention qui lui est imputée.—Ce n'est qu'après le jugement de ces moyens, et lorsqu'ils ont été reconnus admissibles, qu'il y a lieu à surseoir sur la contravention pour attendre le jugement sur le faux. *Arr. du* 24 *mars* 1809, *Mém., tom.* 5, *p.* 102; *autre du* 21 *avril* 1809, *tom.* 6, *p.* 437.

5. Si, dans un procès-verbal, les Employés déclarent qu'ils ont dégusté les boissons, que le prévenu avoue avoir en sa possession, et s'ils évaluent le prix total des boissons laissées à sa garde, il ne peut s'inscrire en faux, en soutenant, 1° que les Employés n'ont pas dégusté; 2° que la quantité portée au procès-verbal est supérieure à la quantité réelle des boissons saisies, ces moyens de faux n'étant pas admissibles, puisqu'ils ne sont pas de nature à justifier la contravention. *Arr. du* 27 *avril* 1810, *Mém., tom.* 7, *p.* 160.

6. Lorsqu'un procès-verbal constate que les Employés ont trouvé du vin caché, et dans un vase d'une capacité inférieure à l'hectolitre, le prévenu ne peut s'inscrire en faux, en opposant, 1° que le vase trouvé chez lui n'était pas totalement rempli de vin; 2° que les Employés avaient déclaré que c'était du bon vin sans en avoir fait la dégustation; ces moyens, en les supposant vérifiés, ne pouvant détruire la contravention, ne sont pas admissibles.—Lorsqu'un procès-verbal constate plusieurs contraventions, les moyens de faux sont inadmissibles s'ils ne sont proposés que sur une partie des contraventions. *Arr. du* 23 *novembre* 1810, *Mém., tom.* 7, *p.* 44.

7. Lorsqu'un procès-verbal constate plusieurs faits relatifs à la même matière, et de chacun desquels il doit résulter une contravention, les tribunaux ne peuvent admettre des moyens de faux qui, en les supposant prouvés, ne détruiraient que certaines contraventions, et en laisseraient subsister d'autres. *Arr. du* 20 *mars* 1812, *Mém., tom.* 7, *p.* 295.

8. De simples dénégations, dénuées de faits et de circonstances, opposées aux faits d'un procès-verbal, ne peuvent être admises comme moyens de faux. *Arr. du* 18 *février* 1813.—Aff. Lombardo.

9. Lorsqu'un procès-verbal constate deux contraventions, les moyens de faux proposés ne peuvent être admis s'ils ne tendent à justifier le prévenu que sur l'une des deux contraventions.—Le tribunal doit, dans ce cas, prononcer le rejet des moyens de faux et donner foi au procès-verbal dans tout son contenu et pour toutes les contraventions qui y sont établies. *Arr. du* 7 *mai* 1813, aff. Leperche.

CHAPITRE IV.

Des Contraintes.

24. La Régie pourra employer contre les redevables en retard la voie de contrainte. *Décret du 1er germinal an 13, art. 43.*

25. La contrainte sera décernée par le Directeur ou Receveur de la Régie; elle sera déclarée exécutoire, sans frais, par le juge de paix (a) du canton où le bureau est établi, et pourra être notifiée par les Préposés de la Régie (b). Le juge de paix ne pourra refuser de viser la contrainte pour être exécutée, à peine de répondre des valeurs pour lesquelles la contrainte aura été décernée. *Décret du 1er germinal an 13, art. 44.*

(a) *Hypothèques.*

1. La contrainte est un titre suffisant lorsqu'elle a été rendue exécutoire par le juge de paix, pour requérir une inscription hypothécaire sur les biens du redevable. *Déc. du Min. des fin., du 22 pluviôse an 10, Mém., tom. 2, p.* 485.

(b) *Signification — Nullités des contraintes.*

2. La signification d'une contrainte doit être faite au domicile du redevable, à peine de nullité. *Arr. du 9 fructid. an 12, Mém., tom. 1, p.* 94.

3. Les nullités de formes dans la signification d'une contrainte, sont couvertes par l'opposition du redevable, lorsque cette opposition est uniquement motivée sur des moyens tirés du fond. *Arr. du 7 août* 1807, *Mém., tom.* 5, *p.* 239.

4. Le désistement de procédure en matière civile pour cause de nullité dans les poursuites, ne prive pas l'Administration du droit de recommencer des poursuites régulières, et de décerner une nouvelle contrainte. *Arr. du 8 mars* 1808, *Mém., tom.* 3, *p.* 292.

5. Une erreur commise dans une contrainte relativement à l'acte sur lequel la contrainte est fondée, n'entraîne pas la nullité de la contrainte. *Arr. du 25 juillet* 1814.

6. La Régie ne peut pas se servir de porteurs de contraintes ou de garnisaires pour le recouvrement des droits. *D. A. n°* 162.

26. L'exécution de la contrainte ne pourra être suspendue que par une opposition formée par le redevable; l'oppostion sera motivée et contiendra assignation à jour fixe devant le tribunal civil de l'arrondissement (a), avec élection de domicile dans la commune où siége le tribunal: le délai pour l'échéance de l'assignation ne pourra excéder huit jours; le tout à peine de nullité de l'opposition. *Décret du 1er germinal an 13, art. 45.*

(a) *Opposition aux Contraintes.*

1. La contestation sur l'opposition à une contrainte doit être portée devant le tribunal dans la juridiction duquel se trouve le bureau d'où la contrainte a été décernée. *Arr. du 5 mai* 1806, *aff. Lenore, Mém., tom.* 2, *p.* 415.

2. Lorsqu'un redevable de la Régie est en état de faillite, les dispositions du Code de commerce sont inapplicables envers le trésor public, dont le privilége ne peut se discuter devant le commissaire de la faillite, mais seulement devant le tribunal appelé à connaître des oppositions aux contraintes. *Arr. du 9 janvier* 1815.—Aff. Bonnet.

3. Les discussions qui peuvent s'élever pour les droits dus par un failli ne sont pas

de la compétence du tribunal de commerce, et doivent être portés devant le tribunal institué pour connaître des oppositions aux contraintes. *Arr. du* 10 *mai* 1815. — Aff. Godin.

27. Les redevables contre lesquels auraient été protestées faute de paiement, des obligations souscrites par eux envers la Régie, par suite de crédits obtenus, seront contraignables par corps (a). *Décret du* 1er *germinal an* 13, *art.* 52.

(a) *Contrainte par corps en matière civile.*

1. La Régie ne peut employer la contrainte par corps pour le recouvrement des droits que dans le seul cas prévu par cet article. *D. A. n°* 470.

2. L'exécution de la contrainte par corps en matière civile est soumise aux formalités prescrites par le Code de procédure civile, liv. 5, tit. 15.

3. Les administrations sont dispensées de faire aucune consignation pour alimens. *Voy.* nomb. 92.

28. Le recouvrement des dix pour cent (des octrois) se poursuivra par la saisie des deniers de l'octroi, et même par voie de contrainte, à l'égard du Receveur municipal. *Ordonn. du* 9 *décembre* 1814, *art.* 74. *Loi du* 28 *avril* 1816, *art.* 157.

29. A défaut de paiement des droits, il sera décerné contre les redevables des contraintes qui seront exécutoires, nonobstant opposition et sans y préjudicier (a). *Loi du* 28 *avril* 1816, *art.* 21.

(a) *Exécution des contraintes nonobstant opposition.*

1. Lorsque la loi prononce qu'une contrainte sera exécutoire nonobstant opposition, les sommes demandées par cette voie doivent toujours être acquittées, en supposant même qu'elles ne seraient pas dues, sauf la restitution si elle est statuée par le jugement définitif sur l'opposition. *Arr. du* 4 *février* 1807, *Mém., tom.* 4, *p.* 406.

2. Les oppositions aux contraintes de la Régie des Contributions indirectes ne peuvent jamais devenir la matière d'une simple ordonnance de référé.—Il ne peut être sursis à la contrainte ; celle-ci est exécutoire nonobstant toute opposition et sans y préjudicier. *Arr. du* 6 *août* 1817.

CHAPITRE V.

Des Instances civiles.

30. Les contestations (a) qui pourront s'élever sur le fond des droits établis (b) ou maintenus par la présente loi seront portées devant les tribunaux de première instance, qui prononceront dans la chambre du conseil, et avec les mêmes formalités prescrites pour le jugement des contestations qui s'élèvent en matière de paiement des droits perçus par la Régie de l'enregistrement. *Loi du* 5 *ventôse an* 12, *art.* 88.

(C'est l'art. 65 de la loi du 22 frimaire an 7, rapporté nomb. 31, qui règle la forme des procédures en matière d'enregistrement).

(a) *Contestations civiles élevées sur des procès-verbaux.*

1. Quoique la Régie ait porté elle-même une affaire devant le tribunal correctionnel, elle peut ensuite, si le fonds du droit est contesté, demander, pour cause d'incompé-

tence, l'annullation du jugement rendu par ce tribunal. *Arr. du* 23 *juillet* 1807, *Mém., tom.* 2, *p.* 529.

2. Lorsque, dans une instance portée devant un tribunal de police correctionnelle, le fonds du droit est contesté, ce tribunal doit prononcer d'office le renvoi devant le tribunal civil. — La Régie peut élever en appel la question d'incompétence, quoiqu'elle ne l'ait pas proposée en première instance. *Arr. du* 16 *juin* 1808, *Mém., tom.* 4, *p.* 460.

3. Toute contestation qui a pour objet de soutenir que l'Administration ou ses Préposés n'ont pas le droit de faire certaines opérations ou d'exiger certaines conditions, ne peut être considérée comme une contestation sur le fonds du droit, et donner lieu, par ce motif, au renvoi devant le tribunal civil. — On doit, au contraire, ne considérer comme contestation civile que celle qui a pour objet de soutenir que le prévenu n'est pas assujéti aux droits et qu'il est dispensé de les acquitter en tout ou en partie. *Arr. du* 8 *juill.* 1808, *Mém., tom.* 4, *p.* 495.

4. Lorsqu'un redevable est poursuivi en raison d'une contravention, il ne peut, pour se soustraire à la peine encourue, élever une contestation sur le fond du droit, si la disposition de la loi est claire et précise, et les tribunaux doivent prononcer immédiatement sur le fait de la contravention soumise à leur jugement, quelles que soient les défenses du prévenu. *Arr. du* 13 *avril* 1809, *Mém., tom.* 5, *p.* 264.

5. Lorsqu'une cour royale renvoie une instance devant un tribunal civil, elle ne peut insérer dans son arrêt un motif duquel il résulte que les droits contestés ne sont pas dus. *Arr. du* 16 *juin* 1809, *Mém., tom.* 5, *p.* 321.

6. Lorsqu'il s'élève en police correctionnelle une question qui présente un doute raisonnable sur le fond du droit, il y a lieu à renvoyer devant le tribunal civil pour décider sur la question concernant le droit. *Arr. du* 31 *juillet* 1812, *Mém., tom.* 7, *p.* 251.

7. Un procès-verbal pour défaut de licence ne peut être renvoyé devant le tribunal civil. — La licence est le brevet qui confère et qui atteste l'autorisation de fabriquer et de débiter; et sa durée étant formellement limitée au dernier jour de l'année où elle est délivrée, il s'ensuit que, dès le premier jour de l'année suivante, le fabricant ou le débitant ne peut plus être autorisé qu'au moyen d'une nouvelle licence, à défaut de laquelle il est en contravention, et passible de l'amende prononcée par l'art. 171 de la loi du 28 avril 1816. *Arr. du* 6 *mars* 1818.—Aff. Héron.

(b) *Fixation—Compensation de droits.*

8. Avant qu'une contrainte soit décernée par l'Administration, les tribunaux ne peuvent, sur la demande d'un redevable, déterminer la quotité des droits qu'il est obligé de payer, et en ordonner le paiement ou la consignation. *Arr. du* 7 *mai* 1806, *Mém., tom.* 1, *p.* 230.

9. Les tribunaux ne peuvent décider que les créances et titres qu'un redevable aurait à répéter de l'Administration, soient admis en paiement des droits acquis au trésor.— La quittance d'un receveur dans laquelle cette compensation aurait été admise, ne libère pas le redevable. *Arr. du* 28 *juillet* 1808, *Mém., tom.* 4, *p.* 502; *autre du* 10 *janvier* 1809, *Mém., tom.* 5, *p.* 123.

31. L'introduction et l'instruction des instances auront lieu devant les tribunaux civils de départemens; la connaissance et la décision en sont interdites à toutes les autorités constituées ou administratives...— L'instruction sera faite par simples mémoires respectivement signifiés (a).—Il n'y aura d'autres frais à supporter, par la partie qui succombera, que ceux du papier timbré, des significations et du droit d'enregistrement des jugemens.—Les tribunaux accorderont, soit aux parties, soit aux préposés de la Régie qui suivront les instances, les délais qu'ils leur demanderont pour produire leurs défenses; ils ne pourront néanmoins être de plus de trente jours.—Les jugemens seront rendus dans les trois mois au plus tard (b) à compter de l'introduction des instances, sur le rapport d'un juge (c), fait en audience publique, sur les conclusions du procureur du Roi; ils seront sans appel (d) et ne

pourront être attaqués que par la voie de cassation (e). *Loi du* 22 *frimaire an* 7, *art.* 65.

(a) *Instruction des procédures. — Plaidoiries.*

1. La production d'un mémoire dans lequel un préposé admet les motifs sur lesquels la partie a formé son opposition, ne peut être considérée comme un acquiescement, surtout si, avant le jugement, il a été produit de nouvelles conclusions.—Les préposés chargés du recouvrement des droits ne peuvent lier l'Administration par de mauvaises défenses. *Arr. du* 21 *avril* 1806, *Mém., tom.* 1, *p.* 157.

2. Dans les instances relatives au recouvrement des droits, les tribunaux ne peuvent, à peine de nullité des jugemens, entendre les défenses verbales des parties. *Arr. du* 13 *janvier* 1807, *Mém., tom.* 4, *p.* 619; *autre du* 28 *février* 1814.—Aff. Julich.

3. Les tribunaux ne peuvent recevoir des mémoires non signifiés ni admettre des observations verbales après le rapport fait à l'audience. *Arr. du* 18 *janvier* 1808, *Mém., tom.* 4, *p.* 685.

4. La disposition qui défend toute plaidoirie dans les affaires de la Régie relatives aux perceptions, ne s'étend pas aux actions en requête civile.—Dans ces actions, l'Administration n'est pas dispensée de produire, en tête de sa demande, une consultation de trois avocats. *Arr. du* 30 *août* 1809, *Mém., tom.* 6, *p.* 486.

5. Un jugement rendu sur mémoire non communiqué ni signifié est nul. *Arr. du* 20 *octobre* 1813.—Aff. Denaix.

6. Un jugement, dans une instance engagée pour validité d'une saisie-arrêt, opérée pour sûreté des droits, doit, à peine de nullité, être rendu sur le rapport d'un juge et sans plaidoirie. *Arr. du* 9 *février* 1814.

7. Un jugement rendu en matière de contribution, sans que le ministère public ait été entendu, est nul. *Arr. du* 15 *mars* 1814.—Aff. Bonneau.

8. La disposition qui défend toute plaidoirie dans les instances concernant les contributions, s'étend même aux actions pour recouvrement des fermages nationaux. *Arr. du* 22 *mars* 1814.—Aff. Steen.

9. Un jugement est nul s'il a été rendu sur plaidoirie, quoique toutes les parties eussent constitué un avoué.—Il est également nul à défaut du rapport d'un juge et des conclusions du ministère public. *Arr. du* 31 *janvier* 1816.—Aff. Quidet.

(b) *Délai pour le prononcé du jugement.*

10. Il n'y a pas déchéance ni prescription, quoique la décision d'une instance en matière civile soit prolongée au-delà du délai de trois mois fixé par cet article. *Arr. du* 4 *mars* 1807, *Mém., tom.* 3, *p.* 152; *autre du* 19 *juin* 1809, *tom.* 6, *p.* 496.

11. Dans une instance civile en recouvrement de droits, l'Administration ne devient pas non recevable à défaut d'avoir mis sa demande en état dans les trois mois. *Arr. du* 2 *août* 1808, *Mém., tom.* 6, *p.* 414.

(c) *Rapport fait à l'audience.*

12. Un certificat extrajudiciaire délivré pour constater qu'un jugement a été précédé d'un rapport fait par l'un des juges, ne peut suppléer la mention que doit contenir le jugement même, de l'observation de cette formalité. *Arr. du* 25 *avril* 1808, *Mém., tom.* 4, *p.* 419.

13. Le défaut de rapport fait à l'audience par un juge donne lieu à la cassation du jugement, et cette nullité peut être invoquée dans l'instance en cassation, quoiqu'on n'en ait fait aucune mention devant les premiers juges. *Arr. du* 13 *décembre* 1809, *Mém., tom.* 6, *p.* 628.

(d) *Cas où il y a lieu à l'appel.*

14. Les jugemens rendus sur les contestations de droits sont rendus en dernier ressort; mais quand il s'agit de recouvremens de revenus ou deniers publics, ils sont sujets à l'appel, suivant la quotité de la somme contestée. *Arr. du* 13 *messidor an* 9, *Mém., tom.* 2, *p.* 696.

15. La disposition qui interdit l'appel dans les instances pour le recouvrement des droits, n'est pas applicable aux jugemens rendus par défaut, contre lesquels la Régie est recevable à former opposition. *Arr. du* 4 *mars* 1807, *Mém., tom.* 3, *p.* 152.

16. Un jugement rendu en dernier ressort ne peut être attaqué par la voie d'appel, sous prétexte qu'il n'est pas qualifié en dernier ressort. *Arr. du* 23 *juin* 1817.—Aff. Damours.

(e) *Pourvoi en cassation en matière civile.*

17. Le délai pour le pourvoi est de trois mois francs, à compter de la notification du jugement à personne ou à domicile, pour toutes les personnes qui habitent en France. *Loi du 1er décembre* 1790.—Dans ce délai, il ne faut compter ni le jour de la signification ni celui de l'échéance. *Décr. du 1er frimaire an* 2.—Quand le jugement que l'on attaque n'a pas été signifié, on est toujours à temps de former le pourvoi : au lieu de la copie signifiée, on joint alors une expédition du jugement. *Réglement de* 1738.

18. Le pourvoi se réalise par le dépôt au greffe de la cour de cassation, d'une requête contenant les fins et moyens de cassation, avec les pièces justificatives, et surtout la copie signifiée ou une expédition authentique du jugement attaqué. *Réglement de* 1738.—La remise de la copie signifiée, ou d'une autre expédition du jugement attaqué, est de rigueur, à peine de nullité du pourvoi, même dans les instances qui intéressent le gouvernement. *Arr. du* 23 *brumaire an* 10, *Mém., tom.* 1, *p.* 359.

19. L'Administration faisant suivre directement les instances en cassation, on va indiquer quelles sont les dispositions que les Directeurs ont à remplir relativement à ces instances.—Lorsqu'un jugement est signifié par la partie, le Directeur doit s'empresser d'adresser à l'Administration la copie signifiée; mais si la partie néglige ou diffère trop long-temps la notification, le Directeur adresse une copie du jugement, sur papier libre, à l'Administration, qui décide s'il y a lieu à déclarer le pourvoi, et qui, dans ce cas, autorise le Directeur à lever une expédition en forme du jugement. *Circ. n°* 147, *Contentieux, Rec., tom.* 4, *p.* 183.

20. L'Administration ne serait pas recevable à se pourvoir contre un jugement qui aurait été signifié sans réserve à sa requête. *Arr. du* 25 *décembre* 1807, *Mém., tom.* 3, *p.* 159.

21. L'exécution volontaire du jugement constitue un acquiescement tacite qui entraîne également la déchéance du pourvoi. *Mém., tom.* 2, *p.* 427.—Dans les instances suivies à la requête de l'Administration, il y a lieu d'agir ainsi qu'il suit : 1re Supposition. Si un jugement qui condamne en dernier ressort la Régie à effectuer une restitution, est signifié à la requête de la partie qui l'a obtenu, avec commandement d'y satisfaire. On doit d'abord exiger caution (*voy.* § 22) : si la caution est fournie, on doit exécuter provisoirement le jugement comme forcé et contraint, sous la réserve expresse du pourvoi en cassation.—2e Supposition. Si le jugement n'est pas signifié, comme il ne peut alors exister de contrainte, la restitution serait un acquiescement. Il convient donc de s'y refuser.—3e Supposition. Si un jugement alloue à l'Administration une partie de ses conclusions et rejette les autres, et si on le signifie pour en suivre l'exécution, ce ne doit être qu'avec réserve expresse de se pourvoir aux chefs qui font préjudice, autrement il y aurait acquiescement.—Si la partie se présente spontanément pour satisfaire au chef du jugement qui la condamne, ses offres ne peuvent être reçues qu'avec les mêmes réserves. *Mém., tom.* 2, *p.* 428.

22. Le pourvoi en cassation, dans les matières civiles, n'est pas suspensif; la cour n'accorde point de surséance. Rien ne peut empêcher l'exécution provisoire du jugement dénoncé. *Loi du 1er décembre* 1790.—Cependant les paiemens à faire par la Régie, par suite de jugemens contre lesquels on s'est pourvu en cassation, ne peuvent avoir lieu que sous caution, d'après la loi du 16 juillet 1793, ainsi conçue : « Il ne sera fait par la trésorerie et par les » caisses des diverses administrations, aucuns paiemens en vertu de jugemens attaqués par la voie de cassation, dans les » termes prescrits par la loi, qu'au préalable ceux au profit desquels lesdits jugemens auraient été rendus n'aient donné » bonne et suffisante caution pour sûreté » des sommes à eux adjugées. »

CHAPITRE VI.

Navigation intérieure.

32. Les contraventions aux lois sur les canaux et la navigation intérieure continueront d'être constatées, poursuivies et jugées suivant

les formes prescrites par la loi du 24 brumaire au 7. *Décret du 1er germinal an 13, art.* 46.

33. Toute personne qui aura aidé ou favorisé la fraude, ou qui aura concouru à des contraventions... ... sera condamnée aux mêmes peines que les auteurs des fraudes et contraventions. *Loi du 14 brumaire an 7, art.* 24.

34. Le juge de paix du canton prononcera sans appel et en dernier ressort lorsque, non compris le droit (l'amende), n'excédera pas cinquante francs, et pour le surplus il renverra aux tribunaux compétens. *Idem, art.* 25.

35. Les procès-verbaux seront affirmés, dans les trois jours, devant le juge de paix du canton, ou devant l'un de ses assesseurs, à peine de nullité.—Ces procès-verbaux feront foi jusqu'à inscription de faux en matière de fraude et de contravention, et en matière de police correctionnelle jusqu'à preuve contraire (a).—Dans les cas qui excèderont la compétence du juge de paix, il sera tenu de renvoyer les procès-verbaux au tribunal qui doit en connaître, pour être l'affaire poursuivie à la diligence du Procureur du Roi près le tribunal.—Les actions résultant des procès-verbaux seront poursuivies dans le mois, à peine de nullité. *Idem, art.* 26.

(a) *Nombre d'Employés nécessaire pour validité de ces procès-verbaux.*

1. Lorsqu'une loi ne détermine pas le nombre d'employés nécessaire pour l'authenticité des procès-verbaux, on doit conclure de ce silence de la loi qu'il suffit d'un seul rédacteur. *Arr. du 29 floréal an 10, Mém., tom. 2, p.* 672.

36. Les contestations relatives au paiement de l'octroi de navigation seront, conformément à la loi du 30 floréal an 10, portées devant le Sous-Préfet dans l'arrondissement duquel le bureau de perception sera situé, sauf le recours au Préfet, qui prononcera en conseil de préfecture. *Arrêté du 8 prairial an 11, art.* 15.

CHAPITRE VII.

Contentieux de la Garantie.

37. L'ADMINISTRATION des Monnaies surveillera les bureaux de garantie relativement à la partie d'art et au maintien de l'exactitude des titres des ouvrages d'or et d'argent mis dans le commerce (a). *Loi du 19 brumaire an 6, art.* 37.

(a) *Contestations sur l'application des poinçons de la garantie.*

1. On doit considérer comme une contestation de la compétence seule de l'Administration des monnaies, les questions élevées devant les tribunaux pour savoir si un ouvrage est susceptible ou non de recevoir, sans détérioration, l'application du poinçon, et la solution de ces questions doit être renvoyée à cette Administration. *Mém., tom.* 3, *p.* 40 et 354.

2. Les tribunaux ne peuvent prononcer

sur les contestations qui s'élèvent devant eux, tant sous le rapport du titre que sous celui de l'art; ils doivent renvoyer à l'Administration des monnaies, et suspendre leur jugement jusqu'à la décision de cette Administration. *Arr. du* 10 *mars* 1810, *Mém., tom.* 6, *p.* 611.

3. Lorsqu'il y a des doutes sur la possibilité de marquer certains ouvrages du poinçon de garantie, et qu'un tribunal a désigné pour experts des Employés de l'Administration des monnaies, le jugement définitif ne peut être contraire à la décision portée dans l'expertise. *Arr. du* 26 *octobre* 1810, *Mém., tom.* 7, *p.* 137.

4. Un tribunal ne peut prononcer la main-levée des ouvrages d'or et d'argent saisis à défaut de marque, qu'après qu'il a été constaté que ces ouvrages n'étaient pas susceptibles de recevoir, sans détérioration, l'empreinte des poinçons. *Arr. du* 4 *septembre* 1814.—Aff. Lansac.

5. Un tribunal ne peut déclarer, sans que la preuve en soit établie, que des ouvrages d'or et d'argent saisis à défaut de marque, ne sont pas susceptibles de recevoir, sans détérioration, l'empreinte des poinçons. *Arr. du* 10 *novembre* 1815.—Aff. Desange.

38. Les Employés des bureaux de garantie feront les recherches, saisies et poursuites dans les cas de contravention à la présente loi (a). *Loi du* 19 *brumaire an* 6, *art.* 71.

(a) *Visite chez les assujétis pour le droit de garantie.*

1. Les Employés des Contributions indirectes pourront entrer en tout temps chez les individus sujets aux droits sur la marque d'or et d'argent. *Art.* 81 *de la loi du* 5 *ventôse an* 12.

2. La loi soumet aux obligations qu'elle prescrit, tous les marchands et fabricans d'or et d'argent, dans le nombre desquels se trouvent nécessairement compris les horlogers, puisqu'ils vendent et fabriquent des boîtes de montres en or et en argent, et qu'ils peuvent vendre des chaînes et breloques. *Circ. de l'Adm. des Monn. du* 1er *prairial an* 8, *Rec., tom.* 1, *p.* 298.

3. La loi ne faisant aucune distinction ni exception, tous les ouvrages d'or et d'argent qui se trouvent chez un marchand ou fabricant, soit dans sa boutique, soit dans son atelier, soit dans tout autre endroit de son domicile, sont nécessairement considérés comme objets de commerce, puisqu'il a la facilité de les vendre quand il en trouve l'occasion; et s'ils ne sont pas en règle, les Employés doivent les saisir et en dresser procès-verbal en se conformant aux dispositions de la loi. *Circ. de l'Adm. des Monn. du* 1er *prairial an* 8, *précitée.*

4. Un brocanteur qui achète et vend des montres et bijoux d'or et d'argent, est assujéti aux dispositions de la loi du 19 brumaire an 6. *Arr. du* 15 *avril* 1808, *Mém., tom.* 4, *p.* 469.

5. Dans le cas où l'on éprouverait, de la part du contrevenant, des violences telles, qu'elles empêcheraient la rédaction du procès-verbal, c'est à l'officier de police qu'il appartient d'employer les moyens que la loi met en son pouvoir pour assurer la tranquillité des Employés. *Circ. timbrée* Contentieux, n° 117, *Rec., tom.* 4, *p.* 175.

6. Le refus d'exercice n'a pas été classé au tableau, parce qu'il ne peut se présenter comme simple contravention en matière de garantie; les Employés étant toujours accompagnés d'un officier de police, celui-ci doit prendre les mesures convenables pour faire cesser toutes les oppositions de la part des assujétis; et si leur opposition ne cédait pas à ces mesures, il y aurait alors un délit de rebellion, et c'est le Code pénal qui serait applicable. *Voy.* Officier de police, p. 90.

39. Lorsque les Employés d'un bureau de garantie auront connaissance d'une fabrication illicite de poinçons, le Receveur et le Contrôleur (a), accompagnés d'un Officier municipal (b), se transporteront dans l'endroit ou chez les particuliers qui leur auront été indiqués, et y saisiront les faux poinçons, les ouvrages et lingots qui en seraient marqués, et enfin les ouvrages achevés et dépourvus de marques qui s'y trouveraient; ils pourront se faire accompagner au besoin par l'Essayeur ou par un de ses agens. *Loi du* 19 *brumaire an* 6, *art.* 101.

(a) *Employés des Contributions indirectes.*

1. Ces Employés ont aussi qualité pour faire tous les actes prescrits par cette loi. *Voy.* ci-après nomb. 45.

(b) *Officier de police.*

2. Les Maires et leurs Adjoints, ainsi que les Commissaires de police, sont maintenant chargés des fonctions de la police administrative. *Loi du 18 pluviôse an 8, et Circ. de l'Adm. des Monn. du 1er prairial an 8, Rec., tom. 1, p.* 280.

3. Les Commissaires de police, les Maires et les Adjoints sont requis : 1° Pour accompagner les Employés dans les visites et recherches à faire chez les marchands et fabricans d'ouvrages d'or et d'argent, domiciliés dans l'arrondissement de la commune, et chez tous autres particuliers faisant clandestinement ce commerce; 2° pour assister à toutes les opérations qui tendent à constater les fraudes sur lesquelles doivent prononcer les tribunaux correctionnels auxquels la loi attribue la connaissance de ces délits; 3° pour protéger les parties intéressées, c'est-à-dire les Employés, dans le cas de refus ou de violence, et les orfèvres dans celui où les Employés s'écarteraient des dispositions de la loi; 4° pour être présens à la rédaction du procès-verbal, veiller à ce que les faits et dires y soient rapportés avec exactitude, et, dans le cas d'omission, faire rétablir les faits ou dires omis; 5° pour, après la lecture du procès-verbal, le signer ou attester, comme ils le jugent le plus convenable, attendu que, sans l'une ou l'autre de ces formalités, ce procès-verbal ne ferait foi en justice que jusqu'à inscription de faux; ce qui ne peut avoir lieu lorsqu'il est signé et attesté d'un fonctionnaire public ayant pour ce qualité, et qui a assisté à toutes les opérations; 6° enfin, pour accompagner les Employés au greffe du tribunal correctionnel, être présens au dépôt des ouvrages saisis, et signer l'acte qui constate ce dépôt. *Circ. de l'Adm. des Monn. du 1er prairial an 8, Rec., tom. 1, p.* 292.

4. Un procès-verbal en matière de garantie est valide, quoiqu'il ne soit pas signé par le Commissaire de police, s'il constate la présence de cet officier aux visites. *Arr. du 25 fructidor an 13, Mém., tom.* 1, *p.* 70; *autre du* 18 *novembre* 1808, *Mém., tom.* 4, *p.* 730.

5. Les Commissaires de police, dans les villes où il y en a d'établis, ont qualité pour remplacer les officiers municipaux dans les fonctions qui leur sont attribuées par l'art. 101 de la loi du 19 brumaire an 6. *Arr. du 8 frimaire an 14, Coll., p.* 12; *autre du* 19 *novembre* 1807, *Mém., tom.* 2, *p.* 730.

40. Il sera dressé à l'instant, et sans déplacer, procès-verbal de la saisie et de ses causes, lequel contiendra les dires de toutes les personnes intéressées (a), et sera signé d'elles (b). Ledit procès-verbal sera remis, dans le délai de dix jours au plus, au procureur du Roi près le tribunal de police correctionnelle, qui demeure chargé de faire les poursuites (c), également dans le délai de dix jours (d). *Loi du 19 brumaire an 6, art.* 102.

(a) *Aveux des Contrevenans.*

Voy. nomb. 7, §. 3.

(b) *Signature des procès-verbaux.*

1. En cas de refus de la part des contrevenans, il en sera fait mention, ainsi que de la sommation de signer qui leur aura été faite.

Voy. Officier de police, §§ 3 et 4.

(c) *Forme des poursuites judiciaires.*

2. Les dispositions du décret du 1er germinal an 13, relatives à la forme des procédures, ne sont pas applicables en matière de garantie. Les poursuites en cette matière doivent être réglées par le Code d'instruction criminelle, d'où il résulte que l'appel d'un jugement de police correctionnelle doit être déclaré au greffe le dixième jour, au plus tard, après celui qui a suivi le prononcé du jugement. *Arr. du 9 juin* 1809, *Mém., tom.* 5, *p.* 278.

(d) *Commencement des poursuites.*

3. L'inobservation de ce délai n'entraîne pas la déchéance et ne peut mettre le contrevenant à l'abri des peines qu'il a encourues. *Arr. du 29 mai* 1813.—Aff. Pavie.

41. Les poinçons, ouvrages ou objets saisis seront mis sous les cachets de l'Officier municipal, des Employés du bureau de garantie présens,

et de celui chez lequel la saisie aura été faite, pour être déposés (a) sans délai au greffe du tribunal de police correctionnelle. *Loi du* 19 *brumaire an* 6, *art.* 103.

(a) *Dépôt des objets saisis.*

1. Les objets en contravention ne doivent, sous aucun prétexte, être laissés à la garde du prévenu, ni d'une caution, ni même dans la maison où ils ont été trouvés; ils doivent être renfermés sur-le-champ dans une boîte ou paquet ficelé, et sous le cachet de l'Officier de police, du Préposé saisissant et du prévenu : si celui-ci refuse, il sera fait mention de son refus. Ces objets seront déposés, *sans délai*, non pas au bureau de la Régie, mais au greffe de la police correctionnelle. *Circ. n°* 117, *Contentieux, Rec., tom.* 4, *p.* 175. *Voy.* §. 3, nomb. 39.

42. Dans le cas où le tribunal prononcerait la confiscation des objets saisis, ils seront remis au Receveur de la Régie (des Contributions indirectes) pour être vendus (a). Il sera prélevé, sur le prix qui en proviendra, un dixième qui sera donné à celui qui aura le premier dénoncé le délit (b), et un second dixième qui sera partageable par parties égales entre les Employés du bureau de garantie (c) : le surplus, ainsi que les amendes, seront versés dans la caisse du Receveur. *Loi du* 19 *brumaire an* 6, *art.* 104.

(a) *Vente d'objets saisis.*

1. Lorsque la confiscation est prononcée par le tribunal, les objets saisis doivent être remis au Receveur de la Régie pour être vendus (dans la forme accoutumée). *Circ. n°* 8, *Rec., tom.* 1, *p.* 513.

(b) *Indicateur en matière de garantie.*

2. Il faut qu'il y ait nécessairement un indicateur pour que le dixième qui lui est dévolu soit payé; mais il suffit qu'il se soit fait connaître du Contrôleur de la Garantie, et que celui-ci l'atteste formellement. *D. A. n°* 501.

(c) *Partage du produit des saisies.*

3. Les Employés de la Régie sont admis au partage dans les saisies auxquelles ils concourent, et jouissent en entier du dixième lorsqu'ils saisissent seuls. *Circ. n°* 56, *Rec., tom.* 3, *p.* 85, *et art.* 8 *de l'arr. du Min. des fin., du* 17 *oct.* 1816.

43. Les mêmes formes et dispositions prescrites par les quatre articles précédens, auront lieu également pour toutes les recherches, saisies et poursuites relatives aux contraventions à la présente loi. *Loi du* 19 *brumaire an* 6, *art.* 105.

44. Tout ouvrage d'or et d'argent achevé, et non marqué, trouvé chez un marchand ou fabricant, sera saisi et donnera lieu aux poursuites par-devant le tribunal de police correctionnelle. Les propriétaires (a) des objets saisis encourront la confiscation (b), et en outre les autres peines portées par la loi. *Idem, art.* 107.

(a) *Propriétaires d'objets d'or et d'argent.*

1. Ces expressions, *les propriétaires des objets saisis*, ne doivent s'entendre que des marchands et fabricans, et non des particuliers, pour les objets destinés à leur usage. *Arr. du* 1er *frim. an* 14, *Coll., p.* 9.

(b) *Confiscation d'objets saisis.*

2. La confiscation des objets saisis pour contravention doit être prononcée, même lorsque le contrevenant viendrait à mourir avant la fin de la procédure. *Mém., tom.* 4, *p.* 680. *Voy.* nomb. 20, § 15.

3. Les contraventions à la garantie des matières d'or et d'argent sont particulièrement demeurées sous l'empire de la disposition de l'art. 31 du décret du 1er germinal an 13; et les tribunaux doivent, en cas de nullité du procès-verbal, prononcer la confiscation des objets saisis lorsque la contravention est constatée par l'instruction. *Arr. du* 17 *ventôse an* 13, *Coll., p.* 3; *autre du* 5 *septembre* 1806, *Mém., tom.* 1,

p. 208; *autre du 22 mai* 1807, *Mém.*, *tom.* 1, *p.* 342; *autre du* 18 *novembre* 1808, *Mém.*, *tom.* 4, *p.* 730.

4. Les mouvemens de montres et les boîtes, une fois réunis, forment, dans la main de l'horloger auquel ils appartiennent, un seul objet, et le mouvement est soumis à la confiscation encourue à défaut de marque sur la boîte au moment de la saisie. *Arr. du* 15 *frimaire an* 14, *Mém.*, *tom.* 1, *p.* 15.

5. Le mouvement fait partie intégrante de la montre, et doit être par conséquent compris dans la confiscation, si la montre y est soumise. *Arr. du* 15 *avril* 1808, *Mém.*, *tom.* 4, *p.* 469.

6. Les montres non revêtues de poinçons trouvées chez un horloger, sont dans le cas de la confiscation, et donnent lieu à l'amende. *Ar. du* 2 *janv.* 1806, *Coll.*, *p.* 17.

7. Un horloger chez lequel on saisit des boîtes de montres achevées et non marquées, ne peut être renvoyé de l'amende et de la confiscation, par le motif qu'il n'était détenteur de ces boîtes que depuis moins de vingt-quatre heures, et qu'elles n'étaient pas étalées, mais renfermées dans un tiroir au moment de la visite des Employés. *Arr. du* 18 *mai* 1815.—Aff. Baron.

8. La confiscation des ouvrages d'or et d'argent pour défaut de marque de garantie, ne peut être étendue aux diamans et pierres qui seraient montés sur ces ouvrages. *Arr. du* 15 *février* 1817.—Aff. Croco.

Voy. les arrêts indiqués nomb. 15, § 2 et suiv., qui, d'après ceux indiqués au § 3 ci-dessus, sont applicables aux procédures en matière de garantie.

45. Les dispositions de l'art. 76 de la loi du 5 ventôse an 12, concernant les condamnations qui doivent être prononcées contre les contrevenans aux (contributions indirectes), et celles de l'arrêté du 5 germinal suivant, relatives à la répartition du produit des amendes (a) et confiscations, et à la faculté de transiger sur les procès-verbaux de saisie, ne sont point applicables aux délits et contraventions concernant la garantie des matières d'or et d'argent, à l'égard desquelles la loi du 19 brumaire an 6 doit être exécutée, sauf en ce qui concerne la perception du droit de garantie qui a été attribuée à la Régie des (Contributions indirectes), dont les Préposés peuvent néanmoins, eux-mêmes, ou concurremment avec les Employés du bureau de garantie, constater les délits et contraventions (b) à la loi du 19 brumaire an 6, et poursuivre la condamnation des peines encourues (c), en remplissant les formalités prescrites par cette loi, sans qu'il puisse être transigé sur ces délits et contraventions. *Décret du* 28 *floréal an* 13, *art.* 1.

(a) *Peines en matière de garantie.*

1. L'amende prononcée par l'art. 76 de la loi du 5 ventôse an 12, n'est pas applicable en matière de garantie, et les dispositions pénales prononcées par la loi du 19 brumaire an 6 doivent seules être suivies. *Arr. du* 3 *janvier* 1806, *Coll.*, *p.* 20; *autre du* 27 *juin* 1817.—Aff. Griffe.

(b) *Employés des Contributions indirectes.*

2. Les Employés des Contributions indirectes ont qualité pour rédiger des procès-verbaux de contravention aux droits de garantie. *Arr. du* 17 *ventôse an* 13, *Coll.*, *p.* 3.

3. En matière de contravention à la loi du 19 brumaire an 6, les Employés des Contributions indirectes peuvent dresser des procès-verbaux sans l'assistance des Employés du bureau de garantie, et ils ne sont assujétis à suivre que les formalités prescrites par cette loi. *Arr. du* 26 *janvier* 1809, *Mém.*, *tom.* 5, *p.* 222.

4. Les procès-verbaux des Employés des Contributions indirectes, pour contraventions aux droits de garantie, ne sont pas soumis à d'autres formalités que celles prescrites par la loi du 19 brumaire an 6. *Arr. du* 18 *novembre* 1808, *Mém.*, *tom.* 4, *p.* 730; *autre du* 25 *février* 1813.—Aff. Holst.

(c) *Poursuites judiciaires.*

5. La Régie des Contributions indirectes a la faculté, concurremment avec le ministère public, de poursuivre la condamnation des peines encourues, et l'appel interjeté par elle est régulier. *Arr. du* 5 *septembre* 1806, *Mém.*, *tom.* 1, *p.* 208; *autre du* 22 *mai* 1807, *Mém.*, *tom.* 1, *p.* 589.

6. Cependant, S. Ex. le Ministre des

finances ayant décidé, le 10 février 1807, que les Employés devaient se borner à constater les contraventions dans les formes prescrites par la loi du 19 brumaire an 6, et laisser le soin des poursuites au ministère public, les Directeurs doivent s'abstenir de se porter partie civile dans ces sortes d'instances. *Circ. n° 117, Rec., tom. 4, p. 175.*

CHAPITRE VIII.

Poudres et Salpêtres.

46. La vente des poudres au public continuera d'être soumise, sous l'exploitation de la direction générale des Contributions indirectes, aux lois, ordonnances et réglemens actuellement en vigueur sur la matière. *Ordonnance royale du 25 mars 1818, art. 3.*

47. La Direction générale des Contributions indirectes demeure spécialement chargée de l'exécution des décrets des 24 août 1812 et 16 mars 1813, relatifs à la recherche et saisie des poudres, soit étrangères, soit fabriquées hors des poudreries du Gouvernement, qui pourraient circuler ou être vendues en fraude dans notre Royaume. *Idem, art. 4.*

48. La Régie des (Contributions indirectes) est spécialement chargée de la recherche des poudres étrangères et de celles fabriquées hors des poudrières du Gouvernement, qui pourraient circuler et être vendues dans le Royaume. *Décret du 24 août 1812, art. 1.*

49. Le prix de celles qui seront saisies par les agens de cette Régie, et qui doivent être remises à l'administration des poudres (a), et payées par elle au prix fixé par les lois et réglemens, ainsi que les amendes des délinquans, sont adjugés à ces agens. *Idem, art. 2.*

(a) *Prises d'échantillons — Dépôt de Poudres saisies.*

1. Lorsque le motif de la saisie portera sur la qualité de la poudre, les Employés auront soin de joindre à leurs procès-verbaux deux échantillons de la poudre saisie. —Chaque échantillon devra être renfermé dans une boîte ou paquet ficelé et revêtu du cachet des Employés saisissans et de celui de la partie saisie. Le procès-verbal fera mention de cette opération et de la sommation faite à la partie d'apposer son cachet sur les échantillons : l'empreinte des cachets sera mise en marge du procès-verbal.—Les Employés devront avoir soin de n'apposer ces cachets qu'avec de la cire molle, pour éviter les accidens que la cire enflammée pourrait occasionner. *Instruct. n° 45, § 20.*

2. Les poudres et objets saisis seront déposés provisoirement chez le Receveur central, d'où ils seront ensuite expédiés sur le point désigné par le Commissaire des poudres. *Idem, § 21.*

3. A l'égard des ustensiles et instrumens propres à la fabrication, l'agent de la Régie des poudres et salpêtres pourra retenir ceux qu'il reconnaîtra pouvoir être de quelque utilité pour l'exploitation qui lui est confiée, à la charge d'en payer la valeur d'après expertise. Les autres objets seront vendus dans la forme prescrite par l'art. 33 du décret du 1er germinal an 13. *Idem, § 24.*

50. La surveillance attribuée par le décret du 24 août dernier à la Régie des Contributions indirectes, sur la fabrication, la circulation et la vente dans toute l'étendue du Royaume, des poudres étrangères ou fabriquées hors des poudreries du Gouvernement, s'exercera aussi de la même manière sur la fabrication, la circulation et la vente des salpêtres. *Décret du 16 mars 1813, art. 1.*

51. Les Employés des (Contributions indirectes) sont autorisés à entrer en tout temps dans les ateliers, fabriques et magasins des fabricans, marchands et débitans, qui, aux termes des lois, sont tenus de justifier de l'emploi des poudres et salpêtres qui sont en leur possession. Ils pourront aussi, conformément à l'art. 83 de la loi du 5 ventôse an 12, faire des visites chez les particuliers soupçonnés de fraude, en se faisant assister par un officier de police. *Idem, art.* 2.

52. Toutes contraventions aux lois et arrêtés concernant les poudres et salpêtres seront constatées par des procès-verbaux (a) rédigés concurremment au nom de l'administration des poudres et au nom de l'Administration des Contributions indirectes.—Toutes les formalités relatives à la rédaction de ces procès-verbaux, et aux suites à y donner, seront conformes à celles qui sont établies par le décret du 1er germinal an 13, pour l'Administration des Contributions indirectes.

(a) *Des Procès-Verbaux.*

1. Les Préposés des Administrations étrangères, et tous autres agens ayant droit de verbaliser, doivent se conformer aux règles qui leur sont propres, pour la rédaction de leurs procès-verbaux ; mais toutes les fois qu'il se trouvera un ou plusieurs Employés des Contributions indirectes, parmi les saisissans, on suivra les formalités prescrites par le décret du 1er germinal an 13. *Inst. n°* 45, § 5.

53. Les instances relatives aux fraudes et contraventions seront portées devant les tribunaux de police correctionnelle, où elles seront suivies à la requête des deux Administrations, par les défenseurs ou Préposés supérieurs de l'Administration des Contributions indirectes, dans les formes propres à cette dernière. *Décr. du* 16 *mars* 1813, *art.* 4.

1. D'après l'ordonn du 25 mars 1818, c'est à la requête de l'administration des contributions indirectes seulement que les instances relatives aux poudres devront être suivies dorénavant, mais cette ordonnance n'ayant rien innové relativement aux salpêtres, les dispositions de l'article ci-dessus, et des art. 6 et 7 (nomb. 55 et 56), doivent continuer à être suivies en ce qu'elles prescrivent sur cette matière.

54. Les tribunaux correctionnels prononceront, dans tous les cas, à raison des fraudes et contraventions, les peines établies envers les contrevenans par les lois et arrêtés relatifs aux poudres et salpêtres. —Lorsque des Employés des (Contributions indirectes) des poudres et salpêtres, des douanes, des agens de police, des gendarmes ou autres agens publics ayant droit de verbaliser, auront seuls découvert la contravention, et opéré la saisie, le produit des amendes et confiscations appartiendra exclusivement aux saisissans.—Lorsque plusieurs Préposés des Administrations, ou agens publics ci-dessus désignés, auront concouru à une saisie, la répartition de l'amende et de la confiscation sera faite par portions égales entre les diverses Administrations et les agens dépendant d'une même autorité, sans égard au nombre respectif des saisissans (a). Les simples particuliers qui auront découvert des contraventions et fait opérer des saisies, de la manière prescrite par le décret du 10 septembre 1808, auront droit, comme les Préposés et agens sus-désignés, à la totalité du produit des amendes et confiscations (b). —Les agens de police et les gendarmes qui ne seront appelés que pour assister à la saisie, n'auront droit à aucun partage des amendes. *Idem, art.* 5.

(a) *Partage du produit des saisies.*

1. Si la saisie est faite concurremment par les Employés de la Régie et par d'autres agens, tels que des officiers de police, des gendarmes, des Employés des poudres et salpêtres, des douanes ou autres agens publics ayant droit de verbaliser, le produit, après le prélèvement des frais, sera divisé en autant de parts qu'il y a d'administrations ou d'autorités diverses au procès-verbal, et le montant de chaque part sera versé, par le Receveur central, à ces administrations, qui en feront ensuite la répartition dans les formes qui leur sont particulières. *Inst. n°* 45, § 28.

2. Les sommes attribuées à la Régie des Contributions indirectes dans les saisies de poudres et salpêtres, seront partagées dans les proportions suivantes; savoir: un quart au trésor, un quart à la caisse des retraites et la moitié aux Employés saisissans. *Circ. n°* 17, *Contentieux, nouv. série.*

(b) *Indications fournies par des particuliers.*

3. Les simples particuliers qui auraient découvert une contravention aux lois sur les poudres et salpêtres, sont autorisés à en faire la déclaration à la mairie, qui fera procéder à la visite des lieux dans la forme établie par le décret du 10 septembre 1808. *Inst. n°* 45, § 18.

55. Les transactions sur procès auront lieu dans la même forme, et d'après les mêmes règles que celles qui sont établies pour la Régie des (Contributions indirectes); mais elles ne pourront être consenties par les Directeurs de cette Régie que provisoirement, et de concert avec les commissaires de l'Administration des poudres. Ces derniers consentiront seuls les transactions dans tous les cas où les Employés des Contributions indirectes n'auraient point contribué à la découverte des délits; mais les arrangemens qu'ils auront faits ne seront définitifs qu'après avoir été approuvés par l'Administration des poudres. *Décret du* 16 *mars* 1813, *art.* 6. *Voy.* nomb. 53, § 1.

56. Les personnes qui, en vertu de commission de la Régie, sont autorisées à avoir en leur possession des poudres et salpêtres, à la charge de justifier de l'emploi, feront cette justification dans les formes qui seront déterminées par des instructions administratives, à la première réquisition des agens de l'Administration des poudres et des Employés de la Régie des Contributions indirectes. *Idem, art.* 7. *Voyez* nomb. 53, § 1.

57. Les formalités relatives aux transports des poudres et salpêtres continueront, comme par le passé, à être remplies dans les lieux de départ, de passage et d'arrivée, par les officiers municipaux; mais les Employés des Contributions indirectes seront prévenus de ces transports par ceux qui les auront ordonnés. *Idem, art.* 8.

Nota. Ceci doit s'entendre des poudres qui circulent pour le service du Gouvernement, celles que la Régie mettra en circulation devant être accompagnées d'acquits à caution.

CHAPITRE IX.

Contentieux des Octrois.

58. Les procès-verbaux (des Employés des Octrois) constatant la fraude seront affirmés devant le juge de paix (dans l'arrondissement duquel siége l'Administration municipale) dans les vingt-quatre heures de leur date, sous peine de nullité (a); et ils feront foi en justice jusqu'à inscription de faux. *Loi du* 7 *frimaire an* 8, *art.* 8.

(a) *Affirmation des Procès-Verbaux en matière d'Octroi.*

1. Il est à remarquer que l'affirmation est la seule formalité qui soit prescrite, à peine de nullité, pour les procès-verbaux qui intéressent les Octrois seulement.

2. Le délai de vingt-quatre heures fixé pour cette affirmation est de rigueur; il se compte de l'heure de la rédaction du procès-verbal. *Arr. du 5 janvier* 1809, *Mém., tom.* 5, *p.* 179.

3. La nullité d'un procès-verbal n'entraîne pas nécessairement l'absolution du prévenu, qui doit être condamné, si la preuve de sa contravention est établie indépendamment du procès-verbal. *Lett. du Minist. de la justice du 7 germinal an 9; autre du 14 germinal an 10, Recueil des Octrois, p.* 197 *et* 203.

59. Le recouvrement des droits d'Octroi sera poursuivi par voie de contrainte, et par corps, contre tout régisseur, fermier, receveurs et autres préposés à la recette desdits droits.—Les contraintes seront décernées par le Receveur municipal, visées par le juge de paix du canton où est située la commune : elles seront signifiées à la requête du maire, et exécutées conformément au tit. 15 du liv. 5 de la première partie du Code de procédure civile. *Décret du* 15 *novembre* 1810, *art.* 1 et 2.

60. Les Préposés de l'Octroi doivent être âgés au moins de vingt-un ans accomplis. Ils sont tenus de prêter serment devant le tribunal civil de la ville dans laquelle ils exerceront, et, dans les lieux où il n'y a pas de tribunal, devant le juge de paix. Ce serment sera enregistré au greffe, sans qu'il soit nécessaire d'employer le ministère d'avoué.—Il est dû seulement un droit fixe d'enregistrement de trois francs (a). *Ordonnance du* 9 *décembre* 1814; *art.* 58.

(a) *Réitération du serment.*

1. En cas de changement de résidence, les Employés ne sont pas tenus à nouvelle prestation de serment; il suffit qu'ils fassent viser leur commission, sans frais, par le juge de paix ou le président du tribunal civil du lieu où ils doivent exercer. *Idem, art.* 59.

61. Les Préposés d'Octroi doivent toujours être porteurs de leur commission, et seront tenus de la représenter lorsqu'ils en seront requis.—Le port d'armes est accordé aux Préposés d'Octroi dans l'exercice de leurs fonctions, comme aux Employés des Impositions indirectes (a). *Idem, art.* 60.

(a) *Port d'armes.*

1. Les Employés des Impositions indirectes ont la permision générale du port d'armes sans être assujétis à la taxe et au renouvellement; mais l'usage du fusil de chasse leur est interdit, à moins d'une autorisation spéciale sujette à rétribution. *Lettre du Min. de la police générale, du* 25 *juillet* 1806, *Rec., tom.* 4, *p.* 20.

62. Il est défendu à tous Préposés d'Octroi, indistinctement, de faire le commerce des objets compris au tarif (a).—Tout Préposé qui favorisera la fraude, soit en recevant des présens, soit de toute autre manière, sera mis en jugement, et condamné aux peines portées par le Code pénal contre les fonctionnaires publics prévaricateurs (b). *Id., art.* 63.

(a) *Commerce défendu aux Employés.*

1. Il est fait pareille défense aux Employés de la Régie des Impositions indirectes. *Circ. n°* 171, *Rec., tom.* 5, *p.* 36.

2. Tout fonctionnaire, tout officier public, tout agent du Gouvernement, qui, soit ouvertement, soit par des actes simulés, soit par interposition de personnes;

aura pris ou reçu quelque intérêt que ce soit, dans les actes, adjudications, entreprises ou régies dont il a ou avait, au temps de l'acte, en tout ou en partie, l'administration ou la surveillance, sera puni d'un emprisonnement de six mois au moins, et de deux ans au plus, et sera condamné à une amende qui ne pourra excéder le quart des restitutions et des indemnités, ni être au-dessous du douzième.—Il sera, de plus, déclaré à jamais incapable d'exercer aucune fonction publique.— La présente disposition est applicable à tout préposé ou agent du gouvernement qui aura pris un intérêt quelconque dans une affaire dont il était chargé d'ordonnancer le paiement ou de faire la liquidation. *Art.* 175 *du Code pénal.*

(b) *Prévarication.*

Les peines prononcées en cas de prévarications sont rapportées ci-après nomb. 102.

63. Toutes contraventions aux droits d'octroi seront constatées par des procès-verbaux (a), lesquels pourront être rédigés par un seul préposé, et auront foi en justice (b). Ils énonceront la date du jour où ils seront rédigés; la nature de la contravention, et, en cas de saisie, la déclaration qui en aura été faite au prévenu; les noms, qualité et résidence de l'Employé verbalisant et de la personne chargée des poursuites; l'espèce, poids ou mesure des objets saisis; leur évaluation approximative (c); la présence de la partie à la description, ou la sommation qui lui aura été faite d'y assister; le nom, la qualité et l'acceptation du gardien; le lieu de la rédaction du procès-verbal, et l'heure de sa clôture. *Ordonn. du* 9 *décembre* 1814, *art.* 75.

(a) *Des procès-verbaux en matière d'Octroi.*

1. Les formalités prescrites par le décret du 1er germinal an 13 ne sont pas applicables aux procès-verbaux rendus en matière d'octroi seulement, et les préposés de cette administration ne sont pas tenus, à peine de nullité, d'indiquer leur domicile dans ces actes. *Arr. du* 5 *brumaire an* 14, *Mém., tom.* 1, *p.* 109.

2. Les formalités prescrites par le décret du 1er germinal an 13 ne sont pas applicables aux procès-verbaux rendus en matière d'octroi seulement. *Arr. du* 27 *février* 1807, *Mém., tom.* 2, *p.* 547.

3. Les Employés sont dispensés de rédiger des procès-verbaux en forme pour les saisies d'objets d'une valeur de dix francs et au-dessous; ils ont la faculté, dans ce cas, de dresser de simples rapports exempts du timbre et de l'enregistrement. *Déc. du Min. des finances, du* 28 *mars* 1809. *Rec. des Octrois, p.* 276.

4. Les gardes-champêtres ne peuvent verbaliser en matière d'octroi qu'autant qu'ils sont munis d'une commission de préposés. *Déc. du Min. de la justice, du* 14 *juin* 1811. *Idem., p.* 324.

(b) *Inscription de faux.*

Voy, § 4, nomb. 23.

(c) *Évaluation des objets saisis.*

5. Le prix des objets saisis pour fraude aux droits d'octroi, doit être établi d'après la valeur commerciale de ces objets dans le lieu de la saisie, et non dans le lieu où les marchandises ont été achetées. *Arr. du* 22 *germinal an* 13, *Mém., tom.* 1, *p.* 182.

64. Dans le cas où le motif de la saisie portera sur le faux ou l'altération des expéditions, le procès-verbal énoncera le genre de faux, les altérations ou surcharges; lesdites expéditions, signées et paraphées du saisissant, *ne varietur,* seront annexées au procès-verbal, qui contiendra la sommation faite à la partie de les parapher, et sa réponse. *Ordonn. du* 9 *décembre* 1814, *art.* 76.

65. Si le prévenu est présent à la rédaction du procès-verbal, cet acte énoncera qu'il lui en a été donné lecture et copie; en cas d'absence du prévenu, si celui-ci a domicile ou résidence connue dans le

lieu de la saisie, le procès-verbal lui sera signifié dans les vingt-quatre heures de la clôture. Dans le cas contraire, le procès-verbal sera affiché, dans le même délai, à la porte de la maison commune. — Ces procès-verbaux, significations et affiches pourront être faits tous les jours indistinctement. *Idem, art.* 77.

66. L'action résultant des procès-verbaux en matière d'octroi et les questions qui pourront naître de la défense du prévenu, seront de la compétence exclusive, soit du tribunal simple de police (a), soit du tribunal correctionnel du lieu de la rédaction du procès-verbal, suivant la quotité de l'amende encourue (b). *Idem, art.* 78.

(a) *Compétence du tribunal de simple police.*

1. D'après l'art. 137 du Code d'instruction criminelle, les contraventions qui sont du ressort du tribunal de simple police, sont celles pour lesquelles l'amende ne s'élève pas au-dessus de quinze francs. — Ainsi, toutes les instances au sujet de saisies d'octroi dont l'estimation est au-dessus de 15 f., ou dans lesquelles il s'agit de l'application de peines prononcées par l'art. 15 de la loi du 27 frimaire an 8, pour opposition aux visites, doivent être portées au tribunal de police correctionnelle.

(b) *Des poursuites.*

2. Quoiqu'un procès-verbal ait été rendu par les préposés de l'octroi, la Régie de l'octroi ne peut appeler d'un jugement rendu contre elle lorsque l'instance a été suivie à la requête du ministère public seul, qui ne déclare pas appel de son côté. *Arr. du 13 mars 1806, Mém., tom. 2, p.* 698.

3. Lorsque deux procès-verbaux de saisie ont été rapportés pour la même contravention, l'un à la requête de la Régie, l'autre à celle du Maire, comme administrateur de l'octroi, celui-ci peut intervenir dans l'instance par voie de tierce-opposition, quoique l'affaire soit portée en appel, et qu'il ne soit pas intervenu en première instance. *Arr. du 18 juillet* 1817. — Aff. Malleux, Duchemin et Dupuis.

67. Les objets saisis par suite des contraventions aux réglemens d'octroi, seront déposés au bureau le plus voisin; et si la partie saisie ne s'est pas présentée dans les dix jours, à l'effet de payer la quotité de l'amende par elle encourue, ou si elle n'a pas formé, dans le même délai, opposition à la vente, la vente desdits objets sera faite par le Receveur, cinq jours après l'apposition à la porte de la maison commune et autres lieux accoutumés, d'une affiche signée de lui, et sans aucune autre formalité. *Ordonn. du 9 décembre 1814, art.* 79.

68. Néanmoins, si la vente des objets saisis est retardée, l'opposition pourra être formée jusqu'au jour indiqué pour ladite vente. L'opposition sera motivée, et contiendra assignation à jour fixe devant le tribunal désigné en l'art. 78, suivant la quotité de l'amende encourue, avec élection de domicile dans le lieu où siége le tribunal. Le délai de l'échéance de l'assignation ne pourra excéder trois jours. *Id., art.* 80.

69. S'il s'élève une contestation (a) sur l'application du tarif, ou sur la quotité du droit réclamé, le porteur ou conducteur sera tenu de consigner, avant tout, le droit exigé entre les mains du Receveur, faute de quoi il ne pourra passer outre, ni introduire, dans le lieu sujet, l'objet qui aura donné lieu à la contestation, sauf à lui à se pourvoir devant le juge de paix du canton; il ne pourra être entendu qu'en représentant la quittance de ladite consignation au juge de paix, lequel prononcera sommairement et sans frais, soit en dernier ressort, soit à la charge d'appel, suivant la quotité du droit réclamé. *Id., art.* 81.

(a) *Contestation civile.*

1. En matière d'octroi, le recours à la juridiction civile ne peut avoir lieu qu'à raison des contestations, soit sur la quotité des droits, soit sur l'application du tarif, et que quand le conducteur de l'objet prétendu passible de l'octroi a recouru, après la consignation du droit, au juge de paix du canton.—Mais lorsque, au lieu de consigner les droits et de recourir au juge de paix, le conducteur refuse de payer, ce refus constitue une contravention, et l'action résultant du procès-verbal, ainsi que toutes les questions auxquelles donne lieu la défense du prévenu, doivent être jugées par les tribunaux correctionnels ou de police, suivant la quotité de l'amende. *Arr. du 7 mars* 1818.—Aff. Touquet et Genouville.

70. Dans le cas où les objets saisis seraient sujets à dépérissement, la vente pourra en être autorisée avant l'échéance des délais ci-dessus fixés, par une simple ordonnance du juge de paix sur requête. *Ordonn.* du 9 *décembre* 1814, *art.* 82.

71. Les Maires seront autorisés, sauf l'approbation des Préfets, à faire remise, par voie de transaction, de totalité ou de partie des condamnations encourues, même après le jugement rendu. Ce droit appartient exclusivement à la Régie des Impositions indirectes, et, d'après les règles qui lui sont propres, toutes les fois que la saisie a été opérée dans l'intérêt commun des droits d'octroi et des droits imposés au profit du trésor. *Idem, art.* 83.

72. Le produit des amendes et confiscations pour contraventions aux réglemens de l'octroi, déduction faite des frais et prélèvemens autorisés, sera attribué, moitié aux Employés de l'octroi, pour être répartie d'après le mode qui sera arrêté, et moitié à la commune. *Idem, art.* 84.

73. Les préposés des octrois sont tenus, sous peine de destitution, d'exiger de tout conducteur d'objets soumis aux impôts indirects, comme boissons, tabacs, sels et cartes, la représentation des congés, passavans, acquits-à-caution, lettres de voiture et autres expéditions; de vérifier les chargemens, de rapporter procès-verbal des fraudes ou contraventions qu'ils découvriront; de concourir au service des impositions indirectes toutes les fois qu'ils en sont requis, sans toutefois pouvoir être déplacés de leur poste ordinaire; enfin, de remettre, chaque jour, à l'Employé en chef des impositions indirectes, un relevé des objets frappés du droit au profit du trésor qui auront été introduits. —Les Employés des Impositions indirectes concourront également au service des octrois, et rapporteront procès-verbal pour les fraudes et contraventions relatives aux droits d'octroi qu'ils découvriront. *Idem, art.* 92.

74. Les préposés des octrois se serviront, pour l'exercice de leurs fonctions, des jauges, sondes, rouannes et autres ustensiles dont les Employés des Impositions indirectes font usage. *Idem, art.* 93.

CHAPITRE X.

OBJETS DIVERS.

Actes administratifs.—Incompétence des tribunaux.

75. Défenses itératives sont faites aux tribunaux de connaître des actes d'administration, de quelque espèce qu'ils soient, aux peines de droit, sauf aux réclamans à se pourvoir (devant le ministre des finances) pour leur être fait droit s'il y a lieu. *Loi du* 16 *fructidor an* 3, 2e *paragraphe* (1).

1. Un comptable en débet ne peut former opposition à la contrainte décernée contre lui, et les tribunaux ne doivent pas en connaître.—C'est devant l'autorité administrative que doivent être portées les réclamations auxquelles l'arrêté qui établit le débet peut donner lieu. *Avis du Conseil d'Etat, du* 8 *ventôse an* 10, *Mém.*, *tom.* 2, *p.* 601.—Les tribunaux ne peuvent annuller la contrainte décernée contre un comptable en débet. *Mém.*, *tom.* 4, *p.* 687.

2. La question de savoir si l'existence d'un cautionnement passé devant une administration est légalement constatée, doit être résolue par l'autorité administrative. *Décret du* 24 *juin* 1808, *Mém.*, *tom.* 4, *p.* 537.

3. Les tribunaux ne peuvent connaître des contestations qui s'élèvent entre les préposés, relativement à l'exécution des ordres émanés de l'administration dont ces Employés dépendent. *Arr. du* 1er *nivôse an* 6, *Mém.*, *tom.* 1, *p.* 149.

4. Avant qu'une contrainte soit décernée par l'Administration, les tribunaux ne peuvent, sur la demande d'un redevable, déterminer la quotité du droit qu'il est obligé de payer, et en ordonner le paiement ou la consignation. *Arr. du* 7 *mai* 1806, *Mém.*, *tom.* 1, *p.* 230.

5. Les tribunaux ne peuvent statuer sur la suffisance ou l'insuffisance des cautionnemens offerts à la Régie, et l'autorité administrative est seule compétente pour juger, dans ce cas, la solvabilité des cautions. *Arr. du* 19 *mai* 1806, *Mém.*, *tom.* 1, *p.* 54.

6. Les tribunaux ne peuvent connaître de la validité d'un paiement reçu par un agent du gouvernement et ordonner la restitution, sans attendre la décision de l'administration à laquelle cet agent appartient. *Arr. du* 28 *octobre* 1807, *Mém.*, *tom.* 4, *p.* 411.

7. Le tribunal qui a renvoyé à l'autorité administrative la décision d'une question préjudicielle ne peut ensuite, en jugeant le fond de la question, prononcer d'une manière contraire à la décision administrative. *Arr. du* 30 *décembre* 1807, *Mém.*, *tom.* 5, *p.* 94.

8. Les tribunaux ne peuvent méconnaître la fixation de capacité des mesures, faite par l'autorité administrative. *Arr. du* 8 *juin* 1808, *Mém.*, *tom.* 4, *p.* 399.

9. Les tribunaux ne peuvent, sans empiéter sur l'autorité administrative, déclarer que les moyens pratiqués par les préposés, pour établir la perception, sont dommageables pour les assujétis.—C'est à l'Administration que doivent être adressées les réclamations de cette nature. *Arr. du* 24 *janvier* 1812, *Mém.*, *tom.* 7, *p.* 195.

(1) On pourra remarquer, par les arrêts rapportés à la suite de la loi du 16 fructidor an 3, dans quel sens on entend faire ici l'application de cette loi.

Timbre de l'Enregistrement.

76. La contribution du timbre est établie (a) sur tous les papiers destinés aux actes civils et judiciaires et aux écritures qui peuvent être produites en justice et y faire foi (b). — Il n'y a d'autres exceptions que celles nommément exprimées dans la présente. *Loi du 13 brumaire an 7, art.* 1.

(a) *Dispositions diverses.*

1. L'empreinte du timbre ne peut être couverte d'écriture ni altérée, à peine d'une amende de 25 francs pour les fonctionnaires publics. *Art.* 21 *et* 26 *de la loi du* 13 *brumaire an* 7.

2. Le papier déjà employé à un acte quelconque ne peut plus servir pour un autre acte, quand même le premier n'aurait pas été achevé, à peine de 100 f. d'amende pour les officiers et fonctionnaires publics. *Art.* 22 *et* 26 *idem.*

3. Il ne peut être fait ni expédié deux actes à la suite l'un de l'autre, à peine de 100 fr. d'amende pour les officiers et fonctionnaires publics. *Art.* 23 *et* 26 *idem.*— Sont exceptés cependant les procès-verbaux et autres actes qui ne peuvent être consommés dans un même jour et dans la même vacation; — les procès-verbaux de reconnaissance et de levée de scellés, qui peuvent être faits à la suite des procès-verbaux d'apposition; — les significations des huissiers, qui peuvent également être écrites à la suite des jugemens et autres pièces dont il est délivré copie. — Il peut également être donné plusieurs quittances sur une même feuille pour à-compte d'une seule et même créance ou d'un seul terme de fermage ou loyer.—Toute autre quittance donnée sur une même feuille n'aurait pas plus d'effet que si elle était donnée sur papier non timbré. *Art.* 23 *idem.*

4. Les actes qui ne sont pas écrits sur papier timbré, ou visés pour timbre, ne peuvent être enregistrés ni présentés en justice. *Art.* 25 *et* 25 *idem.*

5. Le timbre des quittances fournies au gouvernement, ou délivrées en son nom, est à la charge des particuliers qui les donnent ou qui les reçoivent. *Art.* 29 *idem.*

6. Les receveurs de l'enregistrement sont autorisés à retenir les actes en contravention à la loi du timbre, à moins que le contrevenant ne consente à signer le procès-verbal constatant la contravention ou à payer l'amende encourue et le droit. *Art.* 31 *idem.*

(b) *Actes soumis au timbre ou qui en sont exempts.*

7. Les actes de la Régie des contributions indirectes soumis au timbre de dimension, sont : les originaux et copies de significations, les contraintes, les procès-verbaux de contravention, les significations et copies de ces procès-verbaux, les autres actes judiciaires et les transactions.—Les obligations à terme que les redevables sont autorisés à souscrire sont soumises au timbre proportionnel. *Décis. du Minist. des finances, du* 5 *mai* 1807, *Rec., tom.* 4, *p.* 166.—Le papier employé à la signification des contraintes doit, dans tous les cas, être soumis au timbre, n'importe que la somme pour laquelle la contrainte est décernée soit au-dessus ou au-dessous de 25 fr. *Autre décision du* 14 *avril* 1807, *Rec., tom.* 4, *p.* 181.

8. Sont exceptées cependant, d'après l'article 16 de la loi du 13 brumaire an 7, les quittances de frais remboursés aux avoués, celles des fournisseurs et autres parties à qui il est fait des paiemens, lorsqu'il ne s'agit que de sommes de *dix francs et au-dessous.*—*Voy.*, pour les autres exceptions, nomb. 63, § 3, et nomb. 77, § 17.

9. Les greffiers ne peuvent refuser aux administrations publiques des extraits non sujets, ni aux droits ni aux formalités du timbre, des jugemens qu'elles requièrent. —Les greffiers ont seuls le droit de délivrer ces extraits, pour lesquels il leur est accordé une rétribution. *Rec., tom.* 6, *p.* 31. — Ces dispositions ont été confirmées le 20 mars 1816, par une circulaire de S. Ex. Monseigneur le Chancelier aux Procureurs généraux près les Cours royales.—Les extraits de jugemens étaient également dispensés du droit d'enregistrement, mais cette exemption ne peut plus avoir lieu d'après la loi du 28 avril 1816 (sur l'enregistrement), qui porte, article 38, que les jugemens seront enregistrés sur la minute.

Droits d'Enregistrement.

77. Les droits d'enregistrement sont fixes ou proportionnels (a), suivant la nature des actes qui y sont soumis (b). *Loi du 22 frimaire an 7, art. 2.*

(a) *Dispositions générales.*

1. Le délai pour faire enregistrer les actes des huissiers et autres ayant pouvoir de faire des procès-verbaux, est de quatre jours, à peine, s'il s'agit d'un acte soumis au droit fixe, d'une amende de 25 francs, et de plus, d'une somme égale au droit.— L'exploit ou le procès-verbal non enregistré dans ce délai est nul, et l'huissier ou l'Employé responsable de cette nullité. —S'il s'agit d'un acte soumis au droit proportionnel, la peine est d'une amende égale au droit, sans qu'elle puisse être moindre de 50 fr. *Art. 30 et 34 de la loi du 22 frimaire an 7.*

2. Le jour de la date de l'acte n'est pas compté, ni le dernier jour du délai, lorsqu'il se trouve être un dimanche ou un jour de fête solennisé. *Art. 25 idem.*

3. Les huissiers et autres ayant pouvoir de faire des exploits ou procès-verbaux peuvent les faire enregistrer, soit au bureau de leur résidence, soit au bureau du lieu où ils auront fait ces actes. *Art. 26 idem.*

4. On ne peut différer le paiement du droit d'enregistrement sous le prétexte de contestation sur la quotité, sauf à se pourvoir en restitution, s'il y a lieu. *Art. 28 idem.*

5. Les droits sont acquittés par les huissiers et autres ayant pouvoir de faire des procès-verbaux pour les actes de leur ministère. *Art. 29 idem.*

6. Les copies d'exploits et autres actes qui se signifient à partie ou par affiche, peuvent être délivrées avant l'enregistrement. *Art. 41 idem.*

7. La perception du droit proportionnel suit les sommes et valeurs de 20 f. en 20 f. inclusivement et sans fraction. *Art. 2 de la loi du 27 ventôse an 9.*

8. Un procès-verbal est nul s'il n'est pas enregistré dans le délai prescrit par l loi du 22 frimaire an 7. *Arr. du 31 juillet 1807, Mém., tom. 2, p. 449.*

(b) *Actes soumis à l'enregistrement, et droits dont ils sont passibles.*

8. Les procès-verbaux de saisie et contravention doivent, en exécution de l'article 43 de la loi du 28 avril 1816 (sur l'enregistrement), être enregistrés au droit fixe de deux francs. *Déc. du Min. des finances, du 31 octobre 1817.*

9. S'il y a cautionnement par acte distinct ou non du procès-verbal pour remise des objets saisis, il est dû un second droit fixe, mais il n'y a pas lieu à percevoir le droit proportionnel; attendu que ces cautionnemens ne sont que la suite et le complément des procès-verbaux. *Déc. du Min. des finances, du 25 novembre 1806, Mém., tom. 1, p. 78.*—Il n'y a pas cautionnement lorsque les objets sont laissés à la charge du contrevenant; et par conséquent il n'y a pas lieu à un second droit.

10. Si les objets saisis sont mis en fourrière, ou déposés entre les mains d'un tiers, ce dépôt opère un droit fixe; mais il n'est pas dû s'il est fait entre les mains d'un Employé de la Régie.

11. L'assignation ensuite d'un procès-verbal ou en appel, la signification des jugemens ou arrêts, et tous les autres actes des huissiers en matière de simple police ou de police correctionnelle, ne sont soumis qu'au droit fixe d'un franc, conformément au nº 48, article 68 de la loi du 22 frimaire an 7. *Art. 5948 du Journal de l'Enregistrement.*

12. Les jugemens en police correctionnelle portant condamnation à l'amende et à la confiscation sont soumis au droit proportionnel de 50 cent. par 100 fr. *Loi du 22 frimaire an 7, art. 69, nomb. 9, § 2.*— On ne doit percevoir le droit de 2 pour 100 porté par le nomb. 8, § 5 de l'art. 69, que quand les condamnations sont expressément prononcées à titre de dommages et intérêts. *Déc. du Min. des finances, du 1er juillet 1816.* — Ces jugemens ne sont soumis qu'au droit fixe d'un franc, conformément au nº 48, art. 68 de la loi du 22 frimaire an 7, lorsqu'ils ne portent pas de condamnation de somme, ou lorsque la condamnation n'est pas susceptible de produire un droit supérieur.—Cette fixation est applicable aux jugemens de simple police comme à ceux des tribunaux correctionnels. *Art. 5948 du Journ. de l'Enregistrem.*— Lorsque le droit proportionnel a été acquitté sur un jugement rendu par défaut, la perception sur le jugement con-

tradictoire n'a lieu que sur le supplément des condamnations. Il en est de même des jugemens *rendus sur appel.*—S'il n'y a pas de supplément de condamnation, le jugement est enregistré pour le droit fixe d'un franc, qui est toujours le moindre droit à percevoir. *Art.* 69, § 2, *n°* 9 *de la loi du* 22 *frimaire an* 7.

13. Les notifications des contraintes pour recouvremens de contributions sont soumises au droit fixe d'un franc, mais seulement lorsque la somme principale excède 25 fr. *Nomb.* 30, § 1, *art.* 68 *de la loi du* 22 *frimaire an* 7. — Les notifications de contraintes pour les sommes de 25 francs et au-dessous doivent être enregistrées gratis. *Nomb.* 2, § 2, *art.* 70 *idem.*—Le droit est exigible lorsque le montant primitif de la cote excède 25 fr., quelque faible que soit la somme qui donne lieu aux poursuites. *Déc. du Min. des finances, du* 14 *avril* 1807, *Rec., tom.* 4, *p.*181.—Quand le droit est exigible, il est dû autant de fois qu'il y a de personnes à qui la notification est faite, si elles ne sont ni associées, ni cohéritières, ni débiteurs solidaires. *Art.* 68, § 1, *n°* 30 *de la loi du* 22 *frimaire an* 7.

14. Les jugemens en matière de contributions (au civil) sont soumis aux mêmes droits que ceux entre particuliers. *Art.* 39 *de la loi du* 28 *avril* 1816. — Ce droit est de 50 cent. pour 100 fr. lorsque le jugement porte condamnation ou liquidation de sommes. *Art.* 69, § 2, *n°* 9 *de la loi du* 22 *frimaire an* 7. — Les jugemens sans condamnation de sommes, ou dont le droit proportionnel ne s'élèverait pas au droit fixe, opèrent 5 fr. *Art.* 45, *n°* 5 *de la loi du* 28 *avril* 1816.—Les jugemens interlocutoires ou préparatoires ne sont soumis qu'au droit fixe de 3 fr. *Art.* 44, *n°* 10, *idem.*

15. Les ventes faites en vertu de l'article 33 du décret du 1er germinal an 13, comme celle de meubles et effets mobiliers, faites par les huissiers, opèrent un droit de 2 pour 100. *Nomb.* 1, § 5, *art.* 69 *de la loi du* 22 *frimaire an* 7.

16. Les baux passés aux fermiers des bacs et bateaux sont soumis au droit proportionnel d'enregistrement, ainsi que les cautionnemens qui en sont la suite. *Déc. du Min. des finances, du* 19 *janvier* 1808, *Mém., tom.* 3, *p.* 240.

17. Les actes de dépôt au greffe, des moulages, timbres et empreintes des instrumens dont la Régie a adopté l'usage, ne sont soumis à aucun droit de greffe, d'enregistrement et de timbre. *Rec., vol.* 6, *p.* 67.

18. Le décime pour franc est maintenu sur les droits d'enregistrement mentionnés dans les §§ précédens.

Timbre des lettres de voiture.

78. Les Préposés des douanes et les Préposés à la perception des droits d'octroi sont tenus de se faire représenter les lettres de voiture, connaissemens, chartes-parties et polices d'assurance des marchandises et autres objets dont le transport est fait par terre ou par eau, et de vérifier si ces actes sont écrits sur papier (timbré), ainsi qu'il est prescrit par l'art. 5 de la loi du 6 prairial an 7. *Décret du* 16 *messidor an* 13, *art.* 1.—En cas de contravention, ils rédigeront des procès-verbaux pour faire condamner les souscripteurs et porteurs, solidairement, à l'amende fixée par l'art. 4 de la même loi. *Idem, art.* 2.—Pour indemniser les Préposés des soins de cette vérification, il leur sera accordé la moitié des amendes qui auront été payées par les contrevenans. *Id., art.* 3.

1. Les lettres de voiture, connaissemens, chartes-parties et polices d'assurance, peuvent être sur papier de telle dimension que les parties jugeront convenable, sans qu'elles soient tenues de faire usage du papier frappé d'un franc. *Déc. du* 3 *janv.* 1809, *art.* 1. Les propriétaires qui font conduire par leurs voituriers et leurs propres domestiques ou fermiers le produit de leur récolte, ne sont pas tenus de se pourvoir de lettres de voiture timbrées. *Idem, art.* 2.

2. Ce décret n'abroge point la disposition de celui du 15 messidor an 13 relative au partage des amendes. *Lett. du Min. des financ., du* 15 *juin* 1809, *M., t.* 5, *p.* 219.

3. Le simple refus d'un voiturier de représenter une lettre de voiture, sous prétexte qu'il ne lui en a pas été remis, ne

suffit pas pour autoriser les poursuites. Il est nécessaire de produire la preuve matérielle de la contravention par la représentation de la lettre de voiture écrite sur papier libre. *Déc. du Min. des finances, du 9 octobre* 1810.

Saisie des Traitemens et Pensions.

79. Les traitemens des fonctionnaires publics ou employés civils sont saisissables jusqu'à concurrence du cinquième sur les premiers mille francs et toutes les sommes au-dessous; du quart sur les cinq mille francs suivans, et du tiers sur la portion excédant six mille francs, à quelque somme qu'elle s'élève, et ce jusqu'à l'entier acquittement des créances. *Loi du* 21 *ventôse an* 9.

1. Le mot *saisissable* inséré dans la loi signifie qu'un traitement ne peut être arrêté que par voie de saisie, pour laquelle il faut toujours que le créancier ait un titre, soit exécutoire, soit sous signature privée, revêtu de l'ordonnance du juge; ces explications ont été données par les orateurs lors de la discussion.—Le décret du 18 août 1807, ci-après, § 4 et suiv., détermine les formalités que doivent suivre tant les opposans que les comptables.

2. Les traitemens et remises des préposés des octrois ne peuvent être saisis par leurs créanciers que dans les proportions déterminées par la loi du 21 ventôse an 9. *Art.* 61 *de l'ordonnance du* 9 *décembre* 1814.

3. Les pensions de retraite ne peuvent être transportées, cédées, déléguées ou saisies. *Voy. pensions de retraite.*

4. Indépendamment des formalités communes à tous les exploits, tout exploit de saisie-arrêt ou opposition entre les mains des receveurs, dépositaires ou administrateurs de caisses ou de deniers publics, en cette qualité, exprimera clairement les noms et qualités de la partie saisie; il contiendra en outre la désignation de l'objet saisi. *Décret du* 18 *août* 1807, *art.* 1.

5. L'exploit énoncera pareillement la somme pour laquelle la saisie-arrêt ou opposition est faite, et il sera fourni, avec copie de l'exploit, auxdits receveurs, caissiers ou administrateurs, copie ou extrait en forme du titre du saisissant. *Id., art.* 2.

6. A défaut par le saisissant de remplir les formalités prescrites par les art. 1 et 2 ci-dessus, la saisie-arrêt ou opposition sera regardée comme non avenue. *Id., art.* 3.

7. La saisie-arrêt ou opposition n'aura d'effet que jusqu'à concurrence de la somme portée en l'exploit. *Idem, art,* 4.

8. La saisie-arrêt ou opposition formée entre les mains des receveurs, dépositaires ou administrateurs de caisses ou deniers publics, en cette qualité, ne sera point valable si l'exploit n'est fait à la personne préposée pour le recevoir, et s'il n'est visé par elle sur l'original, ou, en cas de refus, par le procureur du Roi près le tribunal de première instance de leur résidence, lequel en donnera de suite avis aux chefs des administrations respectives. *Idem, art.* 5.

9. Les receveurs, dépositaires ou administrateurs seront tenus de délivrer, sur la demande du saisissant, un certificat qui tiendra lieu, en ce qui les concerne, de tous autres actes et formalités prescrits, à l'égard des tiers-saisis, par le titre 20 du livre 3 du Code de procédure civile.—S'il n'est rien dû au saisi, le certificat l'énoncera;—Si la somme due est liquide, le certificat en déclarera le montant. — Si la somme due n'est pas liquide, le certificat l'exprimera. *Idem, art.* 6.

10. Dans le cas où il serait survenu des saisies-arrêts ou oppositions, sur la même partie et pour le même objet, les receveurs, dépositaires ou administrateurs seront tenus, dans les certificats qui leur seront demandés, de faire mention desdites saisies-arrêts ou oppositions, et de désigner les noms et élections de domicile des saisissans et les causes desdites saisies-arrêts ou oppositions. *Idem, art.* 7.

11. S'il survient de nouvelles saisies-arrêts ou oppositions, depuis la délivrance d'un certificat, les receveurs, dépositaires ou administrateurs seront tenus, sur la demande qui leur en sera faite, d'en fournir un extrait, contenant pareillement les noms et élections de domicile des saisissans, et les causes desdites saisies-arrêts ou oppositions. *Idem, art.* 8.

12. Tout receveur, dépositaire ou administrateur de caisses ou de deniers publics, entre les mains duquel il existera une saisie-arrêt ou opposition, sur une partie prenante, ne pourra vider ses mains

sans le consentement des parties intéressées, et sans y être autorisé par justice. *Idem, art.* 9.

13. Les receveurs et administrateurs ne peuvent être réellement autorisés par justice qu'en vertu d'un jugement définitivement exécutoire, ayant acquis force de chose jugée; et c'est à la partie qui réclame l'exécution d'un jugement à justifier qu'il a acquis cette qualité. *Mém., tom.* 3, *p.* 357, *et tom.* 4, *p.* 485.

Vols de caisse.

80. Tout receveur, caissier, dépositaire, percepteur ou préposé quelconque chargé de deniers publics, ne pourra obtenir la décharge d'aucun vol, s'il n'est justifié qu'il est l'effet d'une force majeure, et que le dépositaire, outre les précautions ordinaires, avait eu celle de coucher ou de faire coucher un homme sûr dans le lieu où il tenait ses fonds, et en outre, si c'est au rez-de-chaussée, de le tenir solidement grillé. *Arrêté du* 8 *floréal an* 10.

1. Tout vol de deniers doit être constaté à la réquisition du comptable volé, à l'instant même où celui-ci s'en aperçoit, et au plus tard dans les vingt-quatre heures. —Le procès-verbal doit être dressé par le juge de paix ou l'officier de police le plus voisin du lieu où le vol a été commis, et contenir, 1° déclaration si la pièce où le vol a eu lieu était ou non occupée; 2° une description exacte de la pièce, ainsi que de toutes les effractions faites aux portes, fenêtres, coffres, etc., et celle des moyens employés par les voleurs pour s'introduire; 3° toutes les dépositions, tant à charge qu'à décharge, qui pourraient être reçues par le juge de paix, au moment où il constate le délit; 4° une déclaration faite par le comptable volé, énonçant la quotité des sommes volées, et appuyée d'un bordereau de sa situation, dressé d'après le relevé de ses registres, qu'il fera arrêter et viser par le juge de paix et un Employé de l'Administration, ou le Contrôleur, s'il est sur les lieux; 5° enfin toutes les indications pouvant servir à faire ressortir l'innocence du comptable, et les dispositions qu'il avait faites pour prévenir l'événement. — Si le vol avait été commis avec attroupement et à main armée, le comptable volé devrait, indépendamment des formalités ci-dessus prescrites, s'assurer que le maire ou les adjoints ont, en conformité de l'article 2 du titre 5 de la loi du 10 vendémiaire an 4, fait constater le délit dans les vingt-quatre heures, et en ont adressé le procès-verbal dans les trois jours au procureur du Roi, et s'il n'avait pas la certitude que ces formalités eussent été remplies, le procès-verbal qui aurait été dressé par les juges de paix, maire, etc., ou par lui-même, assisté de témoins, en cas de refus desdits officiers, serait envoyé dans le même délai au procureur du Roi (par l'intermédiaire du directeur). *Circ. n°* 52, *Rec.*, *tom.* 2, *p.* 257.

2. Il ne suffit pas, pour qu'un comptable soit déchargé du débet résultant du vol de sa caisse, que le vol ait eu lieu à son insu, et que les auteurs en aient été connus et punis; il faut encore qu'il ait couché ou fait coucher un homme sûr dans le lieu où il tenait les fonds. *Avis du cons. d'état, du* 20 *pluviôse an* 13, *Mém., tom.* 1, *p.* 95.

Insolvabilité ou absence des redevables.

81. L'insolvabilité ou l'absence des redevables du trésor public seront constatées, ou par des procès-verbaux de carence, dressés par des huissiers, ou par des certificats délivrés, sous leur responsabilité, par les maires et adjoints des communes de leur résidence ou de leur domicile. — Ces certificats seront visés par les préfets pour l'arrondissement du chef-lieu, et par les sous-préfets pour les autres arrondissemens. *Arrête du* 6 *messidor an* 10, *art.* 1 *et* 2.

14

Transactions.

82. Les transactions sur procès seront définitives : 1° avec l'approbation du directeur, lorsque, sur les procès-verbaux de contravention et de saisie, les condamnations de confiscation et d'amende ne s'élèveront pas à plus de 500 francs. (Pour les sommes au-dessus, elles ne seront définitives qu'avec l'approbation du Directeur-général ou du Ministre des finances, suivant la quotité.) *Décret du 5 germinal an* 12, *art* 23.

1. La faculté de rendre les transactions définitives dans le cas prévu par l'article ci-dessus a passé de plein droit aux Directeurs actuels de la Régie. *D. A. n°* 153.

2. C'est le minimum de l'amende ajouté au montant de la confiscation qui doit servir à calculer le produit des saisies lorsqu'on veut déterminer à qui appartient l'approbation des transactions pour les rendre définitives. *Circ. n°* 14, *Contentieux, nouv. série.*—Quand le minimum de l'amende est de 100 fr., la transaction souscrite par le Directeur est définitive si la somme que la Régie a le droit d'obtenir des tribunaux pour confiscation est de 400 f. et au-dessous. *Circ. n°* 199, *Contentieux, Rec., tom.* 6, *p.* 32.—La circulaire n° 14, en arrêtant cette fixation, n'a eu, sans doute, pour objet que de faciliter la liquidation des affaires ; cette disposition ne peut être considérée que comme une mesure d'ordre intérieur qui ne lie pas M. le Directeur général vis-à-vis les parties, et ne peut l'empêcher de prononcer, lorsqu'il le juge convenable, sur les transactions qui deviennent de sa compétence, en prenant pour base des peines encourues, le maximum des amendes.

3. Les transactions doivent être rédigées en double expédition et double copie, et les unes et les autres doivent être signées du contrevenant ou de son représentant, ainsi que du Directeur.—Les deux expéditions doivent être timbrées du timbre de l'enregistrement; celle que le Directeur conserve est destinée à la justification du produit. Les deux copies doivent être sur papier libre ; l'une doit rester aux archives de la direction, l'autre est envoyée à l'Administration avec l'état des saisies. *Circ. n°* 186, *Rec., tom.* 5, *p.* 607.

4. Pour être valables, les transactions doivent être signées du contrevenant, hors le cas où il serait absent, ou qu'il ne saurait pas signer; alors il doit être suppléé par un fondé de pouvoirs muni de procuration régulière, à moins que la personne qui représente le contrevenant ne se porte fort pour lui dans la transaction. *Idem.*

5. Les Directeurs ont seuls qualité pour transiger. Il est défendu à tout autre Employé, quel que soit son grade, d'entrer en négociation avec les prévenus, et de s'immiscer, en aucune manière, dans les transactions. *Circ. n°* 214, *Rec., vol.* 6, *p.* 10.

6. Une transaction provisoire passée par un Directeur après jugement de première instance, ne peut modifier ce jugement lorsque la condamnation excède la compétence du directeur; si la transaction n'a pas reçu l'approbation du Directeur général, elle est comme non avenue, et la cour d'appel ne doit y avoir aucun égard. *Arr. du* 11 *juin* 1807, *Mém., tom.* 2, *p.* 577.

7. Une transaction souscrite par la femme non autorisée de son mari, n'oblige pas celui-ci, mais elle est un aveu formel de la vérité des faits rapportés au procès-verbal; et s'il résulte de ces faits une contravention, le mari en est responsable. *Arr. du* 31 *juillet* 1807, *Mém., tom.* 2, *p.* 449.

8. Une transaction ne peut être viciée par la condition suspensive qui y est insérée, jusqu'à l'approbation de l'autorité compétente. — Il n'est pas nécessaire que l'approbation ou le refus du Directeur général soient donnés au pied de la transaction ; il suffit qu'ils le soient dans la forme établie par l'Administration. *Arr. du* 26 *juin* 1811, *Mém., tom.* 7, *p.* 218.

Employés destitués ou démissionnaires.

83. Tout Préposé destitué ou démissionnaire sera tenu, sous peine d'y être contraint, même par corps, de remettre à la Régie ou à son fondé de pouvoirs, en quittant son emploi, sa commission, ainsi que

les registres et autres effets dont il aura été chargé par la Régie, et de rendre ses comptes. *Décret du 1er germinal an 13, art.* 27.—Les mêmes dispositions sont prescrites à l'égard des préposés des octrois par l'article 64 de l'ordonnance du 9 décembre 1814.

Privilége de la Régie pour les Débets et pour les Droits.

84. La Régie aura privilége à tous créanciers, sur les meubles et effets mobiliers des comptables pour leurs débets, et sur ceux des redevables pour leurs droits, à l'exception des frais de justice, de ce qui sera dû pour six mois de loyer seulement, et sauf aussi la revendication dûment formée par les propriétaires des marchandises en nature qui seront encore sous balle et corde. *Décret du 1er germinal an 13, art.* 47.

1. Le trésor public n'est pas assujéti aux dispositions du Code de commerce pour exercer son privilége sur les biens d'un comptable en état de faillite. *Arr. du* 9 *mars* 1808, *Mém., tom.* 3, *p.* 367.

2. Quoiqu'un particulier qui a vendu un objet compris dans une saisie exécutoire, opérée pour le recouvrement du droit, n'en soit pas payé, il ne peut primer le privilége de la Régie sur le produit de la vente de cet objet. *Arr. du* 17 *octob.* 1814. —Aff. Bouisson.—*Voy.* nomb. 26, § 2, p. 83, et nomb. 89, § 1.

Saisie des Produits.

85. Toutes saisies du produit des droits faites entre les mains des Préposés de la Régie ou dans celles de ses redevables, seront nulles et de nul effet. *Décret du 1er germinal an* 13, *art.* 48.

1. Les droits dont la perception est attribuée à des administrations publiques ne peuvent être saisis, même en vertu d'un jugement qui en ordonne la restitution comme indûment perçus. *Arr. du* 16 *thermidor an* 10, *Mém., tom.* 1, *p.* 349.

Apposition de scellés sur les papiers d'un Comptable.

86. Dans le cas d'apposition de scellés sur les effets et papiers des comptables, les registres de recette et autres de l'année courante ne seront pas renfermés sous les scellés : lesdits registres seront seulement arrêtés et paraphés par le juge, qui les remettra au Préposé chargé de la recette par *intérim*, lequel en demeurera garant, comme dépositaire de justice; et il en sera fait mention dans le procès-verbal d'apposition de scellés. *Décret du 1er germinal an* 13, *art.* 49.

Restitution de droits.—Prescription.

87. La prescription est acquise à la Régie contre toutes demandes en restitution de droits et marchandises, paiement d'appointemens, après un délai révolu de deux années; elle est acquise aux redevables contre la Régie, pour les droits que ses Préposés n'auraient pas réclamés dans l'espace d'un an, à compter de l'époque où ils étaient exigibles.—La Régie est déchargée de la garde des registres des recettes

antérieures de trois années à l'année courante. *Décret du 1er germinal an 13, art. 50.*

1. On ne peut, en matière de perceptions publiques, réclamer l'intérêt sur le montant des droits indûment perçus, et dont la restitution est ordonnée. *Arr. du 11 février 1806, Mém., tom. 1, p. 37.*

2. La prescription d'un an établie en faveur des redevables ne peut s'appliquer aux amendes et condamnations résultant des procès-verbaux. *Arr. du 6 septemb. 1806, Mém., tom. 1, p. 219.*

3. La prescription établie pour la restitution de droits mal à propos perçus ne peut être interrompue par les actes émanés de l'Administration, l'interrupion civile de la prescription ne profitant qu'à celui qui la forme. *Arr. du 30 mars 1808, Mém., tom. 4, p. 414.*

4. On peut percevoir des droits prescrits, et celui qui les a acquittés n'est pas fondé à en demander la restitution. *Mém., tom. 1, p. 352.*

Privilége pour frais de justice sur les meubles et effets mobiliers des condamnés.

88. En conséquence de l'art. 2098 du Code civil, le privilége du trésor public est réglé de la manière suivante en ce qui concerne le remboursement des frais dont la condamnation est prononcée à son profit en matière criminelle, correctionnelle et de police. *Loi du 5 septembre 1807, art. 1.*

1. Nonobstant le privilége accordé au trésor pour les frais de justice, la Régie a le droit d'en poursuivre le recouvrement par voie de contrainte par corps. *Voyez* nombre 18, § 1, p. 78.

2. L'Administration n'a pas, pour le recouvrement des amendes, un privilége contre les autres créanciers des condamnés comme elle en a un pour le recouvrement des frais. *Mém., tom. 4, p. 416.*

89. Le privilége du trésor public sur les meubles et effets mobiliers des condamnés, ne s'exercera qu'après les autres priviléges et droits ci-après mentionnés; savoir : 1° les priviléges désignés aux art. 2101 et 2102 du Code civil; 2° les sommes dues pour la défense personnelle du condamné, lesquelles, en cas de contestation de la part de l'administration des domaines, seront réglées, d'après la nature de l'affaire, par le tribunal qui aura prononcé la condamnation. *Idem, art. 2.*

1. Les loyers et fermages dus aux condamnés doivent être rangés dans la classe des meubles et effets mobiliers, sur lesquels le trésor public exerce son privilége pour le recouvrement des frais de justice. —Quand la créance n'est pas de l'espèce de celles mentionnées aux art. 2101 et 2105 du Code civil, le créancier d'un condamné, quoiqu'ayant un titre antérieur à la condamnation, ne peut détruire le privilége du trésor public, s'il n'a déjà acquis des droits par des exécutions légales. *Arr. du 6 juin 1809, Mém., tom. 5, p. 299.*

Privilége pour frais de justice sur les immeubles des condamnés.

90. Le privilége du trésor public sur les biens immeubles des condamnés n'aura lieu qu'à la charge de l'inscription dans les deux mois, à dater du jour du jugement de condamnation; passé lequel délai, les droits du trésor public ne pourront s'exercer qu'en conformité de l'art. 2113 du Code civil. *Loi du 5 septembre 1807, art. 3.*

1. L'exécution n'est pas nécessaire pour prendre inscription sur les biens d'un condamné, afin d'assurer le recouvrement des frais de justice; il suffit de représenter une expédition du jugement, quand bien même les dépens n'y seraient pas liquidés, parce que l'évaluation doit en être faite dans le bordereau; elle peut même y être portée à une somme plus élevée que celle des frais connus, afin d'assurer le recouvrement de ceux qui seraient encore ignorés ou qui seraient encore à faire. *Déc. du Min. de la justice, du 3 septembre 1808, Mém., tom. 4, p. 621.*

91. Le privilége mentionné dans l'article 3 ci-dessus ne s'exerce qu'après les autres priviléges et droits suivans :—1° les priviléges désignés en l'art. 2101 du Code civil, dans le cas prévu par l'art. 2105; —2°. les priviléges désignés en l'art. 2103 du Code civil, pourvu que les conditions prescrites pour leur conservation aient été accomplies; —3° Les hypothèques légales existantes indépendamment de l'inscription, pourvu toutefois qu'elles soient antérieures au mandat d'arrêt, dans le cas où il en aurait été décerné contre le condamné, et, dans les autres cas, au jugement de condamnation;—4° les autres hypothèques, pourvu que les créances aient été inscrites au bureau des hypothèques avant le privilége du trésor public, et qu'elles résultent d'actes qui aient une date certaine antérieure auxdits mandat d'arrêt ou jugement de condamnation;—5° les sommes dues pour la défense personnelle du condamné, sauf le réglement, ainsi qu'il est dit en l'art. 2 ci-dessus. *Loi du 5 septembre 1807, art. 4.*

Alimens.

92. Les détenus en prison à la requête de l'agent du trésor public, ou de tout autre fonctionnaire, pour cause de dettes envers l'Etat, recevront la nourriture comme les prisonniers à la requête du ministère public.—Il ne sera fait aucune consignation particulière pour la nourriture desdits détenus. *Décret du 4 mars 1808, art. 1 et 2.*

Vente d'animaux et objets périssables.

93. Les animaux et tous objets périssables, pour quelque cause qu'ils aient été saisis, ne peuvent rester en fourrière, ou sous le séquestre, plus de huit jours.—Après ce délai, la main-levée provisoire pourra être accordée.—S'ils ne doivent ou ne peuvent être restitués, ils seront mis en vente, et les frais de fourrière seront prélevés sur le produit de la vente, par privilége et préférence à tous autres. *Décret du 18 juin 1811, art. 39.*

94. La main-levée provisoire des animaux saisis et des objets périssables mis en séquestre, sera ordonnée par le juge de paix ou par le juge d'instruction, moyennant caution et le paiement des frais de fourrière et de séquestre. — Si lesdits objets doivent être vendus, la vente sera ordonnée par les mêmes magistrats.—Cette vente sera faite à l'enchère au marché le plus voisin, à la diligence de l'administration (poursuivante). — Le jour de la vente sera indiqué par affiches vingt-quatre heures à l'avance, à moins que la modicité de l'objet ne détermine le magistrat à en ordonner la vente sans formalité, ce qu'il exprimera dans son ordonnance.— Le produit de la vente sera versé

dans la caisse de l'administration (poursuivante) pour être disposé ainsi qu'il sera ordonné par le jugement définitif. *Idem, art.* 40.

Bouteilles et demi-bouteilles.

95. Dans toutes les opérations relatives aux taxes établies par le présent titre, les bouteilles seront comptées chacune pour un litre; les demi-bouteilles chacune pour un demi-litre, et les droits perçus en raison de ces contenances. *Loi du* 28 *avril* 1816, *art.* 145.

1. Toutes les règles relatives aux futailles sont applicables aux dames-jeannes d'une capacité supérieure à vingt-cinq litres. *D. A. n°* 12.

Contestations pour le jaugeage des boissons.

96. Toute personne qui contestera le résultat d'un jaugeage fait par les Employés, pourra requérir qu'il soit fait un nouveau jaugeage en présence d'un officier public, par un expert que nommera le juge de paix, et dont il recevra le serment. La Régie pourra faire vérifier l'opération par un contre-expert qui sera nommé par le président du tribunal d'arrondissement; les frais de l'une et de l'autre vérification seront à la charge de la partie qui aura élevé mal à propos la contestation. *Loi du* 28 *avril* 1816, *art.* 146.

1. En cas de contestation sur le jaugeage, on ne doit pas se refuser à ce que la contenance des futailles soit vérifiée par l'empotement; mais ses résultats, s'ils diffèrent de ceux obtenus par les Employés, ne peuvent être invoqués pour faire taxer de faux l'énoncé d'un procès-verbal. *D. A. n°* 419.

Arrestation des fraudeurs et colporteurs de Tabacs.

97. Les Employés des contributions indirectes, des douanes, des octrois, les gendarmes, les préposés forestiers, les gardes-champêtres, et généralement tout employé assermenté, pourront constater la vente des tabacs en contravention à l'art. 172, le colportage, les circulations illégales, et généralement les fraudes sur le tabac; procéder à la saisie des tabacs, ustensiles et mécaniques prohibés par la présente loi; à celle des chevaux, voitures, bateaux et autres objets servant au transport, et constituer prisonniers les fraudeurs et colporteurs dans le cas prévu par l'article précédent. *Loi du* 28 *avril* 1816, *art.* 223.

1. Les cas prévus par l'art. 222 sont ceux de vente en fraude à domicile et de colportage, indiqués n°s 12 et 13, 10e tableau.

2. Lorsque les Employés auront arrêté un colporteur ou vendeur de tabac de fraude, ils seront tenus de le conduire sur-le-champ devant un officier de police judiciaire, ou de le remettre à la force armée, qui le conduira devant le juge compétent, lequel statuera de suite, par une décision motivée, sur son emprisonnement ou sur sa mise en liberté.—Néanmoins, si le prévenu offre bonne et suffisante caution de se présenter en justice, et d'acquitter l'amende encourue, ou s'il consigne lui-même le montant de ladite amende, il sera mis en liberté s'il n'existe aucune autre charge contre lui. *Loi du* 28 *avril* 1816, *art.* 224.

3. Les Employés n'ont pas qualité pour constituer un individu prisonnier dans la maison d'arrêt; et lorsqu'ils arrêtent un prévenu, ils doivent le conduire sans délai devant le procureur du Roi ou son substitut, ou, en cas d'éloignement, devant l'officier de police judiciaire le plus voisin, ou

le remettre entre les mains de la force armée pour le conduire devant l'autorité compétente. — Le procureur du Roi ne peut se dispenser de décerner le mandat de dépôt, même lorsque le procès-verbal serait entaché de vice de forme, ou qu'il ne pourrait lui être représenté, si d'ailleurs il existe d'autres indices de la contravention, tels que l'aveu du prévenu, la représentation des objets de fraude dont il a été trouvé porteur, etc. *Lettre du Min. de la justice, du* 9 *mai* 1811, *Rec., vol.* 6, *p.* 40.

4. Les maires, leurs adjoints et les juges de paix étant au nombre des officiers de police judiciare, ils sont toujours à portée des Employés, dans le cas où ceux-ci ne pourraient conduire eux-mêmes le prévenu devant le procureur du Roi ou le remettre entre les mains de la force armée. — Si le prévenu arrêté offrait caution ou demandait à transiger, il pourrait être conduit devant le Directeur, conformément à l'article 1er de l'ordonnance du 31 décembre 1817.

5. Les préposés dénommés dans l'article 223 ci-dessus, ou tous autres individus qui arrêteront ou concourront à arrêter des colporteurs ou vendeurs de tabac de fraude, recevront une prime de 15 francs par chaque personne arrêtée, quel que soit le nombre des saisissans. — Cette prime ne sera acquittée qu'autant que les contrevenans auront été constitués prisonniers, ou qu'amenés devant le Directeur des contributions indirectes, ils auront fourni caution ou auront été admis à transation. *Ordonnance du* 31 *décembre* 1817, *art.* 1er. —Lorsque les tabacs saisis ne seront pas jugés propres à la fabrication, il sera accordé aux saisissans, à titre de prime, 30 f. par 100 kilogr. *Art.* 3 *idem.*

Soupçons de fraude. — Visite chez les particuliers non sujets à l'exercice.

98. En cas de soupçon de fraude à l'égard de particuliers non sujets à l'exercice, les Employés pourront faire des visites dans l'intérieur de leurs habitations, en se faisant assister du juge de paix, du maire, de son adjoint ou du commissaire de police, lesquels seront tenus de déférer à la réquisition qui leur en sera faite, et qui sera transcrite en tête du procès-verbal. Ces visites ne pourront avoir lieu que d'après l'ordre d'un Employé supérieur, du grade de contrôleur au moins, qui rendra compte des motifs au Directeur du département. — Les marchandises transportées en fraude, qui, au moment d'être saisies, seraient introduites dans une habitation pour les soustraire aux Employés, pouront être suivies par eux, sans qu'ils soient tenus, dans ce cas, d'observer les formalités ci-dessus prescrites. *Loi du* 28 *avril* 1816, *art.* 237.

1. Le défaut de transcription en tête du procès-verbal de la réquisition faite à l'officier de police par les préposés, n'entraîne pas la nullité du procès-verbal. *Arr. du* 21 *février* 1806, *Mém., tom.* 1, *p.* 112.

2. Le défaut de présence d'un officier de police aux visites chez les particuliers non sujets à l'exercice, ne vicie pas les actes des Employés; il donne seulement le droit à ces particuliers de s'opposer aux visites jusqu'à l'arrivée de l'officier dont la loi exige la présence. *Arr. des* 30 *et* 31 *juillet* 1807, *Mém., tom.* 2, *p.* 449 *et* 478; *autre du* 31 *décembre* 1807, *tom.* 3, *p.* 114.

3. Lorsque les Employés jugent convenable de ne pas interrompre des vérifications commencées de jour dans une maison, avec l'assistance d'un officier de police, ils peuvent les continuer pendant la nuit. *Arr. du* 20 *mai* 1808, *Mém., tom.* 5, *p.* 161.

4. En cas de soupçon de fraude, les Employés peuvent faire des visites, avec l'assistance d'un officier de police, pour les droits établis par la loi qui autorise ces visites comme pour ceux qui peuvent être établis postérieurement. *Arr. du* 22 *décembre* 1808, *Mém., tom.* 4, *p.* 760.

5. Les Employés, quoique accompagnés d'un officier de police, ne peuvent faire des visites, dans le domicile d'un particulier non sujet à l'exercice, qu'aux heures où la loi permet à cet officier d'y pénétrer lui-même. *D. A.* n° 184.

Rebellion.

99. Les rebellions ou voies de fait contre les Employés seront poursuivies devant les tribunaux, qui ordonneront l'application des peines prononcées par le Code pénal, indépendamment des amendes et confiscations qui pourraient être encourues par les contrevenans.—Quand les rebellions ou voies de fait auront été commises par un débitant de boissons, le tribunal ordonnera, en outre, la clôture du débit pendant un délai de trois mois au moins, et de six mois au plus. *Loi du 28 avril* 1816, *art.* 238.

1. Toute attaque, toute résistance avec violence et voies de fait envers...... les préposés à la perception des taxes et des contributions...... agissant pour l'exécution des lois...... est qualifiée, suivant les circonstances, crime ou délit de rebellion. *Art.* 209 *du Code pénal.* — Les peines, en cas de rebellion, sont celles prononcées par les articles 210, 211 et 304 du Code pénal; elles sont indiquées au § 2 de la note 93, p. 58.

2. Les individus qui ont exercé des violences envers les préposés peuvent être poursuivis et punis correctionnellement, sur le simple procès-verbal du maire de la commune, quoique les préposés eux-mêmes n'aient point rédigé de procès-verbal. *Mém., tom.* 4, *p.* 613.

3. La Régie ne peut conclure à l'application des articles du Code pénal; c'est exclusivement le ministère public qui peut prendre de pareilles conclusions. *Arr. du* 13 *février* 1807, *Mém., tom.* 2, *p.* 592.

4. Des violences et voies de fait exercées par les conducteurs d'un chargement, contre les préposés, au moment où ceux-ci, étant dans l'exercice de leurs fonctions, les interpellent de déclarer ce qu'ils transportent, forment une présomption suffisante pour établir que les prévenus opéraient une fraude, et que leur opposition à l'exercice des préposés, ainsi que les violences et voies de fait dont elle a été accompagnée, avaient pour but et pour effet d'empêcher la saisie des objets de fraude. *Arr. du* 23 *juill.* 1812.

Répartition du produit des saisies.

100. Les Employés n'auront aucun droit au partage du produit net des amendes et confiscations; un tiers de ce produit appartiendra à la caisse des retraites, les deux autres tiers feront partie des recettes ordinaires de la Régie. — Néanmoins les Employés saisissans auront droit au partage du produit net des amendes et confiscations prononcées par suite des fraudes et contraventions relatives aux octrois, aux tabacs et aux cartes. — A Paris, et dans les villes où l'abonnement général autorisé par l'art. 73 sera consenti, les communes disposeront relativement aux saisies faites aux entrées, par les préposés de l'octroi, du tiers affecté ci-dessus à la caisse des retraites de la Régie. *Loi du 28 avril* 1816, *art.* 240.

1. Les Employés de la Régie ont encore droit au partage, 1° dans les saisies pour fraude à la circulation des boissons, aux huiles et aux voitures publiques. *Art.* 126 *de la loi du* 25 *mars* 1817.—2° Dans les saisies en matières de poudres et salpêtres, garantie, sels, douanes, ainsi que dans les amendes pour contravention aux lois sur le *timbre* des lettres de voiture. *Circ. n°* 17, *timbrée Contentieux, nouvelle série.*

2. Dans les saisies faites chez les débitans de boissons, quelle que soit la nature de la fraude, s'il y a en même temps défaut de représentation des expéditions prescrites pour la circulation des boissons, les Employés saisissans doivent jouir de l'avantage que leur assure l'art. 126 de la loi du 25 mars 1817, et participer en conséquence au partage du produit des amendes et confiscations. *D. A. n.°* 358.

3. Ils en sont exclus dans les saisies pour fraudes et contraventions aux droits d'entrée sur les boissons, et à la navigation. *D. A. n.°s* 269 *et* 376.

4. Les Employés de la Régie d'un grade supérieur à celui de Contrôleur, sont exclus du partage, même dans les saisies auxquelles ils auraient concouru personnellement, à moins qu'ils n'y soient admis par une décision spéciale. *Arrêté du Min. des finances du 17 octobre 1816, art. 2.* — Les Directeurs sont autorisés à prendre part dans les saisies opérées en matière de sels. *Circ. n° 17, Contentieux, nouv. série.* — *Voy.* §. 14 ci-après.

5. Dans les cas où les Employés de la Régie sont admis au partage, il s'effectue de la manière suivante : un quart au trésor public, un quart à la caisse des retraites, et la moitié aux Employés saisissans. — Les Contrôleurs ambulans ou de ville, quand ils concourent aux saisies, jouissent de deux parts d'Employés. *Art. 1, idem.*

6. Lorsque la contravention est constatée par des préposés étrangers, concurremment avec les Employés de la Régie, la moitié revenant aux saisissans est partagée par tête. Si les Employés de la Régie sont exclus, la part qui leur est attribuée dans cette moitié, est versée; savoir : deux tiers au trésor, un tiers à la caisse des retraites. *Idem, art. 4.*

7. Les préposés étrangers à la Régie jouissent, en quelque matière que ce soit, de la moitié attribuée aux saisissans, lorsqu'ils opèrent seuls, et le partage doit s'en effectuer entre eux d'après les formes et dans les proportions particulières à l'administration à laquelle ils appartiennent. *Art. 3, idem.*

8. Dans les saisies faites par les troupes ou par la gendarmerie, seules ou concurremment avec les Employés de la Régie, la portion revenant aux troupes est calculée à raison d'une part de préposé pour chaque militaire, et de deux parts pour chaque officier ou sous-officier. — Cette portion est versée entre les mains de l'officier commandant chargé d'en faire la répartition suivant le mode réglé par le Ministre de la guerre. *Art. 5, idem.*

9. Les gendarmes ne sont pas autorisés par la loi à requérir l'exhibition des expéditions dont les boissons doivent être accompagnées en cours de transport ; mais lorsque, par des motifs particuliers à la nature de leur propre service, ils mettent les Employés de la Régie à même de constater une fraude ou une contravention quelconque, on doit leur accorder, sur le produit des amendes et confiscation, la part allouée aux indicateurs. *D. A. n.° 238.*

10. Les Employés des octrois doivent être considérés relativement au partage des saisies, comme préposés étrangers. *D. A. n.° 89.*

11. En cas de saisie commune à l'octroi et aux contributions indirectes, le produit net de l'amende et de la confiscation doit être partagé par portion égale entre les deux Administrations. — Si la saisie est opérée par les Employés de la Régie seuls, ils ont droit au partage dans la moitié revenant à l'octroi, suivant le mode de répartition en usage dans cette administration ; la moitié revenant à la Régie, est partagée; savoir, un tiers à la caisse des retraites, et deux tiers au trésor. — Si la saisie est opérée par les Employés de l'octroi seuls, ils jouissent dans la moitié revenant à la Régie, de la portion revenant aux saisissans. — Dans les saisies faites concurremment, la portion revenant à chaque administration est partagée entre les deux classes des préposés, conformément aux règles ci-dessus établies. — Dans les villes où l'abonnement général du droit de détail a été consenti, la caisse municipale profite du quart alloué à la caisse des retraites. *Arrêté du Min. des finances du 17 octobre 1816, art. 6.*

12. Il est accordé en toute saisie (*Voy.* cependant nomb. 42), à titre d'indemnité, à celui qui a dénoncé les fraudes ou les contraventions, un tiers du produit net des amendes et confiscations, pourvu que le dénonciateur se soit fait connaître à l'Administration ou au Directeur avant la saisie. *Idem, art. 7.*

13. Les Employés de la Régie n'ont pas le droit de saisir en matière de douanes dans l'intérieur; mais lorsqu'ils ont conduit, devant les fonctionnaires désignés par la loi, l'objet de fraude arrêté par eux en circulation, ils ont droit aux cinq septièmes de la part dévolue aux saisissans et aux indicateurs; s'ils n'ont fait qu'indiquer un dépôt frauduleux, ils n'ont alors part qu'à la portion d'indicateur. — Les sommes revenant aux Employés dans ces sortes de saisies, et dans celles d'octrois, sont reçues par le Receveur central; la répartition en est faite aux Employés sans autre prélèvement que le quart affecté à la caisse des retraites. *Circ. n° 17, Content., nouv. série.*

14. Dans les saisies en matière de sels, la portion restante après les prélèvemens pour le trésor et la caisse des retraites, doit être partagée dans la proportion d'un tiers pour le Directeur, et les deux tiers aux Employés saisissans. — Si c'est

une amende pour double droit, le tiers alloué ci-dessus au Directeur du lieu de la saisie, est dévolu à celui du lieu où l'acquit-à-caution a été délivré, et les deux tiers alloués aux Employés saisissans appartiennent ; savoir : un tiers aux Contrôleur et Employés de la saline, et un tiers aux Contrôleurs spéciaux des sels à l'étranger. *Cir. n° 17, Contentieux, nouv. sér.*

Il n'est rien changé aux répartitions en matière de garantie. *Arrêté du Min. des fin. du 17 oct. 1816, art. 8. Voy. nomb. 42.*

Foi due aux actes inscrits sur les portatifs.

101. Les actes inscrits par les Employés, dans le cours de leurs exercices, sur leurs registres portatifs, auront foi en justice jusqu'à inscription de faux. *Loi du 28 avril 1816, art. 242.*

1. A l'égard des débitans de boissons, les Employés sont tenus de consigner sur le registre de ces assujétis le résultat de leurs exercices, ainsi que les paiemens, ou de mentionner dans leurs actes le refus qu'aura fait le débitant de se munir dudit registre, ou de le représenter. *Art. 55, même loi.*

2. Les tribunaux ne peuvent, par de simples conjectures, supposer qu'une mention faite sur le portatif y a été insérée après coup, et sur ce motif refuser la foi due aux actes qui y sont inscrits, lorsqu'ils ne sont pas attaqués par la voie de l'inscription de faux. *Arr. du 8 juillet 1808, Mém., t. 4, p. 667.*

Prévarication.—Poursuites des Employés.

102. Les Préposés ou Employés de la Régie, prévenus de crimes ou délits commis dans l'exercice de leurs fonctions, seront poursuivis et traduits, dans les formes communes à tous les citoyens, devant les tribunaux compétens, sans autorisation préalable de la Régie : seulement le juge instructeur, lorsqu'il aura décerné un mandat d'arrêt, sera tenu d'en informer le Directeur des impositions indirectes du département de l'Employé poursuivi ; le tout conformément aux dispositions de la loi du 8 décembre 1814, article 144. *Loi du 28 avril 1816, art. 244.*

1. Tous fonctionnaires...., tous percepteurs de droits, taxes, contributions, deniers, revenus publics ou communaux, et leurs commis ou préposés qui se seront rendus coupables du crime de concussion, en ordonnant de percevoir ou en exigeant ou recevant ce qu'ils savaient n'être pas dû, ou excédant ce qui était dû pour droits..., ou pour salaire ou traitement, seront punis ; savoir, les fonctionnaires ou les officiers publics, de la peine de la réclusion, et leurs commis ou préposés d'un emprisonnement de dix ans au moins et cinq ans au plus.—Les coupables seront de plus condamnés à une amende dont le maximum sera le quart des restitutions et des dommages-intérêts, et le minimum le douzième. *Article 174 du Code pénal.*

2. La plainte en concussion ne peut être admise à raison d'une perception prétendue illégale, lorsque cette perception est fondée sur un procès-verbal non argué de faux. *Arr. du 28 nivôse an 13, Mém., t. 1, p. 179.*

3. Le préposé d'une administration, chargé de vérifier la conduite et la gestion d'un comptable, ne peut être actionné en justice par action civile et pour injures verbales, relativement aux informations qu'il est obligé de prendre pour remplir l'objet de sa mission. *Arr. du 29 germinal an 9, Mém., t. 4, p. 521.*

Autorités civiles et militaires.

103. Les autorités civiles et militaires, et la force publique, prêteront aide et assistance aux Employés pour l'exercice de leurs fonctions, toutes les fois qu'elles en seront requises. *Loi du 28 avril* 1816, *art.* 245.

1. La même disposition est prescrite à l'égard des préposés des octrois par l'article 65 de l'ordonnance du 9 décembre 1814.

Avances pour frais de justice.

104. La Régie des Contributions indirectes continuera à faire l'avance des frais de poursuites et des droits de timbre et d'enregistrement, dans toutes les affaires poursuivies à sa requête et dans son intérêt. *Ordonnance du* 22 *mai* 1816, *art.* 4.

1. Dans les procédures pour rebellion, injures ou insultes envers les Employés, l'Administration fait l'avance des frais de justice, même en matière criminelle, sauf son recours contre les condamnés; en conséquence les mandats et exécutoires sont délivrés sur elle. *Déc. du Min. des finances du* 30 *mai* 1807, *Rec., vol.* 5, *p.* 64.

2. Dans les instances en matière de garantie où le ministère public agit seul et en son nom, s'il succombe, chaque partie doit payer ses frais, mais alors c'est à la Régie des contributions indirectes à acquitter ceux faits par le ministère public. *Lettre du Min. des fin. du 9 juillet* 1811, *Mém., t.* 7, *p.* 92.

3. La Régie est tenue de lever une expédition authentique des arrêts contre lesquels elle exerce le pourvoi en cassation, et de faire l'avance de droits de timbre et d'enregistrement, tant de l'arrêt que de la déclaration du pourvoi. *Déc. du Min. de la justice, en date du* 20 *janvier* 1818.

4. Lorsque le Ministère public poursuit seul, il ne peut être condamné aux frais faits par la partie contre laquelle les poursuites sont dirigées. *Arr. du* 30 *juin* 1814.

Promulgation des lois.

105. A l'avenir, la promulgation des lois et de nos ordonnances résultera de leur insertion au Bulletin officiel. *Ordonnance du* 27 *novembre* 1816, *art.* 1.

106. Elle sera réputée connue, conformément à l'article du Code civil, un jour après que le Bulletin des lois aura été reçu de l'imprimerie royale par notre Chancelier Ministre de la justice, lequel constatera sur un registre l'époque de la réception. *Idem, art.* 2.

107. Les lois et ordonnances seront exécutoires, dans chacun des autres départemens du royaume, après l'expiration du même délai, augmenté d'autant de jours qu'il y aura de fois dix myriamètres entre la ville où la promulgation en aura été faite et le chef-lieu de chaque département, suivant le tableau annexé à l'arrêté du 25 thermidor an 11. *Idem, art.* 3.

1. Voir le tableau annexé à la circulaire timbrée *Divisions territoriales* n° 17.

2. Lorsqu'une loi établit une perception nouvelle sans spécifier l'époque à laquelle elle doit commencer, le paiement des droits est dû aussitôt que la loi est devenue exécutoire dans le département. *Arr. du 26 janvier 1806, Mém., tom. 2, p.* 482.

108. Néanmoins, dans les cas et les lieux où nous jugerons convenable de hâter l'exécution, les lois et ordonnances seront censées publiées, et seront exécutoires, du jour qu'elles seront parvenues au Préfet, qui en constatera la réception sur un registre. *Id., art.* 4.

1. Par une ordonnance du 18 janvier 1817, il a été réglé que l'exécution ne daterait néanmoins que du jour où les lois ou ordonnances seraient imprimées et affichées en vertu d'un arrêté spécial des préfets; mais ce mode particulier de publication, réservé pour les cas extraordinaires, sera sans doute rarement applicable aux matières qui forment les attributions de la Régie; et, à moins d'une notification expresse de M. le Directeur général ou de celle de M. le Préfet, les Directeurs devront toujours se conformer à la règle générale. *Circ. timbrée Divisions territoriales*, n° 17.

Pensions de retraite.

109. Il ne sera reçu aucune signification de transport, cession ou délégation de pensions de retraite affectées sur des fonds de retenues. —Le paiement desdites pensions ne pourra être arrêté par aucune saisie ou opposition, à l'exception des oppositions qui pourraient être formées par le propriétaire du brevet de la pension. *Ordonnance royale du 27 août 1817, art. 1 et 2.*

1. Un arrêt en date du 28 août 1815, rendu par la Cour de cassation, section civile, avait déjà décidé que les pensions de retraite acquittées par les caisses des administrations, sont insaisissables comme celles acquittées directement par le trésor public.

Observation générale.

On terminera cette seconde partie par une réflexion reproduite plusieurs fois dans le Mémorial du Contentieux, au sujet de quelques arrêts qui paraissent modifier certaines formalités ou en exiger l'observation moins rigoureuse lorsqu'elle n'est pas prescrite à peine de nullité. Les Employés ne doivent pas s'autoriser de ces arrêts dans la pratique; ils doivent y voir, au contraire, la preuve qu'ils ne peuvent s'écarter sans danger des termes de la loi, même dans les circonstances qui paraissent indifférentes, puisque la moindre déviation peut donner lieu à des procédures souvent très-longues et toujours nuisibles à la Régie, quel qu'en soit le résultat.

FIN DE LA DEUXIÈME PARTIE.

TROISIÈME PARTIE.

MODÈLES DE PROCÈS-VERBAUX.

N° 1. *Saisie de Boissons pour fraude aux droits de circulation.*

L'AN mil huit cent le à la requête de monsieur le Conseiller d'Etat Directeur-général de l'Administration des contributions indirectes, dont le bureau est établi à Paris, à l'hôtel de l'Administration, rue Sainte-Avoye, poursuite et diligence de M. , Directeur de ladite Administration, à , y demeurant, rue , n° , où il fait élection de domicile, pour la suite du présent procès-verbal.

Nous soussignés (*noms, grades et résidence des Employés verbalisans*), ayant serment en justice, et porteurs de nos commissions, CERTIFIONS qu'étant dans l'exercice de nos fonctions, en surveillance sur la route qui conduit nous avons vu, se dirigeant du côté de , une charrette tirée par un cheval, conduite par un seul individu, et chargée de deux tonneaux qui nous ont paru pleins de liquide; ayant fait connaître nos qualités au conducteur, nous lui avons demandé ce que renfermaient ces deux tonneaux; sur sa réponse qu'ils étoient pleins de vin, nous l'avons interpellé de nous déclarer ses nom, prénoms, profession, domicile, le lieu du chargement et celui de la destination desdits tonneaux, a répondu , ayant percé chacun desdits tonneaux, il en est sorti effectivement du vin rouge que nous avons goûté et fait goûter audit sieur , et qu'il a reconnu, ainsi que nous, être franc et marchand; sommé ledit de nous représenter les congés, passavans, acquits-à-caution ou autres expéditions de la Régie des contributions indirectes dont il doit être porteur, a répondu ; et, attendu la contravention dudit à l'art. (1), nous lui avons déclaré, en vertu de l'art. 17 de la même loi, la saisie desdits deux tonneaux de vin, de la charrette et du cheval, et que nous allions conduire le tout à notre bureau, situé , où lesdits vins seront jaugés, estimés et déposés; l'avons sommé de nous accompagner, pour assister auxdites opérations, ainsi qu'à la rédaction de notre procès-verbal, à quoi il a acquiescé. En conséquence, lesdits deux tonneaux ayant été à l'instant transportés sur la même charrette à notre susdit bureau, nous les avons jaugés, et reconnu qu'ils contenaient ensemble hectolitres litres de vin, que nous avons évalués, de concert avec le sieur , à la somme de , et nous les avons confiés à la garde du sieur , Receveur, lequel s'en est chargé, avec promesse, de les représenter à toute réquisition de justice. Nous avons encore fait observer audit que la charrette et le cheval n'étant saisis que pour sûreté de l'amende qu'il a encourue, nous lui en donnerions main-levée, moyennant caution solvable, ou la consignation d'une somme de six cents francs, maximum de ladite amende (2),

---

(1) Pour transport de boissons sans expédition *(art. 6)*; pour transport de boissons avec expédition qui n'est pas conforme au chargement *(art. 10)*; pour transport de boissons par une route ou à une destination autre que celle indiquée par l'expédition, ou avec une expédition dont le délai est expiré *(art. 15)*; pour refus de représenter les expéditions qui doivent accompagner les boissons en cours de transport *(art. 17 de la loi du 28 avril 1816)*.

(2) S'il fournit caution, *voyez* le procès-verbal n° 2. S'il refuse de consigner et de donner caution, *voyez* le n° 3.

et ledit ayant aussitôt déposé la somme de entre les mains dudit sieur , Receveur, qui le reconnaît, nous lui avons accordé la libre disposition de son cheval, ainsi que de la voiture : DE TOUT QUOI nous avons dressé le présent procès-verbal dans le bureau , en présence du Receveur et celle du sieur , leur en ayant donné lecture, avec sommation de le signer; le Receveur a promis le faire (ainsi que ledit ou non ledit , qui a répondu ne savoir ou ne vouloir). Clos ledit procès-verbal lesdits jour et an, à heures du , duquel nous avons remis copie audit qui a signé (*ou* refusé de signer) avec nous et le Receveur.

N° 2. *Saisie commune pour fraude aux droits d'entrée et d'octroi.*

L'an mil huit cent le à la requête de monsieur le Conseiller d'Etat Directeur général de l'Administration des contributions indirectes, dont le bureau est établi à Paris, rue Sainte-Avoye, et de monsieur (*noms et qualités du Maire*), au nom de la ville de , poursuite et diligence de M. , Directeur des contributions indirectes à , y résidant, rue , n° , où il fait élection de domicile pour la suite du présent; nous soussignés (*noms, grades et résidence des Employés*), assermentés en justice, et porteurs de nos commissions, CERTIFIONS qu'étant dans l'exercice de nos fonctions à , nous avons remarqué sur la route de , se dirigeant vers l'intérieur de , un individu conduisant une charrette atelée d'un cheval; l'ayant arrêté comme il venait de franchir notre barrière, nous lui avons fait connaître nos qualités, et nous lui avons demandé s'il ne portait rien de sujet à la déclaration et aux droits, nous a répondu ; voulant nous assurer de la sincérité de cette réponse, nous avons soulevé et nous avons aperçu sacs, que nous avons reconnu, après en avoir fait l'ouverture, être pleins de fruits secs; ayant transporté lesdits sacs dans notre bureau, où nous avons fait entrer ledit particulier, nous avons procédé, en sa présence, à la vérification et pesée des fruits, et reconnu, ainsi que lui, que c'étaient des fruits secs propres à la fabrication du cidre, et qu'ils pesaient kilogrammes; interpellé ledit particulier de nous déclarer ses nom, prénoms, profession et demeure, et de nous dire pourquoi il n'avait pas fait sa déclaration à l'entrée, a répondu : attendu la contravention à l'art. 24 de la loi du 28 avril 1816, et à l'art. du réglement particulier de l'octroi, nous lui avons déclaré procès-verbal et saisie desdits kilogrammes de fruits secs, que nous avons estimé, de gré à gré avec lui, à la somme de et dont nous avons constitué gardien le sieur , Receveur audit bureau d , qui s'en est chargé, avec promesse de les représenter à toute réquisition de justice. Nous avons déclaré, en outre, audit qu'il serait poursuivi en police correctionnelle pour la confiscation des fruits saisis et pour le paiement de l'amende de 100 francs à 200 francs qu'il a encourue, conformément à l'art. 46 de la loi du 28 avril précitée; et que, pour sûreté de ladite amende, nous saisissions également sa charrette et son cheval, qui seraient mis en fourrière, à défaut par lui de consigner ladite somme de 200 francs ou de nous fournir une caution solvable (1), *nous a présenté pour caution le sieur* (nom, prénoms, profession et demeure), *lequel, ici présent, après avoir pris connaissance du procès-verbal, s'est rendu volontairement garant et caution solidaire dudit , à qui, par ce moyen, nous avons laissé la libre disposition de la charrette et du cheval susmentionnés.* DE TOUT QUOI nous avons rédigé le présent procès-verbal dans notre bureau d , en présence du Receveur, dudit (*contrevenant*) et dudit (*caution*), leur en ayant donné lecture, avec invitation de le signer; le

---

(1) S'il consigne l'amende, *voyez* le procès-verbal n° 1. S'il refuse de consigner et de donner caution, *voyez* n° 3.

Receveur a promis le faire, ainsi que le sieur (*la caution doit toujours signer*): le sieur (*contrevenant*) a promis également (*ou* refusé). Clos le présent procès-verbal les susdits jour, mois et an, à heure , et remis copie au sieur (*contrevenant*), ainsi qu'au sieur , sa caution, qui a signé avec nous et le Receveur, ainsi que ledit (*ou non ledit*).

N° 3. *Saisie commune pour fraude aux droits de circulation, d'entrée et d'octroi, en voiture suspendue.*

L'AN (*le surplus comme au n° 2*).

CERTIFIONS qu'étant dans l'exercice de nos fonctions ordinaires à la barrière d , nous avons vu venir du dehors, se dirigeant sur notre barrière, pour entrer dans , un cabriolet particulier atelé d'un cheval conduit par une personne de nous inconnue, qui, sans s'arrêter devant notre bureau, l'a dépassé, et continuait à s'acheminer dans
Soupçonnant que ledit cabriolet pouvait contenir des objets de fraude, nous nous en sommes approchés; et, après avoir fait connaître nos qualités au conducteur, nous l'avons prévenu que nous désirions faire la visite de son cabriolet, pour nous assurer s'il ne renfermait aucun objet soumis aux droits, et nous l'avons à cet effet invité, aux termes de l'art. 31 de l'ordonnance du 9 décembre 1814, à nous suivre chez M. le Commissaire de police; à quoi ayant acquiescé, nous nous sommes tous ensemble acheminés par la rue d : mais à peine avions-nous fait cinquante pas, que le susdit conducteur a fait arrêter son cheval, et nous a déclaré qu'il était inutile d'aller plus loin, qu'il conduisait en effet des boissons, et qu'il ne mettait aucun obstacle à ce que nous en fissions la recherche; à ces mots, nous avons rétrogradé. Arrivés devant le bureau, le susdit conducteur est descendu de son cabriolet, dont ayant aussitôt, d'après son autorisation, fait la visite, nous avons découvert dans le coffre deux boîtes de fer-blanc qui le remplissaient en entier, et paraissaient avoir été faites exprès: présumant que ces boîtes renfermaient des boissons, nous les avons extraites, et n'ayant pas découvert autre chose de suspect, nous les avons portées dans notre bureau pour en faire la vérification. Ouverture faite desdites boîtes, nous avons reconnu et fait reconnaître audit particulier qu'elles renfermaient de l'eau-de-vie, que nous avons mesurée, pesée et reconnue, ainsi que lui, être à degrés de qualité franche et marchande, et en quantité de litres. Interpellé ledit particulier de nous déclarer ses nom, profession et demeure, le lieu du chargement et celui de la destination desdites eaux-de-vie, et de nous représenter l'expédition de la Régie des contributions indirectes dont il devait être porteur, a répondu ; et, attendu la contravention dudit sieur aux articles 6 et 24 de la loi du 28 avril 1816, et à l'art. du réglement particulier de l'octroi, nous lui avons déclaré saisie desdits litres d'eau-de-vie, que nous avons estimés de gré à gré avec lui à la somme de , et nous les avons confiés à la garde du sieur , Receveur de l'octroi, lequel s'en est chargé, avec promesse de les représenter à toute réquisition de justice: nous avons de plus déclaré audit qu'en vertu des articles 17 et 27 de la loi du 28 avril précitée, nous lui saisissions également son cabriolet et son cheval; mais que cette saisie n'ayant lieu que pour sûreté de l'amende qu'il a encourue, nous lui en donnerions main-levée, moyennant caution solvable ou consignation de la somme de 1,000 francs, montant de ladite amende (1). *Nous ayant répondu qu'il ne pouvait ni consigner ladite somme ni fournir une caution, nous lui avons fait connaître que lesdits cheval et cabriolet, que nous avons estimés de concert avec lui; savoir: le cabriolet à et le cheval à seraient*

---

(1) S'il fournissait caution, voyez ce qui est mis en caractères italiques dans le procès-verbal n° 2; et s'il consigne l'amende, voyez celui n° 1.

mis en fourrière chez le sieur , aubergiste à , qui en sera constitué gardien, et nous l'avons prévenu qu'à défaut d'avoir satisfait aux causes de la présente saisie, dans le délai de huit jours, fixé par l'art. 39 *du décret du* 18 *juin* 1811, *la vente dudit cheval sera poursuivie conformément à l'art.* 40 *du même décret.* De tout quoi, etc.

Nº 4. *Saisie commune pour fraude aux droits d'entrée et d'octroi par escalade.*

L'AN, etc. (*comme pour le nº* 2).

CERTIFIONS que, sur les heures d étant dans l'exercice de nos fonctions à , nous avons aperçu plusieurs personnes, dont l'air préoccupé a éveillé nos soupçons et nous a engagés à les surveiller attentivement; après divers mouvemens, nous avons vu l'un desdits particuliers jeter par-dessus le mur quelque chose que nous avons présumé être une échelle de corde, car il s'en est servi au même instant pour grimper sur le mur, et nous l'avons vu ensuite tirer à lui quelque chose que nous n'avons pas pu bien distinguer, et qu'il a laissé descendre de l'autre côté du mur en dedans de (1) ; ne doutant plus que ces hommes ne fussent occupés à introduire des boissons, ou autres objets en fraude des droits, deux de nous, les sieurs , se sont détachés pour aller, en passant par la barrière d , de l'autre côté du mur; après avoir attendu le temps nécessaire pour qu'ils pussent y arriver, nous nous sommes approchés des susdits particuliers aussi secrètement qu'il nous a été possible; et aussitôt que nous avons aperçu que nous étions découverts, nous nous sommes élancés sur eux assez à temps pour saisir un de ceux et celui qui se trouvait sur le mur, à l'instant où il venait d'en descendre précipitamment; les autres ayant pris la fuite, nous n'avons pu les atteindre; demandé à ces deux hommes ce qu'ils faisaient là, ont répondu ; demandé aussi ce que renfermaient plusieurs sacs que nous avons trouvés à leurs pieds, ont répondu qu'ils contenaient des petits barils remplis d'eau-de-vie; nous nous sommes alors emparés desdits sacs, au nombre de , et de l'échelle de corde qui était restée au mur, et nous avons transporté le tout, accompagnés des prévenus arrêtés, à notre bureau d , où étant, nous avons sommé lesdits particuliers de nous déclarer leurs noms, prénoms, profession et demeure, le lieu où ils avaient pris lesdits sacs, et leur destination, ont répondu
En cet instant sont également arrivés les sieurs , qui ont aperçu deux hommes au même endroit où le sieur , l'un des prévenus, avait descendu l'objet que nous avions remarqué. Ces deux hommes ayant précipitamment pris la fuite, lesdits sieurs n'ont pu les atteindre; mais ayant cherché au pied du mur, ils y ont trouvé un sac de même forme que ceux précédemment saisis en dehors; nous l'avons présenté aux prévenus, en les sommant de nous dire s'ils le reconnaissaient, ont répondu . Ouverture faite de tous les susdits sacs, nous en avons extrait petits barils contenant en totalité litres eau-de-vie à degrés, bonne, franche et marchande, ainsi que nous l'avons reconnu par les mesurage, pesée et dégustation que nous en avons faits; lesdits l'ayant reconnu également, nous les avons invités à nous représenter les expéditions de la Régie des contributions indirectes dont

---

(1) Il n'est pas nécessaire, pour qu'il y ait fraude par escalade, que les contrevenans soient surpris escaladant les murs de leur personne; la seule action d'introduire les objets soumis aux droits en les jetant par-dessus les murs, suffit pour caractériser cette fraude; et les personnes qui jettent ces objets depuis le dehors, comme celles qui les ramassent en dedans, sont passibles de la peine de six mois de prison. C'est ainsi que le tribunal de police correctionnelle du département de la Seine a décidé cette question dans plusieurs circonstances.

ils devaient être porteurs, ont répondu . Attendu la contravention manifeste aux articles 6 et 24 de la loi du 28 avril 1816 et à l'art. du réglement de l'octroi, nous leur avons déclaré procès-verbal et saisie desdits litres eau-de-vie et objets susdésignés, et nous les avons estimés de gré à gré avec eux à la somme de , les prévenant que les eaux-de-vie et les sacs seraient déposés entre les mains de M. , Receveur, lequel, ayant été présent à notre vérification, s'en est effectivement chargé comme gardien, avec promesse de les représenter à toute réquisition. Nous avons de plus déclaré auxdits , qu'en vertu des articles 19 et 46 de la loi précitée, ils avaient encouru, outre la confiscation et une amende de 100 francs à 600 francs, une peine correctionnelle de six mois de prison, et qu'en conséquence nous allions les remettre entre les mains de la force armée pour être conduits devant M. , à qui serait en même temps remise l'échelle de corde susmentionnée pour servir de preuve au procès. De tout quoi nous avons immédiatement dressé notre procès-verbal dans le bureau susdésigné, en présence du Receveur et celle desdits sieurs ; leur en avons donné lecture à tous les trois, avec sommation de le signer; le Receveur a promis le faire, non les sieurs , qui ont dit ne savoir. Clos le présent procès-verbal à heures les susdits jour, mois et an, et nous en avons remis copie à chacun desdits , après avoir signé avec M. , Receveur.

Et de suite nous avons requis l'assistance d , de service à , auxquels nous avons remis les sieurs , pour être conduits devant M. . Nous leur avons également remis une copie de notre procès-verbal et l'échelle de corde qui y est mentionnée, pour être déposés en même temps à , et ont lesdits signé avec nous pour leur charge et garde, les jour, mois et an que dessus.

N° 5. *Procès-verbal pour vente en détail de Boissons sans déclaration préalable, sans enseigne et sans licence.*

(*Transcrire ici le modèle n°* 31).

L'an mil huit cent, etc. (*le surplus comme au modèle n°* 1).

Nous soussignés (*noms, grades des Employés*), à la résidence de , accompagnés de M. , qui a déféré à la réquisition dont copie est transcrite en tête du présent, Certifions qu'étant informés par les plaintes de plusieurs débitans, et par d'autres indices, que le sieur se livrait à la vente en détail des boissons, sans déclaration, nous nous sommes transportés dans son domicile, situé rue , n° ; étant entrés (*indiquer toutes les circonstances propres à établir la contravention, désigner la qualité et la quantité des boissons à mesure qu'elles sont trouvées, la déclaration des buveurs et des personnes achetant des boissons, etc.*); demandé audit pourquoi il vendait du vin en détail sans en avoir fait la déclaration préalable, sans s'être muni d'une licence et sans avoir placé une enseigne devant sa maison, a répondu ; interpellé de nous conduire dans sa cave, nous y avons trouvé pièces de que nous avons jaugé et goûté, reconnu et fait reconnaître audit contenir de vin, bon, franc et marchand; sommé de nous représenter les expéditions de la Régie qui ont dû accompagner lesdites pièces, a dit ; sur quoi nous lui avons fait observer qu'il était en contravention à l'article 50 de la loi du 28 avril 1816, pour s'être livré à la vente en détail des boissons sans déclaration, sans enseigne et sans licence; en conséquence, nous lui avons déclaré procès-verbal et saisie tant (*la totalité des boissons trouvées dans la maison et dans la cave*) formant, suivant le jaugeage que nous en avons fait en sa présence, litres, que nous avons évalués de gré à gré avec lui à la somme de et que nous avons confié à sa garde, sous la promesse qu'il nous a faite de les représenter, ou leur valeur, à toute réquisition de justice. Et avons sur-le-champ rédigé le présent procès-verbal dans (*telle chambre de la maison*) dudit en sa présence et celle de M. , qui a assisté à toutes nos opérations; leur ayant donné lecture dudit procès-verbal avec sommation de le signer, M. a promis le faire, non ledit , qui a refusé, disant . Avons clos le présent à heures d et en avons laissé copie audit après l'avoir signé avec M.

N° 6. *Procès-verbal pour défaut de renouvellement de Licence.*

L'AN, etc. (*comme au modèle n° 1*).

CERTIFIONS qu'étant dans le cours de nos exercices chez le sieur (*nom, prénoms, profession et demeure de l'assujéti*), et qu'après avoir réglé l'état de ses boissons et constaté sur notre portatif les ventes qu'il a faites depuis jusqu'à ce jour, nous lui avons demandé si, conformément à l'article 171 de la loi du 28 avril 1816, et aux avertissemens que nous lui avions donnés et réitérés, il s'était pourvu d'une licence pour l'année courante, et nous l'avons invité à nous en faire la représentation, a répondu Nous lui avons fait observer qu'il était en contravention à l'article 171 précité de la loi du 28 avril 1816, et nous lui avons déclaré procès-verbal de cette contravention, le prévenant qu'il serait poursuivi en police correctionnelle, tant pour le paiement de la licence que pour celui de l'amende de 300 francs qu'il a encourue. Nous avons aussitôt rédigé notre procès-verbal chez ledit , dans ; lui en ayant donné lecture avec invitation de le signer, a Clos ledit procès-verbal dans le lieu ci-dessus désigné, à heures ; remis copie audit

---

N° 7. *Procès-verbal constatant un excédant de Vin chez un marchand en gros.*

L'AN, etc. (*comme au n° 1*).

CERTIFIONS qu'étant dans le cours de nos exercices dans les magasins du sieur , marchand en gros à , rue , n° , nous avons vérifié en sa présence qu'il existait dans ledit magasin pièces de vin, contenant, d'après notre jaugeage, ainsi qu'il le reconnaît, litres, que, d'après les déclarations qu'il avait faites au bureau de les , il avait enlevé de son magasin, à destination de diverses personnes, pièces contenant litres, ce qui forme un total de pièces pour litres. Nous lui avons fait observer que, d'après le dernier acte de notre portatif, dressé à la suite de notre exercice en date du , il restait à ses charges pièces pour litres; que, par conséquent, il avait reçu depuis ledit exercice litres de vin, pour lesquels nous l'avons invité à nous représenter les expéditions de la Régie qui ont dû les accompagner lors de leur introduction chez lui Nous ayant représenté , nous lui avons fait observer de nouveau que lesdits ne portaient que litres, qu'il manquait encore des expéditions pour litres, et nous l'avons invité à nous en faire la représentation; mais il nous a répondu qu'il n'en avait pas d'autres; à lui demandé pourquoi il avait un excédant de litres, a répondu Nous lui avons fait remarquer que, nonobstant ces explications, il était en contravention à l'article 100 de la loi du 28 avril 1816, en ce qu'il avait introduit dans son magasin litres de vin sans expédition, ainsi que cela se trouve démontré par le mesurage, la dégustation et le décompte que nous en avons fait en sa présence; qu'ainsi il avait encouru l'amende de 50 francs à 300 francs, prononcée par l'article 106 de la loi du 28 avril précité et la confiscation desdits litres de vin, dont nous lui avons déclaré saisie, les ayant évalués de gré à gré avec lui à la somme de nous les avons laissés à sa charge et garde, sous la promesse qu'il nous a faite de les représenter, ou leur valeur, à toute réquisition de justice. De tout quoi nous avons rédigé aussitôt notre procès-verbal dans le susdit magasin, en présence dudit , à qui nous en avons donné lecture, avec invitation de le signer, ce qu'il a promis. Fait et clos à heures du et remis copie audit qui a signé avec nous.

N° 8. *Procès-verbal chez un Brasseur pour un entonnement fait avant l'heure fixée, et pour fabrication d'un brassin sans déclaration, avec enlèvement des objets saisis.*

L'an, etc. (*comme au n° 2 si le brasseur est soumis à l'octroi; dans le cas contraire, comme au n° 1*).

Certifions qu'en suite de la déclaration de mise de feu faite le au bureau de la Régie de , par le sieur , brasseur dans cette ville, de laquelle déclaration il résulte qu'il devait procéder aujourd'hui, à heures, à l'entonnement d'un brassin provenant de sa chaudière n° , nous nous sommes transportés à heures dans sa brasserie située rue , n° , à l'effet d'assister audit entonnement; étant arrivés, et parlant à , nous lui avons fait connaître l'objet de notre visite; mais il nous a dit que l'entonnement avait déjà eu lieu et qu'il venait d'être achevé à l'instant même. L'avons invité à nous représenter l'ampliation de la déclaration susrelatée; à quoi ayant satisfait, nous lui avons fait remarquer que l'entonnement était fixé pour heures du , que cette heure n'était pas encore sonnée; que par conséquent il était en contravention à l'article 120 de la loi du 28 avril 1816, de quoi nous lui avons déclaré que nous dresserions procès-verbal, auquel serait jointe l'ampliation susmentionnée, que nous avons à cet effet paraphée *ne varietur*. Continuant nos exercices, nous avons invité ledit à nous représenter les bières nouvellement fabriquées, il nous a indiqué pièces, placées ; examen fait desdites pièces, nous avons reconnu qu'elles étaient pleines de bière encore guillante; et, d'après le jaugeage que nous en avons fait, qu'elles contenaient litres, quantité approximative et ordinaire du produit de chaque brassin de la chaudière n° ; ayant vérifié la cuve guilloire, nous avons cru remarquer qu'il y avait eu en guillage une plus grande quantité de bière que celle ci-devant désignée, nous l'avons également fait remarquer audit , et nous lui avons demandé s'il n'avait pas d'autre produit à nous représenter; sur sa réponse négative, nous lui avons déclaré que nous entendions faire des recherches plus exactes, et nous l'avons invité à nous accompagner, à quoi il a consenti; après avoir parcouru nous sommes entrés dans , où nous avons trouvé pièces; ayant procédé à leur vérification, nous avons reconnu et fait reconnaître audit qu'elles étaient pleines de bière encore guillante, et qu'elles contenaient, d'après notre jaugeage, litres; interpellé de nous dire d'où provenait cette bière, a répondu ; mais nous lui avons fait remarquer qu'elles ne pouvaient provenir que d'un second brassin fait sans déclaration, ce qui établit une nouvelle contravention de sa part à l'article 120 de la loi du 28 avril 1816, pour laquelle il a encouru, conformément à l'article 129 de la même loi, l'amende de 200 francs à 600 francs, et la confiscation desdits litres de bière, dont nous lui avons déclaré la saisie, et que nous avons évaluée de gré à gré avec lui à la somme de ; nous lui avons encore déclaré qu'attendu les difficultés existant déjà entre lui et la Régie, nous effectuerions, immédiatement après la rédaction de notre procès-verbal, le transport de ladite bière au bureau de où elle serait mise en dépôt à la charge de M. , Receveur, qui en en sera constitué gardien; nous l'avons invité à nous accompagner et à être présent audit dépôt, ce qu'il a Nous avons aussitôt rédigé, etc.

NOTA. *On opérera le transport et le dépôt des objets saisis conformément au modèle n° 23.*

N° 9. *Découverte d'une distillerie sans déclaration.*

(*Transcrire ici la réquisition modèle n°* 31).

L'AN, etc. (*comme au n° 2 si l'octroi est intéressé; dans le cas contraire, comme au n°* 1).

CERTIFIONS que, sur l'avis à nous donné qu'il existait une distillerie non déclarée dans la maison du sieur , commune de , nous avons adressé à M. le Maire de ladite commune la réquisition dont copie est transcrite en tête du présent, et de lui accompagnés, nous nous sommes transportés chez ledit sieur , où étant et parlant à , nous lui avons fait connaître nos qualités et l'objet de notre transport, lui demandant s'il était vrai (*qu'il ou M.*) fît fabriquer des eaux-de-vie, et que, dans ce cas, il eût à nous justifier de la déclaration qu'il avait dû faire en exécution de la loi du 28 avril 1816, et à nous représenter la licence dont il avait dû se munir, a répondu qu'en effet ; nous ayant introduits dans (*désigner les chaudières, alambics et autres ustensiles reconnus, les matières en préparation, celles déjà fabriquées, en indiquer le degré et la mesure, dire si le feu est allumé ou non, détailler enfin toutes les circonstances qui établissent la fabrication, ainsi que les allégations et justification du prévenu*); attendu la contravention aux articles 138 et 139 (ou 138 et 141) de la loi du 28 avril 1816, nous lui avons déclaré procès-verbal, ensemble la saisie (*des eaux-de-vie*), que nous avons évaluées de gré à gré avec lui à la somme de , et que nous avons laissées à sa charge, sous la promesse qu'il nous a faite de les représenter, ou leur valeur, à toute réquisition. De tout quoi nous avons rédigé, etc.

N° 10. *Procès-verbal divisé en deux vacations pour fabrication d'Huiles sans déclaration.*

(*Copier ici la réquisition modèle n°* 31).

L'AN, etc. (*comme au n° 1 si les huiles ne sont pas imposées au tarif de l'octroi; dans le cas contraire, comme au n°* 2).

CERTIFIONS qu'ayant été instruits que le sieur avait fait un approvisionnement assez considérable de (*indiquer les graines ou les fruits*), et qu'il se livrait d'ailleurs au commerce des huiles, nous nous sommes transportés dans sa maison, située rue , n° , accompagnés de M. , qui a déféré à notre réquisition, dont copie est transcrite en tête du présent; arrivés chez ledit , que nous avons trouvé, nous l'avons informé de l'objet de notre transport, et nous l'avons invité à nous accompagner dans les recherches que nous nous proposions de faire; ayant acquiescé à notre invitation, nous sommes d'abord entrés (*indiquer toutes les circonstances, décrire les grains, fruits et autres substances propres à la fabrication, les moulins et instrumens qui y sont employés, les huiles déjà fabriquées celles en fabrication, etc.*); et, attendu l'heure avancée de , qui nous empêche de terminer la description des objets susmentionnés, nous avons notifié audit que nous nous réservions de continuer notre présent procès-verbal demain à heures du matin; nous l'avons invité à être présent à la même heure, ainsi que M. ; et après avoir réuni tous les susdits objets dans (*telle chambre ou magasin*), en avoir fermé en-dedans les (*croisées ou autres ouvertures*) et nous être assurés qu'elles sont en bon état, nous avons scellé la porte d'entrée au moyen d'une bande de papier fixée avec de la cire rouge, et aux deux extrémités de laquelle nous avons apposé notre cachet, dont l'empreinte est en marge du présent, ledit invité à y apposer également le sien, a répondu , Nous lui avons encore notifié que les scellés demeureraient à sa charge et garde, et qu'il serait responsable de leur conservation, aux peines de droit, à quoi il a consenti; et aussitôt nous avons dressé le présent, dont nous avons donné lecture audit , ainsi qu'à M. ; ils ont promis signer avec nous. Fait et clos au lieu susdésigné à heures; remis copie audit après avoir signé avec

Le à heures du matin, même requête et diligence, par continuation de notre procès-verbal commencé le , nous soussignés , assistés de M. , nous étant rendus chez le sieur , que nous avons trouvé, après avoir reconnu tous ensemble que les scellés apposés hier sur étaient sains et entiers, nous sommes entrés et nous avons continué nos opérations comme suit (*procéder à la reconnaissance, mesurage ou pesée des objets de fraude, en faire la description*); demandé audit pourquoi il faisait fabriquer des huiles chez lui sans en avoir fait la déclaration, à l'effet de soumettre sa fabrication à la surveillance de la Régie, conformément à l'article 98 de la loi du 25 mars 1817, a répondu ; nous lui avons fait observer qu'il était en contravention à l'article précité, et qu'il avait encouru, conformément à l'article 109 de la même loi, une amende de 100 francs à 200 francs, et la confiscation des huiles ci-devant désignées, en quantité de , dont nous lui avons déclaré saisie, et après les avoir évaluées de gré à gré avec lui à la somme de , nous les avons laissées, etc. (*la fin comme au n° 5*).

N° 11. *Fabrication de cartes de fraude par un cartier commissionné.*

(*Transcrire ici la réquisition modèle n° 31*).

L'AN, etc. (*comme au n° 1*).

CERTIFIONS qu'ayant eu lieu de soupçonner que le sieur , maître cartier commissionné à , se livrait à la fraude, nous nous sommes transportés chez lui, rue , n° , accompagnés de M. , dont nous avons requis l'assistance, afin de prévenir toute difficulté dans les recherches que nous nous proposions de faire, tant dans le domicile dudit sieur que dans les autres parties de la maison qu'il habite; y étant arrivés et parlant à , nous l'avons informé de l'objet de notre transport, et nous l'avons invité à être présent à nos visites, à quoi il a consenti; après avoir fait d'inutiles recherches dans les ateliers déclarés dudit sieur , ainsi que dans son habitation personnelle, nous lui avons demandé s'il n'était possesseur d'aucun autre local, a répondu que non. Ayant fait inviter (*le propriétaire ou principal locataire*) à se rendre auprès de nous, est intervenu le sieur , ainsi qu'il nous a déclaré être; nous lui avons fait connaître l'objet de nos recherches, et nous lui avons demandé si le sieur n'avait la jouissance d'aucun autre local, le prévenant que nous avions l'intention de poursuivre nos perquisitions dans toute la maison, et que, dans le cas où nous découvririons un atelier clandestin, il serait lui-même en contravention à l'article 16 de l'arrêté du 19 floréal an 6; nous ayant dit que le sieur tenait encore à loyer une chambre au étage, nous nous en sommes fait désigner la porte, et nous avons invité ledit sieur à nous en faire l'ouverture, ce qu'ayant fait, nous sommes entrés accompagnés de lui, et nous avons reconnu (*indiquer si des ouvriers étaient occupés à fabriquer, faire la description des matières fabriquées et en préparation, des moules, etc., fermer les objets de fraude sous enveloppe, les cacheter, inviter le prévenu à apposer son cachet, etc.*). Nous avons fait reconnaître audit qu'il était en contravention à l'article 12 de l'arrêté du 19 floréal an 6, et à l'article 1er du décret du 9 février 1810; nous lui avons déclaré procès-verbal et saisie desdits , le prévenant que le dépôt en serait effectué entre les mains de M. (*noms, qualités et demeure du gardien*), qui en sera constitué gardien, à quoi nous l'avons invité d'être présent, ce qu'il a ; de tout ce que dessus nous avons rédigé notre procès-verbal dans la chambre susdésignée, en présence dudit sieur et de M. , leur en ayant donné lecture avec invitation de le signer; M. a promis le faire, non ledit , qui a refusé. Ainsi clos et arrêté les jour, mois et au que dessus à heures, ledit procès-verbal, dont nous avons laissé copie au sieur (*le prévenu*), et avons signé avec M.

Le transport des objets saisis sera fait suivant le modèle n° 23.

N° 12. *Saisie d'une voiture à destination fixe, pour transport de paquets non enregistrés sur la feuille de route.*

L'AN, etc. (*Le surplus comme au n° 1*).

Certifions qu'étant dans l'exercice ordinaire de nos fonctions à nous avons vu, arrivant à , sur les heures d la diligence d Voulant nous assurer si les formalités prescrites par les lois étaient exactement remplies et les droits exactement payés, nous nous sommes approchés du conducteur, et, après lui avoir fait connaître nos qualités, nous l'avons invité à nous représenter la feuille de route et le laissez-passer dont il devait être porteur en exécution de l'article 5 du décret du 14 fructidor an 12 et de l'article 117 de la loi du 25 mars 1817; ayant obtempéré à cette réquisition, il nous a remis, 1.° un laissez-passer portant le n.° délivré à le que nous lui avons rendu après nous être assurés de son identité; 2°. une feuille de route portant le n.° datée de le et signée laquelle a été par nous paraphée *ne varietur*, pour être annexée au présent, et portait paquets enregistrés n.os à diverses adresses. Demandé au conducteur s'il ne transportait aucune autre marchandise que celles indiquées ci-dessus, a répondu Nous l'avons prévenu que nous voulions en faire la vérification; mais que, pour ne pas compromettre le service des voyageurs, nous allions l'accompagner jusqu'au bureau de déchargement. Arrivés audit bureau, situé rue n.° en même temps que ladite voiture et le conducteur, que nous avons toujours accompagnés, s'est encore présenté un particulier, qui nous a dit être Nous lui avons aussi fait connaître nos qualités et l'objet de notre visite, à laquelle ayant procédé en sa présence et celle du conducteur, nous avons reconnu sur ladite voiture, outre les paquets ci-dessus mentionnés et inscrits seuls sur la feuille de route plusieurs autres paquets non enregistrés et ainsi détaillés: Sommé le susdit conducteur et de nous déclarer leurs noms, prenoms, professions et demeures, et pourquoi ils avaient entrepris le transport desdits paquets sans les avoir enregistrés, ont repondu Nous leur avons alors fait observer qu'ils étaient en contravention à l'article 5 du décret du 14 fructidor an 12 précité, nous leur avons déclaré procès-verbal de cette contravention, les prévenant qu'ils seraient poursuivis en police correctionnelle pour le paiement de l'amende prononcée par l'art. 122 de la loi du 25 mars qu'ils ont *encourue*, ainsi que pour le remboursement des droits fraudés. De tout quoi nous avons rédigé, etc.

N° 13. *Saisie d'une voiture faisant un service d'occasion sans déclaration.*

L'AN, etc. (*comme au n° 1*).
CERTIFIONS qu'étant en surveillance à l'entrée de la ville de , nous avons remarqué qu'une voiture qui paraissait faire un service public n'était pourvue d'aucune estampille (*dans le département de la Seine on ajouterait :* ni d'aucun des numéros de la police qui en tiennent lieu), et voulant nous assurer si elle avait été soumise aux droits et à la déclaration, en exécution de la loi du 25 mars 1817, nous nous en sommes approchés, et, après avoir fait connaître nos qualités, tant au conducteur qu'aux personnes qui se trouvent au nombre de dans l'intérieur, nous avons interpellé celles-ci de nous déclarer si elles étaient propriétaires de la voiture et des chevaux qui y sont atelés; l'une de ces personnes nous ayant répondu que non, qu'elle avait été reçue moyennant pour être conduite de à , nous avons fait remarquer cette réponse au conducteur, nous l'avons sommé de nous déclarer ses nom, prénoms, profession et demeure; et s'il avait fait sa déclaration au bureau de la Régie des contributions indirectes, de nous en justifier par la représentation de son laissez-passer, a répondu Nous lui avons fait observer qu'il était en contravention à l'article 117 de la loi du 25 mars 1817 précitée, et qu'en vertu de l'article 120 de cette loi nous lui déclarions procès-verbal et saisie, 1° de ladite voiture (*indiquer le nombre des places et le signalement*); 2° des harnais et des chevaux. Nous avons modérément estimé le tout, de concert avec ledit , à la somme de , et nous lui en avons offert main-levée moyennant caution solvable; mais nous ayant représenté qu'il était hors d'état de satisfaire présentement à cette obligation, et qu'un retard lui serait préjudiciable, ainsi qu'aux voyageurs, nous avons consenti à lui accorder ladite main-levée, et nous la lui avons accordée en effet, sous sa caution juratoire, et sous la promesse qu'il nous a faite de représenter lesdits objets, ou leur valeur, à toute réquisition de justice. De tout quoi, etc.

N° 14. *Procès-verbal d'arrestation d'un colporteur de tabacs.*

L'an, etc. (*le même préambule qu'au n° 1*), nous soussignés débitant de tabac dans la commune d y demeurant, assermenté en justice et porteur de ma commission, et garde-champêtre de la même commune, y demeurant, également assermenté en justice et porteur de la marque distinctive voulue par la loi, CERTIFIONS qu'ayant été instruits qu'un individu colportait et cherchait à vendre du tabac, nous nous sommes acheminés vers où nous présumions devoir le rencontrer. En effet, étant parvenus nous avons vu un particulier de nous inconnu porteur d'un sac et tenant une balance à la main; nous en étant approchés, nous lui avons fait connaître nos qualités, et nous lui avons demandé ce que renfermait le sac dont il était porteur, a répondu D'après cette réponse, nous nous sommes emparés dudit sac, et, l'ayant ouvert, nous avons reconnu qu'il renfermait du tabac en non revêtu des marques de la Régie. Interpellé ledit particulier de nous dire ses nom, prénoms, profession et demeure, et de nous déclarer d'où provenaient ces tabacs, a répondu demandé pour quel usage était la balance qu'il tenait à la main, a répondu demandé encore s'il avait d'autres tabacs et dans quelle maison ils étaient placés, a répondu ; mais cette réponse ne nous ayant pas paru sincère, nous l'avons invité à nous suivre à l'auberge d où nous soupçonnions qu'il était logé; y étant arrivés avec lui, le sieur aubergiste, l'a reconnu, et nous a déclaré qu'il était arrivé ce matin chez lui avec un cheval qu'il conduisait et sur lequel étaient deux sacs; que l'un de ces sacs était déposé et qu'il était sorti avec l'autre il y a environ . Ayant invité le sieur à nous conduire vers le cheval dont il venait de nous parler, il nous a introduits dans son écurie, où nous avons vu un cheval (*signalement du cheval*); demandé audit si ce cheval lui appartenait, a répondu nous étant fait conduire dans la chambre où était le second sac, nous l'avons en effet trouvé, et, l'ayant ouvert, nous avons reconnu qu'il contenait du tabac en dépourvu de marques de la Régie; demandé audit si ces tabacs lui appartenaient également, et s'il avait à nous représenter des expéditions de la Régie des contributions indirectes, a répondu et attendu la contravention manifeste à la loi du 28 avril 1816, nous lui avons déclaré procès-verbal et saisie tant du cheval ci-dessus indiqué que des deux sacs renfermant des tabacs, des balances et de poids de la livre et de ses subdivisions, dont il était porteur. Ayant procédé à la reconnaissance des tabacs, le sieur nous a prêté une romaine dûment étalonnée, avec laquelle nous avons, toujours en présence dudit , pesé les susdits tabacs, qui se sont trouvés en quantité, savoir, de kilogrammes dans le sac dont ledit était porteur lorsque nous l'avons rencontré, et de kilogrammes dans le second; nous avons enfermé dans celui-ci les balances et poids, après les avoir pliés ensemble et recouverts de papier, et nous avons fermé l'un et l'autre desdits sacs avec une ficelle, dont nous avons fixé les extrémités avec de la cire rouge, sur laquelle le sieur , l'un de nous, a apposé son cachet, dont l'empreinte est en marge du présent; sommé ledit d'y apposer également le sien, a répondu . Toutes ces opérations étant terminées, nous avons déclaré audit que, pour aujourd'hui, le cheval resterait en fourrière chez le sieur ; que les deux sacs renfermant les tabacs, balances et poids, seraient déposés chez le sieur , l'un de nous, qui s'en est provisoirement constitué gardien, et que demain le tout serait conduit par nous à et serait mis à la disposition de M. le directeur des contributions indirectes susdésigné, qui est chargé d'en poursuivre contre lui la confiscation, ainsi que l'application de l'amende de 300 à 1000 fr. prononcée par l'article 222 de ladite loi du 22 avril 1816; que, quant à lui, nous allions, en conformité des articles 223 et 224 de la même loi, nous assurer de sa personne et le conduire devant M. le maire de cette commune (ou devant M. le juge de paix du canton), chargé de statuer sur son emprisonnement (1), dans le cas où il serait hors d'état de fournir une caution solvable pour le maximum de ladite amende ou d'en consigner le montant: nous étant transportés, accompagnés dudit , dans le bureau du sieur (*le débitant de tabac*), nous y avons effectué le dépôt provisoire des deux sacs ci-dessus désignés, et nous y avons rédigé le présent procès-verbal en présence dudit à qui nous en avons donné lecture, avec invitation de le signer, ce qu'il a clos ledit procès-verbal à heures du , et remis copie audit après l'avoir signé.

Le lendemain, on ferait le transport des objets saisis conformément au modèle n° 23.

N° 15. *Procès-verbal pour fraude au droit de navigation.*

L'an, etc. (*comme au* n° 1), je soussigné , receveur au bureau de navigation de , où j'ai ma résidence, certifie que cejourd'hui à heures du , étant sur les bords du , j'ai vu dans l'enceinte

---

(1) En conduisant le prévenu devant le juge de paix, les Employés affirmeront leur procès-verbal et le feront immédiatement enregistrer. S'il y avait de la gendarmerie dans le lieu de la saisie, on lui ferait la remise du prévenu, comme au n° 4, au lieu de le conduire devant le juge de paix.

du une barque que plusieurs personnes étaient occupées à décharger. M'étant approché de ladite barque, j'ai demandé quel en était le patron : s'est alors présenté un individu qui m'a dit être le patron de la barque et se nommer ; interpellé de me dire où il avait opéré son chargement, a répondu ; l'ayant invité à me représenter la quittance des droits qu'il avait dû payer au bureau de et à me remettre le laissez-passer qui a dû lui être délivré, a répondu ; je lui ai fait alors observer qu'il était en contravention à l'article (*citer l'article de l'arrêté spécial à chaque bassin*), et qu'il avait encouru l'amende de prononcée par l'article ; je l'ai prévenu que j'allais me retirer à mon bureau pour dresser procès-verbal, l'invitant à me suivre pour en entendre lecture et retirer copie : étant arrivé audit bureau, et le sieur ne s'étant pas présenté, j'ai rédigé mon procès-verbal les jour, mois et an que dessus.

N° 16. *Plainte pour refus de paiement du droit de passe d'un Bac.*

Cejourd'hui est comparu par-devant nous , maire de la commune d , le sieur , fermier du bac d , lequel nous a dit qu'il y a environ heures ; le sieur , demeurant à , s'est présenté pour passer la rivière dans ledit bac avec un cheval ; que, sur la demande qu'il lui a faite de la somme de , suivant la fixation arrêtée par le tarif, il lui a répondu qu'il la lui remettrait à l'autre bord ; mais qu'y étant arrivés, il lui avait refusé formellement de lui faire ce paiement, disant (*indiquer toutes les circonstances qui ont accompagné le refus*), et ledit sieur nous ayant requis de dresser acte de sa déclaration, aux fins de poursuivre par les voies de droit le paiement de ladite somme, nous avons rédigé le présent, qu'il a déclaré sincère et véritable dans tout son contenu, après lecture à lui faite ; et avons signé avec ledit sieur , ce , les jour, mois et an que dessus.

N° 17. *Procès-verbal pour fraude aux droits de Garantie.*

L'an mil huit cent le à heure du nous soussignés (*noms, prénoms, qualités et demeures des Employés*), ayant serment en justice et porteurs de nos commissions, certifions qu'étant informés qu'un marchand ambulant d'objets de bijouterie et d'orfévrerie les exposait en vente dans la maison du S aubergiste, située rue n.° où il est logé, et désirant nous assurer si lesdites objets étaient revêtus du poinçon voulu par la loi, assistés de M. (*indiquer le nom et la qualité de l'officier de police*), requis par nous à cet effet, nous nous sommes transportés dans ladite maison du S que nous avons d'abord rencontré, et que nous avons invité à nous indiquer la chambre occupée par ledit marchand ; à quoi ayant adhéré, il nous a conduits à la chambre .° où, étant entrés, nous avons trouvé un individu de nous inconnu qui, sur notre invitation de nous déclarer ses noms, prénoms, profession et domicile, nous a répondu lui avons aussitôt fait connaître nos qualités, et que l'objet de notre transport est de procéder à la visite et examen des ouvrages et marchandises d'orfévrerie et bijouterie qu'il a dans son commerce, afin de nous assurer s'ils sont revêtus du poinçon de garantie du titre voulu par la loi, le sommant de nous représenter lesdits ouvrages et de nous ouvrir ses armoires, tiroirs, malles et bijoutières. Le S adhérant à notre réquisition (*dans le cas où il refuserait, la visite ne doit pas être suspendue; l'officier doit requérir à l'instant un serrurier pour l'ouverture des portes et armoires; il est fait mention de toutes ces circonstances dans le procès-verbal*), et nous ayant représenté les ouvrages et les marchandises qu'il avoit en sa possession. nous avons reconnu (*expliquer pièce par pièce, soit les articles qui ont été trouvés dépourvus de marque de la garantie, soit ceux revêtus d'une marque ou empreinte dont les Employés suspectent la légalité, soit enfin ceux qui présentent une apparence quelconque de contravention*)· ayant fait remarquer audit que pour les objets sus-énoncés il a négligé d'exécuter la loi du 19 brumaire an 6, et qu'il est passible des peines qu'elle prononce, il a déclaré (*faire mention des dires du contrevenant*), et attendu que les objets ci-dessus spécifiés sont en contravention aux art. de ladite loi du 19 brumaire an 6, nous en avons déclaré saisie audit et les avons soigneusement renfermés en sa présence, au nombre de pièces, dans une boîte qui a été de suite ficelée et scellée de cire rouge, avec empreinte de notre cachet, de celui (*de l'officier de police*) et de celui dudit (*ou non de celui dudit qui a refusé de le mettre. quoique requis*). lui avons encore déclaré que nous allions faire de suite le dépôt de ladite boîte au greffe du tribunal civil, conformément à l'art. 103 de la loi précitée. De tout quoi nous avons rédigé à l'instant, et sans désemparer, le présent procès-verbal, qui, après lecture, a été signé par nous Employés sus-nommés, par M. (*l'officier de police*), qui a toujours été présent à nos opérations, et par ledit (*ou non par ledit qui a refusé, disant*)

N° 18. *Rapport de saisie d'objets d'une valeur de 10 francs et au-dessous, pour fraude à l'octroi.*

L'AN le avant (*ou* après) midi, en vertu de la décision de S. Ex. le Ministre des finances, du 28 mars 1809, nous (*nom, prénoms et qualités*), étant de service à (*indiquer le poste ou bureau*), porteurs de nos commissions et assermentés, avons (*rapporter ici toutes les circonstances de la fraude, le nom du contrevenant, l'espèce de l'objet saisi, sa valeur, la déclaration de la saisie de la même manière que dans un procès-verbal ordinaire*), dont nous avons aussitôt rédigé le présent rapport, que nous déclarons sincère et véritable.

A les jour, mois et an que dessus.

NOTA. Il serait superflu de donner des modèles de procès-verbaux en matière d'octroi seulement, ceux donnés pour les saisies communes devant remplir cet objet, puisque les formalités prescrites par l'ordonnance du 9 décembre 1814 sont presque littéralement les mêmes que celles prescrites pour les procès-verbaux des Employés de la Régie.

N° 19. *Procès-verbal des Employés d'octroi pour défaut de timbre sur une lettre de voiture.*

L'an mil huit cent , le , à la requête de M. le directeur-général de l'administration de l'enregistrement et des domaines, poursuite et diligence de M. , directeur de ladite administration à , rue , n° , où il fait élection de domicile pour la suite du présent, nous soussignés, Employés de l'octroi de la ville de , y demeurant, assermentés en justice et porteurs de nos commissions, agissant au présent en vertu du décret du 19 messidor an 13, CERTIFIONS que cejourd'hui à heures du , s'est présenté à , où nous étions de service, un voiturier conduisant , lequel, sur la sommation que nous lui avons faite de nous exhiber les lettres de voiture dont il pouvait être porteur, nous en a représenté une datée de , le , adressée au sieur , à , portant expédition de et signée par , ayant reconnu qu'elle n'était revêtue d'aucun timbre, nous l'avons fait remarquer audit voiturier, qui a dit se nommer et demeurer à . Nous l'avons prévenu que nous allions rapporter procès-verbal contre lui et contre le sieur susdénommé, souscripteur de ladite lettre, afin de les faire condamner solidairement au paiement de l'amende de trente francs prononcée par l'article 26 de la loi du 13 brumaire an 7, à la restitution des droits, au décime et aux frais; et, de fait, nous avons aussitôt rapporté le présent procès-verbal, auquel nous avons annexé ladite lettre de voiture non timbrée que nous avons paraphée *ne varietur* (1). Fait et clos dans notre bureau d , les jour, mois et an que dessus, à heures d

Affirmé dans les vingt-quatre heures devant le juge de paix.

N° 20. *Affirmation.*

PARDEVANT nous (*nom, qualité et domicile du juge de paix* ou *de son suppléant*), le procès-verbal ci-dessus a été affirmé sincère et véritable par les Employés soussignés, après qu'il leur en a été donné lecture.

Fait à le à heures d

N° 21. *Notification du procès-verbal.*

L'AN mil huit cent le à heures d , nous, dénommés et qualifiés au procès-verbal ci-dessus, au requis que dit est, nous étant transportés au domicile dudit , situé à , et parlant à , nous lui avons lu et signifié le susdit procès-verbal, avec sommation de le signer, ce qu'il a Nous lui en avons laissé copie, ainsi que du présent, et avons signé.

N° 22. *Affiche du procès-verbal.*

L'AN mil huit cent le à heures d , nous, dénommés et qualifiés au procès-verbal ci-dessus, au requis que dit est, certifions qu'attendu l'absence du sieur , que nous avons vainement cherché pour lui donner lecture et copie dudit procès-verbal, nous nous sommes transportés à la porte de la mairie d , où étant, nous avons affiché copie dudit procès-verbal et du présent exploit, et avons signé.

N° 23. *Acte de transport pour opérer le dépôt des objets saisis.*

Et de suite, lesdits jour et an, a midi, nous (*au moins deux des Employés-rédacteurs*), dénommés et qualifiés au procès-verbal ci-dessus, et, d'autre part, à la requête que dit est, CERTIFIONS avoir fait charger les saisis par ledit procès-verbal, et les avoir accompagnés et fait conduire à où étant et parlant à , nous lui avons déclaré (*en présence* ou *en l'absence du prévenu*), que nous allions

---

(1) Si le voiturier réclame copie du procès-verbal ou de la lettre de voiture, elle lui sera délivrée sur papier timbré, à ses frais.

mettre en dépôt, à sa charge et garde, les saisis par le susdit procès-verbal. Ledit sieur ayant reconnu l'état des , a consenti à en demeurer gardien et a promis de les représenter à toute réquisition de justice. En foi de quoi il a signé avec nous dans le susdit à heures a midi.

N° 24. *Acte de mise en fourrière des moyens de transport.*

Et de suite, lesdits jour et an, a midi, nous soussignés (*au moins deux des Employés-rédacteurs*), dénommés et qualifiés dans le procès-verbal ci-dessus, à la requête qui dit est,

Certifions avoir conduit (*accompagnés* ou *en l'absence du sieur*), les saisis et retenus, comme il est expliqué audit procès-verbal, chez le sieur , aubergiste à , et parlant à , nous lui avons déclaré que nous laissions à sa charge et garde lesdits , évalués à , à quoi il a consenti, se chargeant, comme dépositaire de justice, avec promesse de les loger, nourrir et entretenir selon l'usage, et ce, moyennant la somme de pour chaque jour, prix ordinaire et débattu entre nous; il a promis en outre de ne livrer lesdits qu'à notre réquisition ou consentement, ou au consentement et réquisition de l'Administration. En foi de quoi nous avons signé avec ledit

---

N° 25. *Acte de cautionnement des moyens de transport saisis* pour garantie de l'amende, *lorsque la main-levée en est accordée après la clôture du procès-verbal.*

Cejourd'hui s'est présenté devant nous le sieur , lequel a dit que, par suite du procès-verbal du , il a été procédé à la saisie de qui ont été consignés en fourrière chez le sieur , pour sûreté de l'amende réclamée par l'Administration des contributions indirectes pour le fait de la contravention à la loi du arguée par ledit procès-verbal; que le comparant offre, pour obtenir la remise des objets saisis, de fournir caution solvable du *maximum* de l'amende réclamée, et de payer en outre au sieur , aubergiste, les frais de fourrière tels qu'ils ont été réglés et convenus avec lui, et ce avant la reprise desdits objets; et de fait ledit comparant nous a présenté pour caution le sieur , de nous bien connu, lequel, ici présent, s'est rendu et constitué caution dudit sieur , et s'est obligé solidairement avec lui, et sous la même peine, au paiement de la somme de (1) *faisant le* maximum *de l'amende réclamée et* encourue par ledit , pour les causes énoncées au procès-verbal susdaté; et, au moyen de la soumission du sieur et du paiement fait par ledit directement au sieur , des frais de fourrière dus jusqu'à ce jour, nous avons à l'instant fait remettre et délivrer audit sieur qui le reconnaît, et en décharge (*le dépositaire*) et tous autres qu'il appartiendra lesdits . De tout quoi nous avons dressé le présent en notre bureau de , lesdits jour et an, et avons signé avec lesdits sieurs , après lecture à eux faite. (*Cet acte doit être dressé sur papier timbré et enregistré dans les quatre jours.*)

---

(1) Si les moyens de transport saisis étaient d'une valeur inférieure au maximum de l'amende, on dirait : *montant de l'évaluation desdits , laquelle somme est imputable au paiement de l'amende.*

N° 26. *Acte de cautionnement des moyens de transport saisis*, et dans le cas de la confiscation, *lorsque la main-levée en est accordée après la clôture du procès-verbal.*

L'AN mil huit cent le s'est présenté devant nous le sieur lequel nous a dit que, par suite du procès-verbal du il a été procédé sur le sieur à la saisie de qui ont été consignés et mis en fourrière jusqu'au prononcé de leur confiscation, à laquelle l'Administration des contributions indirectes a conclu par ledit procès-verbal, pour le fait de la contravention à la loi du et qu'il nous offrait pour en obtenir la remise, de fournir caution solvable de la somme de à laquelle lesdites ont été évaluées par le procès-verbal susdaté, et de payer en outre au sieur aubergiste, les frais de fourrière échus, tels qu'ils ont été réglés et convenus avec lui, et ce avant la reprise desdits ; et de fait, ledit comparant nous a présenté pour caution le sieur demeurant à rue n.° de nous bien connu, lequel, ici présent, s'est rendu et constitué caution pour ledit et s'est obligé, solidairement avec lui et sous les mêmes peines, au paiement de la somme de valeur desdits dont la confiscation a été encourue par ledit pour les causes énoncées au procès-verbal susdaté, et au moyen de la soumission, etc. (*le surplus comme au modèle précédent*).

N° 27. *Requête pour demander l'autorisation de vendre des animaux mis en fourrière.*

A Monsieur le Juge de paix d

Requiert , Directeur des contributions indirectes à , au nom de son administration, qu'il vous plaise ordonner, conformément aux art. 39 et 40 du décret du 18 juin 1811 (1), 1° qu'il sera procédé le , à la vente au plus offrant et dernier enchérisseur, d (*désigner les animaux dont la vente est poursuivie*) , saisi le en vertu de l'article par les Employés de la Régie à sur le sieur , qui en a refusé la remise sous caution à lui offerte par le procès-verbal; 2°. que le prix de la vente restera déposé dans la caisse de la Régie pour recevoir la destination qui sera ordonnée par le jugement définitif à intervenir; et vous ferez justice. A , le

---

N° 28. *Assignation en suite d'un procès-verbal.*

L'AN, etc. (*Même préambule qu'au n° 1*).

Nous soussignés , avons donné assignation (2) au sieur ,

---

(1) S'il était nécessaire que la vente fût promptement faite, on dirait 1° Qu'il soit procédé à la vente d , saisis le, etc.
2 Qu'attendu la faible valeur desdits , qui serait insuffisante pour couvrir plus long-temps les frais de fourrière, la vente sera faite sans formalité, et que le prix en restera, etc.

(2) S'il y a plusieurs prévenus par suite du même procès-verbal, on les indiquera tous dans l'original de l'assignation en disant : *Avons donné assignation 1° au sieur , demeurant à , en son domicile, où nous nous sommes exprès transportés, parlant à ; 2° au sieur , demeurant à , en son*

demeurant à , en son domicile, où nous nous sommes exprès transportés, parlant à , à comparaître en personne à la première audience du tribunal civil de , jugeant en police correctionnelle, trois jours francs après la date du présent, et en tant que de besoin à toutes les audiences suivantes jusqu'à jugement définitif, pour répondre sur et aux fins du procès-verbal dressé par nous le , dûment enregistré, signifié (1) et affirmé, procéder, voir prononcer la confiscation de , *se voir condamner en d'amende* (2), en conformité de l'article et aux dépens (3), sans préjudice des peines qui pourraient être encourues à raison de toutes autres contraventions résultant soit du procès-verbal, soit de l'instruction de la procédure; au paiement de tout quoi il pourra être contraint par toutes voies, même par corps. Et avons à cet effet, parlant comme dessus, laissé audit copie du présent, avec déclaration que M. , avoué près ledit tribunal, occupera pour la Régie; et avons signé.

N° 29. *Acte de vente d'objets saisis.*

L'AN, etc. (*comme pour le n° 1*).

Je soussigné , entreposeur-receveur central des contributions indirectes à , assermenté en justice, CERTIFIE qu'en conformité de l'article 33 du décret du 1er germinal an 13, après affiches signées de moi et apposées tant à la porte de la maison commune qu'à celle de l'auditoire du juge de paix, le , j'ai procédé cejourd'hui, à heures , comme il est dit ci-après, et en présence du public rassemblé dans , à la vente au plus offrant et dernier enchérisseur, de , saisis par procès-verbal du , sur le sieur , et acquis à la Régie en vertu (*du jugement rendu le par* , ou *de la transaction souscrite le , par le sieur*). Lesdits ayant été mis à prix à , valeur à laquelle ils ont été estimés par le procès-verbal de saisie, ont été adjugés et délivrés à M. , demeurant à , dernier enchérisseur, au prix de , qu'il a payé comptant, ainsi que les frais de vente. La vente étant terminée, j'ai signé avec ledit sieur , acquéreur.

N° 30. *Acte de rachat d'un objet saisi par l'octroi.*

L'AN mil huit cent le , sur la demande faite par le sieur de racheter (*désignation des objets*), saisis sur (*lui*, ou *tel voiturier ou domestique, etc.*) le par (*procès-verbal* ou *rapport*) des Employés (*de tel poste ou bureau*), lesdits objets lui ont été remis, ainsi qu'il le reconnaît, moyennant paiement, conformément à la loi, de la somme de , montant de leur

---

domicile, où nous nous sommes également transportés, parlant à ; 3° au sieur , etc.

(1) Si le procès-verbal n'a été signifié que par affiche, il n'est pas de rigueur d'en donner copie au prévenu en tête de l'assignation, mais il serait bien de le faire.

(2) S'il y a plusieurs prévenus solidaires, on dira, dans l'original de l'assignation : *S'ouïr les susnommés condamner solidairement en d'amende*; et dans la copie : *S'ouïr le sieur condamner. solidairement avec les sieurs , en d'amende.*

(3) Si les moyens de transport sont saisis pour sûreté de l'amende, on ajoutera : *Ouïr dire qu'il sera procédé à la vente des moyens de transport saisis, pour le prix qui en proviendra être versé dans la caisse de la Régie, en déduction ou jusqu'à concurrence de l'amende.*

estimation. Ledit sieur a en outre payé la somme de pour les frais dudit procès-verbal. Fait au bureau de , les jour, mois et an que dessus et avons signé (*signature du Receveur et du contrevenant*).

N° 31. *Réquisition au Commissaire de police, etc., en vertu de l'article 237 de la loi du 28 avril 1816.*

Nous soussignés , Employés (1) des contributions indirectes à la résidence d , en vertu de l'art. 237 de la loi du 28 avril 1816, requérons M. (*le Commissaire de police, le Maire, son Adjoint ou le Juge de paix*) de nous assister dans la visite que nous nous proposons de faire chez , d'après les ordres (2)

Fait à , le

N° 32. *Déclaration de pourvoi en cassation.*

Cejourd'hui est comparu au greffe de la Cour (*le Directeur ou l'avoué de la Régie*), lequel a déclaré se pourvoir en cassation contre l'arrêt de la Cour jugeant en appel de police correctionnelle du , pour les torts et griefs qu'il en résulte, protestant de nullité de tout ce qui serait fait au préjudice du présent, et, après lecture, a signé avec nous, greffier.

N° 33. *Requête en cassation.*

Le Conseiller d'Etat Directeur général des contributions indirectes, poursuite et diligence de M , Directeur de la même Administration dans l'arrondissement d , expose que la Régie a été obligée de se pourvoir contre un arrêt de la Cour Royale de , le , qui, etc.

Les moyens de cassation que la Régie propose contre cet arrêt, consistent 1° etc., etc. Ce considéré, il plaise à la Cour de casser et annuler l'arrêt dont il s'agit, rendu par la Cour royale d , le , renvoyer la cause et les parties devant une autre Cour Royale pour être jugé de nouveau, condamner les défendeurs aux dépens.

Fait à

---

(1) Si les recherches étaient faites par les Employés de l'octroi, on dirait : Nous soussignés Employés de l'octroi de , y demeurant, autorisés par l'art. 92 de l'ordonnance du 9 décembre 1814, et en vertu, etc.

(2) Désigner le chef de service, s'il est du grade de Contrôleur au moins ; à défaut, le Directeur de l'arrondissement.

FIN.

TABLE

DES MODÈLES.

FIN DE LA TABLE DES MODÈLES.

TABLE.

A.

B.

C.

E.

F.

G.

H.

I.

J.

L.

M.

N.

O.

P.

R.

S.

T.

U.

V.

FIN DE LA TABLE.

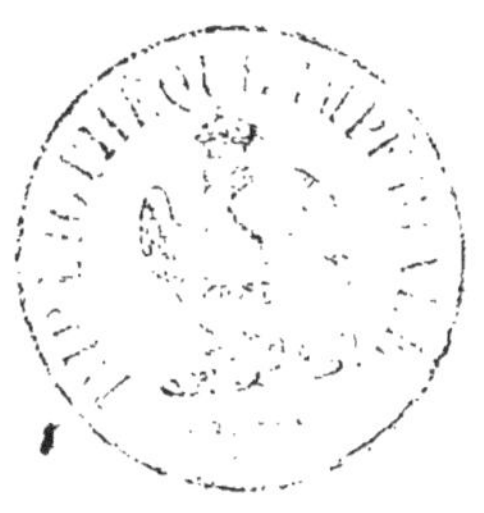

www.ingramcontent.com/pod-product-compliance
Lightning Source LLC
LaVergne TN
LVHW050415160826
845677LV00002BA/392

* 9 7 8 2 0 1 3 0 9 7 9 9 4 *